Incongruous *Entertainment*

Incongruous

DUKE UNIVERSITY PRESS   DURHAM AND LONDON 2005

Entertainment

CAMP, CULTURAL VALUE, AND THE MGM MUSICAL

Steven Cohan

© 2005 DUKE UNIVERSITY PRESS
ALL RIGHTS RESERVED
PRINTED IN THE UNITED STATES OF
AMERICA ON ACID-FREE PAPER ∞
DESIGNED BY REBECCA GIMÉNEZ
TYPESET IN CYCLES AND AREPO BY
TSENG INFORMATION SYSTEMS
LIBRARY OF CONGRESS CATALOGING-
IN-PUBLICATION DATA APPEAR
ON THE LAST PRINTED PAGE
OF THIS BOOK.

CONTENTS

ACKNOWLEDGMENTS

*N*o less than an MGM musical, this book had its moments of important if unacknowledged collaboration, and now is the moment to say so. To begin with, my thinking about camp and the musical benefited enormously from the instruction I received from my undergraduate and graduate students the several times I taught this genre. While I send a big, fat, collective thank you to them all, let me single out Karen Hall, Tim Connelly, and Cristina Stasia. Additionally, I had the welcome opportunity to present portions of chapters as lectures or at conferences during the years when I researched and drafted the manuscript, and the thoughtful response of these audiences to my arguments greatly helped me to crystallize my thinking. I especially learned from and still recall the conversations I had with Susan Edmonds (about camp taste), Murray Pomerance (about *Bathing Beauty*), Jane Feuer (about Gene Kelly), Bruce Babington (about male dancers), Adrienne McLean (about Judy Garland), Matthew Tinkcom (about Garland fandom as well as about MGM overall), Barbara Klinger (about home video), and Sean Griffin (about everything musical). Pam Robertson Woczik gave me helpful bibliographic direction when I started the project and momentarily didn't know where to turn next. David Boxwell shared a fun news item with me. Amy Villarejo, Amy Lang, and Roger Hallas contributed through our conversations while I wrote. David Leone was in many ways an inspiration for my work. Heartfelt thanks to Linda Shires and Crystal Bartolovich, who each offered valuable criticism when I was designing the book's plan and formulating its methodology. Ina Hark, as always, provided a reliable sounding board every step of the way.

The labor of writing this book was considerably eased by leave time and a grant for illustration costs which I received from the College of Arts and Sciences at Syracuse University. In the same vein, I want to thank Bob Gates, chair of my department while I wrote this book, for his consistent support of my scholarship. My gratitude also goes go to Ron and Howard Mandlebaum and the staff at Photofest for their help in finding illustrations (Ron, whom I worked most closely with, knows his musicals and was invaluable), and to the librarians at the Margaret Herrick Library of the Academy of Motion Pictures Arts and Sciences, where I began my research. I owe a warm thanks to Ken Wissoker, my editor at Duke University Press, whose confidence in this project never flagged, to his assistant, Courtney Berger, and to the two anonymous readers who read the manuscript with so much interest and as much rigor.

Aside from these debts, I also owe a personal thanks to my mother Lillian, my late father Albert, and my aunt Dolly (my own Auntie Mame) for sharing their love of musicals with me when I was a child—and for continuing to do so when I was supposedly all grown up. Thanks, too, to Harry, Shari, Roman, and Alex.

Portions of this book were previously published in different form. An early, condensed version of chapter 3 appeared as "Dancing with Balls in the 1940s: Sissies, Sailors, and the Camp Masculinity of Gene Kelly" in *The Trouble with Men: Masculinities in European and Hollywood Cinema*, edited by Phil Powrie, Ann Davies, Bruce Babington, and published by Wallflower Press (London, 2004). The first but incomplete version of chapter 6 appeared as "Judy on the Net: Judy Garland Fans and 'the Gay Thing' Revisited." in *Key Frames: Popular Cinema and Cultural Studies*, edited by Matthew Tinkcom and Amy Villarejo, and published by Routledge (London, 2001). I thank the publishers for giving me permission to include this material, and the editors for their helpful criticism when I first formulated these two chapters.

Finally, I dedicate this book to Allen Larson and Josh Stenger. Thank you for your unwavering friendship, intellectual inspiration, and camp fellowship: you're really hep, too.

*M*ainstream fare in the studio era, the MGM musical is today considered an outdated, niche commodity—it has become camp. Camp itself dates back to the time of the closet, the same period when musicals flourished at MGM. In response to that era's oppression and censorship of homosexuality, camp allowed for the ironic, self-reflective style of gay men passing as straight, who kept a "straight face" so as not to let outsiders in on the joke, while simultaneously winking at the initiated in shared acknowledgment of it. *Camp* can be defined as the ensemble of strategies used to enact a queer recognition of the incongruities arising from the cultural regulation of gender and sexuality. The flamboyance of camp when inflected as style, taste, wit, parody, or drag may seem the antithesis of passing, but to be flamboyant was a fundamental component of the joke. Camp strategies for achieving ironic distance from the normative have always exploited the slippery space between a "posture" and an "imposture," between "resembling" and "dissembling"—in one way or another, camp signaled the queer eye for a straight guise. Now out of the closet and made more visible, camp continues to bear this significance today as a queer practice and, in academic circles, as queer theory.

By now, too, the camp reputation of the musicals produced by Metro-Goldwyn-Mayer during the 1930s, 1940s, and 1950s—the studio era—is pretty much taken for granted as a consequence of the genre's cultish value for gay men. "In gay subcultural argot," Brett Farmer observes, "the term *musical* has long been used as a coded reference to homosexuality; to describe someone as 'musical' or 'into musicals' is to describe them as homosexual" (74). This association has been well-known for some time. The movie *Can't Stop the Music* (1980) referenced MGM's musicals visually and in dialogue as a coded acknowledgment of the Village People's source in gay culture, which this disco musical was reluctant to name directly at the risk of alienating a general audience, who nevertheless stayed away in droves. No such decoding is required today. The musical's affiliation with gay cult tastes is enough of a truism for a film or television series simply to mention it as the automatic sign of a character's gayness. Recognizing this connection, the 2003 independent film about a group of misfit teens attending a summer drama school, where they put on musicals, was simply called *Camp*. The title's play on words was so transparent that it ceased to register as a pun.

The cultural marginality of the MGM musical in the present day is a far cry from its prominence during the studio era, when the genre epitomized the best of show business, serving as a medium for bringing together talents from stage, vaudeville, radio, and the recording industry along with film stars in two hours of spectacular family entertainment. Their camp reputation notwithstanding, many of these old films have since been canonized as the epitome of MGM's golden age, receiving new commercial value on cable and home video as classics. On the other hand, for young moviegoers unable to recognize either their classic or cultish worth, these same musicals are an inaccessible as well as obsolete form of entertainment, only recoupable as nostalgia by (or oftentimes with) an older generation of grandparents.

These striking differences in value for the musicals—as family fare, classics, nostalgia, or gay cult—do not mark as great a disjunction between past and present as one may think. Reading the MGM musical through camp illuminates the continuities as well as discontinuities in what it represented as "wholesome" entertainment during the studio era and what it represents now, well over half a century later, as "incongruous" entertainment. Camp already informed the manufacturing of these extravagant, escapist films—it was a key element in the crafting of their entertainment values during their moment of production—and contemporary marketing and reception of the films more openly recognize their camp appeal. This continuity brings out how the MGM musical's history locates significant demarcations of value according to public recognition of its legibility *as* a camp product. Camp, that is to say, has a history too, and it greatly contributed to the cultural value which the MGM musical initially carried and continues to bear.

Although many studios produced musicals which have a strong camp following today—the Busby Berkeley musicals from Warner Bros. and Carmen Miranda musicals from Twentieth Century–Fox come immediately to mind—there are compelling reasons why I concentrate exclusively on MGM's output. Of all the majors, the Culver City studio made the greatest investment in the genre as its trademark, producing more musicals on an annual basis and retaining more talent under contract for that purpose. In the public mind MGM unofficially stood for "More Great Musicals," the roaring lion guaranteeing the best and the biggest, the most lavish and expensive entertainment regardless of who produced and directed or who starred and costarred. Of great consequence for this reputation, the studio employed a large number of homosexual, lesbian, and bisexual artists and craftspeople to collaborate on musicals, most famously but not exclusively in the Arthur Freed unit, a factor discussed in the first chapter. Their contribution to the consistency of MGM's signature product has only begun to be recognized in accounts of the gay men and women working in Hollywood (Mann, Ehrenstein) and to be appreciated as a closeted labor force which articulated its presence through a distinctive camp style (Tinkcom, *Working Like a Homosexual*).

MGM's identification with the musical genre is as firmly in place today, in no small part because, unlike its rivals from the studio era, the Metro-Goldwyn-Mayer of Culver City has effectively ceased to exist except in name only; its past glories therefore remain indelibly etched into its famous name. On eBay auction pages, merchandise related to old musicals is sometimes linked to MGM in titles or descriptions, whether or not this studio was actually responsible. The prestige of *Singin' in the Rain* (1952) keeps alive this special association of musicals and the roaring lion, as do *That's Entertainment!* (1974) and its two sequels (1976, 1994). Regardless of corporate ownership, marketing of the film library on cable, CD, and home video still privileges MGM as the singular producer of the genre.

Incongruous Entertainment follows the time span I have just been sketching. The first half treats the middle decades of the twentieth century, paying closest attention to the 1940s, when MGM turned out one expensive musical after another and perfected its discernible camp style. This section examines that style (chapter 1), female star turns (chapter 2), and Gene Kelly's dancing (chapter 3). The book's second half looks past the studio era, concentrating on the MGM musical's later and more dubious renown as an outdated form of entertainment with unmistakable camp valences. This section examines the canonical and cult reputations of *Singin' in the Rain* (chapter 4); the repackaging of the musicals in the first and third *That's Entertainment!* as well as on cable, CD, and home video (chapter 5); and Judy Garland fandom on the Internet (chapter 6). Taken together, these six chapters demonstrate how the histories of the MGM musical and camp overlap, mutually informing each other.

Before going any further to establish the basis for viewing this interaction, I should first clarify my use of the terms *gay*, *homosexual*, and *queer*, which comprise the field of reference for any discussion of camp. In the interest of stylistic variety, and also following the example of scholars whose work has been of importance to this book, I often use the three terms as if they are synonymous, while nonetheless trying to maintain precision in my word choice whenever possible. To a certain extent, in common usage all three terms signify a person whose sexual orientation deviates from the heterosexual norm. Yet each marks out significantly different positions toward, even values for, nonconformist sexualities, particularly as a ground of identity. *Gay* has connotations of identity politics and the post-Stonewall rights movement, designating a subcultural affiliation and social presence through sexual orientation. *Gay*, moreover, is commonly used as an adjective or plural noun to avoid sexism, referring to both men and women. But the word brings with it an earlier history of covert homosexual self-identification before Stonewall, too. *Queer* bears an even more plural meaning, referring to people of any nonheterocentric sexual or gendered self-identification: one does not have to be homosexual or lesbian to be queer since the category includes bisexual and transgendered persons. In referring to gender or sexual nonconformity, *queer* also carries forward its history as a pejorative and denigrating cultural label, the opposite of straight.

Contemporary usage aims to invert this history by repoliticizing the queer's disturbance of dominant culture's regulating norms as affirming, empowering, transgressive. *Homosexual*, functioning like *gay* as a noun and an adjective, refers more specifically to same-sex desire and activity, and it still retains negative associations due to its history as a clinical diagnosis of pathological inversion. In my own view, the three terms comprise something of a semantic continuum as used today: from same-sex desires and acts (*homosexual*), to the socialized persons orienting their identities and affective bonds around their homosexuality (*gay*), to the wider cultural location and value of gender/sexual dissidents (*queer*). This continuum explains why the terms are so often used interchangeably in academic writing, which well understands that sexuality, the individual, and culture are inextricably, dynamically, and historically bound up together.[1]

Of course these definitions are ad hoc and somewhat impressionistic on my part; what needs to be stressed is that these three terms did not have the same referential specificity in the middle decades of the last century that they have in the present. According to historian George Chauncey, during the first half of the twentieth century sexual preference did not determine identity across the board for all men. As often as it referred to same-sex intimacy, *homosexuality* signified a type of gender behavior, an effeminate demeanor. Men who acted on their homosexual desires did not necessarily self-identify as "gay"—as happened more automatically after the emergence of identity politics and the gay liberation movement—but they were called "queer" if found out or were suspected of being "queer" if they had an effeminate manner. This historical sense of what *gay, queer,* and *homosexual* referred to in the past, for individuals as well as in the culture, needs to be kept in mind when we think about camp and the MGM musical.

CAMP AS A HISTORICAL PRACTICE

Although the musicals produced by MGM may now seem obviously campy, that description immediately raises questions. Just what is being seen as camp, and, more to the point, what determines this reception, when, and for whom? Is it simply a mocking affection for the films as outlandish artifacts, enabled by historical distance from their moment of production? As the vantage point of the present denaturalizes older codes of gender and style, it does seem to be more apparent that these musicals push to the extreme an obsolete aesthetic standard. Viewed as an antiquated cultural form, the musicals then seem most legible through what Barbara Klinger calls "mass camp": a "sensibility [which] entered mainstream culture ready to adore the mediocre, laugh at the overconventionalized, and critique archaic sex roles" (139). Mass camp, which I discuss further in chapter 4, is "safe," readily available as a "hip" or "chic" consumer taste for old films now out of fashion, and smugly superior to nostalgia because it lacks "the 'stigma' of subcultural affiliation" (140). Spectators watching MGM musicals today as mass camp relish their unintentionally laughable over-the-top attractions, detaching the films from their original contexts. This kind of laughter negates whatever historical relation the musicals may have had at the time of their production to camp, which was already a highly developed and sophisticated practice, albeit with a decidedly *unsafe* subcultural affiliation as a queer idiom.

In many respects, the general currency of *camp* as a recognizable term, a way for audiences to describe their pleasure in films that are so old they are bad and so bad they are good, has resulted from the gradual erasure of its materiality as a queer practice over the past decades. Susan Sontag's 1964 "Notes on Camp," still the most regularly cited piece on the topic, first brought the term to the notice of intellectuals, and the essay's subsequent longevity—it accompanied the term *camp* into the mainstream—has set the limits on how camp has since been understood. Evaluating it as a dismissal of high culture, Sontag describes camp as "a sensibility" which views the world apolitically in terms of style. Camp style, she observes, exalts "artifice and exaggeration" (53) and satisfies a taste for the extravagance of "art that proposes itself seriously, but cannot be taken altogether seriously because it is 'too much'" (59). Sontag makes only passing acknowledgment of "the peculiar relationship of Camp taste and homosexuality" (64), dedicating the essay to Oscar Wilde and remarking that camp shows "how to be a dandy in the age of mass culture" (63). Sontag does not pursue what camp style has to do with expressions of sexual dissidence except to link both camp and dissidence with elitist posturing. Rather, her choice of the word *peculiar* in mentioning camp's relationship to homosexuality implies Sontag's motivation, not altogether sympathetic, in singling out camp as an example of a "sensibility" as opposed to an "idea," her declared point in musing on this topic. "To name a sensibility, to draw its contours and to recount its history," she states, "requires a deep sympathy modified by revulsion" (53).

Two decades later, Andrew Ross's 1988 "Uses of Camp" rightfully saw Sontag's ambivalence about camp sensibility as a symptomatic response to "the massive reorganization of cultural taste that took place in the course of the sixties" (74). Although Ross understands full well the historical significance of camp for the "traditional" gay sensibility (73), he is primarily concerned with how, via the Pop movement, it came to function economically as the "rediscovery of history's waste" (66). The emergence of camp as a new category of taste, Ross argues, "more than anything else, shaped, defined, and negotiated the way in which intellectuals of the sixties tried to 'pass' as newly enlightened subscribers to the Pop aesthetic in the attractive, throwaway world of immediacy created by the mass culture industries" (55). Certain artists such as Andy Warhol layered the new Pop aesthetic with an awareness of how that intellectual "passing" concerned taste and sexuality alike, but for the most part it represented a transformation of camp's meaning as a distinctive queer style.[2]

In focusing on the cultural environment which ultimately resulted in the phenomenon of mass camp, Sontag's and Ross's essays document the heterosexual appropriation of camp style and taste from a homosexual milieu. What emerged from this rerouting of camp into the mainstream, Moe Meyer comments in the introduction to his 1994 anthology, was not camp itself but "the camp trace," its recuperation as an unthreatening "queer aura" giving special value to straight tastes within the domain of heterosexuality (5). Meyer himself defines camp as the "strategies and tactics of queer parody" (9), a definition which in his view makes it inseparable from queer identities: camp parody provides the performative ground through which a queer identity gets enacted. Furthermore, he attributes camp's political "power" to "its ability to be conscious of its future as an appropriated commodity." But unlike Ross, Meyer maintains that camp is a "product" of "queer agency" because it "selects and chooses which aspects of itself will be subsumed into dominant culture" (17)—a political understanding of camp which various ACT UP groups exploited in their street demonstrations during the late eighties and early nineties.

Though Meyer, in contrast with Sontag and Ross, seeks to reclaim the intractable queerness of camp, the three accounts are worth placing side by side. All three offer valuable commentary about the circulation of camp, but each critic also tries to see it as a coherent object, focusing on what camp *is*: a sensibility made evident in an excessive style, a category of taste reinvesting outmoded commodities with new value for consumer culture, a performance of queer agency. Taken together, these three essays recount how what camp signified by the end of the last century—as style, surplus value, or parody—had evolved along with the greater assimilation of homosexuality and identifiable gay tastes into the mainstream. Whereas camp once distinguished queer from straight responses to popular culture, mass camp now more homogeneously legitimizes any guilty pleasure, the self-conscious consumption (and, from the viewpoint of manufacturers, exploitation) of commodities that deliver an affect in excess of their apparent objective value. For that matter, mass camp has since mutated into *trash* and *cheese*, the more postmodern terms of choice for describing the hip consumption of throwaway commodity culture from the position of self-conscious alienation which disavows a guilty pleasure while indulging in it: putting a preference for absurd or vulgar mass-produced commodities in air quotes, so to speak (Glenn, 16–18). On an episode of RuPaul's cable talk show devoted to the topic, even camp filmmaker John Waters explained that he himself prefers *trash* to *camp*, for the latter term calls to his mind "two older gentlemen in an antique shop talking about Rita Hayworth."[3]

Waters's seeming repudiation of camp is complexly layered, as his own camp wit always is. His example means to recognize the obsolescence of camp, its antiquated place in popular culture, where it marks a generational divide amongst gay men. Yet the concrete nature of his illustration, not to mention the occasion of his presence on a talk show hosted by a drag queen with crossover success as a singer and celebrity, just as strongly alludes to another story about camp, its ongoing history as a queer discourse of social identity and group cohesion.

From the 1920s through the 1960s, camp was the code and custom of the closet, in Chauncey's words, both "a cultural *style* and a cultural *strategy*" (290). Working against, while acknowledging, the imperative to pass as straight, camp gave homosexual men a distinctly queer idiom through which to articulate their censored, usually precarious cultural location. Camp allowed them to "make sense of, respond to, and undermine the social categories of gender and sexuality that served to marginalize them," and it did so by exposing the artifice of the social order which categorized them as "unnatural" (Chauncey, 290). When Michael Bronski defines camp as "the reimagining of the material world into ways and forms which transform and comment upon the original," he has this historical perspective in mind as the source of camp's purpose of "[changing] the 'natural' and 'normal' into style and artifice" (42). Thus, like Meyer and Chauncey, he disagrees with Sontag that camp is apolitical. "Because it has been used by gay people as a means of communication and survival," Bronski writes, "camp is political. And because it contains the possibility of structuring and encouraging limitless imagination—to literally create a new reality—it is not only political, but progressive" (43).

Whatever was political and progressive about camp, however, can be seen only by historicizing it as a cultural practice, not by valorizing it as a utopian or revolutionary theory. Even for those not otherwise disadvantaged, such as middle-class or wealthy urban white males, camp sought to reclaim language and representationality as well as public spaces from a heteronormative mainstream culture that rendered homosexuality invisible except as a structuring absence for defining "manliness" in opposition to "womanliness," whether in gendered or sexual terms. "The only process by which the queer [was] able to enter representation and produce social visibility," as Meyer puts it (11), camp remained contiguous to mainstream culture and its own coding of heteronormality because the latter provided the point of reference, the motivating circumstance, for the double function of camp as a style and a strategy of passing.

All that said, the materiality of camp as a practice has been notoriously difficult to pin down. For it should be evident by now that "camp is not a thing," as sociologist Esther Newton observes. "Most broadly it signifies a *relationship between* things, people, and activities or qualities, and homosexuality" (105). Newton's ethnographic study, *Mother Camp* (based on interviews and field observation in Chicago and Kansas City, primarily conducted in 1965–66 for her dissertation), looks closely at the practices and social ordering of female impersonators—doing drag in their occupations of showgirls or working girls—before the liberation movement initiated by the 1969 Stonewall riot in New York City. What Newton found is still enormously useful in honing in on the coordinates of camp as it was practiced during the era of the closet, when it was not limited to drag on the one hand or to unmarried gentlemen conversing about a favorite female star on the other.

According to Newton, camp is situational, "inher[ing] not in the person or thing itself but in the tension between that person or thing and the context or association" (107). Camp therefore resists objectification and appears to an outsider as highly subjective, even idiosyncratic. "Informants," she reports, "stressed that even between individuals there is very little agreement on what is camp because camp is in the eye of the beholder, that is, different homosexuals like different things, and because of the spontaneity and individuality of camp, camp taste is always changing. This has the advantage, recognized by some informants, that a clear division can always be maintained between homosexual and 'straight' taste" (105). For all its variety and mutability, however, Newton still found that camp cohered around certain "strong themes," which "are intimately related to the homosexual situation and strategy." These are: incongruity, "the subject matter of camp"; theatricality, "its style"; and humor, "its strategy" (106).

Camp, Newton explains, takes its content from the incongruity of the juxtaposed binary systems regulating gender and sexuality via their coding of cultural value and hierarchy. "Masculine-feminine juxtapositions are, of course, the most characteristic kind of camp, but any very incongruous contrast can be campy. For instance, juxtapositions of high and low status, youth and old age, profane and sacred functions of symbols, cheap and expensive articles are frequently used for camp purposes" (107). Asserting style over content then enacts perceptions of incongruity: "Importance tends to shift from what a thing *is* to how it *looks*, from *what* is done to *how* it is done . . . The kind of incongruities that are campy are very often created by adornment or stylization of a well-defined thing or symbol" (107). Reinforcing the "exaggerated, consciously 'stagey'" style is an underlying dramatic form, which "always involves a performer or performers and an audience," and which "is suffused with the perception of 'being as playing a role' and 'life as theatre'" (107). Here, Newton comments, camp and drag can "merge and augment each other" (107), that is, insofar as "the double stance toward role, putting on a good show while indicating distance (showing that it is a show) is the heart of drag as camp" (109). Finally, camp is meant to be fun, though not with the intent of trivializing either the perception of incongruity or the style of representing it. Rather, in aiming to make people laugh at "one's incongruous position" (109), the camp idiom of juxtaposition through overadornment and theatricality provides "a continuous creative strategy for dealing with the homosexual situation, and, in the process, of defining a positive homosexual identity" (110).

Even though Newton records the extent to which camp and drag were often intricately related in the subculture inhabited by her interviewees, she takes care to differentiate between "the drag queen" and "*the* camp" (56) whom she describes as "a homosexual wit and clown" (100). The distinction is worth noting. Yes, both the drag queen and the camp "are expressive performing roles" (104) and "are intimately related" (105). But, Newton remarks, "strictly speaking, the drag queen simply expresses the incongruity," being concerned primarily "with masculine-feminine transformation," "while the camp actually uses it to achieve a higher synthesis," being concerned more "with what might be called a philosophy of transformations and incongruity" (105). Additionally, in contrast with the drag queen, who had a lower status for bearing "the visible stigmata of homosexuality" (105), the camp was "the cultural and social focus of male homosexual groups" (56). This factor cut across class divisions since groups with differing social standing all had in common their coherence around the camp and the perspective on incongruity which he voiced or enacted.

Newton's observations help to clarify how camp operated in practice even when inflected as a drag queen's style of gender hyperbole and exaggerated theatricality. Drag supplied one element of the camp repertoire but by no means comprised its entirety. Doing drag at night in clubs, bars, or parties was campy because it foregrounded the constructedness of femininity as distinct from a sexed body, but so, in its way, was passing in the daytime or at theaters or the opera. Appearing to be straight required a gender impersonation not un-like drag because it meant "fulfilling (or not violating) all the requi-sites of the male role as defined by the 'straight' world." Amongst gay men, the word *drag* was often used "in this broader sense, even to include role playing which most people simply take for granted" (Newton, 108). Far from being the expression of an innate femininity that motivated same-sex desire—the scientific explanation of homo-sexuality as a gender inversion at this time—"letting your hair down," as the saying went, by doing drag or exaggerating effeminacy in tone or manner was inseparable from the need to pass; indeed, camp situ-ated drag as a reaction to and commentary on the social imperative to pass and the incongruity of the gender ideology it reinforced.

Accounts of Seattle's Garden of Allah, a gay cabaret in opera-tion from 1946 to 1957, give a good picture of how drag and pass-ing coexisted along a spectrum of visibility and invisibility. Follow-ing the day's custom, which was influenced by straight stereotypes of working-class origin, the men and women patronizing the Gar-den adhered to rigid gender binaries in imitation of heterosexual re-lations. Thus the femme lesbian and butch homosexual (or "trade" hetero or bisexual) did not stand out in the crowd as noticeable gen-der impersonators, in contrast with their role-playing counterparts, the butch lesbian and femme (or "queen") homosexual. "You did not see feminine lesbians then because they looked like everyone else," one male patron recollects. "You saw only the masculine women and feminine men. Everyone was still in the closet" (Paulson, 40).[4]

The cultural conundrum of seeing/not seeing queerness was the stuff of camp—and also the source of its fun. As Newton points out, whereas the drag queen could make use of camp hyperbole to ex-aggerate the incongruity of a masculine-feminine binary, the camp's outlook was more fully and subtly expressed in humor. Camp wit took various forms of verbal play: the snappy retort or putdown, the coded innuendo, the double-barreled pun, the misleading pronoun or reference to one's church or family, the pilfered and then twisted cultural allusion. If drag was contingent on the gender ambiguity of passing, so was the camp's semantic ambiguity, which disrupted the apparent transparency of language.

Camp wit exploited the ambiguity of straight discourse in order to articulate a queer perspective of social as well as sexual relations. It provocatively challenged the legitimacy of perceived intent, exposing the larger cultural field in which words bore meanings beyond their confining straight context. The "double entendre" in particular, Chauncey observes, "made the double life possible. It allowed men to construct a gay world in the midst of but invisible to the straight world" (286). For instance, as John Clum remarks when analyzing how the word *gay* operates as camp in the song lyrics of Cole Porter, in the 1930s and '40s the word itself "was a coterie term, used only by some urban homosexuals," its new meaning only "for those in the know." In mainstream usage, *gay* still bore its traditional, if now vacated, sense of "happy, colorful, energetically frivolous, hedonistic" (73)—as when an MGM trailer claimed that *Broadway Melody of 1940* (with a Porter score, incidentally) was "big as Broadway and twice as gay!" In contrast with contemporary usage, the word *gay* could go either way, even in the same instance, depending on its audience. The resulting semantic ability to break into what would otherwise appear to be a secure discursive location marked the word's camp valence, allowing *gay* literally to pass as "straight" in Porter's lyrics (and, perhaps, in the trailer as well). Impossible to recognize unless one were "in the know," camp intrusions in the circuits of semantic exchange depended on a straight audience missing the point or refusing to hear or see beyond what common sense dictated.

Disrupting the relation of language, meaning, and intent rearranged what counted as being "inside" as opposed to "outside." In the very act of speaking to those included within the privileged circle of semantic exchange, camp also addressed the hypothetical person left out of the loop, "who views the object 'normally'" (Robertson, 17). Although well-established theatrical slang for gays by 1920 and in more widespread use beyond strictly show-business circles by 1945 (Robertson, 3), *camp* was still a "gay word not yet known to outsiders" (Bérubé, 90). As such, camp was a tactic of survival for individuals, certainly. But even more importantly, it forged a collective subcultural identity, which explains the centrality of the camp across social divisions in Newton's account and also the clarity with which the term could name a discernible sensibility or taste for those in the know. "When gay men engaged in camp before Stonewall," Daniel Harris recalls, "they often did so as a way of laughing at their appropriation of popular culture for a purpose it had never been intended to serve: that of identifying themselves to other homosexuals and triggering in their audience instantaneous recognition of stock expressions, gestures, and double-entendres that strengthened the bonds that held them together" (19–20). As the mass medium of popular entertainment and cultural representation to which gay men had direct access, the movies and their stars supplied a rich source of readily available and immediately recognizable straight material for camp to rework toward more communal, queerer ends. Smuggling homosexual content into a seeming heterosexual environment, camp developed its own system of referentiality which could then be used to initiate a sexual exchange in public because it offered an alternative discourse for "communicating their forbidden desires"—for instance, through recoded cultural allusions such as a mutual passion for Judy Garland (D. Harris, 20).

This is also how, paradoxically, in its own way camp wove a cloak of invisibility, functioning, Matthew Tinkcom comments, "as an alibi (in the sense of being elsewhere)" (*Working Like a Homosexual*, 5). A shared taste for musicals or film stars like Garland or Hayworth supplied one such alibi as the excuse for homosexuals interacting around an "innocent" common interest while at the same time signaling to each other another shared interest as well. The coded texture of camp discourse made it hard to discern by outsiders except, possibly, as an esoteric and feminizing appreciation of artifice and theatricality.

Far from confirming an inherent homosexual sensibility, the taste signaled by camp discourse was therefore a form of "learned behavior" (D. Harris, 21), socializing men as homosexuals in relation to both the heteronormative world and the unseen queer culture present within it. To be legible, camp required initiation, some form of acculturation. "What may be difficult for younger gay men to understand [today]," Clum points out for those no longer in the know, "is that homosexuality was not often discussed, nor was there necessarily any sex. But there was a support system and a social world of common interests, a major one being musical theater in all its mani-festations . . . That is, gayness was not only a sexual preference (the sex didn't exist for me and my friends until much later) but a cultural milieu" (22–23). Crucial to maintaining that milieu was the custom of intergenerational mentoring, a common element in many biogra-phies of gay men recounting this period of time. Older men consid-ered it a social obligation to take in hand a youth new to the city, teaching him "how to camp"—as well as instructing him in passing, taking him to the theater, introducing him to other men, advising him how to evade police—and as "repayment" the protege was ex-pected to "assume the same role for others" later on (Loughery, 73).

A similar process of socialization in "the argot, the folklore, and the rich variety of the gay life"—though less intergenerational, since the "older men, in this case [were] thirty or thirty-five"—character-ized the homosexual cliques formed during World War II, the origin of friendships which lasted long after the war (Loughery, 143). One ex-GI, interviewed for the documentary *Coming Out Under Fire* (1991), based on Allan Bérubé's book, remembers: "There was a group of us who met and hung out together. I knew they were homosexual, although I never spoke to another man about it, because they were funny, and they were gay, and they were happy, and they knew show biz." For these men, the camp reworking of "bits and pieces of popu-lar culture" in conversation, letters, and mimeographed news sheets was central both to their passing in the military and their differ-entiation from the heteronormality presumed by the military (Bé-rubé, 86).

The *Coming Out* documentary features one mimeographed news-letter—the title changing from "The Myrtle Beach Bitch" to "The Myrtle Beach Belle" to "The Bitches' Camouflage"—which has a car-toon ad soliciting subscribers with the question, "Isn't it campy? Don't forget to order your copy today." Camping allowed for mutual identification, helping gay servicemen to "create and expand a little social space for themselves within a society that tried to keep them invisible, isolated, and silent" (Bérubé, 87). Men expressed a camp outlook in their behavior—swishing when working as MPs and tell-ing the "girls" to line up, as one gay GI recalls in the documentary—and also in their language—borrowing the "vernacular of Dorothy Parker" for letters, as another remembers (using overinflected words such as *darling, ghastly, divine* or phrases such as *I could spit* after describing uncomfortable heat or living quarters). Camping enacted their recognition of the incongruous position of queers in relation to the military, at once more liberated and more censored than in civilian life. The writer of "The Myrtle Beach Bitch" describes how the newsletter was all "gay stuff," explaining there was nothing "normal" about it. Then he turns his statement around, recalling that he and his friends would joke that *they* were the only normal people around: "The rest of the world's queer," they used to say. "We're not."

At the same time, that queerly normal world was getting larger. As many historians have documented, the war years were a milestone in forging a hitherto unavailable, for many even unthinkable, sense of community among homosexuals and lesbians. Moreover, what Bérubé recounts in his discussion of the camp informing many army drag shows is how World War II began the process of bringing camp "out," placing it in more direct contact with a straight audience than was the case for the covert but nonetheless active homosexual subculture in big cities before the war. The drag shows encouraged by the military to provide entertainment for all-male audiences gave ample opportunities for camping in public, for foregrounding the complementary significance of passing and drag as each illuminated the incongruous opposition of "normal" and "queer," of heterosexual and homosexual, made more emphatic—yet also even more slippery—in military culture.

To be sure, the exaggerated impersonation of femininity by men in army shows was not just an import from drag nightlife but a convention carried over from vaudeville and theater. The lack of illusionism in the burlesque style of army drag ostensibly helped to place GI audiences at a safe distance from the gender slippages and implied homoeroticism of shows which reiterated heterosexual values but had men standing in for women. Still, when doing an all-male production of *The Women* or broad impersonations of Carmen Miranda or the Andrews Sisters, many gay performers used their facility with camp wit to turn the tables on their audiences.[5] For one of his examples, Bérubé cites a trio at a Georgia base who wrote a show-stopping song for their drag act that overtly incorporated "gay slang and ended each verse with increasingly mocking and ironic questions about 'camp.' " Their song then finished with the suggestion that the audience's "naivete" in failing to get the trio's camping was "even campier" than the performance itself (90–91).

In sum, whether it took the form of drag, wit, taste, cultural re-coding, or an outright satire of straights' blindness to a queerness standing with hands on hips right before their eyes, the objective of camp was not to produce a meaning or context per se but rather to perceive the relation of meaning and context as mediated by the marginalized and incongruous cultural location of homosexuality. Appropriating the terms of straight culture's representations of gen-der normality but deploying them for queerer purposes (camarade-rie, cruising, consuming), camp style was a strategy for articulat-ing ironic awareness of the multiple codes regulating straightness and queerness alike. In denaturalizing the ideological construction of gender and sexuality, moreover, camp recognition of incongruity did not invert the homologous boundaries of visible/straight/natural and invisible/queer/unnatural but located one side of the polarity in direct tension with the other.

The stance toward incongruity defined camp as a practice, a style and strategy inextricable from passing. With its sights set not-so-squarely on incongruity, "camp plays with notions of seriousness and absurdity," as Scott Long comments, "not to deny them but to re-define them. It is dialectical, not deconstructive, so to speak" (80). For this reason, camp did not amount to a "philosophy" of incon-gruity, as Newton concludes, so much as it enabled practitioners to assume a subjective position of "an *engaged* irony which (as the best definition of camp puts it) allows one a strong feeling of involvement with a situation or object while simultaneously providing one with a comic appreciation of its contradictions" (Glenn, 15). Evident in what Newton analyzes as the subject, style, and strategy of camp, and embodied in the perspective of the camp as a social role, the stance of ironic engagement bespoke a dialectical perception of the incon-gruities through which culture regulates value—sexual values, gen-der values, semantic values, economic values, aesthetic values, *and* entertainment values. Thus, when Tinkcom describes camp as "a phi-losophy not so much of sexuality but of commodity culture" (*Working Like a Homosexual*, 33), I take him to mean that camp inscribes an out-look which problematizes, because it well discerns, how value oper-ates as a system of exchange. This understanding is what enabled the various elements of camp to cohere as a viable social practice more than as a fully worked-out "philosophy."

Historically, camp's dialectical perception of the dominant culture's own representational codes for heteronormality allowed it to function so well as a strategy of passing, while the stance of ironic engagement gave it the potential as a style to interrupt, then redefine the seemingly stable relations of form to content, surface to depth, margin to center, reception to intentionality, consumer to commodity. Because camp so thoroughly depended on ironic humor for its cultural transactions, it is still most tangibly evident as an overly aestheticized or theatricalized style, the goal of which is to deliver the witty verbal or visual *effect*: the inflated depreciation that slyly amounts to ironic appreciation on revised terms. More subtly and powerfully, because its irony affords a position of engagement, not alienation, camp also needs to be understood as the formation of a queer *affect*: of taking queer pleasure in perceiving if not causing category dissonance, whether in representations of heterosexual normality, the values that reiterate it, or the commodities that derive from it. As a practice of everyday queer life, which articulated a dialectical view of cultural productions of all sorts, starting with gender and sexuality, camp intervened in the value-making process of cultural productions, but it did so in order to reinvest in them queerly.

At its most affective, camp recognized the queer as social excess— the surplus value of straight culture, so to speak—while providing the rationale or alibi for his being "too much" through style, taste, and parody, the assertion of a dissident sensibility distinct from the mainstream yet located within it. Camp's ironic engagement with this ideological contradiction could be deadly serious, a mode of critiquing or at least disturbing the circuits through which cultural values maintained the stability of a rigorously heterosexualized world, but it was not a utopian or revolutionary transformation of that world. Its stance toward culture derived from "an epistemology of the closet" (Sedgwick) which post-Stonewall identity politics displaced in the seventies. By the 1980s, as I pointed out in starting this account, a straighter and more homogenous version of camp as a cultish taste had become recognized, even embraced, by mainstream culture as mass camp. For the generation of gay men coming out after Stonewall, in the meantime, the more complex, queerer inflection of camp bore the stigma of the closet's oppressiveness and was considered to be a fatality of the closet's opening.

At the 2002 Broadway premiere of *Hairspray*, the musical version of John Waters's 1988 film, *Daily Variety* reported that the filmmaker "took exception to that four-letter word" even before it appeared in all of the glowing reviews the next morning. "No one uses the word 'camp' anymore," the article quotes Waters saying at the post-performance party. "Only executives in Hollywood use it, as code for 'gay,' like 'sporty' means lesbian" (Hofler, 33). While this coding is indeed now in place, and camp no longer unifies gay communal identity as it once did, reports of "The Death of Camp," as Daniel Harris titles his first chapter of *The Rise and Fall of Gay Culture*, do appear greatly exaggerated. In both the mainstream and gay press, and among journalists and some academics, most often the obituary is meant to exemplify the break between pre- and post-Stonewall styles of social self-representation through a new formation of gay tastes meant to move beyond the closet as the occasion for camp—whether that amounts to the macho "clone look" of the 1980s or the Abercrombie and Fitch style of the present day or even a younger generation's veneration of pop stars in place of Judy Garland. Yet regardless of how it is updated, critiqued, or repudiated, camp remains a topic central to and definitive of gay culture. His objection to the four-letter word notwithstanding, Waters himself guest-starred in an insightful and funny episode of *The Simpsons* ("Homer's Phobia," broadcast on the Fox network on 18 February 1997) which confirmed the ongoing currency of camp beyond Hollywood executives. If the obituary is to be believed, then, this may be the longest a-dying since Desdemona.

CAMP AND THE MUSICAL

Given the longstanding equation of gay camp fandom with musicals, was it simply historical coincidence that the era of camp as a distinctive queer practice and the period when MGM stood for "More Great Musicals" occurred simultaneously? At first glance, the answer would have to be, yes. A camp dialectical perspective of heteronormality, viewing it as contiguous with an inescapable queerness, openly contradicts the musical genre's own formal conventions and ideological premises.

Musicals were manufactured as wholesome entertainment for mainstream audiences, so they are permeated by heterosexual values, beginning with the highly conventionalized plots subordinating songs to the fortunes of a romantic couple. According to Rick Altman's comprehensive analysis in *The American Film Musical*, the couple inspires the genre's structural logic. A male/female pairing organizes a dual focus for an entire film in order to make clearer how matching segments (paralleled numbers, scenes, shots, dialogue, settings, and so on) outline a lateral pattern existing beneath the narrative's linearity. The dually focused structure associates the male figure with one constellation of values (wealth, age, and tradition, say) and the female with another (beauty, youth, and modernity, say), and the couple's eventual union in a musical's closure then enacts the reconciliation of those secondary oppositions, "previously seen as mutually exclusive," in order to satisfy the formal and ideological purposes of "reducing an unsatisfactory paradox to a more workable configuration, a concordance of opposites" (27).

In Altman's account there is nothing campy, let alone queer, about a musical, starting with the "seemingly gratuitous" numbers, which turn out to be "instrumental in establishing the structure and meaning of the film" (27). The lateral pattern structured by the genre's dual focus predicts how, by the finale, male and female will combine as a couple, the two partners complementing each other precisely because of their sexual difference; numbers then mean something in reference to the film's overall structure, which is also to say that they are totally enclosed by the structure's binary logic and heterocentric universe. "The whole point in overdetermining the musical's dualistic structure," Altman writes, "is precisely to make sure that the spectator will sense the film's overall patterns without analysis" (45). Yet in enacting a vision of social harmony to make a myth out of the ritual of courtship, as Altman notes (27), the dual focus also mystifies the ideological work performed by the genre's smoothing over of irreconcilable cultural oppositions as symbolically laid out in this formally calibrated structure, beginning with the presumption that the primary difference in culture is a heterosexual one.

The genre's dually focused concentration on sexually differentiated oppositions certainly seems grist for the mill of camp's thematic, stylistic, and strategic purposes as Newton describes them, readily illuminating the incongruity of this binarized structure. Given the overdetermined heterosexual bias of musicals, however, such a camp response would appear to be breaking the rules, willfully ignoring the proper conventions and "overall patterns" staring one not so gaily in the face. "The sensibility of camp-*recognition*," Eve Kosofsky Sedgwick remarks, "always sees that it is dealing in reader relations and in projective fantasy (projective though not infrequently true) about the spaces and practices of cultural production" (156). But because of the significance of numbers, which interrupt, arrest, or exceed the flow of narrative more often than they stimulate it, the musical, I think, is one of those cases where camp recognition results from seeing the potential for ironic engagement in a film's textual specificity—starting with the genre's own incongruous binary logic—rather than from projection. Just as it standardizes form, generic convention regulates the meanings made available by a text but does not exhaust or entirely control them. Altman himself understands that film genres work this way. And his own claim that the dual focus requires a lateral rather than linear view of the numbers in relation to the narrative can as easily be turned toward camp recognition without willfully disregarding a musical's generic or textual integrity.

Brett Farmer heads in this direction when he describes in terms of fantasy the by-now legendary gay spectatorial investment in the musical. He starts from the premise that, to achieve its intense affective bond with the genre, gay spectatorship requires "active and quite extensive processes of resistance and negotiation" of the musical's heterosexual material (79). The gay audience undertakes a "reordering" of the apparent economy of a musical's preferred meaning as dictated by its closure on the couple, finding pleasure instead in excess, those marginal moments in any musical which undermine the genre's overdetermined ideological agenda and consequently "open it up to alternative interpretations" (81). Generically privileged as a site of excess due to its spectacle, the musical number in particular ends up being more gratuitous than not, a "fertile point of reference" (81)—in Farmer's view, "one of the closest analogues in mainstream cinema to a desubjectivised fantasmatic fluidity" (93). Gay spectators, he posits, seize on the number's representation of gender ambiguities and desires not limited to heterosexual objectives. True, Farmer recognizes that "it is more than possible to ignore or suppress these potentialities and to read the musical number 'straight,' engaging and interpreting its erotic scenarios as exclusively heterosexual, if not heteronormative." But that does not make it impossible "to read the musical number 'otherwise,'" that is, from the position which defines a spectator as gay and not straight, without investment in "the frameworks of compulsory heterosexuality" and so more ready "to acknowledge and realize the shifting potentials for queer desire signaled in and by the excesses and unconventionalities of the musical number" (94).

As his language indicates, Farmer approaches the matter of gay spectatorship psychoanalytically, more as an intense, unconscious engagement at the level of "gay-identified fantasies and desires" (81) than as one involving camp, which in his book he treats in a separate chapter on female stars. But despite his attention to musicals as scenarios of queer fantasy, Farmer's explanation suggests crucial points of convergence with camp. What he theorizes about gay fantasmatic investments in a musical through its numbers resembles the affect of camp as an ironic engagement with ideological incongruity through an exaggerated theatricality. Each can be said to concentrate on "the disruptive, centrifugal dimensions of spectacle and excess over and against the homogenizing, centripetal forces of narrative ordinarily prioritized in and by conventional, 'straight' (in both sense of the word) reading practices" (96). Likewise, Farmer's explanation of how gay spectatorship works from within a musical's own text to resist the heterosexualized trajectory toward closure parallels how camp dialectically reimagines the binary thinking of dominant culture that marginalizes homosexuality. Each can be described as "an active reordering of the text that is both a refusal and a redefinition of the preferred meanings . . . [a] style of negotiated reading practice [which] produces a radically restructured semiotic economy" (80).

My point is that camp, viewed as an affective response and as a reading practice, enacts in a social arena what Farmer claims gay spectatorship connects with more unconsciously and privately. In much the same way, what he argues about the number's doubled legibility as straight and "otherwise" mirrors the camp strategy of passing. For the camp valence of a number to appear, whether as the fluidity of queer fantasy or as an ironic engagement with incongruity, this other perspective on the number's content has to be incorpo-

rated somewhere, somehow into the film's own style of representation—that is, assuming that the other meaning is not simply being
"projected" onto the film, it has to have a textual materiality of its
own even if a noncamp viewer fails to see it.

Still, I have to admit that a difficulty arises when applying Farmer's
explanation wholesale to a historicized account of camp and the
MGM musical. His theorization of gay spectatorship offers a productive direction for thinking about musicals in terms that exceed the
genre's binary structural logic and declared heterosexual bias. Yet
his own understanding of contemporary gay spectatorship (his expressed project) takes for granted a sense of a subcultural and psychic identity which, as already pointed out, does not automatically
translate back to the middle decades of the last century. Camp articulated a collective social bond among queer men, but we still have to
imagine their spectatorship of musicals varying along a spectrum of
complicated relations to dominant culture. After all, queer men invested in the heterosexual regime to some extent, however conflicted
and ironically viewed, because of the power of the imperative to pass.
Even after saying that, camp reception of the musical during this era
can only remain speculative. Little ethnographic evidence of camp
spectatorship of musicals from the studio era survives except as the
odd anecdote here and there in autobiographies and memoirs, themselves often mediated by a contemporary recognition of gay identity.

Camp production of musicals at MGM, on the other hand, is another matter altogether. As I discuss in chapter 1, close inspection
of the industrial and aesthetic protocols determining the production
of musicals in Culver City reveals how they combined, in the films'
mise-en-scène and aggregate form, to address a possible camp spectator with an invitation to read the straight representational content
"otherwise." Without recapitulating here what that chapter covers
in detail, I can at least illustrate textual inscriptions of this invitation by looking at two iconic moments of camp in the history of the
MGM musical: Judy Garland's performances of "The Trolley Song"
in *Meet Me in St. Louis* (1944) and "The Man That Got Away" in *A
Star is Born* (1954), her comeback vehicle at Warner Bros. four years
after the much publicized termination of her contract with MGM. I'll
begin with the latter because not only is it a sublime camp number, it
appears in a film from the studio era which recognizes the camp va-

lences of both Garland and the MGM musical. The multilayered context supplied by *A Star is Born* for "The Man That Got Away" bears as crucially on my argument as the number itself does when first examined as an isolated segment.

CAMP AS "THAT LITTLE SOMETHING EXTRA"

Early in *A Star is Born*, Norman Maine (James Mason) watches Esther Blodgett (Garland) perform "The Man That Got Away" in a jam session with members of the Glenn Williams Orchestra at the Downbeat Club. Garland's intense delivery and tight, often jerky arm gestures punctuate the lyrics' most expressive moments, and the number is staged and photographed to represent the spontaneity, expressiveness, and intimacy of her character's singing. As Richard Dyer comments, "The authenticity the number is after really has nothing to do with what Esther/Garland is singing about—it is the authenticity of her capacity to sing that is at stake" ("*Star is Born*," 139). The performance is consequently defined through "markers of authenticity" to indicate the singer's lack of control (the redundancy of Garland's gestures and facial expressions), lack of premeditation (the singing occurs spontaneously in improvisational rapport with the band), and privacy (the number is done simply for its own sake, not for an audience) (138–39). So strong is the goal of making Esther's authenticity seem transparent that midway through, at an emotional highpoint in the lyric, Garland rushes toward the camera and momentarily goes out of focus. The blurred image lasts for just a few seconds but it indicates that her performance is being caught in the act, not manufactured by movie technology or crafted by a director's or actor's art, despite the obvious way that band members are physically positioned around the singer and visually subordinated to her through lighting so that she dominates the frame at every point.

The authenticity which the number establishes may seem the antithesis of camp, as Dyer states (132–33).[6] Yet throughout the number Garland also sings, looks, and moves with full awareness of the band; the blocking suggests that she does not express the song's powerful emotions rawly but performs them with great intensity in collaboration with the musicians. At the number's close, as the band plays the melody's final notes, Garland looks up dreamily, her face

PHOTOFEST

Judy Garland sings "The Man That Got Away" in *A Star is Born* (Warner Bros., 1954).

registering a quite different emotion than when singing. Ironically, given the torchy delivery, her expression at this point is somewhat eerily reminiscent of Dorothy wistfully thinking about what lies over the rainbow in *Wizard of Oz* (1939). Then Garland winks at the saxophonist and trombone player seated near her, the gesture signaling her approval or possibly a break with the song's persona, and she smiles, revealing a new pleasure derived from having just performed the song extremely well without regard to its unhappy content. Further underlining the number's value as a deliberated performance of emotionality, "The Man That Got Away" is placed too early in the plot of *A Star is Born* to imply a parallel with the character's off-stage feelings. Esther Blodgett is a hardworking and satisfied professional vocalist, her ambitions and passions yet to be stirred up by Norman Maine. At least in terms of what we can assume about her from the film so far, she takes on the song's heartbroken, embittered persona as a fictive role and does so without drawing on past emotional experience to supply the feelings she expresses so intensely.

Paradoxically, what "The Man That Got Away" authenticates is how the star vocalizes the representation of powerful emotions by shaping them through a performance style that theatricalizes transparency and then naturalizes the theatricality. This number, which became a Garland signature second only to "Over the Rainbow," is readable as evidence of the performer's intense involvement in the song's emotional content and, simultaneously, as evidence of her equally intense detachment from it. The dialectical positioning of Garland/Esther's engagement with and distance from the number is the source of its powerful camp affect.

I cite this example from a Warners musical as textual evidence of MGM camp because any number featuring Judy Garland can never be all that much of a digression from either Metro-Goldwyn-Mayer or camp, and to be just as sure, at the time of its release in 1954 *A Star is Born* was already unthinkable without reference to Garland's career at MGM, as I shall discuss in a moment. But even when analyzed in its own terms as an isolated segment, "The Man That Got Away" perfectly exemplifies what Jack Babuscio describes as the "double aspect of a performance" central to camp:

> Thus, camp as a response to performance springs from the gay sensibility's preference for the *intensities* of character, as opposed to its content: what the character conveys tends to be less important than *how* or *why* it is conveyed . . . This theatricalisation of experience derives both from the passing experience (wherein, paradoxically, we learn the value of self while at the same time rejecting it) and from a heightened sensitivity to aspects of a performance which others are likely to regard as routine or uncalculated. It is this awareness of the double aspect of a performance that goes a long way to explain why gays form a disproportionately large and enthusiastic part of the audience of such stars as, most notably, Judy Garland. (46)

Babuscio mentions Garland as his most notable example, attributing her "disproportionately large" gay following to the camp quality arising from her intense singing style, which brings out in some viewers a heightened sensitivity to the art of appearing artless.[7] Thus he locates the source of camp in Garland's intensity as it overwhelms the content of a filmic character or song's persona so that "what the character conveys tends to be less important than *how* or *why* it is conveyed." As importantly, somewhat like Newton, Babuscio locates camp "awareness" of theatricalization as a mode of authentification (what "others are likely to regard as routine or uncalculated") in both the performance and its audience—or more accurately, in a gay audience alert to slippages in that dualism and responsive to the ways that a Garland performance heightens without resolving the "double aspect" of self-presentation as an act of performing ("how" and "why" the style conveys in its intensity as opposed to "what" it conveys as content). In his insightful study of Garland, Dyer, too, finds her significance for gay men in their shared "recognition of the theatricality that the gay sensibility is attuned to," by which he means, more complexly, a sensibility holding together "qualities that are elsewhere felt as antithetical: theatricality and authenticity," but also "intensity and irony, a fierce assertion of extreme feeling with a deprecating sense of its absurdity" (*Heavenly Bodies*, 154).

Both Babuscio and Dyer seek to explain how Garland's performance style appeals to "the gay sensibility," a sensibility historically structured by camp, as Babuscio's contextualization of his remarks in "the passing experience" indicates and as Dyer also acknowledges in his commentary. "The passing experience" substitutes theatricality for authenticity while sustaining the dualism as a camp perspective on self-representation, viewing identity as a social performance which resists synchronizing style (gender demeanor as the signifier of a public self) and content (sexual orientation as the signified of a private self), but instead exploits their asymmetry. Camp in this regard is a semiotic exchange but not necessarily a semantic one. "It is precisely this (unrestful) holding together of antitheses," Fabio Cleto remarks, "that makes camp irreducible to a set of features, for it works by *contra*diction, by *crossing* statements and their possibility of being. Intentions, seriousness, and their correlates (politics and agency) are there, and yet they are only present in a queer articulation: not one that will concede itself as a classifying tool, but rather as a puzzled, questioned issue" (29). "The Man That Got Away" exemplifies such "a queer articulation" because the number is performed, staged, and filmed so as to allow Garland/Esther's singing to be legible as authentic and theatrical at the same time; the number cannot be reduced to either style or content but builds on their tension. As in her dramatic scenes, in her singing Garland's intensity would not support such a strong camp valence without the ballast of her naturalistic acting, seemingly untrained and transparently expressive. The camp affect of "The Man" does not arise because the singer's theatricality displaces her authenticity but, on the contrary, because each side of the dualism, in effect, "passes" as the other: theatricality *is* authenticity in this number, and vice versa.

Through the camp dialectic structuring Garland's electrifying performance of "The Man That Got Away," this sequence in *A Star is Born* establishes that Esther Blodgett has the exceptional talent to become a big star of musicals. As crucially, the film also achieves this end through Norman's subsequent account of the performance's impact on him. His importance in watching her performance cannot be underestimated. Norman/Mason, in fact, is positioned as a spectator of almost every one of Esther/Garland's numbers, and it appears that he falls deeply in love with her by watching her perform: Esther's singing of "The Man" first attracts Norman's interest in her as more than a sexual dalliance; her singing of a television commercial reunites them after he has been shanghaied by the studio for a location shoot; her singing of "Here's What I'm Here For" prompts his proposal; her singing of "It's a New World" stands in for the consummation of their marriage on their honeymoon; her singing of "Someone at Last" cheers him up as he tries to stay sober when unemployed; her singing of "New World" a second time consoles him as he prepares to drown himself in order to prevent Esther from sacrificing her film career to save him.

Although we do not witness Norman's spectatorship during "The Man That Got Away," on its completion we learn that his pleasure when watching was as intense as the singer's performance. The number begins with the band quietly playing its introduction as parallel shots link Norman and Esther, spectator and singer. A far shot of Norman at the back of the nightclub rhymes with a similar shot of Esther and the band on the stage floor; with a cut back to Norman in a medium shot at frame left, a waiter moves from the rear of the club toward the front, and the camera tracks with him back to Esther, now in a medium shot at frame right. Following the trombone player's bluesy vamp, she begins singing, and the camera then stays fixed on her. Afterward, Norman tries to describe the powerful affect of watching her sing. "There are certain pleasures that you get," he explains. "Little, little jabs of pleasure." He goes on to compare his pleasure to that of watching an expert boxer, bullfighter, or ballet dancer. Esther herself dismisses Norman's extravagant praise. Laughing uncomfortably at several points, she wryly concludes that he may not be as sober as they both had thought at the start of their conversation. But he persists. "You've got that little something extra Ellen Terry talked about," Norman continues. "Ellen Terry, a great actress long before you were born. She said that's what star quality was, that little something extra. Well, you've got it."

"That little something extra," which instills "little, little jabs of pleasure" in Norman as Esther sings "The Man That Got Away," is more than confirmation of her star quality, or a reminder of Garland's for that matter. He emphasizes not the authenticity of her singing or its emotional content, but its theatricality, his appreciation of her vocal form. "I'm trying to tell you how you sing," he explains when comparing the performance to fishing or prizefighting. "Do you mean like a prizefighter or a fish?" Esther replies (and Garland's reading of the line fully brings out a camp inflection of her self-deprecating reduction of his praise). The "little, little jabs of pleasure" Norman then mentions arise from his examples of watching a display of stylish, professional expertise: "If you'd never seen a bullfighter in your life, you'd know a great bullfighter the moment he stepped into the ring. From the way he stood, the way he moved. Or a dancer. You don't have to know about ballet. That little bell rings inside your head, that little jolt of pleasure." With a smile, he adds, "Well that's what happened to me just now. You're a great singer."

What Norman refers to in terms of his pleasure as well as Esther's star quality suggests that he watches "The Man That Got Away" as a camp spectator. Esther's emotional performance of the unhappy song does not move him to tears, but to intense—jabbing, jolting—pleasure. The style of her performance amplifies the song's content with "something extra," something in addition to the lyric that adds depth to the singing itself as the authentification of her star quality, not of her heartbreak. That "something extra" is the camp affect of the number, on-screen for Norman and off-screen for the audience. I do not mean to suggest that *A Star is Born* characterizes Norman Maine as a gay spectator of Esther (though the character does have queer resonances, as when he sees her made-up for her screen test, comments that she sat in the makeup chair "for an hour too long, honey" and then does a makeover to restore her "natural" look).[8] Rather, my point is that the film is rather explicit in having him appreciate the value of her singing for its camp dialectic. According to Norman's explanation, Esther's greatness lies in the way she stands, the way she moves: as Babuscio would say, not from *what* she sings but from *how* she sings it.

Norman may be the only spectator watching "The Man That Got Away" within the film but his account of the number authorizes recognition of its camp affect by a moviegoing audience. Ronald Haver, responsible for the 1983 reconstruction of *A Star is Born* that restored footage cut after the film's first-run engagements, takes his cue from Norman when explaining his own intense response. Haver recalls first viewing the shortened version while in high school: "I can remember vividly being open-mouthed in awe at the sound of Garland singing 'The Man That Got Away' . . . I was sixteen when I first saw *A Star is Born*, and it was one of my primal moviegoing experiences, the kind of epiphanic film that burrowed itself into my subconscious and reverberated there" (238). He talked to his classmates afterward and found that "none of them, it seemed, had quite the experience with the film [he] did" (239).

Haver appears to forget his open-mouthed awe, though, and goes on to describe his different experience of *A Star is Born* so that it appears more normalized. He attributes his intense response first to the theater's wide screen and stereophonic sound, then to his uncommon and precocious interest in the film industry, which gave him a more "sophisticated" knowledge (and moviegoing taste) than was usual for a teen. After discussing with his teacher the apparent flaws in the narrative, Haver guessed that the emphasis on Garland at the expense of Mason indicated "there seemed to be something missing about Norman" because of the cuts made to the film, accounts of which he had read in the trade press (239). All the same, suggesting that more than curiosity about Norman is at stake, Haver quotes the entire "little something extra" speech to motivate what would turn out to be a long-standing obsession with restoring the film to its original length. "So it was with me and *A Star is Born*," he reflects. "I wanted more of those 'little jabs of pleasure,' the nuances of characterization, the hundreds of directorial details with which Cukor had so delicately imbued the film" (240). Although throughout his book Haver retrospectively (and to my mind, too repeatedly, protesting more than he needs to) accounts for his intense response to *A Star is Born* not as a Garland fan but as an admirer of George Cukor, which could just be splitting hairs, what led him to experience the film differently than his classmates on that first momentous viewing was his engagement with its camp affect through Garland, much as Norman engages with Esther on-screen.

Shaped by the camp dialectic informing both Garland/Esther's performance and Norman/Mason's spectatorship, "The Man That Got Away" condenses as its frame of reference the camp appeal of the MGM musical, at least when starring Judy Garland. Despite its being a remake of a 1937 film, *A Star is Born* is inseparable from Garland's years at MGM. Moss Hart interviewed her while writing the screenplay, and his most significant alterations of the 1937 version, incorporating some of her anecdotes, occur in the first half, which uses Norman's witnessing of Esther singing "The Man That Got Away" as the narrative pivot (Haver, 45).[9] Behind the scenes, Garland was not the sole former MGM employee. Many of the people working on *A Star is Born* had previously labored at MGM, mainly for the Freed unit, and they were a mix of straight and queer: director George Cukor, lyricist Ira Gershwin, the initial vocal arranger Ralph Blane (who had written scores for several musicals, such as *Meet Me in St. Louis*), costumer Mary Ann Nyberg, orchestrator Skip Martin. Irene Sharaff, Academy Award in hand for *An American in Paris* (1951) after contributing to many MGM films, did both costumes and sets for "Born in a Trunk," possibly at Garland's suggestion (Haver, 191). When cameraman Sam Leavitt left because of another commitment, that big production number was photographed by Harold Rossen, who had done *Wizard of Oz* and *Singin' in the Rain* (Haver, 194). Most crucially, perhaps, Roger Edens, Garland's mentor and Arthur Freed's longtime assistant, created "Born in a Trunk" and worked out "Someone at Last" with Garland at her home, although his MGM contract prevented him from taking a credit (Haver, 179–80, 189–90). Beyond the personnel, the film's production implied another layer of referentiality to MGM: as *A Star is Born* went over budget and behind schedule, the inevitable speculation began appearing in gossip columns that Garland was up to her "old tricks," repeating the behavior that had caused the termination of her MGM contract.

Association of Garland with her former studio, moreover, was exploited by Warner Bros. The publicity campaign laid out in the press book, like the contents of the program distributed with premiere engagements in Los Angeles and New York City, focused attention on Garland's MGM career to document her stardom chronologically and to mark out the four-year absence from the screen which this musical now corrected. The theatrical trailer followed the same promotional strategy, albeit without mentioning rival MGM by name, when announcing a great artist's triumphant return to the screen. Reviews as well as trade paper articles dwelled on Garland's comeback in this film following her dismissal from her longtime studio and triumphant return to vaudeville with her record-breaking engagement at the Palace theater on Broadway. With this context around the film, *A Star is Born* was immediately legible as being "as much a plot about Garland's suffering and difficulties, her performance in spite of it all, as it is about Esther Blodgett's rise to fame" (Staiger, 174).[10]

A reading of Garland's comeback in 1954 through her indelible association with MGM is encouraged from within *A Star is Born*, too, because it incorporates her history at that studio as a continuous frame of reference, as much so in the numbers as in dialogue, plot situations, and Norman Maine's characterization as an addicted performer dropped by his studio for being too undisciplined and disruptive of production schedules. By virtue of its numbers as well as its plot, Gerald Mast calls *A Star is Born* "a retrospective history of Judy Garland" (275). "Born in a Trunk" and "Someone at Last" incorporate motifs from Garland's career, and even refer to more recent successes at her former studio, *An American in Paris* and *Singin' in the Rain*. The first number, done "in the grand MGM style, with Oliver Smith's sets [*sic*] and Irene Sharaff costumes, just like the big MGM ballets" (Mast, 280), borrows its structure from "The Broadway Ballet" in *Singin' in the Rain* (Haver, 190), and the second names *American in Paris* as its object of parody as Garland single-handedly mimes the type of big production number identified with MGM.

The self-reflexivity in those two numbers may have been due to the uncredited guiding hand of Roger Edens. But even without Edens's input, "Gotta Have Me Go with You," Garland's first number, establishes visual and choreographic continuity with "Get Happy" from her final MGM musical, *Summer Stock* (1950), as Jane Feuer observes; and the progression from this first number to the second one, "The Man That Got Away," then "parallels the movement from Garland's MGM persona to her exposure to the public," with the latter number's "histrionic excess and awkward gestures which would not have been tolerated at MGM" announcing a new and different Judy Garland. Because the number's emotional intensity occurs without any plot or character justification other than to establish Esther's great talent, its "motivation," Feuer concludes, "is almost entirely extra-filmic," making most sense as an "acknowledgement of the MGM-Garland demystification" (*Hollywood Musical*, 119)—another way in which Garland's performance is less transparent than first appears, authenticated as camp through the artifice of style.

In serving this purpose, "The Man That Got Away" works as a riposte, an overintensification of the torchy ballad of heartfelt longing such as "Over the Rainbow" which appears in so many of Garland's MGM musicals. "The Man" does not repudiate the MGM style so much as it transposes the relation of performing style and song content. For it is less the case that the studio did not tolerate the "histrionic excess and awkward gestures" distinguishing the *Star is Born* number than that this particular style was reigned in at MGM for Garland's ballads but let loose in up-tempo songs, such as "The Trolley Song" in *Meet Me in St. Louis*, a belting number that was just as much of a Garland standard in her MGM fare. In fact, citing Babuscio's thinking about Garland's intensity and camp, John Clum calls this famous number from *St. Louis* a "classic camp moment" because of "the extreme of anxiety she is projecting while singing an inane song" (150). The critic makes this observation in passing, but, because of their very different emotional registers, a comparison of "The Trolley Song" with "The Man That Got Away" as exemplary Garland camp numbers is worth considering.

"The Trolley Song" similarly produces the "double aspect" of camp by orchestrating an incongruity between the heightening of affect through Garland's performance and the number's less important narrative purpose. Repeating simple rhymes set in a steady cadence to simulate the trolley ride, the song's chorus verbalizes the car's clanging noise and bumpy motion, which then provide the metaphors with which Garland's character, Esther Smith, describes what her heart feels like when, in the motivation for her solo, someone

Judy Garland sings "The Trolley Song" in *Meet Me in St. Louis* (MGM, 1944).

yells out, "Hiya, Johnny!" and she sees the boy next door, John Truett (Tom Drake), belatedly arriving and running after the trolley. However, as far as concerns the plot, "The Trolley Song" is an odd number to include at this juncture because it does not bring the couple any closer together than they were in the previous scene. Rather, "The Trolley Song" concludes with Truett/Drake's puppy-dog look at Esther/Garland as she smiles self-consciously and turns away— as if to disavow the outburst of emotion which the song has occasioned—followed by a fade-out to the Halloween sequence, which does result in the couple's long-anticipated first kiss.

Is there any reason for "The Trolley Song" to be in *Meet Me in St. Louis* other than to have Garland perform a star turn expected by her audience, this time offering a bouncy number to complement her first solo? The more plaintive and introspective "Boy Next Door" articulates Esther's feeling for John Truett, and this number is implicitly addressed to him, while explicitly acknowledging that she cannot violate convention by openly declaring her desire since they have yet to meet. "The Trolley Song" purports to mark the next stage in their relationship. The lyrics describe the scene of Garland's character sitting demurely on the trolley with her "high starched collar" and her "hair piled high," anxiously awaiting the moment when the boy next door, "in a light brown derby and a bright green tie," takes the adjacent seat and holds her hand in his. In contrast with the first solo, however, the lyrics in this number do not reveal anything new about Esther's private feelings—we already know she is infatuated with Truett. Furthermore, before Esther herself sings, the chorus recounts what will happen: how the ride begins with the expectation of "a jolly hour riding on the trolley" but will end up with someone losing her heart instead. The lyrics do not recount the action which the number stages—Esther's awareness of Truett's arrival and progress upstairs to the top of the trolley where she awaits him demurely—so much as determine it, as if Esther and John were actors following a script, which of course Garland and Drake are themselves doing.

As the solo begins, furthermore, how can we ignore the discrepancy between what the lyrics describe and what we as an audience see? Esther's own lace collar is not high up her neck, and she wears her auburn hair down; John likewise is not wearing a brown derby or a green tie. These unsynchronized details only begin to suggest how the number jars with its ostensible plot function. Whereas the lyrics describe Esther as passively genteel when she sees the boy next door on the trolley—she "started to yen," so she "counted to ten," and then "counted to ten again"—the initial agitation, then exuberance of Garland's delivery reverse the song's declared containment of her desire. As notably, although the lyrics indicate that Esther's attention is concentrated on Truett, she sings "The Trolley Song" to the members of the chorus, never to him; at one point, she even conducts their singing with her hands. Their recitation of the lyrics, repeating in the second person what Esther has declared in the first person, acknowledges their position as her audience. That the number is addressed to them, not Truett, theatricalizes the authenticity of Esther's desiring. When the chorus sings the lyrics back to her, their communal acknowledgment of her performance emphasizes the number's camp value as a theatricalization of authentic feminine desire which exceeds the "proper" heterosexual roles scripted by the song.

"The Trolley Song," then, does more than simply build on a disparity between content and style. This number is as much of a "classic camp moment" as "The Man That Got Away" because it too sustains content and style in a dialectic tension. Garland's singing adds female agency to a song that purports to contain it, and the audience on the trolley expands the song's address beyond the boy next door, legitimating the singer's emotional excess while implicitly acknowledging how it is achieved through a theatricalized expression. With Garland's emotional delivery simultaneously readable as both authentic and theatrical, "The Trolley Song" even appears to stage a kind of passing in the way that private self and public mask blur.

This camp resonance accounts for the number's important status in the Garland canon—with "Over the Rainbow" and "The Man That Got Away" it completed the triptych comprising the standard overture at her post-MGM concerts—and it may even help to explain why a curious legend about the filming of "Trolley Song" still persists: that during production, a crewmember who knew Garland happened upon the set and shouted, "Hiya, Judy!", his interruption forever recorded on the soundtrack, or so many fans (and some film trivia experts) continue to believe, insisting they hear the phrase during the number. This account of someone familiar with Garland breaking into the illusionism of the number's representational content is an impossibility, since its soundtrack was prerecorded and played back during the shoot, so what motivates the legend is the distortion of "Hiya, Johnny!" on the monaural soundtrack. Nonetheless, the legend speaks to the number's camp dialectic, which authenticates the performance of female desiring as a theatricalization, making it a song much more about Judy than about Johnny. This legend fancifully reinscribes in the very materiality of the film and its moment of production an audience's recognition of "that little something extra" in the number, namely, its camp affect.

"The Man That Got Away" and "The Trolley Song" readily illustrate my claim that camp has a material existence in musicals, but they will work *too* well as examples if they leave the impression that the dialectic shaping them was confined to Garland alone. I have more to say about her performance style in a very specific type of camp number in the second chapter, where I go further to suggest its continuity with other female stars singing and dancing at MGM, and I shall be discussing Gene Kelly and camp in the third chapter. But even in the limited terms introduced so far, a camp dialectic can easily be seen in the musical performances of a star other than

Garland. In Fred Astaire numbers, the dancer's body often works similarly to Garland's voice in focusing attention on the "little some- thing extra" arising from the tension between his authenticity in em- bodying self-expressiveness through dance and his theatricality in staging that meaning as a dance.

In Astaire's case, the correlative to Garland's excessive intensity is his ineffable combination of physical grace and agility, which give his lithe yet thin body its sense of being weightless as it moves through space. His prop dances, for instance, motivate the content of his cho- reography by supplying the occasion for a seemingly improvised solo that is anything but danced on the spot. Using whatever objects are at hand, often as a substitute for his absent partner in a mock roman- tic duet, these numbers are, of course, tightly choreographed dances but, even with that knowledge disavowed by the film's fictive world, they still signify much more than pure spontaneity on Astaire's part.

Consider as a very brief illustration "Sunday Jumps," one of Astaire's solos in *Royal Wedding* (1951). This number is set in a ship gymnasium as Tom Bowen (Astaire) waits for his sister, Ellen (Jane Powell), to show up for a rehearsal. Astaire's costume is worth noting right away for its contrast with the gym setting: he wears a pale blue shirt and slacks, a pinkish cravat, a necktie of similar color knotted around his waist instead of a belt, and bright red socks to draw at- tention to his feet. While waiting, Astaire starts a metronome and begins practicing tap steps, but stops after a few moments to see if his absent partner is approaching. She never shows, and, accidentally gripping a coat tree as he turns back into the room, Astaire begins dancing with it instead. He glides the coat tree on its base along the floor, tips it with his foot, spins it around, and so forth. As Astaire alternately treats the prop as a lightweight female surrogate and as a heavy inanimate object physically contrasting with and resisting his body, the choreography parodies conventions of a romantic duet with a real female partner, beginning with the riff on a signature step, the Astaire double helix (Mueller, 324–25).

When he tries to lift the coat tree to conclude this duet, however, Astaire has trouble raising it. His apparent lack of physical strength then instigates the second part of this number, a workout in the gym to "bulk up" so he can perform the lift successfully. After flexing his arms and bending his knees to warm up, Astaire cautiously investigates the various training apparatuses (weights on a pulley, parallel bars, vaulting horse, punching bag, indian pins). The equipment appears to daunt and befuddle him but he masters each apparatus to execute a dazzling little routine with it, what John Mueller refers to as the number's "screwball surprises" (325). The workout over, Astaire returns to the coat tree and can now execute the lift without difficulty, twirling with the heavy object held behind his neck like a barbell. Then he lowers the coat tree toward the ground, tilts and cradles it in his arm, posing with it much as he has done with female partners at the end of numerous romantic duets, and the "duo" take their bow to imaginary applause.

What joins the two parts of the number together is the choreography, which overwhelms the content with Astaire's style. His dancing creates a sense of improvisation by the way he begins each of his moves with a "feminizing" gesture in response to the bodybuilding machinery. These gestures—both hands clasped to his face to convey his intimidation or one hand on a hip to indicate his scrutiny, butt extended outward like a bustle, feet dangling in the air while he grips the parallel bars, a sashaying jaunt when he strolls over to a machine—seamlessly turn into his brand of graceful dancing. Likewise, he does not strike the punching bag with his fists but elegantly extends his leg and kicks it with a dance step. The number is irrelevant to Astaire's character in the plot but, as it parodies gender stereotypes by crossing them, it adds its own "little something extra" to the dancer's being light on his toes. "Sunday Jumps" juxtaposes a male body's normalizing masculinization (the bodybuilding workout defining the body through its strength and muscularity) with the dancer's queerer connotations of feminization (the ease and agility with which Astaire turns the workout into an impromptu dance that, resulting from the same kind of discipline and regularity as an athlete exercising, makes the dancer's effete-looking body seem lighter than air yet never emasculated). This dialectic shapes how Astaire can at once embody and enact an alternative form of masculinity through his dancing. Authenticating his theatricalized body as natural grace and vice versa, the camp affect of Astaire's dancing in "Sunday Jumps" draws on a "double aspect" of a musical star's performance that compares with Garland's singing in "Man That Got Away" and "Trolley Song."

3

4

6

5

7

8

Fred Astaire flexes his
muscles in "Sunday Jumps."
Royal Wedding (M G M, 1951).
Frame captures.

These examples just begin to define the textual materiality of camp in the MGM musical, which the following chapters will now explore further and with greater complexity. Functioning as this book's central topic as well as providing me with a dialectical stance of my own for reexamining the musicals critically and historically, camp offers an opportunity for taking a fresh look at the values attributed to this studio's prodigious output of "more great musicals," a body of unparalleled achievement that, for many, represents the apex of the genre as a popular art form. Most obviously, as the Garland and Astaire numbers indicate, camp encourages reconsideration of the musicals' representations of gender and sexuality, but it also helps to place these representations in closer proximity to other issues, seemingly unconnected to camp, which were just as crucial in regulating heteronormality during the studio era, such as stardom and labor, ethnicity and race. Furthermore, camp situates the films in their industrial production, marketing, and ongoing consumption on home video, and it raises still additional questions about the presumed heterosexualization of the studio-era audience and homosexualization of contemporary fandom. Approaching the musicals through camp therefore does not limit the scope for understanding their own formal strategies and cultural significance but, on the contrary, expands the vantage point from which we can more seriously appreciate their ongoing if shifting extra-added value in being "twice as gay" during the past half-century: pleasuring audiences with their expressions of unbridled joy while giving their high spirits a decidedly queer twist. Seen either way, these musicals are truly incongruous entertainment.

Chapter One

IMPROBABLE STUFF: CAMP AND

THE MGM HOUSE STYLE

*I*n her autobiography, Esther Williams recalls the audience response to the 1944 sneak previews of her first musical, then titled *Mr. Coed*:

> The comment cards filled out by the audiences all over southern
> California were not just positive, they were glowing. There was
> every indication that MGM had a big hit on their hands. What the
> moviegoers liked best, of course, was the improbable stuff that
> had little to do with the script. They were wild about the swim-
> ming numbers, especially the water carnival musical extravaganza
> at the finale, and they were enthusiastic about me, too. As a result,
> a decision was made on the third floor. When the picture was re-
> leased, it was no longer *Mr. Coed*. The new title was *Bathing Beauty*,
> and I got to share top billing with Red Skelton. (115)

The trailer which Metro-Goldwyn-Mayer fashioned for the retitled musical, produced by Jack Cummings and directed by George Sidney, was designed to feature "what the moviegoers liked best, of course," namely, "the improbable stuff that had little to do with the script." The trailer describes *Bathing Beauty* as "A show so BIG—so GLORI-OUSLY beautiful . . . It will set a NEW STANDARD in screen achieve-ment!" To support its grand claim, the trailer displays the somewhat eclectic assortment of talents gathered together for this musical: radio comedian Red Skelton, Harry James's swing band with Helen Forrest, Xavier Cugat's Latin band with Lina Romay, former Hit Pa-rade organist Ethel Smith, Colombian singer Carlos Ramirez, and newly top-billed Esther Williams featured with the obligatory assembly of "girls! Girls! GIRLS!" in the "Aqua-Ballet," hailed as "the most Dazzlingly Color Spectacle Ever Filmed!" Clips from the big water ballet—showgirls dancing on stage, followed by a line of swimmers moving in perfect synchrony in the pool below—open the trailer. Introducing the film's two leads, snippets of plot scenes with the red-haired comic and muscular swimming star follow in quick succession. These give fleeting glimpses of Williams posed in her bathing suit, then of Skelton performing in a pink tutu to "Dance of the Sugar Plum Fairies" and resisting his costar's aggressive lovemaking. The latter two excerpts are taken out of context (for in the film Skelton's drag and reluctance to kiss Williams are narratively motivated), but then plot seems insignificant to this coming attraction: afterward follow a string of clips featuring the many musical artists rounding out the cast and another preview of the grandiose spectacle of the aqua-ballet. In short, according to the trailer, *Bathing Beauty* promises to be irresistible camp entertainment on all counts.

As I mentioned in the introduction, the Hollywood musical's camp fan base has been equated almost exclusively with gay men. Their fascination with the musical is often attributed to the genre's exaggerated style and its great female stars, particularly when the two elements combine in the oversized, outlandish spectaculars of the sort typified by Esther Williams's "aquamusicals" for MGM, beginning with *Bathing Beauty*. "The Hollywood musical," Paul Roen observes when introducing his first of two volumes cataloguing movie camp, "is a genre which, by definition, exudes camp." Musicals, he explains, not only allow people suddenly to burst into song but they are "all awash with glitter, tinsel, and garish artifice" (11–12). David Van Leer makes the same claim, though he reverses the equation. "Camp," he states, "imitates the hyperbole of musicals and popular movies as well as other visual extravagances like overstated decor and fashion, and especially cross-dressing" (20). Whether the musical "exudes" camp or camp "imitates" the musical, it follows from both observations that, if camp had not had its own historical existence as a cultural practice, the Hollywood musical would surely have had to invent it, and vice versa.

Camp and the musical seem a perfectly matched couple, as fated to be mated as Astaire and Rogers, Garland and Rooney, Kelly and Sinatra, or Williams and water, but their pairing, while axiomatic today, did not stand out as noticeably when the genre dominated studio production in terms of profits, expense, shooting schedules, labor, and for MGM, reputation. At the Culver City lot, musicals were handled by three specialized units—headed by Arthur Freed, Joe Pasternak, and Jack Cummings—which between them turned out six to ten films annually.[1] Throughout the 1940s and until the mid-1950s, their musicals, Freed's in particular, often made the difference between profit and loss for MGM's corporate owner, Loew's. The three units could deliver a reliable product because the producers had unrestricted access to major and minor stars along with all the studio artists and craftspeople who developed projects for them on a daily basis.

The musical served as Metro's signature product, so much so that the studio became solely identified with the aesthetic evolution of the integrated musical which seamlessly blends story and spectacle. As the trailer for *Bathing Beauty* illustrates, however, what MGM marketed was the genre's oversized spectacle, achieved by a combination of oftentimes very diverse musical elements with the aim of dazzling the spectator's eyes and ears, not of advancing the story. The studio's reputation rested on its musicals' lavish production values. These included not only extravagant sets and outlandish costumes, the saturated look of Technicolor, major stars like Esther Williams and Judy Garland, leading songwriters like Cole Porter and Irving Berlin, and all those "girls! Girls! GIRLS!" but also spots for big dance numbers or dream ballets, for minor comics like Rags Ragland, for contract players who later became big stars, like June Allyson, or those who never did, like Ray McDonald, for second-string performers who always had a specialty number or two, like Ann Miller and Virginia O'Brien, for African American talent in isolated segments, primarily Lena Horne but also the likes of Stump and Stumpy (James Cross and Eddie Hartman), for popular bands like Harry James's and Xavier Cugat's—and let's not forget José Iturbi!

During the heyday of musicals production at the Culver City studio in the 1940s, when each new film was, like *Bathing Beauty*, promoted for its size and grandeur, its "Dazzlingly Color Spectacle,"

MGM routinely designed product with its large roster of contracted talent in mind. More often than not, the studio planned musicals around a formal principle of aggregation rather than integration. An aggregate form includes numbers "as a series of self-contained highlights that work to weaken the dominance of a homogenous, hierarchical narrative continuity" (Rubin, 18). It harks back to the genre's stage origins in what Martin Rubin calls a "Tradition of Spectacle" — from older formats such as P. T. Barnum's American Museum, the minstrel show, the three-ring circus, and Buffalo Bill's Wild West Show, to newer ones such as vaudeville, burlesque, the annual Ziegfeld Follies revues, and the aquacade where Esther Williams got her start. In any of its many incarnations, this tradition specializes in "feelings of abundance, variety, and wonder" (4), the dazzle *Bathing Beauty*'s trailer tells audiences to anticipate.

Whereas an aggregate form accumulates numbers without regard for narrative unity or continuity, an integrated form places numbers in support of narrative, so they seem to derive from and remain bound to a plot and its characters. With the exception of revues, no single musical purely adheres to one form or the other, of course. In conformity with the standards of classical Hollywood filmmaking, almost all MGM musicals tell a story, even if simplified to make room for numbers. The history of the musical, however, is usually viewed as a progression from the primitiveness of aggregation to the maturity of integration, as epitomized by MGM's output in the 1940s and 1950s. "The integrated structure lends itself easily to supporting the American musical as art," Sean Griffin comments when summarizing the critical consensus, "providing the sense of a unified and cohesive work in which all the pieces are in concert with each other" (23). This view minimizes the genre's enduring "vaudeville tradition" — "a standardized plot broken up by various performers (who often play little or no part in the narrative) coming out and doing numbers" (29). For Griffin, an aggregate aesthetic distinguishes Fox's musicals from MGM's, typically held in higher regard because of their integrated structure. Yet as the genre emerged out of studio practices from the 1930s through the 1950s, even at MGM it built on "a shifting and volatile dialectic between integrative and nonintegrative elements" (Rubin, 12) — between the contrasting cinematic values of story and spectacle, respectively.[2] That dialectic, central to the films' alternative history of camp appeal, is crystallized in MGM's house style, which *Bathing Beauty* exemplifies; it is present in the form of the studio's musicals as well as their distinctive look, and made most evident when the aggregate energies of numbers, viewed individually and collectively, visually and contextually, pull against aesthetic conventions centered on an expectation of integration.

The MGM house style helps to account for the musicals' camp reputation because the style's formal tensions correspond with (in the sense of paralleling but also of addressing) the dialectical operation of camp as an ironic engagement with the incongruities of the dominant culture's representational systems and hierarchical value codings, particularly but not exclusively with respect to gender and sexuality. As I shall show, *Bathing Beauty* well illustrates how the MGM style can draw racialized ethnicity into this dialectic, too. The house style incites category dissonance, visualizes it as the juxtaposition of cultural binaries, emphasizes it through overadornment and exaggerated theatricality, and aims it with humor and wit. Let me clarify right away, however, that my objective is not to locate a camp intention on the part of individual filmmakers, even though I will consider the input of the studio's considerable gay labor force working behind the scenes. Rather, I concentrate on the house style's own representation of cultural incongruities for evidence of how, at their moment of collaborative production, the musicals were already addressing the possibility of a camp spectator watching alongside a mainstream audience. Furthermore, I am understanding "house style" to combine all the key elements of the MGM brand: the mise-en-scène's display of artifice and excess interacting with other crafted elements of spectacle, such as performance and choreography, and the formal arrangement of numbers with narrative. As a means of establishing the basis for putting together camp and the MGM musicals historically through their distinctive studio look, I now follow a route that will lead me to the "fairies" in the studio's famous Arthur Freed unit, Lucille Ball's tangling with some cat-women, the significance of the aggregate form for MGM, and eventually back full circle to Esther Williams's swimming pool, Harry James's horn, and Xavier Cugat's maracas.

The labor force working at MGM when musicals dominated the studio's production schedules was, in discrete circles at least, fully versed in the idiom of camp. Much of this labor force remains anonymous. In the departments responsible for the specialized work that went into the making of a musical, the people involved exceeded the credits on any given motion picture, since only the department head and his or her senior assistant was listed. According to William J. Mann's history of gay and lesbian labor in Hollywood, the hegemony of homosexual workers was pronounced in certain units and absent in others, with the distinction based on gender stereotypes of the job and reinforced by hiring practices: the more technical the task (camera, sound, set construction), the more rigidly heterosexual the environment.

For instance, the art decoration department (responsible for the architectural design of sets) was predominantly heterosexual, though headed by Cedric Gibbons, a man rumored to be homosexual despite having been married twice. But the set decoration unit—headed by Edwin B. Willis, married once but not heterosexual—was accepted as an occupation suitable for gay men, who comprised about a third of the total workers in the division. This distinction was industry-wide, but "the trend was most obvious at MGM, where [among the set decorators] homosexuals were considerably higher in the pecking order" (Mann, 217). At MGM, the same applied to research, which, with the exception of two secretaries, was an all-gay enclave who worked closely with the set dressers on decor and props. The research department head, Elliot Morgan, recalled the conviviality among them: "Oh, my, yes, camp humor certainly did bounce off the walls" (197). As for the properties division, "the standing joke around Hollywood was that whenever anyone would ask where to get the best antiques in Los Angeles, they were told the MGM prop department"—all four fully stocked floors (219). Of all departments, though, "the most obvious and undisguised gay ghetto in Hollywood remained wardrobe" (227). At MGM wardrobe included queer fashion designers (Walter Plunkett, Irene Sharaff, Gile Steele, possibly Adrian) but also their assistants, sketch artists, fitters, sewers—*everyone* in wardrobe was rumored to be queer, even if they were not (236–37).

Aside from wardrobe, the most recognized queer presence on the Culver City lot was in the Arthur Freed unit, including many of its important directors, composers, arrangers, and choreographers, all interacting closely with the studio's set dressers, researchers, and costumers. Nicknamed "Freed's fairies" (Mann, 270, Ehrenstein, 82), the unit's queer reputation still holds fast. A 2000 special issue of *Daily Variety* on "Gay Hollywood" charts an eight-decade chronology of gay and lesbian milestones, and it lists, as one of only two exceptional moments in the forties, "the Arthur Freed unit at MGM, aka 'Freed's fairies'" for their "many musical classics," beginning with the 1944 production of *Meet Me in St. Louis* (11 October 2000, A3). Freed, a renowned lyricist before he started producing, was not himself homosexual, but his assistant, Roger Edens, was. Edens, who started working for MGM in the mid-1930s, arranged and wrote musical scores for the films, decided which numbers to include or exclude and where or how to place them, and ran day-to-day operations for Freed, eventually receiving an assistant producer credit. The Freed musical as it evolved into MGM's most prestigious and reliable line of product would have been unthinkable without Edens.

"Freed's fairies" seems to me a double-edged honorific; it designates begrudging, even disdainful or prejudicial recognition of a visible queer niche within the otherwise conservative studio. The nonconformity of the unit's members troubled nervous straight outsiders, but their value for MGM's reputation as the supreme producer of musicals could not be denied. The nickname may call to mind a group of effeminate men working together to put on a show in the best tradition of MGM's musicals with Judy Garland and Mickey Rooney, but the homosexual, bisexual, and effete men associated with the Freed unit differed amongst themselves in their openness at the studio and in private life, just as they by no means resembled each other in demeanor or conformed as a group to the "fairy" stereotype.

Edens and dancer-choreographer-director Charles Walters, who according to all accounts maintained long-term same-sex relationships, were both tallish, good-looking, clean-cut men—that is, straight-looking in appearance—in contrast with the more diminutive, flamboyantly artistic Vincente Minnelli, who came to Metro from the New York stage, where he had worked as a costume and set designer. At the time he made *Meet Me in St. Louis*, studio publicity described the director as "a slight, sensitive young man" (*Who's Who at Metro-Goldwyn-Mayer*, 179). One contract dancer interviewed in the Garland biography shown on the Arts and Entertainment cable channel recalls Minnelli arriving in Culver City complete with his "green eye shadow and the purple lipstick and the tam, etc." She adds, "We didn't think he would marry Judy or anyone else" (*Judy Garland: Beyond the Rainbow*). It is worth reiterating that sexual preference—for some, the desire of the moment regardless of the partner's gender—did not necessarily mean that all the men and women working here thought of themselves as homosexual or lesbian, and certainly not as "gay" in the contemporary sense, so much as nonconformist: more bohemian, modern, liberal, or antiestablishment in their sexual outlook. Playwright and screenwriter Arthur Laurents describes the Hollywood scene immediately after World War II as "very sexual," commenting: "It didn't matter whether you were straight or gay or bisexual. If a new attractive person came to town, the other stars felt free to call up and say, 'Come on over and let's fuck.' And they did. They all did" (quoted in Kaiser, 60). I think it is safe to assume that the same attitude toward sexuality extended to people in the industry who were not stars and whose liaisons attracted less notice.

More important than a source of gossip about sexual activity, the Freed unit was, at least within the relative world of Hollywood, something of a liminal space in Culver City, where, regardless of the sexual partnering, queer and straight outlooks intermingled, influencing each other's work: their meeting place was camp. Edens sustained a close professional and personal relationship with jazz arranger and vocal coach Kay Thompson, always recalled for her "style" and "sophistication"—code words even then for camp—as well as for her bravura sense of the well-timed oversized gesture.[3] Edens and Thompson mentored Judy Garland, shaping her singing style, and they wrote, arranged, and/or planned numbers for her; the pair remained the greatest influences on the star, and probably her two closest personal friends, for the rest of her life.

The Edens-Thompson collaboration did not limit itself to Garland, although the star's performances show the influence of their camp attitudes most directly, nor was it confined to production of musicals. As a birthday present for Freed, the two commissioned their portrait "purposely done in the style of a *Harper's Bazaar* cover" (Fordin, 122), which pays homage to the magazine's haute couture style but from the ironic distance of camp. The pair shared the same birth date and, from 1943 through 1947, when Thompson left Metro to start her nightclub act, they hosted a joint birthday party, the highpoint of which were competitive blackout sketches, rehearsed in advance with secrecy and featuring each host performing with guests such as Garland and songwriter Ralph Blane (Fordin, 215). Indeed, the socializing of the Freed unit has become legendary, from the annual Edens-Thompson birthday celebrations to Gene Kelly's weekend charade parties at his house to more formal affairs. Accounts of the continuous socializing still allude to the camp ethos informing its tone. In the A&E Garland biography, scenic designer Tony Duquette mentions one party where Garland and Thompson sang while Oscar Levant played the piano. "Judy said, 'Oh, Kay, let's sing *real loud*,'" and the phrase became "one of our family statements. When we really wanted to have a good time, we'd say, 'Oh, let's sing *real loud*!'"

The camp style perfected by the collaborative efforts of the Freed unit's "family" sings real loud, too, although the style, while noted for the lavishness of its mise-en-scène, has not received serious or sustained attention as camp in analyses of the MGM canon. The one exception is Matthew Tinkcom's insightful study in his book on camp, *Working Like a Homosexual*. The style of Freed musicals, he claims, was outlandish and over-the-top, camp through and through, but it distinguished the MGM brand, so the style was accepted because it suited corporate strategies of product differentiation. By the same token, Tinkcom argues, the style enabled the queer artisans and workers at the studio to mark their labor as "queer" because it was recognizable as camp by those "in the know." Circulating to general audiences "under the more general idea of [the films] being 'stylized or witty'" (48), the style capitalized on "the dissembling abilities of camp" (50), giving a Freed musical its "multivalence, in that it can be consumed by queer and nonqueer consumers alike for retaining camp features or not" (46). Even at the time of their release, then, the musicals, produced by the studio's most prestigious unit and manufactured by people referred to within the industry then and now as "Freed's fairies," could, on one hand, offer escapist family entertainment seemingly committed to wholesome, normative values through plots, and even numbers, figured around the centrality of a heterosexual couple. On the other hand, the same musicals could deliver a camp affect for an audience who did not align itself with those values and who took great pleasure in the visual strategies with which, as Tinkcom puts it, "camp style marks a critical commentary upon the narrative of heterosexual bonding" (48). Much as the word *gay* itself meant both "excessively joyful" and "homosexual" during this era, the excessive style of the musicals signified lavish, escapist entertainment *and* a queer affective relation to the conventions of representation organizing that entertainment as a camp alibi of sorts.

In illustration, Tinkcom singles out three extravagant Freed musicals directed by Minnelli in the 1940s — *Ziegfeld Follies* (filmed in 1944, released in 1946), *Yolanda and the Thief* (1945), and *The Pirate* (1948) — and examines them in sequence as a specialized project developing a self-conscious camp style of visual excess, one which luxuriates at every moment in the films' mise-en-scène so that the incongruous theatricality of the spectacle effortlessly overwhelms story concerns. A filmed revue, *Ziegfeld Follies* obviously has no narrative to contain the "camp visual field" (57) created by the outlandish art direction, set decoration, costuming, and lighting for the musical numbers, so the camp here stands out most strikingly as an assertion of style over content. While the other two musicals recount a narrative, they deploy the same visual style as *Ziegfeld Follies*, reversing the conventional subordination of spectacle to story. The mise-en-scène does not distinguish between narrative and number but instead treats the entire film as if it were, in effect, one continuous number. In all three musicals, Tinkcom shows, the style allows for a camp perspective that views the heterosexual activity represented in numbers as fantastic, surreal, even unbelievable, in dangerously close proximity to queer desire, and dialectically set against the fantastic mise-en-scène.

Recalling from the introduction what Brett Farmer claims about numbers as sites of fantasy, and my own contention that his argument has strong parallels to camp irony and affect, it does not seem incidental that Tinkcom concentrates on Minnelli musicals with a mise-en-scène denoting a dreamlike landscape. From a straight perspective, the camp here is improbable stuff indeed. Yet that's the point: for to be successful as camp, these musicals also had to pass — they had to be equally or at least superficially legible through a heterosexual lens. Thus as *Yolanda* and *The Pirate* focus on a romantic couple (Fred Astaire and Lucille Bremer in the first instance, Judy Garland and Gene Kelly in the second) and gesture toward narrative integration by not stylistically bracketing plot from numbers, the films' seeming adherence to convention easily distracts the eye from what it could otherwise see.

All the same, the lackluster box-office performance of *Yolanda* and *The Pirate*, rare failures for the Freed unit when balanced against the expense of making them, indicates that the camp aspect may have been too apparent here. The Garland biography on A&E alludes to this when the Peter Graves voiceover comments about the troubled production of *The Pirate*: "This time Minnelli's vision went awry, and Garland herself came to realize that *The Pirate* was being produced for an audience that might not exist." Yet while small in number and not acknowledged publicly, that audience *did* exist, and Minnelli and company addressed it. The Freed-Minnelli musicals were "gay" in *both* senses of the word, and their camp affect resulted from recognition of the double valence which their style could so readily bear for filmmakers and audiences alike. As Graves's remark also implies, a reluctance to name this other audience, at least officially and historically, sustains the closeted value of the style's camp address.

THINK PINK BUT WATCH THE FEATHERS

Tinkcom's own purpose in focusing on Minnelli as a camp auteur tends to view the director as the primary source of the Freed camp style. Minnelli was certainly responsible for his films, and their mise-en-scène predicts musicals and melodramas he directed afterward, so there is an undeniable degree of continuity to his authorship. Further, Minnelli was known to be often more interested in the art direction of his films than anything else.[4] But as Tinkcom and other chroniclers of the Freed unit like Hugh Fordin also make clear, many hands contributed to the look of these films.[5]

The collaborative effort behind a Freed musical extends to Tinkcom's examples, notably *Ziegfeld Follies*. Directed by Minnelli, Judy Garland's number, "The Great Lady Has 'an Interview,'" sends up the inflated star image of the studio's reigning grande dame, Greer Garson. More subtly, according to Tinkcom, the number depicts "an important relation of queers to the figure of Judy Garland," acknowledging how in the mid-1940s she was already perceived (at least by members of the Freed unit) as "a star capable of bonding with her 'camp followers'" (58–59). The choreography stages a noneotic rapport between Garland and the all-male dancing ensemble, gentlemen of the press who interview the Great Lady while paying homage to her Greatness. Their dancing has them interacting with each other more than with her—at times the boys of the press/chorus even push Garland aside as they get caught up in the camaraderie of their high stepping. The number gives every impression of knowing already what Daniel Harris would write five decades later: "The answer to the proverbial question, 'why did gay men like Judy Garland so much?' is that they liked, not her, so much as her audience" (18). Reinforcing the choreography's camp perspective on the boys as well as their diva, Tinkcom goes on to point out, is the "refined vulgarity" of the surrounding decor. "Paradoxically spare and yet overwrought," the mise-en-scène of the star's mansion blurs distinctions between high and low taste, vulgarity and refinement, in the manner in which camp humor renegotiates the apparent divisions of cultural categories in terms of style (59). The style's incongruity supplies a visual analogue for the camp star's relation with the boys of the press, her fans, as staged by the dancing.

Tinkcom calls this number one of Minnelli's most "elegant" and "mocking" achievements in *Ziegfeld Follies* (57), and I shall have much more to say about it in the next chapter. For now my point is that its camp style extends beyond mise-en-scène alone to combine visual, choreographic, performative, and aural elements. The dancing, the decor, the lyrics and Garland's overtheatricalized reading of them, the vocal arrangement of her patter with the boys as the number slides in and out of singing, all contribute to the elegance (and eloquence) of "The Great Lady" as a camp number. Yet Minnelli was not solely responsible. He filmed it, deciding, for instance, how to stage, photograph, and light Garland's entrance to heighten the parodic effect of the glamour she impersonates, but before shooting began, the number was written and arranged by Edens and Thompson, the latter performed the number with its camp vocal inflection and exaggerated gestures for Garland to imitate, which the star did exactly, and Charles Walters choreographed the dancing (Fordin, 139–40).

More crucial for the camp style which saturates *Ziegfeld Follies,*

George Sidney, not Minnelli, began as the musical's director, filming with choreographer Robert Alton, set designer Jack Martin Smith, and costumer Helen Rose a big production number written by Freed and Edens, "Here's to the Girls." After the number was shot, Sidney resigned from the picture, and Minnelli succeeded him. This number remains in the film, placed after the prologue as initially planned, and it is unforgettable camp, as much as everything else Minnelli went on to do. In the prologue, Florenz Ziegfeld (William Powell) looks down from heaven and imagines one last glorious edition of his Follies, beginning with a "pink number, yes, a beautiful pink number with beautiful pink and white blue-eyed girls." Pink, white, and blue-eyed this number surely is, with the addition of 1,200 ostrich feathers dyed to match: "Here's to the Girls" pushes Ziegfeld's own imagery of Anglo American beauty past the point of excess, if that can be possible, juxtaposing straight and queer perspectives of the Follies' idealized version of femininity in a dialectic visualization of female spectacle which elevates "the Girls" to a camp apotheosis.

Representing the quintessential showgirl turn in a Ziegfeld revue, "a variation on the fashion runway, an exhibition of outstanding evening gowns during a slow parade of beauties and musical accompaniment" (Mizejewski, 93), "Here's to the Girls" begins with Fred Astaire, in silver and gray top hat and tails, offering a vocal salute to the showman's legendary glorification of the American girl in all her "variety" (i.e., she comes in different hair colors). As Astaire sings that "this is the mixture/ to start the picture," a half-dozen showgirls make their entrance. They wear pink and silver sequined gowns, slit to show off their legs, and a silver top hat like Astaire's but with pink ostrich plumes for feminizing adornment. Featured dancer Cyd Charisse, in a pink tutu but sans ostrich feathers, follows the showgirls and dances *en pointe*, as the other women arrange themselves behind her, form a circle around her, and pose in a tableau with her, and then Astaire partners Charisse in several turns as he finishes his song.

Astaire disappears. With a shift in the musical arrangement, a large stage curtain opens to reveal a circus setting. The centerpiece is a massive contraption, a pink merry-go-round swathed in layers of diffuse cloth for the lighting to shine through as ersatz sunbeams. Another group of showgirls, also costumed in pink gowns with silver sequins sparkling in the artificial light, sit on live white horses with female attendants in short white uniforms standing by each horse. As the carousel revolves, the women pose on the horses with the same mannequin look, so they all seem identical except for their costumes, which differ slightly in design. With each turn of the carousel, the women's oversized headpieces become progressively more extravagant—and more overwhelming of the women's bodies as each showgirl gets her moment of solo screen time.

The carousel stops turning with the appearance of Lucille Ball, one of the musical's top-billed stars. Her pink feathered headdress, setting off the dyed henna color of her hair, is coordinated with a long pink feathered cape and the sequins in the brocade of her gown above the waist are shaped like metallic feathers. She's glamorous in the Ziegfeld sense, but with all the feathers, real and simulated, when first seen she looks like a bird-woman. To top it off, Ball is standing atop Silver—yes, the Lone Ranger's Silver. The horse's tail is braided with pink satin bows, and a pink ostrich feather is pinned between his ears, coordinating his look, like that of the other horses, with the showgirls. (Silver's trainer, by the way, sued MGM for "defamation of character"—the horse's, presumably—when *Life* magazine put a

Fred Astaire, Cyd Charisse, and a carousel of showgirls. *Ziegfeld Follies* (MGM, 1946).

Lucille Ball
astride Silver
in *Ziegfeld
Follies* (MGM,
1946).

photo of Ball and her companion on the cover with the exclamation, "Silver is a sissy!" [Fordin, 127n]). Ball steps down from the horse and models her bird-woman ensemble for the showgirls, then exchanges her ostrich cape for a whip.

Moving past the carousel, Ball comes on a circus menagerie, its black bars highlighted by a deep red background, complete with smoke and flames. Inside the cage are eight cat-women. They wear black caps with a widow's peak and cat ears attached, and their slinky black costumes expose legs, back, and sides of the waist as they writhe in the red light. They push their way through the bars, the lighting continuing to shine flushed tones on the exposed parts of their bodies while keeping Ball bathed in a white spot. She maneuvers the cat-women to the circus ring, where she proceeds to tame them. Holding the whip to assert her authority as the cats threaten her—they claw in the air with their artificially long, red varnished finger-nails—Ball hypnotizes these femmes feline, who now sway more sub-

Lucille Ball tames the cat-women in *Ziegfeld Follies* (MGM, 1946).

missively to the movement of her arms and the rhythm of the music. Their dance finishes when the cat-women encircle Ball and do back-bends, at which point the camera returns to the carousel, then moves back to include the showgirls circling Cyd Charisse on the right and the cat-women posed behind Lucille Ball on the left. Charisse dances on her toes again and Ball cracks her whip in counterpoint as the number concludes, with the two areas of the circus setting brought together: the Glorified Girls on the merry-go-round, joined by their counterparts in the Astaire segment, make ironic contact with their queerer mirror image, the ferocious cat-women being seduced into submission by Lucille Ball. An off-screen chorus reprises the song lyrics, reminding us that this is the mixture that starts the picture— and quite a mix it has turned out to be!

This big production number can be read straight, for example through its conformity to what Nadine Wills refers to as the generic convention of the "'110 per cent woman': a female body where sex and gender are so codependent, stereotyped and stylized that the final product is an excessively delineated femininity" (121). Wills argues that, whenever the camera in a musical peers between a dancer's legs or she accidentally exposes her undergarments while twirling or doing kicks, the inevitable and generically standard "crotch shot" establishes how "musical spectacle [is] a site of femininity rather than of heterosexuality" (122). That is, the convention has the purpose of defining femininity as a fabrication of excessive womanliness, inscribing the masquerade on the defining area of the female body, suggesting to Wills that musicals are not generically preoccupied with heterosexual differentiation, as critics have supposed, but with regulating femininity through its performance. In this number from *Ziegfeld Follies*, Sidney's camerawork treats the women more respectfully, in part because of their function as showgirls/mannequins and not a chorus line; but one can still view "Here's to the Girls" in the light of what Wills describes. There are no actual crotch shots here, but the number conforms to a representation of femininity that follows in the tradition of Ziegfeld stage shows, with their celebratory equation of whiteness and the production of female glamour (Mizejewski, 9–10).

Yet the visual excess orchestrated by "Here's to the Girls," along with the juxtaposition of the merry-go-round and cat-women segments, allows for a camp view of this production of femininity, too. The excess on display here focuses attention not only on 110 percent femininity in a self-consciously theatricalized setting, enabling artifice to exceed nature, but on the problematic value of heterosexual femininity in this spectacle of hundreds and hundreds of ostrich feathers, glamorized white showgirls astride "sissy" white horses, and cat-women facing the whip. Once Astaire departs the number, the sexual difference initially visualized through his vocalizing as it contrasts with the showgirls' muteness (not to say with their feathered top hats) disappears too, that is, until Lucille Ball trades her feathered cape for a whip. The number is still all-female, but Ball's interaction with the cat-women unexpectedly raises some queer intimations, to say the least. The erotic mobility glimpsed in the parodic staging of butch/femme and s/m lesbian play, visually exemplified in Ball's prop and the cat-women's long and sharpened red fingernails, is incongruous with the static mannequins positioned on the carousel as objects of an absent if implicitly heterosexual male gaze.

As if this camp perspective of the showgirl glorified by the Follies were not plain enough, after the unsuccessful preview Edens added a send-up of the send-up (which he cowrote), "Bring on those Wonderful Men" with Virginia O'Brien.[6] Photographed in three-quarter shot almost throughout, O'Brien is costumed in pink and white sequins like the showgirls riding on the merry-go-round but with the addition of large feathered cuffs on her sleeves; furthermore, her own oversized feather headdress, seeming to sprout out of the crown of her head from the way it is positioned, forms an arch around her. Seated sideways on a noticeably fake white horse, her draped skirt outlining her legs like billowing pants, O'Brien sings, in her signature deadpan style, of her "plan / to glorify the American Man." Her unbridled sexual desire for any male—"a dark or a light one," she doesn't care because she has "a terrible yen / for the wonderful M-E-N"—even includes "you, in the third row," turning the tables on the ostensible straight spectator of the 110 percent woman while also allowing for surrogate recognition of a desiring queer male with a similar yen for the "M-E-N." This number—along with "Girls," the only one not to have a title card with cast and additional credits—was not directed by Sidney or Minnelli but most likely by Norman Taurog, since he did the new material and retakes without credit following the first preview (Fordin, 145; the laser-disc boxed set, though, lists the coda's direction as "uncredited").

The opening sequence of "Here's to the Girls"/"Bring on those Wonderful Men" is consistent with what Minnelli does in the rest of *Ziegfeld Follies*. While his work is more subtle in its use of style as commentary, the opening sets a camp tone, alerting audiences to read all of the successive musical numbers for their visual incongruity and exaggerated theatricality if they are to catch the ironic wit informing this MGM version of the Ziegfeld tradition. More to the point, this sequence illustrates, first of all, how the camp style identified with the Freed unit draws on choreography and performance along with color, set design, and costuming: all enhance the spectacular value of numbers to bring out the incongruity of a musical's heterosexual bias, here epitomized in the requisite showgirl extravaganza and the parodic coda with O'Brien. Second, the collaborative authorship of this *Ziegfeld Follies* sequence indicates how the camp style of a Freed musical was not limited to Minnelli's direction but extended to the unit's work as a whole: if not as pronounced and sustained as in *Ziegfeld Follies, Yolanda,* and *The Pirate,* it is still evident in Sidney's *The Harvey Girls* (1946), Busby Berkeley's series of musicals with Garland and Rooney, the early Gene Kelly-Stanley Donen collaborations, and Charles Walters's *Good News* (1947) and *Easter Parade* (1948). Along with the considerable input of the set designers and costumers, Edens's hands-on participation accounts for camp elements in the Freed style regardless of who directed, and so do Alton's and Walters's choreography.

The collaboration that musicals required, finally, makes it difficult to single out the Freed unit as an exclusive source of camp style for the studio, as Tinkcom maintains (41). The Freed musicals *are* spectacular camp, to be sure, and within the Metro hierarchy the unit itself was perceived as an elite group—"The Royal Family" was its other nickname at the studio, a label with its own camp implications—but many of the same artists and craftspeople now firmly associated with Freed (Alton, Walters, Donen, costume designers Irene Sharaff and Walter Plunkett, set decorator Edwin B. Willis and his assistants, and so on) also worked for Jack Cummings and Joe Pasternak. Kay Thompson did not work exclusively for Freed, and Garland and Kelly made some musicals outside the unit as well.

While Freed had almost exclusive use of people like Roger Edens and Minnelli, camp connoisseurs both, MGM produced more musicals than the other studios because it had more units dedicated to manufacturing the genre on a regular basis, drawing on its large contracted labor force of specialized talents and skills, all working before, behind, and ahead of the camera in the production-line manufacturing of films. Their efforts helped to constitute the regularized product with the MGM brand, regardless of which unit was responsible, and that brand was camp. What Tinkcom points out, quite rightly, about the multivalent camp style perfected in the Freed musicals directed by Minnelli should therefore not distract from the style's continuity with, rather than distinction from, the rest of the studio's output. After all, Freed's production of *The Pirate,* a camp triumph but box-office failure, was followed the next year by Pasternak's equally unsuccessful and comparably campy, if less subtle and sublime, *Kissing Bandit* (1949).

There are certainly differences between each producer's output. Who can deny that Freed's musicals represent MGM at the top of its game or that Pasternak's efforts to include opera stars and classical pianists side by side with the likes of Esther Williams or teen star Jane Powell often sink his to the level of kitsch? Nevertheless, as the genre developed at Metro to serve as its signature product under the administration of Pasternak and Cummings as well as Freed, the studio's musicals all conformed in one way or another to a distinctive studio look, highly polished but excessively stylized and overblown, at least in the numbers, which characterized the MGM logo and were exploited in publicity as a primary selling point. The musicals were planned with their entertainment values always in mind, superseding the importance of narrative integration and justifying the inclusion of numbers simply by virtue of their aggregation. This industrial purpose, which caused a pervasive if variable tension between integrative and aggregate forms in the manufacturing of musicals as studio product, contributed to the house style's camp signification, too. The style signified to some audiences money lavishly spent on a musical's spectacle while allowing for recognition by others of a camp sensibility at work in the style. Its double valence, the potential to be legible as camp commentary or noncamp entertainment, was thus a result of industrial and aesthetic intentions combining.

SHOW ME THE SPECTACLE

The MGM musical's camp appeal had a material basis in its production as mass entertainment. Hence my insistence on looking beyond the accepted standard of integration for the studio's signature, especially as represented by the work of the Freed unit. Otherwise, with its progression traced according to an aesthetic of integration, the musical's history at MGM gives every impression of being antagonistic to camp readings; the integrative aesthetic binds to a narrative frame those marginal moments of spectacular excess which, as we saw in Brett Farmer's theorization of gay investments in the genre, open up musicals to camp pleasures. To be sure, because of the failure of *The Pirate* and *Yolanda*, Tinkcom notes, referring to *An American in Paris* (1951) and *Singin' in the Rain* (1952), that "later Freed productions of the 1950s would herald a compromise between camp visual style and tighter narrative integration . . . the later productions would more carefully balance the camp visual elements . . . with the demands for 'streamlined' (i.e., assertively heteronormative) narrative" (40). But even when their visual and musical elements were "streamlined" with the goal of narrative integration, the Freed musicals simultaneously served aggregate purposes.

Nowhere is the commercial value of aggregation more in evidence than in the unit's successful all-star biopics. *Till the Clouds Roll By* (1946) and *Words and Music* (1948) simply replaced the tired vaudeville sketches of *Ziegfeld Follies* with fictionalized plot lines about Jerome Kern and Rodgers and Hart, respectively, as the thin connecting tissue between numerous numbers performed by guest stars from the studio's roster of talents, the sole reason for these musicals. In both the teaser trailer and press book for *Words and Music*, studio promotion boasted that this musical combined, count 'em, "22 terrific Rogers and Hart tunes," "2 exciting love stories," "5 great Broadway musicals rolled into one," "14 spectacular girl-filled production scenes," "14 sensational singing and dancing stars," *and* "Color by Technicolor." Now that's aggregation!

The biopics may seem exceptions, but more fully integrated Freed musicals respected the requirement of aggregation even when keeping it in check. *The Harvey Girls* gives every appearance of motivating numbers through a well-constructed narrative, but then why is Ray Bolger in this film? His character seems to have slipped through the cracks of the screenplay, appearing suddenly and without narrative explanation as another newcomer arriving with the Harvey Girls in the "Atcheson, Topeka, and Santa Fe" production number. It can be inferred that he has come from somewhere in the East to take over the blacksmith's shop, but otherwise Bolger has no character to speak of and seems to be in the musical, finally, only to perform his comic dance number later on, a parody of the masculinity represented by the cowboy town. Virginia O'Brien, included as Bolger's nominal love interest, has more character motivation, but she disappears from the narrative midway through, also without explanation (she took a leave from the production because she was pregnant). No one, neither the characters nor the audience, seems to notice her absence or to miss her, indicating that O'Brien's purpose, too, is primarily to deliver her solo specialty number, when, revealing a skill belied by her gender, she takes over blacksmith duties from the inept Bolger. Nor is there any reason for Kenny Baker and Cyd Charisse to appear in this Judy Garland musical except, that is, to have the tenor sing a romantic ballad and the ballerina to dance to its melody (yeah, and in a western saloon no less).

Even *Meet Me in St. Louis*, heralded as the musical which put all elements of the Freed unit in place and established a model of integration, front-loads all but two of its numbers before it gets to any sort of plot complication. In reverse fashion, *The Band Wagon* (1953) effectively brings its backstage plot to a halt once the right show goes on the road in the last half hour, turning into a mini-revue of back-to-back numbers. In other Freed musicals acclaimed for their integration—*The Barkleys of Broadway* (1949), *Royal Wedding* (1951), *American in Paris*, and *Singin' in the Rain*—the set-piece fantasy ballet or opening-night show number, sometimes driven by special effects, is a convention deriving from the fantasy numbers in *Yolanda* and *The Pirate* by way of Gene Kelly's show number, "Slaughter on Tenth Avenue," in *Words and Music*. These big numbers disrupt the integrative form to offer a pleasure other than that of following a story: namely, watching the spectacle purely as a spectacle. And Freed's own determination to include Oscar Levant's piano solos in *Barkleys* and *Paris* is not that different from Pasternak's use of José Iturbi along with Kelly, Frank Sinatra, and Kathryn Grayson in *Anchors Aweigh* (1945) or of Lauritz Melchior along with Jimmy Durante, Xavier Cugat, and Esther Williams in *This Time for Keeps* (1947).

For all their adherence to integration, the Freed musicals mentioned betray signs of the product's economic use to the studio as an aggregate form compiling numbers for their entertainment value more than anything else. The importance of aggregation to the MGM musical derived from studio protocols set in place by the *Broadway Melody* series, to which Freed contributed as lyricist.[7] The first *Broadway Melody* (1929), an Oscar winner for best picture, established the genre's importance for Metro's reputation.[8] With *Broadway Melody of 1936* (1935) the studio revived the title as a franchise for its new star, dancer Eleanor Powell. Her musicals, which most often costarred a nonsinger such as Robert Taylor, drew on an assortment of talent in numbers that digressed from an otherwise nonmusicalized romance plot. As Edens recalled two decades later, the "slam bang finale" of *Broadway Melody of 1936* was "like a little revue," with "Broadway Rhythm" divided into five sections to feature Frances Langford, Vilma and Buddy Ebsen, dancers June Knight and Nick Long Jr., and, of course, Powell, "and audiences went wild over it" (Johnson, 179).

Cummings's production of *Broadway Melody of 1938* (1937) went even further with its mix of several standards and a new score by Freed and partner Nacio Herb Brown. It includes extraneous numbers for Sophie Tucker (her trademark, "Some of These Days"), a young Judy Garland (singing "You Made Me Love You" to a photograph of Clark Gable), Charles Igor Gorin (excerpts from *Barber of Seville* and *Carmen*), and hoofers Buddy Ebsen and George Murphy as Powell's best pals (the three do a lively dance, with Powell impersonating a stable boy, and she teams up with Murphy to sing and tap to "I'm Feeling Like a Million," which in a properly dual-focused musical should have been performed with her leading man). The musical then brings this cast together, minus lover-boy Robert Taylor, for another extravagant "slam bang" finale which appears to have no end, "Your Broadway and My Broadway" (where Powell also dances in male attire). The Powell-Taylor coupling is reasserted only afterward with a big close-up — of the two stars and a racehorse. Don't ask.

The final entry in the series, *Broadway Melody of 1940* (1940), teams Powell with Astaire and Murphy for producer Cummings in a style somewhat predicting the Freed unit's. This film more seamlessly integrates several star duets and solo turns as well as two elaborate production numbers that appear to have a narrative purpose but defy logic in the best tradition of the series — and it still makes room for several vaudeville performers in spots that stop the story cold. MGM's adherence to an aggregate format continued during the 1940s with the studio's version of the wartime canteen musicals featuring major stars in specialty numbers, Pasternak's *Thousands Cheer* (1943) and *Two Girls and a Sailor* (1944), as well as Cummings's *Broadway Rhythm* (1944) — an effort to revive the Broadway series without Powell but featuring Murphy — and Freed's *Ziegfeld Follies*, planned as MGM's celebration of its twentieth anniversary. After the war Freed perpetuated the format, as noted, with his musical biopics. At that time competition from the blockbuster Broadway book musical gave narrative integration a more paramount aesthetic and commercial value, but for all that, the studio still turned out, like clockwork, its popular Esther Williams spectaculars and the Jane Powell musical trips to Rio, Paris, the Catskills, or wherever. Furthermore, MGM still crafted big-budget musicals around an ensemble cast. Cummings's *Lovely to Look At* (1952), a remake of *Roberta* (1935), makes room for Kathryn Grayson and Howard Keel to sing, Marge and Gower Champion to dance, Ann Miller to tap, Red Skelton to do his schtick, and a fashion show directed (without credit) by Minnelli.

Assembling a lavish array of talent of all sorts and making sure they had an opportunity to perform was as economically important to the studio's house style as the lavish mise-en-scène. Overscale in size, spectacle, cast, and pretensions of grandeur as well as over-the-top in its mise-en-scène, an MGM musical represented its entertainment value as an excess in its own right. Since the musicals were for the most part still understood as narratives, numbers served contradictory purposes: even when they moved the story, they stopped it momentarily as spectacle, more often than not allowing for a double reading of their content. This is certainly how show numbers work. The story accounts for, say, Fred Astaire and Jane Powell performing on stage together as fictional characters throughout *Royal Wedding* while, on their own terms as spectacle, the numbers exceed this narrative context. In this Freed musical the songs, the dramatis personae and performing styles adapted by the entertainers to suit the songs while playing sibling characters, the staging and choreography, and not least, the mise-en-scène all give extra performative texture to the numbers' camp theatricality as a show within the narrative. To borrow Esther Newton's phrasing, these numbers put on a show while showing it is a show, and such self-reflective awareness easily allows for camp irony.

In the case of a seemingly integrated musical like *Royal Wedding* (and really, any example would serve my purpose), the show numbers then heighten the nonnarrative value of other numbers which appear to arise spontaneously from the story, as when Astaire rehearses in the ship's gym or dances on the ceiling or when Powell sings love songs to Peter Lawford. This is not to claim that an integrative aesthetic was not a conscious concern in a Freed musical's planning. Edens himself complained about musicals "in which the plot and the songs have nothing to do with each other." He called his own contributions to MGM musicals "strictly plot songs which cannot be taken away from the movie and put on the hit parade." Yet as he went on to explain how "songs in film musicals should be part of the script itself," by which he meant that the numbers can't "live away from the movie itself—you have to see the action," he described their appeal as spectacle, mentioning as an example how Astaire sings "and then *bursts* into that wonderful walk of his" (Johnson, 180).

Cinematic handling of numbers insist on this added nonnarrative value for show and nonshow numbers alike. Prerecording, a strategy first tried on *Broadway Melody*, then used on every musical afterward, enhances a vocal performance beyond what a live performer can achieve while spatially exceeding the fictive space imagined on screen; because the singer's voice was recorded at a closer distance to the microphone, the sound editing of the prerecorded track always increases the volume to make the singing louder than the dialogue of narrative scenes (A. Williams, 151). Additionally, the standard convention for editing a musical performance was to shift from the indirect viewpoint of narrative scenes to direct address (Feuer, *Hollywood Musical*, 35–42). Simulating the intimacy of a live performance, this convention further determines that numbers, by definition and through their execution, will pull against integrative purposes. When a singer or dancer faces the camera directly to do a number, whether in a show setting or not, the performance breaks the narrative fiction's illusionism. In *Royal Wedding*, Astaire and Powell play fictive characters, but through the direct address of their numbers they entertain audiences as themselves, that is, as their extrafilmic personae, the supertalented dancer and soprano with their MGM history behind them. No matter if the musical goes on to restore the illusionism afterward, as *Royal Wedding* does, the numbers momentarily expose the performance's affinity with camp as a comparable theater of passing.

The tension arising between aggregation and integration in the formal composition of MGM's musicals brings a dialectical perspective to the mise-en-scène that amplifies the numbers' camp visual style. The MGM standard of aggregation, the hallmark of its product's appeal as spectacular entertainment in all senses, interacted with the equally important standard of creating a lavish visual style, or in place of that an outrageous or excessive conceit for the choreography, to guarantee the musicals' double valence as camp or noncamp. In practice, every musical produced at MGM during the height of the genre's economic significance for the studio was designed so that its trailer could exclaim, as does the one for *Bathing Beauty*, "From Metro-Goldwyn-Mayer comes your Greatest Entertainment!" This promise addressed viewers who liked their musicals straight, but it did not exclude those who preferred them otherwise. *Bathing Beauty* is a perfect case in point. "Produced in the lush, lavish manner which is as familiar as the Metro trademark," as *Variety*'s review noted at the time ("Sten."), this musical readily displays how the house style worked to camp effect in more standard MGM product, the sort not usually mentioned in the same breath as the Freed unit's achievements.

THE CAMP DIALECTIC OF *BATHING BEAUTY*

For a musical with two stars lacking strong singing and dancing abilities, *Bathing Beauty* has a lot of numbers—ten, not including the one where Red Skelton dances in his pink tutu. None is integrated with the narrative, nor do any of them advance a dual focus on the central couple formed by Esther Williams and Skelton. On the contrary, the specialty acts, not the stars, perform almost every one of the numbers, most already familiar tunes designed to capitalize on the crossover popularity from radio, records, and stage shows of the era's dance bands and their singers. These performers play themselves and, while the aggregation of their numbers gets in the way of the narrative, they supply the entertainment segments which make *Bathing Beauty* a bona fide musical.

The comedic romance plot, in the meantime, allows for a camp reading on its own terms, suggesting that an aggregate form does not have to make narrative entirely irrelevant to an appreciation of the camp house style. *Bathing Beauty* recounts the farcical efforts of an unathletic, effeminate male to be wed in more than name only to a tanned, muscular female who works as the swimming instructor at a women's college. The groom dresses in women's clothing, and the first item he packs for his honeymoon is a hot-water bottle. And the bride? Well, at one point the bride is shown reclining on the floor with her spinsterish dean, the pair toasting marshmallows in the fireplace as they scheme to get rid of the groom.

All the while this is happening, the "improbable stuff that had little to do with the script," as Williams recalled the many musical numbers in *Bathing Beauty*, appears to divert attention from, and thereby contain, the plot's staging of this couple's gender instability. With the exception of the aquaballet in the finale, planned for the film after Williams was cast opposite Skelton, the show numbers at first glance do exactly the opposite of what I have been arguing throughout this chapter: the aggregate format contains the camp plot through numbers that offer, at regularized intervals, moments of relief from camp. Numbers spotlighting Harry James's or Xavier Cugat's orchestras just don't seem to allow for the same camp recognition as a splashy water ballet with Esther Williams and her synchronized swimmers.

Yet these show numbers are not quite as straight as they first seem. Instigated by the star couple's delayed consummation of their marriage, which takes place near the start of the film, the comedic plot pressures the couple's heterosexual conformity on the basis of their more visible gender nonconformity, encouraging a camp reading apart from the numbers. The numbers, themselves stylized excessively according to tropes of racialized ethnicity as well as gender, intersect with this plot dialectically, establishing the ground for a more complex camp reading. These two modes of addressing a camp spectator then coalesce around the aquatic figure of Esther Williams. With this argument in mind, it is therefore worth setting *Bathing Beauty* alongside Griffin's defense of the Fox musical's vaudeville tradition as a progressive alternative to the integrated form presumably dominating MGM's production of the genre at this same time. He maintains that the integrated form privileged at MGM elides racial difference in the interest of presenting a utopian view of Americana, typified by *Meet Me in St. Louis* (released the same year as *Bathing Beauty*) and the other canonized Freed musicals that followed it. The Fox vaudeville musicals of this period, according to Griffin, have more potential for social criticism because the appearance of specialty performers like the Nicholas Brothers and Carmen Miranda—their numbers rarely integrated into narratives centered on Alice Faye or Betty Grable—opens gaps in the "construction of the films through which various hegemonic norms can momentarily be critiqued and up-ended" (31). *Bathing Beauty* not only illustrates the same aggregate energies characterizing the MGM style *as* camp but also exemplifies how this camp style could incorporate race and ethnicity into its dialectical treatment of gender and sexuality.

A vehicle for the two stars, *Bathing Beauty* builds on the milquetoast and athletic personae crafted for Skelton and Williams by MGM as the studio's versions of Paramount's Bob Hope and Twentieth Century-Fox's Sonja Henie, respectively. This makes it impossible to think about the plot apart from Skelton's established and Williams's emerging star personae, especially since their first appearance is at a country club swimming pool in California, where college swimming instructor Caroline Brooks (Williams) exhibits her expertise in the water, and her fiancé, songwriter Steve Elliott (Skelton), shows his lack of prowess: he can't swim. Despite their aquatic incompatibility, they marry, both planning to resign their jobs afterward. Then comes the inevitable complication. In order to separate the couple so that Steve will complete the score needed for an upcoming show, nightclub owner George Adams (Basil Rathbone, of all people—in a musical!) contrives to have a Latina showgirl, Maria Dorango (Jacqueline Dalya), pose as the songwriter's wife, dragging with her three red-headed boys supposedly bearing Spanish names. Intending to get the marriage annulled because of her husband's supposed bigamy, Caroline returns to her job at the women's college in New Jersey, where Steve's rival for her affections is a former beau, a prissy botany professor inseparable from his Great Dane, Duke. Steve follows his bride and discovers that a clause in the college's charter actually allows for the admittance of men. Taking advantage of this loophole, Steve enrolls. He has a motive for being the only male student in this all-female school—it's his only way of being near Caroline to win her back—but his presence nonetheless causes suspicion. "Why should a man wish to become a student here?" one professor asks when learning of this highly unorthodox freshman. The tipsy lawyer trying to break the charter's loophole puts the matter more directly when Steve happens to meet him in the bar of Adams's nightclub: "What kind of man would want to go to a women's college?"

What kind of man? As if to answer, *Bathing Beauty* plays up Skelton's sissy persona with several jokes involving his gender confusion, one or two repeated from an earlier musical with the comedian, *Ship Ahoy* (1942). "She's my husband. I mean I'm her wife," the hapless husband mutters in frustration to a hotel operator when trying to phone his bride after she leaves him. The plot also gives Skelton more than one opportunity to do comic drag. Along with his appearance in a tutu when he attends eurhythmics class, he does a pantomime for the college girls of a woman waking up and putting on her makeup (the kind of extraneous Skelton vaudeville sketch often included in his MGM films). In a more sustained sequence, Skelton hides in Williams's closet, confined there by the growling Duke who will not let him leave, while the clock ticks toward curfew. Desperate not to be expelled, Skelton resorts to wearing Williams's clothes, putting on a full outfit—a blue tailored suit, fur stole, and hat with feather and veil—in order to make his escape from Duke (who is actually the butchest male in this film), presumably by convincing the dog he is Caroline. This dog-and-drag act raises explicit questions about Skelton's masculinity yet again. Rushing into his room while still in his wife's clothes, Steve finds George waiting for him, and the latter immediately asks, not too delicately, "Don't you think you're carrying this girl business a little too far?"

The replacement of *Mr. Coed* with *Bathing Beauty* as the musical's title neatly condenses the gender problematic set in motion by the plot's requiring Skelton to carry the "girl business" too far. The plot, in other words, is legible—and risible—as camp because it reiterates the masculine/feminine slippage occurring during the war years, when images of "the strong, independent, even *masculine* woman" and of "effeminate men as women" were popularized on film, whether treated dramatically or comically (Mann, 240; see also Woll, 98–102). Though it makes no reference to wartime, *Bathing Beauty* addresses cultural fallout from the sexual instability resulting from the war's deregulation of gender roles (hence the first title, *Mr. Coed*), but covers up this anxiety by asserting the primacy of male heterosexual desire for an unimpeachable feminine female (hence the second title, *Bathing Beauty*).

Here the obstacle separating the couple—namely, the fraudulent first wife—works as more than a plot device. For why does she have to be Latina? Her ethnicity helps to determine, albeit indirectly, the camp value of Esther Williams in the spectacular water ballet that closes the film. Maria Dorango appears every inch the bad carbon copy of Carmen Miranda—she bursts in right after the marriage ceremony, shouting, "Zees man is my hooz-ban!"—but at this point an audience already knows that hers is a double impersonation. The scene immediately before the wedding, when Adams arranges the ploy, reveals that Maria Dorango is really one Mary Donovan from Brooklyn, who has assumed the Latina persona to advance her stage career. With this imposter's exaggeration of ethnic femininity disclosed right away as a type of masquerade, Williams's character, Caroline, is not only the authentic bride but also represents the more authentic form of femininity—the all-American girl without any kind of deceptive artifice or intent whatsoever. Even so, the emphatic doubling of a female's masquerade (Mary as Maria as Mrs. Elliott), excessive as far as the plot is concerned, can make one think twice about Esther Williams's personification of all-American femininity, too.

When Williams first swims in *Bathing Beauty*, her expertise in the pool—as she alternates between the breaststroke and backstroke, goes underwater, then dives in and out, skipping along as if water were her natural element—stands out in comparison with the effeminacy of the film's male characters. From then on until the finale, we only see her "dry," in professional suits or evening dress, even though she teaches swimming. After he reunites with Caroline and Maria/Mary returns to cause more confusion, Steve finally delivers the score to George Adams, but only on the condition that Caroline star in the show, which conveniently turns out to be an aquacade (just as she conveniently turns out to be a performer). "How does she look in a bathing suit?" George asks. "How does she look in a bathing suit?" Steve replies. "Is he kidding?" This rhetorical question, directed to the audience via Skelton's close-up as well as to George in the plot, assumes that, once she exchanges her tailored suits for a one-piece, Esther Williams's unmistakable all-American girlishness will shine through in the aquacade. However, Williams does not easily serve this representation. To be a bathing beauty— really no more than a Ziegfeld showgirl in a swimsuit—she also has to perform femininity, and this performance is not all that different from Mary Donovan's masquerade, just less pronounced because it is not doubled or marked as ethnic.

Any assurance that Esther Williams simply looks good in a bathing suit is complicated by the star's undeniable athleticism and muscularity. She has a more imposing physique than any of the men in *Bathing Beauty*, and the bathing suit accentuates it. Not surprisingly, doubt about her conventional femininity underlined Williams's star image when she headlined at MGM. Catherine Williamson examines how, from the start of her movie career, Williams's image "as an athlete, a physically powerful woman," had to negotiate "cultural anxieties about strength and gender" in order not to appear too butch and lesbian. The star's success was due to "the brilliant way she merged 'femininity' and 'athleticism' into an aesthetically pleasing yet politically innocuous form," with publicity substituting her "humorous blurring of genus" (is she more human or more marine animal?) for the more difficult implication of gender confusion that her muscular femininity implied (8–10).

At the time of *Bathing Beauty*, the publicity mill had not yet been cranked up to full speed, that discursive framework was not yet in place, and the "cross-gender anxieties associated with the muscular female body" (10) were not yet repressed from Williams's image.[9] These anxieties get shown most strongly when *Bathing Beauty* displays the couple's sexual difference: in the swimming pool. Caroline can swim but Steve cannot, requiring her to rescue him in the film's last moments following the aquaballet, when, having found out about the Maria Dorengo scheme, Steve chases George into the pool and, remembering he cannot swim, sinks to the bottom. Caroline pops out of the water, pulls Steve up by the hair, they kiss, then he pulls her under, implying the consummation that has been delayed throughout—though since he cannot swim, we can only speculate that she will still have to hold him up, especially down there.

Williams, in short, is not a bathing beauty but a beautiful swimmer, and therein lies the gap between her image and its meaning, why she is still remembered as the "mother of synchronised swimming and queen of camp" (Zuiderveld). This reputation testifies to the indelible effect on her star image of *Bathing Beauty*'s spectacular finale, choreographed by John Murray Anderson, who had already worked with the swimmer on Billy Rose's Aquacade.

The aquaballet does not begin in water, which is surprising given that its purpose is to present Williams to the audience as a new type of musical star, one who swims while looking good in a bathing suit. Instead, the production number opens with a tight close-up of a trumpet's bell, the camera moves back to reveal Harry James, then a group of trumpeters with him, then the entire company with singer Helen Forrest, all performing against a backdrop with a lime green and orange-yellow sunburst intersected by aqua and forest green stripes. On the stage next to the orchestra, showgirls—wearing billowing tiered pink gowns, circlets of shells on their heads and leis of the same around their shoulders—emerge swinging to the beat of James's music. Dancing to the right of the stage, they gesture toward a second bandstand, and the camera reveals Xavier Cugat and his singer Lina Romay, who join in the music making. Traveling to a pool below the stage, the camera then records the line of swinging showgirls reflected in the water.

This shot prepares for the entrance of the swimmers. In long pink jackets resembling the showgirls' gowns, the swimmers line up, then disrobe, revealing bathing suits colored half pink, half green. Arms overhead, they dive into the pool one after the other, and the camera views their synchronized line from a diagonal angle to show its depth. As Harry James and company continue to swing, the swimmers travel the length of the pool still in a line; then, after a cut back to the showgirls on stage, the swimmers join in the dancing: clapping, somersaulting, matching their arm movements to those of the showgirls. When a second group of swimmers dives in the water, the pool is rocked by water dancing—a rather odd sight since what we see are swimmers treading water while waving their arms in unison to the swing beat and finishing with more somersaults.

The somersaults cue the next part of the number. With the music changing from swing to a classical waltz, Esther Williams finally arrives. She emerges from below the stage on a hydraulic lift in the shape of two white seahorses facing each other. Six elegant, statuesque showgirls, paired up according to the monochromatic color (black, blue, orange) of their long gowns and wide-brimmed chapeaux—in these costumes, they look out of place in the aqua setting, as if they had wandered in from the *Ziegfeld Follies* shoot—assist Williams as she removes robe and other accessories to reveal her white one-piece bathing suit, inset with tiny sparkling mirrors to catch the lights. Williams dives in the water, swims past paralleled lines formed by the swimmers, and heads underwater, an overhead shot revealing the foam caused by kicking swimmers with Williams visible in the middle.

Somewhat abruptly, the aquaballet now changes course. Williams finds a water lily, and the camera cuts back to the surface, where we see a single lily encircled twice by arrangements of additional lilies. The swimmers enter this floral pattern, and in the manner of Busby Berkeley an overhead shot reveals a human lily. Another cut returns to Williams, who picks up the plant, smells its fragrance, stands in the water with a view of the showgirls dancing behind her, and dives back into the pool. Now underwater again, Williams glides through the legs of swimmers, who have formed two revolving pinwheels, and then does some somersaults. For the finale, Williams bursts to the surface, and we can see the dancers standing on stage behind her, frozen in a pose, their arms reaching in the air to make a V. She swims past spouting fountains, then retraces her path as flames burst up in the center of each spray. The camera moves back to set the final tableau: with fire and water shooting up toward the sky, Williams rises from a lift in the pool, posing as the swimmers move toward her, and a curtain of water ends the number, the dancers still swinging on the stage. In fact, they never seem to stop dancing, since they still appear on stage doing the same steps when Skelton jumps into the pool after the number is over.

The water ballet's straight motivation may be to deliver the crotch shot, many of them in fact, but its grandiose spectacle exceeds this purpose, exaggerating the visual incongruities brought out by the style. The number demands camp recognition for it to make any sense at all. The very introduction of swimming in a musical number is an incongruous idea in and of itself, since it involves neither singing nor dancing; further, synchronized swimming aims to conform the body to the precision of machinery or a production line but in a fluid medium which activates reflexive bodily movement along with physical skill and discipline. In order to visualize its overall conceit equating swimming with dancing, the aquaballet parallels the line of showgirls with the line of swimmers, while belying their comparability. Water is simply much less stable for regularizing movement than a stage floor. Williams reports that pillars were added to the pool's set design before shooting in order to give the

The aquaballet in *Bathing Beauty* (MGM, 1944). Top photo: The synchronized swimmers form a water lily, while showgirls pose in the background. Bottom photo: Esther Williams rising from the water in the finale.

swimmers marks to hit after they dived in and to break up the viewing plane as a means of concealing momentary but still visible rifts
in the synchronized line when a swimmer was off (112). The paralleling of showgirls and swimmers thus has the effect of juxtaposing
the more static arrangement of the showgirls' dancing above water,
always in line and doing the same steps, with the swimmers' movement in the water, even when synchronized—however hard the choreography and camerawork at others times objectifies their bodies in
the manner of Berkeley's similar water number, "By a Waterfall," in
Warners' *Footlight Parade* (1933).

But the pairing of showgirls and swimmers is not the only source
of visual incongruity which this spectacular production number
stages. It builds through a series of incongruous juxtapositions, beginning with James and Cugat appearing on opposite bandstands,
then arranging the swinging dancers on one side of the performing
area and synchronized swimmers on the other, then contrasting Williams's singular freestyle swimming with the ensemble work of the
other swimmers, finally concluding with orgasmic eruptions of fountains succeeded by flames as Williams glides serenely and confidently
across the pool's surface. Such dualisms dominate the stylization
of the number at every turn. The swimmers wear complementary
colors (pink and green) and they form two pinwheels underwater,
just as the six showgirls with Williams when she enters are chromatically doubled according to their costumes and the seahorses on
the lift are twinned. The visual dualisms are present sequentially as
well as concurrently. The dancers are fixed in position when Williams
swims in the finale, then she strikes a statuesque pose as she rises out
of the water and the swimmers approach her with great splashing.
Additionally, the music changes from swing to classical, the set combines natural and mechanical elements (the pool and the stage), the
choreography deploys physical expertise (swimming) and technical
special effects (the lifts on stage and, in the pool, the fountains with
flames inside). As noticeably, the stage is heterosexualized as a space
(James's and Cugat's orchestras perform alongside the showgirls),
while the swimming pool (where only women perform) is not. At the
same time, the dualisms blend together with unsettling visual effect,
as when the swimmers mimic dancers but what they do cannot be
called "dancing," or when they form the figure of a lily in Berkeley-

esque fashion on the water's surface and the image changes back, via montage, into a real plant.

The style here certainly works to set off Williams as the number's star by exempting her from the dualism motif for the most part (her white costume, her vertical movements in the water, the freedom and individuality expressed by her solo swimming). Yet the number, while marking Williams as female, fails to authenticate her femininity, instead theatricalizing her body in the water as a dynamic and unrestrained, not static, one. Nor does the style safely heterosexualize Williams through her swimming, since it incorporates the gender anxieties which Williamson references, clearly on display in the sequence beginning with the lily's transformation into an overhead Berkeleyesque pattern and back into a lily which Williams presses to her face, and concluding with her swimming underwater through the entwined legs of the corps de water ballet. In this sequence, as the "aqua-choreography" shifts back and forth between literalizing and symbolizing the crotch shot through the synchronized swimmers, the number marks Williams's difference and places her in erotic conjunction with the women, queering what the bathing beauty and the swimming pool signify for the plot's gender problematic. The number's style imagines the idea of pairing from every possible angle without ever resorting to the one dualism expected of a musical: a heterosexual coupling.

NYLONS OR MARACAS — OR TRUMPETS?

The other numbers in *Bathing Beauty*, most lacking as lavish a mise-en-scène and all on a much smaller scale than the aquaballet, seem more resistant to camp recognition. Taken at face value, these numbers visualize the superiority of American music even when it appropriates from other cultural sources. The numbers thus set up various polarities of musical styles (swing/Latin bands, hot/sweet arrangements, traditional/modern songs) as references to the genre's conventional valorization of popular entertainment through an opposition of authentic and inauthentic musical expressiveness. Organist Ethel Smith first performs a traditional standard from 1914, "By the Waters of the Minnetonka," for the college girls before their music class begins, then immediately follows with a hotter number from "below the border," "Tico, Tico." The college girls—played by the same contract dancers who worked in the opening number of *Ziegfeld Follies* (and confirming that they have indeed mastered the blank mannequin stare to perfection)—join in, and this "South American jive" incongruously mates Smith's organ sound with the beat of tambourines, conga drums, and maracas.

Either individually or in their aggregation, the many show numbers in *Bathing Beauty* are nonetheless amenable to camp if only because their stylization exaggerates the dualistic thinking supporting the implied parallel between the authenticity of American popular entertainment and that of the heteronormality supposedly confirmed by the end of the sissy-boy-meets-loses-regains-all-American-girl plot. Much in the same spirit as Smith's specialty spots, Skelton's one number, "You Take the High Note," is a swing improvement of "Loch Lomond," the traditional Scottish ballad being taught in the music class. Because he has fallen asleep out of boredom, Skelton gets the assignment of writing a better version overnight; with permission to use any backup he wishes, Skelton brings Harry James and orchestra and a few other surprises, so the number performed in the classroom turns into a full-fledged stage performance, with the entire faculty, including Williams, there to watch. The number is also about pairing up, as it turns out. The lyrics use singing as a conceit for describing heterosexual coupling: if the female takes the high note and the male the low note, they'll "make sweet music together." Without Williams, though, the duet loses the conventional purchase the number might have had, at least from the lyrics, in evoking the generic dual focus to forge more of a bridge to the plot. Instead, Skelton performs with Jean Porter (playing classmate Jean Allenwood). The first verse indicates the casting may be a means of protecting Skelton's voice, since Porter sings it and he joins in with her only at its finish. Successive verses begin to blur the sexual difference of high and low notes, however, just as they give Skelton more to do: if she sings in his key, and he sings in hers, they "won't be off key together." Then they repeat the first verse but exchange places in the high/low note duality.

At this point Skelton and Porter leave the stage singing as a couple and the routine appears to be concluded, but it is not. Rather, it keeps adding performers two by two, with the multiplication of couples prompting additional verses. Skelton and Porter return with Janis Paige and Carlos Ramirez, making a quartet out of the duet; then Helen Forrest and Buddy Moreno appear from the bandstand to form a sextet; and finally Harry James and Ethel Smith join in to create an octet, the former playing "hot" on his trumpet and the latter playing "sweet" on her organ (with corresponding close-ups of his horn and her feet on the pedals). As these additional couples join in, the arrangement starts to alternate between cross- and same-gendered vocal partnering. Furthermore, the choreography plays with the gender mobility afforded by the multiple coupling, ending with a chorus line that, according to the lyrics, means to top the Rockettes. First all eight performers, arms linked together, kick up their legs, then the four women form a line and kick, then the men do the same and don't do a bad job. When all eight join arms again, the line spins out of control, and Skelton barrels toward the classroom window. Pulled back by classmates in the audience, he gushes, "Isn't that redhead fellow wonderful?" only to realize, "That's me!" and rushes back to the stage for the number's finish: four couples, the men bending a knee for the women to sit on. Skelton's momentary self-consciousness of the performance as a performance means to turn the joke narcissistically on the comedian, but it also calls attention to the number's camp attitudes toward the idea of high note/low note heterosexual coupling: who would ever expect to see Harry James kicking his legs like a Rockette, arm-in-arm with Skelton, Ramirez, and Moreno?

It's an eclectic male chorus line, too, mixing Anglo and Latin performers. I mention this because ethnicity is a recurring element in the other numbers, which contrast James's swing with Cugat's Latin-American music. The ethnic juxtaposition of their respective musical styles is marked out by the East/West Coast settings of their numbers and the instruments appearing as a metonymy, verbally and visually, of each orchestra leader's special skill: the trumpet for James, the maracas for Cugat. Except for when he has to dance like a Rockette, James is treated with all due respect in *Bathing Beauty*. His numbers, "The Trumpet Blues" and "Hora Stacato," are chromatically cool in their visual design, the light sparkling off the brass instruments. Both numbers use trick photography to focus on James's trumpet-playing, either to have him remain in place while behind him the camera moves quickly across the orchestra, or to have him seem to be in two places at once on the bandstand, at the start and end of a traveling shot.

By contrast, Cugat's numbers, "Bim Bam Bum" and "Alma Llanerna," are more hotly colored and dynamically staged and edited; here, the Spanish songs, choreography, large cast, and vivid costuming draw on stereotypical tropes of ethnic authenticity while simultaneously exaggerating the performers' theatricality. Whereas James's orchestra wears suits, Cugat's featured players wear ruffled sleeves. Whereas Helen Forrest coolly sings the torchy "I Cried For You" with the backing of James's Music Makers, Lina Romay vivaciously performs the up-tempo "Bim Bam Bum" with Cugat's orchestra to display her "hotchcha" sexuality as a Latina ethnic. The Cugat numbers also more strangely delineate the space between performance and audience within the film. "Bim Bam Bum" appears self-contained, photographed on a soundstage, but on its finish the number turns out to be set in a country club, performed for a crowd of all-white swimmers frolicking in a pool well below the stage. "Alma Llanerna" is fully staged in a nightclub as a peasant dance with singer Romay, while Skelton, waiting for Cugat to get off stage, listens to it over the telephone on the other side of the continent.

Standing out as stylistically different from James's, Cugat's numbers in *Bathing Beauty*, the first of ten MGM musicals to feature him in the 1940s, were obviously crafted to satisfy the era's craze for Latin American rhythms and dances. As clearly, his numbers display a straightforward—and noncamp—ideological valence, which is why they may seem to differ in significance from the aquaballet. Cugat's appearance as a specialty act in *Bathing Beauty* and his many other musicals, including four more with Esther Williams, follows from the film industry's commitment to the federal Good Neighbor Policy as a means of addressing the Latin American audience during and immediately after the war. The Production Code Administration even hired a specialist, Addison Durland, to vet scripts for accurate, respectful treatment of Latin Americans. Not surprisingly, the policy resulted in ideological compromise, balancing a goal of "authenticity" with the racial hierarchies of those nations' own cultural elites, who wanted to show their countries as urban, clean, and white, and with the studios' own "desire to have Latin characters retain their traditional comic or exotic functions" (O'Neill, 375).

The already prevalent "stereotype of fiery and tempestuous Latin women" (372), in the form of Lina Romay's musical persona and Mary Donovan's Latina impersonation, was exempt from Durland's scrutiny; he further assumed that inclusion of a Latin American star such as Cugat or Ramirez "was somehow automatically immune from offensive or problematic representations" (376). The "good neighborly" Latin or Latina ended up representing a "safe" cultural other in comparison to the German or Japanese other of wartime, and musicals incorporated this ethnic type by simultaneously privileging Latin American stars as a source of entertainment while marginalizing them from the narrative (López, 414).

The film industry's pan-Americanism through the use of Latin settings or, as in *Bathing Beauty*, the inclusion of Latin entertainers had a particular economic end: increasing the product's appeal in the American hemisphere without weakening the domestic market. But how Latinness was represented on film also participated in what Matthew Frye Jacobson has analyzed as an ideological shift in the United States, beginning in the 1920s, whereby the cultural and legal constitution of whiteness went from being multiraced (as, say, in "Mediterranean" or "Slavic" white "races") to being singular ("Caucasian"). By mid-century, *ethnicity* marked cultural more than racial differences, which is to say that "peoples still defined as racial groups were also tacitly marked by a degree of difference that was more than merely cultural." As for ethnicity, it "provided a paradigm for assimilation which erased race as a category of historical experience for European and some Near Eastern immigrants. Not only did these groups now belong to a unified Caucasian race, but race was deemed so irrelevant to who they were that it became something possessed only by 'other' peoples" (110). This is why, in supervising scripts for the PCA, Durland capitulated to external demands that Latin American nations be represented as white. Yet this shift did not occur all at once, and "residual traces" of an older racial ideology "persisted" at this time too (93), as evident in Durland's other compromises. Latins on film were still doubly marked: representing a cultural ethnicity affiliated with Southern European origins, while still signifying racial otherness as skin color.

The ideological ambiguity of ethnicity as a marker of racial/cultural differences determined the comic value of Cugat, Romay, and

Ramirez as dark Latin types in *Bathing Beauty*, not the least when they perform with fair-skinned Red Skelton, who shares their narrative scenes. More significantly, their numbers show the Latin performers as simultaneously raced *and* ethnic, other but not other, and this gloss helps to determine their potential for a camp reading of ethnicity as a cultural performance of identity not all that different from Esther Williams's watery version of femininity in the aquaballet. In the way they are performed and filmed, the Latin numbers contrast with the unmarked but visible whiteness of James's "Hora Stacato," introduced as a Jascha Heifetz violin concerto drawn from traditional gypsy music but with the "violin fireworks transcribed to the trumpet," and of blonde Ethel Smith's appropriation of "some South American jive" for her organ in "Tico, Tico." These latter numbers spotlight the specialty performer as a translator of ethnic music into a North Americanized sound. Cugat's numbers, on the other hand, may be almost as North Americanized, but they retain the Spanish language, and, as production numbers, they are more carnivalesque in setting, costuming, and choreography. The Latin numbers are not queer, but neither are they straight in the sense in which, by comparison, James's and Smith's numbers signify the greater comfort of white, North American entertainment.

This North/Latin American duality is made explicit when Carlos Ramirez breaks with his otherwise foolish, asexual character to sing "Te Quiero Juste" accompanied by members of Cugat's orchestra. The number showcases Ramirez's romantic baritone voice while visually differentiating him as Latin from the white members of the California country club. Having written the love song for Williams, Skelton now needs someone to sing it, and he warns his friend, "[You'd] better put my heart and soul into it." Why Skelton wrote the lyrics in Spanish when Ramirez speaks English is never made clear; but no explanation is needed, of course, since this is just an excuse to include the number, so the diminutive Ramirez follows the statuesque Williams around the pool, singing in Spanish. That she has little idea of what he is singing about may explain why she keeps backing away as if he were stalking her. Clearly not dressed for a country club, Ramirez seems out of place here except for the fact that Williams's matador swimming robe matches the design of his and the strolling band's costumes. Taking off the robe, she dives into

14

Carlos Ramirez
serenades Esther
Williams with
"Te Quiero Juste."
Bathing Beauty
(MGM, 1944).

PHOTOFEST

the pool, swimming to a reprise of the song; with the Spanish verses gone, the melody now functions as her swimming theme, "Magic Is the Moonlight," which it did extrafilmically, too (E. Williams, 109).

In this number, the proximity of Latin ethnicity to the star, whom MGM was already promoting in 1944 as "probably the ideal embodiment of American girlhood" (*Who's Who at Metro-Goldwyn-Mayer*, 35), points up the indisputable whiteness of the feminine ideal Williams embodies while effacing its own raced connotations of whiteness. However, the number's incongruous mixture of Spanish love song/swimming reprise somewhat disturbs the North/Latin American hierarchy supporting the naturalizing of whiteness as propped up by the Hispanic subordinate. Indeed, raced ethnicity may come too close to unraced North Americanness in the California country club. For shortly after this number, *Bathing Beauty* not only introduces Maria Dorango/Mary Donovan, but the film also takes an unexpected geographic turn and heads northeast, unexpected only because an opening card states: "We don't know if this story actually happened—but if it *did* happen—it couldn't happen in a nicer place than California." But some twenty minutes in, following Cugat's first number and Ramirez's solo, the plot abruptly relocates to New Jersey when Skelton goes off in pursuit of Williams at the aptly named Victoria College. Although Ramirez accompanies Skelton, the change in locale nonetheless sets up the distinction, as far as concerns the successive nightclub numbers, between the whiteness of the Northeast, where James's performances are all set, and the ethnic mixing of the West Coast, where Cugat remains until he appears for a moment in the aquaballet.

Even while confined to the west after the action moves east, Cugat continues to perform in *Bathing Beauty*, and his final number, "Alma Llanerna," is the most incomprehensible representation of Latin American ethnicity in the entire film. This production number has an incongruous mise-en-scène which mixes together peasant ethnicity with nightclub elegance. Behind a blue scrim the Cugat orchestra is shown in silhouette, with a glittering chandelier above and a vase of flowers in the foreground; the camera moves in on the vase, which turns out to be part of a single tall pillar connected to—nothing. Latin peasants come out dancing as couples, miming some kind of ritual folk celebration as they reach Cugat and a group of violinists arranged in a line behind him on steps. The camera moves up to catch the entire orchestra playing under the chandelier, then focuses on the xylophone player, after which the peasant chorus sings, and finally Romay, in long pigtails and a multicolored skirt, appears with two gauchos for her solo. The editing cuts back and forth from peasants to orchestra, for instance moving from Romay's swirling skirt to Cugat and violinists; and Romay and her partners are also shot in silhouette behind the blue scrim. After these three do a flamenco-style dance, the number ends with the camera pulling back to take in the whole scene: the lone pedestal with the flowers, the chandelier above, a large ornate window framing Romay and the gauchos, the violinists and peasant dancers on steps, the rest of the orchestra below them.

"Alma Llanerna" confirms Ana M. López's observation that, in the Good Neighbor films, Hollywood performed the work of ethnography, producing, rather than reflecting, the relation of cultural texts to ethnicity; the films did not represent ethnics but created imagery of non–North American otherness for audiences to experience *as*

15

The finale of "Alma Llanerna" with Xavier Cugat, Lina Romay, and company. *Bathing Beauty* (MGM, 1944).

ethnicity (405). This was certainly how MGM represented its Latin performers to the moviegoing public. In *Who's Who at Metro-Goldwyn-Mayer*, a pocket-sized paperback book of two hundred pages celebrating the studio's twentieth anniversary in 1944, the biography of Cugat mentions the orchestra leader's birth in Spain but ignores that he was raised in and identified with Cuba, representing him as European by virtue of his birthplace and his later musical training in Spain and Italy. For all that, the profile still depicts him as the quintessential Latin good neighbor: "On the M-G-M lot he greets everyone as 'amigo' and everyone is his friend" (156). Furthermore, whereas the profile of Harry James features the trumpeter's upbringing by circus performers and Southern roots but stresses both his artistry (he is not only fond of classical musical but is influenced by it, and he does not shave his mustache in order not to injure his lip) and his all-American love of baseball (the James band's softball team is "as famous as their swing") (158), Cugat's profile notes his early career as a newspaper cartoonist in Los Angeles but defines him ethnically through his music, the "Latin-American melodies [played] for Yankee ears." MGM credits Cugat with "popularizing the rumba in the United States" and attributes to him "a campaign to make the samba, tango, and other South American dances popular in the United States" as well (156). Similarly, even though Romay's profile recounts that she was born in New York and raised in Detroit among other U.S. cities (her father was a Mexican consulate), it highlights how her surname, pronounced correctly or not, "denotes a dark-eyed Latin beauty," an ethnicity evident in her love of colors, "the brighter the better," and possibly even in her pet cocker spaniel's name, "Negra" (118).

The Latin numbers in *Bathing Beauty* do this same kind of cultural work for U.S. consumption, to be sure, but they also stand out as incongruously "ethnic." They are indeed "improbable stuff"! Not only are they overstylized, calling too much attention to their theatricalization of ethnicity as a cultural production on a par with the camp treatment of femininity in the aquaballet, but these numbers also touch on the plot in a way that causes additional awareness of the performers' Latinness as a hyperbolic ethnicity and associates it with camp passing. Cugat may play himself in caricature (he even opens the film by drawing his cartoon signature) and be geographically isolated from most of the narrative action, but he is also the fictive character responsible for Maria Dorango's presence and the delayed marital consummation which the Latina pretender causes. When she makes her first appearance Dorango wears a costume closely resembling that of Cugat's troupe in their first number, "Bim Bam Bum," indicating that she is probably a member of his company. The connection returns immediately following "Alma Llanerna." After Skelton listens to this number on the telephone, he asks if Cugat knows any more about Dorango's whereabouts, and the orchestra leader replies that she not only has disappeared, but she stole his last pair of maracas to boot. Romay then jumps in to exclaim that, worse, the imposter stole her last pair of nylons, and as Skelton hangs up, we hear them arguing over which is the more serious theft: "Maracas!" "Nylons!"

The exchange obviously trivializes their talent and implicitly neuters Cugat, but it also brings back a reference to ethnicity as an artifice of represented otherness, linking Cugat and Romay to the ethnic masquerade of Mary Donovan (herself not characterized as an ethnic but as a Brooklynite). For that matter, Skelton is himself in drag during this entire scene, still wearing Williams's clothing, implying another comparability of gender and ethnic impersonations. Finally, the arbitrary way in which "Alma Llanerna" gets inserted in the narrative, with Skelton only hearing it because he happens to telephone Cugat, causes the number's visual absurdities to rub against its supposed authenticating use of ethnic tropes. Skelton tells Cugat, "Your number sounded wonderful." Yet if audiences were to follow Skelton's lead and listen with their eyes closed to Cugat's Latin sound as if it were on radio, they would miss the number's hyperbolic visualization of ethnicity, and they would also shut their eyes to its camp. What this framework for hearing/viewing "Alma Llanerna" suggests is that *not* paying attention to the number's incongruity in representing "authentic" Latin ethnicity is to watch the number as noncamp entertainment.

The many numbers in *Bathing Beauty*, in sum, build a camp coherence of their own through their aggregation as well as their excessive visual style. The comic plot derives from disturbances to gender normality, upsetting the masculine/feminine dualism that regulates the difference between queer and straight, while the show numbers— whether directly, in the case of Cugat's, or indirectly as a structuring absence, in the case of James's—visually incorporate tropes of ethnicity to establish the North/Latin American dualism which in its turn reveals how the aquaballet is just as concerned with making a spectacle of femininity to idealize a whiteness marked neither as raced nor as ethnic. Thus the ballet begins with the two bands on each side of the stage, while letting James dominate musically. The finale, in this sense, may stop the plot in the interest of spectacle but it serves as the point where cultural preoccupations of the plot and the numbers come together, visualizing the nonraced, nonethnic image of the bathing beauty as the lynchpin of heteronormality—and giving that image its delicious camp spin.

Disconnecting the plot from numbers, the aggregate form of *Bathing Beauty* thus addresses a potential camp audience through that conjunction of gendered and ethnic representations and the value codings which underwrite them. This musical's camp dialectic derives from the multiple ways in which its ten numbers stylize their content out of a logic of juxtaposition while pushing this logic to excess. Except for the aquaballet, a camp perspective does not thoroughly inform each and every number but is the effect of their aggregation. The film's camp self-awareness, moreover, does not substitute a queer reading of all the numbers for a straight one but mediates the ostensibly straight plot (its heterosexual romance) and its queer resonances (the various gender instabilities problematizing the romance) from the ironic vantage point of the numbers' stylistic incongruities.

If the camp style seems an imposition on the musical's content and its ideological agenda, well, that *is* the point of camp, but the style is nonetheless part of the musical's textual materiality, resulting from the collaboration of queer and straight personnel manufacturing *Bathing Beauty* in accord with studio protocols for the product and in complicity (whether resistant or conformist) with the historical field in which the musical was produced and then received. The multiple sources of the style, moreover, account for the contradictions that make this musical's otherwise straight-seeming entertainment so visibly incoherent. But by the same token, I am not suggesting that the MGM house style offers a fully worked-out critique either of its era's gender or ethnic ideologies—certainly not in the manner in which I, writing as a critic, have put the numbers together to make the incongruities of *Bathing Beauty* more fully intelligible. Rather, I am arguing that the style renders the incongruity of the numbers more apparent to those in the know—that is to say, those watching the musical in 1944 for its stylized entertainment and not its heterosexual agenda—which encourages recognition that the ideological regulation of gender and ethnicity *is* being interfered with, and done so in the name of camp. When Esther Williams recalls that "what moviegoers liked best, of course, was the improbable stuff," she was no doubt thinking about the numbers' appeal as escapism from wartime hardships and consumer shortages. This appeal drew on their lavish, outlandish imagery and gratuitous motivations with respect to the plot; but those same features also made the numbers "improbable" in a way that corresponded with their camp value, too.

Chapter Two

*T*he number begins as gentlemen of the press arrive to interview a celebrated Lady—"America's pride and joy / The prettiest, wittiest glamour girl by far"—played by a young MGM star whose girl-next-door persona at that time was not very glamorous at all. As the men sing her praises while dancing, the Lady mimes narcissistic enjoyment of her glamorous features while pointing them out. She is all motion. With her head bobbing as if too loosely fastened to her neck by a diamond choker, her gesturing overly animated and excessive in drawing attention to her body, the Lady's frantic movements call to mind a puppet without strings, a Judy with too much punch. Circling around the manic Lady, the interviewers claim in unison that they do not want to learn the banal details of her life, such as whether or not she takes lemon in her tea. To oblige them, the Lady confides, "The facts I give / Are genuinely, intimately feminine," segueing into the song's chorus, which recounts how "most of all / A lady loves to love."

Although this description may initially suggest that the number in question is Judy Garland's "The Great Lady Has 'an Interview,'" written by Roger Edens and Kay Thompson and choreographed by Charles Walters for *Ziegfeld Follies* (1946), in fact, it is Debbie Reynolds's "A Lady Loves," written by Joseph Myrow and Mack David and choreographed by Robert Alton for *I Love Melvin* (1953). Designed to capitalize on the success of *Singin' in the Rain* (1952) by reteaming Reynolds with Donald O'Connor, *I Love Melvin* is decidedly B fare as far as MGM musicals go. It was produced by George Wells and directed by Don Weiss, so with the exception of Alton's choreography, *Melvin* was not overseen by any of the major personnel responsible for making musicals at the studio. Despite the added expense of some location shooting in New York City, this is one of those rare MGM musicals that, at a meager running time of seventy-seven minutes, seems eminently suitable for the second half of a double bill.

I Love Melvin nonetheless offers pleasures expected of the MGM brand. It features inventive staging of Reynolds's numbers by Alton, spectacular hoofing from O'Connor, and a rather goofy treatment of the backstage plot concerning Judy LeRoy's (Reynolds) inspired plan of how to break out of the chorus. The besotted Melvin Hoover (O'Connor), a photographer's assistant working for *Look*, follows Judy around with the excuse of doing a photo story about an ordinary chorus girl's life, and she makes him promise to put her on the cover of *Look*'s next issue. "Now *there* is an earth-shaking notion!" Melvin's boss (Jim Backus) exclaims sarcastically when pitched the idea. "A girl on the cover of a magazine! They'll go mad, I tell you, mad!" The *Look* editor uses the photograph of a prize-winning racehorse instead, requiring Melvin to fake a sample issue with Judy's picture in the animal's place. His ruse gets out of hand and he runs away, with the result that Judy *does* end up on *Look*'s cover, though not for the purpose originally imagined, when the editor agrees to help publicize her search for the missing Melvin.

Featuring a girl's picture on the cover did sell magazines all the time, but the plot premise of *I Love Melvin* is actually quite pertinent to the musical genre. As one variation of the fashion-show display imitating Florenz Ziegfeld's stage revues from earlier in the century, the "girl on the cover of a magazine" was a common enough conceit for elaborate production numbers meant to feature showgirls in glamorous costumes. Professional models pose along with Rita Hayworth in Columbia's *Cover Girl* (1944), and "The Girl on a Magazine Cover" with Ann Miller is a Follies number on the New Amsterdam roof in MGM's *Easter Parade* (1948). "A Lady Loves," which opens *I Love Melvin*, parodies the Ziegfeld definition of femininity through fashion. The number takes place in a salon where the Lady—garbed in hot pink and showing lots of leg, feathers in her hair, glittering diamonds on her wrists—makes her entrance down a runway of stairs in

16

Debbie Reynolds lists all the things "A Lady Loves" in *I Love Melvin* (MGM, 1953).

the manner of a Ziegfeld showgirl. Admired by gentlemen in top hats and capes as well as the boys from the press, she reveals the secrets of her femininity to these sugar daddies all the while being interviewed. Much like Lana Turner's character Sheila Hale (née Regan) in *Ziegfeld Girl* (1941), the Lady discloses right off the bat that she prefers "expensive clothes and pretty jewels / And furs and French chapeaux," "loves a penthouse / Where she'll be content to play," and most of all "adores the subtle phrase / That it's the man who pays."

Judged by its lyrics, the number seems a knock-off of "Diamonds Are a Girl's Best Friend" from the 1949 stage hit *Gentlemen Prefer Blondes* (the film version with Marilyn Monroe was released several months after *Melvin*). Following the same logic as "Diamonds," "A Lady Loves" equates femininity with the unabashed coveting of expensive things. And like "Diamonds," the *Melvin* number confirms Pamela Robertson's observation that "the comic gold digger," almost always a chorus girl on stage or in film, is camp's female equivalent of the dandy—"its original personification, its defining voice" (58). Reynolds performs "Lady Loves" with too much self-conscious animation to be taken seriously as either poised showgirl mannequin or sexy gold-digging siren. The star's nonstop energetic miming is just too often out of step with the dancers, her smirking just too noticeable as she races to keep up with them. For example, after promising to give "the genuine, intimately feminine" facts, she abruptly extends her arms high in the air and seems about to take off in flight. Reinforcing her frantic miming, Reynolds overenunciates the lyrics and her breathing, as when she puts stress on each syllable of "genuinely, intimately feminine," drawing even more of a gap between what the song expresses and how it is performed.

The number's setup does this as well, framing Reynolds's dancing and delivery with additional layers of performing. At first "Lady Loves" is presented as a musical number being filmed with Big Movie Star Judy LeRoy in a studio just like MGM. From the moment the sound technician plays back the prerecorded track, the song's glamorous, gold-digging persona is acknowledged to be a manufactured image, distinct from the movie star doing her impression of that Lady. After the director yells "cut," the star receives the acclaim of every member of the crew as well as a surprise visit from longtime MGM star Robert Taylor, who drops by to confess his undying passion. Their kiss is interrupted by the revelation that the entire sequence is an aspiring chorus girl's dream of movie stardom, brought to a halt by a mother's wake-up yell. Judy LeRoy (née Schneider) is still living at home with her parents and contributing to the family's income. What is more, she is no alluring Ziegfeld showgirl with gold-digging potential, since her job on Broadway is to play a football. For that matter, this number immediately follows the credits, which begin with Debbie Reynolds writing the film's title in lipstick on a dressing-room mirror. So can we ignore that the young, tomboyish star performing the multiple poses of "Lady Loves" is herself one of "the kids from Singin' in the Rain" (as the trailer for Melvin refers to the two leads), where her character's lack of glamour and innate talent are juxtaposed with the inauthenticity of glamorous silent screen star, Lina Lamont (Jean Hagen)?

In this opening number, I Love Melvin establishes its continuity with MGM's production of the musical genre as it focused a camp lens on the glamour of female stardom. The choreography of "A Lady Loves" alludes not only to Garland's "Great Lady" segment in Ziegfeld Follies but to the many numbers she did with the boys in the chorus, and it evokes as well comparable dance numbers featuring other MGM stars, such as Eleanor Powell and Ann Miller, which destabilize the constructed ideal of feminine glamour established by the Ziegfeld revues. Additionally, with "Lady Loves" introducing the plot about a chorus girl who hopes for her big break by appearing on the cover of *Look* magazine (since she is never going to get it by playing a football!), *I Love Melvin* follows the conventions by which MGM musicals set up a dialectic between glamour and stardom on the one hand and an ingenue's talent, hard work, and gender nonconformity on the other. For MGM musicals, these latter qualities make a Garland, Powell, or Reynolds the exemplar of show business values precisely because she stands for a more authentic type of female entertainer. Yet, paradoxically, these musicals represent her authenticity in highly theatrical star turns that mock glamour and, consequently, deviate from the cultural norm of "genuine" femininity otherwise upheld by movie stardom and the Ziegfeld revue alike.

This chapter examines the camp valences of female star turns in the MGM musical. The special type of number I am singling out complicates what has become a truism about the camp appeal of female stars: that, as Daniel Harris puts it, "in the homosexual's imagination, Hollywood divas were transformed into gay men, undergoing a strange sort of sex change operation from which they emerged as drag queens, as men in women's clothing" (12). I don't dispute that cross-gendered identification contributes to gay men's fascination with musicals and their divas. However, collapsing camp and stardom into the latter's potential for appropriation by drag obscures what, during the era of their production, musical numbers which parody glamour could stage about femininity for women as well as queer men by relying on camp strategies.

A camp number such as "Lady Loves" does more than acknowledge how femininity is constructed out of artifice because, through Reynolds's performance and interaction with the boys in the chorus, the number associates the star with an ironic outlook on gender conformity much like that distinguishing the camp figure from the drag queen, to return to Esther Newton's comparison of the two social roles in mid-century homosexual circles. "The drag queen," she states, "simply expresses the incongruity [of masculine-feminine transformation] while the camp actually uses it to achieve a higher synthesis," the wit enabled by his stance as a queer clown-philosopher (105). No doubt the camp outlook informing star turns can be attributed to the queer people writing, arranging, directing, choreographing, costuming, and/or decorating MGM's musicals, and I do not ignore the influence on such numbers of Roger Edens, Charles Walters, and Robert Alton in particular. My primary concern in this chapter is the result of their collaborative behind-the-scenes labor, the numbers centering on a female star who enacts a camp's recognition of the incongruities arising from glamour's operation as a cultural mechanism of heterosexualization. Given the MGM musical's history, it should come as no surprise that Judy Garland's example figures most prominently in this discussion, which pays close attention to her numbers in *Ziegfeld Girl* and her "Great Lady" spot in *Ziegfeld Follies*, but I also seek in the final section to trace the continuity between her camp star turns and those of other key female performers working at the studio, including Lena Horne.

ZIEGFELD GLAMOUR

The Ziegfeld reputation bore commercial value as a point of reference for many of MGM's musicals, implied every time the studio promoted the "girls! Girls! GIRLS!" on display in a big production number like the Esther Williams aquaballet in *Bathing Beauty* (1944). The reference was more than implied on several occasions. For *Broadway Melody* (1929) Metro invented a fictive version of Ziegfeld (the producer Zanfield), but by the time of *The Great Ziegfeld* (1936) and its follow-up films, *Ziegfeld Girl* and *Ziegfeld Follies*, the studio had licensed the showman's name, exploiting his official theme, "The Glorified American Girl." All three Ziegfeld musicals lavishly reproduce the producer's trademark style with numbers illustrating beauty as a pageant of women decked out in fantastic gowns, jewels, feathers, and headpieces: "A Pretty Girl is Like a Melody" in the first, "You Stepped Out of a Dream" in the second, and the previously discussed "Here's to the Girls" in the third. In each number a male singer (respectively Dennis O'Keefe with Allen Jones's voice, Tony Martin, Fred Astaire) celebrates female beauty and anonymous showgirls appear in a procession to authenticate the truth of what he sings. As crucially, through their example, the showgirls redefine the universal value of "beauty" hailed by the song, embodying it as glamour.

Given the commercial prestige of Ziegfeld-styled production numbers for MGM, it is worth recalling what the showgirls' glamour historically signified in the Follies during its life on Broadway from 1907 to 1931. As Linda Mizejewski documents, the Ziegfeld girl's visual elaboration of a male voyeuristic fantasy should not detract from this iconic figure's contribution to the new industry of celebrity and its creation of glamour, "not [as] an illusion or abstraction but [as] a real way of thinking and perceiving desire and sexuality" (46). Borrowing from but also determining the commercial development of haute couture runways on the one hand (Ziegfeld even added bona fide fashion models starting in 1915) and department store displays on the other, the Follies's tableaux of showgirls helped to define the status and look of women in early-twentieth-century public space. Mizejewski identifies three features of the Ziegfeld girl's embodiment of glamour that bear on this discussion: the glamour was work, it was white, and it was comparable with female impersonation.

First, the Ziegfeld girl's glamour provisionally stabilized the conflicted implications of her status as a working woman freed from domesticity by virtue of her weekly wage. "Despite the public relations imagery of the 'lady' and her elegant stage appearance," Mizejewski remarks, "the Ziegfeld Girl was nevertheless part of the 'liberated' showgirl continuum that glamorized a busy, prominent career (albeit a short one) for a single woman" (87). Her "girlhood," glorified as such by the Follies's motto, meant she was youthful and unmarried yet, contradictorily, her work in the show meant she was eroticized and sexually knowing. On-stage as an element of the fashion tableaux, the racy yet respectable Ziegfeld girl tamed "women's work" by connecting it to "appearance and decor," thereby evading "questions of authority and education." Off-stage in the press's narrativization of her private life, always suggesting the association of chorus girls with gold digging, even prostitution, she "represented a fantasy solution to the real problems of working-woman life" by ending her career "in marriage to a special member of the audience," that otherwise unavailable, elusive millionaire whose eye she first caught while appearing on stage (74). The Ziegfeld girl thus epitomized a constellation of reversible dualisms: "consumer/consumability, working girl/gold digger; chorus girl/call girl" (190).

Second, in working to embody glamour, the Ziegfeld girl's value as theatrical entertainment did not result from individual talent, the province of the musical and comedy acts alternating with the showgirl numbers in the revue format, but from her relative anonymity, homogeneity, and regulation. Along with the grind of rehearsing and performing, not to mention the producer's well-known surveillance of his employees, the Follies's showgirl numbers relied on a corps of disciplined bodies for the glamorous stage effect. The Ziegfeld walk (half runway pose, half pageant strut down a staircase), the artificial positioning in relation to architectural decor, the costumes that required an effort to wear and often restricted motion (particularly once they started to represent consumable objects or exotic locations), the organization of women according to height and shape, even a suntanning prohibition—all contributed to the Ziegfeld girl's uniformity as a hierarchized category of classed, heterosexualized, and Anglo femininity. Setting the showgirl numbers in contrast with "Jewish, ethnic, and African American comedy, including blackface" (6), the revue structure constituted glamour as "an enclave of whiteness within a far more racially and ethnically mixed montage of images and stereotypes" (11). The Ziegfeld girl's disciplined public body produced whiteness *as* glamour, Mizejewski claims (9–10), affixing it to "contended sites of definition" regarding Americanness (184)—that is, to homologous distinctions being drawn at that time between gender, sexuality, class, race, and nation.

Third, during the era of the revues, the showgirl's condensation of femininity, working, and whiteness was already rife with potential for camp recognition of the artifice by which Ziegfeld branded glamour. After all, a Ziegfeld show closely resembled, in method as well as effect, the illusionism of professional female impersonators popular at the same time, such as Francis Leon and Julian Eltinge. In her book Mizejewski reproduces a 1912 newspaper cartoon which, in a series of panels following Eltinge's transformation from one gender to the other, observes how "the middle-aged man [at the start] and the fashionable, wasp-waisted woman [at the end] are separated only by corsetry." The same, Mizejewski comments, can be said of the showgirl: "Both are performances of the 'perfect lady,' emphasizing authenticity, respectability, femininity, fashion" (105). The striking parallel indicates how, even then, the so-called authentic and imitative expressions of glamour could easily be "turned inside out," made reversible to disclose the central proposition of either "perfect lady," namely, "that sex and gender are *only* a matter of behavior and dress" and, hence, a matter of "performance and imitation" (106). While the revues themselves did not highlight the connection—when the Follies included female impersonation it did so for comedy in the burlesque tradition—the parallel nevertheless lays the basis for the Ziegfeld show's secondary history of availing the fantastically costumed showgirl to appropriation by professional and amateur drag acts. Her own presence on the Ziegfeld stage was already an act of gender impersonation, another type of passing in the culture, suggesting to Mizejewski how "the basics of camp . . . neatly summarize basic assumptions of the Ziegfeld enterprise that made it so successful and so enduring" (197).

In their sheer visual extravagance alone, the MGM musicals reproducing Ziegfeld glamour appear to know this, too, as my discussion of *Ziegfeld Follies* and the studio style in the previous chapter already began to indicate. "Here's to the Girls" dwells to excess on the artificial, disciplined look required by "authentic" femininity, just as it reduces the showgirl's "variety" to a homogenized whiteness, and the mannequins' miming of the beauty extolled by Astaire's song implies the common ground they share with female impersonation. The number pushes that latter implication even further through the juxtaposition of the mannequins on the carousel and the cat-women, which enlarges the pageant's scope beyond the song's content, staging the suggestively deviant sexuality being contained by the spectacle. I now want to pursue an equally important point: the MGM staging of Ziegfeld glamour widened the historical gap between Ziegfeldness as the musicals' point of reference and inspiration, and their recreation of it. *Ziegfeld Girl* vividly displays the conflicted representation of glamour which results, alternating, often wildly, between the obfuscation of nostalgic renewal on the one hand and the camp parody shaping Judy Garland's star turns on the other. Since the latter view refracts, and is therefore unthinkable without, the former, let me examine each in turn.

Ziegfeld Girl was a Pandro S. Berman production under the direction of Robert Z. Leonard, who also did *Great Ziegfeld*, with numbers staged by a rather sedate (for him) Busby Berkeley. The film may have "emblazoned the brand name" Ziegfeld Girl for widespread circulation, supplanting the more generic term *showgirl* (Mizejewski, 1), but it did so rather belatedly. By the time MGM recycled the Ziegfeld girl as an icon of glamour in its musicals, the showgirl glorified in the Follies had passed her moment of greatest popular currency. Before Ziegfeld died in 1932, his revues had lost money due to a combination of out-of-hand expenses and diminished audience interest in his repeated formula. With Ziegfeld's death, his name functioned as *vaudeville* did in musicals, as shorthand for the era before the advent of talkies, when the musical genre itself came to dominate the entertainment industry.

"Built upon the *greatness* of the most fabulous name in the world of *entertainment*," the *Ziegfeld Girl* trailer consequently boasts, and this thinking informs the film, too. Despite the fact that its mise-en-scène could as easily represent 1941, when the film was released, *Ziegfeld Girl* begins with a title card recalling "that fabulous era—when Florenz Ziegfeld glorified the American Girl, and New York wore her over its heart like an orchid—while she lasted." The figurative language collapses the American Girl into a metonymy of her Ziegfeld costume, picturing her as something exotic yet fragile which the city "wore" until it wore her out. The title card invokes the Ziegfeld girl's fabulousness along with her era's, and so recreates the forgotten value of her glamour as a nostalgic memory of her cultural influence and the pre-Depression conditions enabling it.

The card records the first of many such disjunctions between the Ziegfeld girl's incarnation in the past and MGM's efforts to reify her glamour in the present. For in wrapping its title figure in nostalgia—and ultimately in Judy Garland—*Ziegfeld Girl* delivers an incomprehensible package, immediately evident in the narrative's splitting of the eponymous girl into three characters. The film follows three unknowns, charting their eventual outcomes as Follies performers: gold digging and alcoholism (Sheila, the Lana Turner character), flirtation with the leading man but reconciliation with the estranged husband (Sandra, the Hedy Lamarr character), and bona fide stardom outside the chorus line (Susan, the Judy Garland character). Uniting these three character arcs is the overall dramatization of the backstage labor that goes into the production of glamour, the economy of sexual exchange feeding on it, and the difficulties of embodying it successfully. Even while mystifying the Ziegfeld project, this narrative highlights the process of impersonation required of glamour. "I'm two people," the Lana Turner character insists, as if that explains why she could be so fatally attracted to the fringe benefits of Follies life and still be in love with her working-class boyfriend, trucker James Stewart. However, the narrative dances around the question of female subjection to the Ziegfeld enterprise as a culturally sanctioned institutionalization of desirable femininity. It makes the Follies responsible for success when the girl has talent (Susan) but blames her when she succumbs to the sexual temptations of economic and familial/marital independence, either to dally in adultery (Sandra) or to burn herself out (Sheila).

In recounting these three stories, moreover, *Ziegfeld Girl* oscillates between the fallen-woman melodrama and the backstage musical. MGM's trailer for *Ziegfeld Girl* promoted it as a star-laden musical with "Songs! 10 of 'em . . . and every one a hit!" Among the female leads, though, only Garland can carry a musical; Turner and Lamarr have more to do in the narrative, but in the numbers they simply pose as part of the tableaux. Hence in generic terms the film assigns different values to the three characters and their portrayers, matching Garland with one set of conventions and Lamarr and Turner with another. The generic hybridity becomes most divisive in the finale, which cuts from Susan's opening night as a headliner, when she performs a number saluting Ziegfeld girls of past shows, to Sheila watching in the audience, leaving her seat when she becomes ill, collapsing in the theater lobby, finally dying. By placing the emotional weight of closure on Sheila's melodramatic outcome, even though Turner herself is fourth billed, the film shortchanges what, according to protocols of the musical, should have been a climactic big finish with Garland (Dyer, "Four Films," 70).

A layering of extrafilmic references compounds the mixed signals given off by these narrative and generic uncertainties. *Ziegfeld Girl* not only builds on the emerging star personae of the three leads (Dyer,

68), but also matches their fictive characters to well-known Zieg-feld girls: sexy good-bad girl Sheila/Turner evokes Lillian Lorraine, the disturbed showgirl and mistress of Ziegfeld, whose public alco-holic outbursts caused her departure from the Follies; ex-vaudeville trouper Susan/Garland echoes Marilyn Miller, the Ziegfeld proté-gée who rose from the ranks to become a major star in his book shows; and exotic, statuesque Sandra/Lamarr alludes to Dolores, the most famous of the producer's models imported from the fashion salon (Mizejewski, 171). Even more disconcertingly—and further dis-placing Garland from the climax along with the "authentic" Zieg-feld girl of the past as the film's historical referent—the finale quotes MGM's biography of the showman by incorporating fragments of numbers from *Great Ziegfeld*, introduced as "souvenirs" of the Fol-lies "of yesteryear": "You Gotta Pull Strings," "You Never Looked So Beautiful," and a circus number with a chorus line of Rockettes-like dancers. Then *Ziegfeld Girl* reprises its own "You Stepped Out of a Dream," with this melody setting the rhythm of Sheila's final walk down a staircase, when she leaves the balcony and triumphantly demonstrates to herself that, though fired the year before for being a drunk and now struggling for breath, she still has what it takes. After the disgraced Ziegfeld girl's last gasp, Susan/Garland reappears in blonde curls and Marie Antoinette costume so that she can be matched to footage from *Great Ziegfeld* with Virginia Bruce—playing Audrey, the Lillian Lorraine replica and *not*, as might be expected, the Marilyn Miller imitation—atop the tiered wedding-cake tableau (and thus in Garland's place) at the end of "A Pretty Girl is Like a Melody," but with the soundtrack of "You Never Looked So Beauti-ful" attached to the inserted imagery.

All of this dizzily embedded quotation of celebrity lore and er-satz Ziegfeld spectacle is instant nostalgia, but nostalgia for a glam-our now being *re*manufactured by MGM. The conflation of pseu-doreferents causes *Ziegfeld Girl* to sag from the weight of its own tautological imaging, signaling, as Mizejewski puts it when also noting the allusions and insertions, "the sheer impossibility of lo-cating and occupying that mythical position, the Ziegfeld Girl" of the title (173). In its convoluted referentiality, this nostalgically re-membered "glamour" is like a bouncing ball, skipping from one allu-sive/elusive real/fictive figure to another—as if the film were franti-

Judy Garland pays camp tribute
to "Ziegfeld Girls" in *Ziegfeld Girl*
(MGM, 1941). Frame captures.

cally seeking that final, fitting embodiment of its title. Why? Because the closure puts forward the most incongruous Ziegfeld girl of all: Judy Garland.

From the finale's vantage point, it appears that the musical genre, by rights the appropriate venue for reproducing Ziegfeld spectacle, poses a problem for a stable representation of the Ziegfeld girl's renewed value as an icon of glamour—or at least a musical does so when featuring the star who was fast becoming the cornerstone of MGM's hefty investment in the genre. Richard Dyer has analyzed how Garland's lack of glamour, and hence failure at femininity, was a central element of her star persona at MGM. When she started at the studio as an adolescent, her emotionally powerful voice registered discordance with her body, since she was considered the pudgy little girl with the disproportionately big voice. As a teen and then a young adult, she possessed the talent warranting stardom but had an unorthodox body according to filmic standards—less than five feet tall with a short neck and practically no waist, she was all chest and legs and could not easily hide her propensity to sudden weight gains— so her nonconformity with the studio glamour mill was "structured into her image and her films" via unflattering costuming and belittling or self-deprecating dialogue (*Heavenly Bodies*, 165). Often used to cruel effect, at its most benign the negative comparison intended, as in *Babes in Arms* (1939), to characterize her as youthful, ordinary, lively: the girl living next door to Mickey Rooney who happened to have been born in a trunk. "I know I'm no glamour girl," she says to an absent Rooney during the spoken interlude of "I Cried for You." "But maybe someday you'll find out glamour isn't everything." Nevertheless, the fact that Garland was not as glamorous as her contemporaries at the studio, like Lana Turner, still marked her body as a site of deficiencies, even though her films showed her using her powerful voice to transcend the lack through her authenticating intensity.

Ziegfeld Girl follows suit but also depicts, for the first time, a teenaged Garland character maturing into an independent young adult with a career of her own. More importantly, her numbers here indicate how, for her emerging adult persona (she was eighteen when this film was in production), her lack of glamour could be turned inside out as camp by people crafting material for her, notably her vocal coach and mentor Roger Edens, who was responsible for Garland's two specialty stage numbers in this musical as in almost all her others.

The camp shaping a Garland star turn does not necessarily reside in the number's content, which more often than not concerns heterosexual themes, but in the performative stance taken toward the content. Again, one way a Garland number produces camp affect is by registering an emotional intensity which overwhelms the song's lyrics or narrative placement, signifying authenticity while theatricalizing it. The specialty stage numbers in *Ziegfeld Girl* indicate another way her star turns would henceforth draw on camp. They use glamour as a self-theatricalizing trope, allowing Garland to perform how and why her distinctive style has, along with her energy and intensity, an ironic edge that makes her superior to a beautiful showgirl's staid passivity: instead of being nonglamorous, Garland is acting it.

A good illustration is the first portion of the *Ziegfeld Girl* glamour finale, written by Edens for Garland to represent her character's opening-night triumph as the newly top-billed star of the Follies. Titled "Ziegfeld Girls," it begins with the frame filled with balloons, top to bottom, side to side; then the camera pans downward to reveal "the newest crop of Mr. Ziegfeld's girls / The ladies who parade for you in tons of plumes and feathers." From behind the balloons Garland makes her entrance, dressed in a short-skirted tutu with extra layers of gauzy material here and there, and matching supersized puffs on her head and one arm. (Perhaps the outfit was meant to go with all the balloons, but today she looks like she could be the little dancing figure in a musical commercial for a bath wash product.) One hand on her waist, she bends and pushes her hips to the side, mimicking the conventional pinup pose of a chorine.

Garland's costume, shorter size, and chorus-girl stance set her apart from the elegant long-flowing debutante gowns, comparative height, and languid posturing of the ensemble, and her role in the number is not to join the group but to sing its praise, although her hymn to beauty takes a considerably different tone than previously heard in Tony Martin's "You Stepped Out of a Dream." Since the audience already knows "the figures," Garland sings, they might as well "know the facts" about this year's new vintage of showgirl.

As the girls recount their origins, exemplifying how a Ziegfeld girl comes from all walks of life around the country, their recitations alternate with Garland's wry annotations. For instance, she notes that "one girl worked in a bookstore / But," and here Garland shakes her head and raises the pitch of her voice, "she never read a book." "To be a puhh-fect Ziegfeld girl," she further intones, placing a hand on her breastbone for jesting emphasis (and using her Eleanor Roosevelt voice from "My Day" in *Babes in Arms*), "you needn't have much knowledge." Rather, the Follies is "a school / Where beauty enters in the rough / And comes out labeled glam-ah." With the last line, she turns to look at a nearby showgirl for illustration. Her gaze traveling up from the taller woman's shoulders to her head, Garland raises her brow in mocking overstatement.

Throughout, as Garland weaves in and out of the tableau, the showgirls take their status as Ziegfeld girls at face value, while her inflected voice and animated hand gestures contrast with their monotones and immobile faces. Visual comparison with the ensemble may measure Garland's inferiority by making her appear out of place in a showgirl number, starting with that silly costume, but because the delivery of Edens's material makes perfectly clear that her performance is being underlined as a performance of her difference, she shows up the showgirls and cuts them down to below her size, finding the whole enterprise of "glam-ah" and her odd-girl-out role in it "puhh-fectly" amusing.

Ultimately, in preparation for the montage from *Great Ziegfeld*, Garland has to back away from her send-up of glamour, more earnestly singing, "It's the Ziegfeld girl who stands out in the cast." The "souvenirs" of the glorious Ziegfeld past that follow suggest that a pretty girl is more of a memory than a melody since *Ziegfeld Girl* itself makes no further effort to recreate the Follies anew.[1] When Garland returns in the finale's closing moments, she stands wobbly on the wedding-cake platform and is absurdly outfitted to resemble not only Virginia Bruce, but Mrs. Ziegfeld herself, Billie Burke as Glinda in *Wizard of Oz* (1939).

Despite her awkwardness on the platform, Garland sports a big, wide smile as she sings along with the chorus. A sign of discomfort or defensiveness on her part? Perhaps. One may certainly find a pathos in this final image which overwrites both the parody of glamour in

"Ziegfeld Girls" and Garland's performance of the number. According to Adrienne McLean, "Garland's filmed body exhibits signs that bespeak a suffering that is physical as well as psychic" (4). Often constrained by corsets and choreography that ill-served the limitations of her build, Garland appears on film to "indeed have a special, somatically apparent relationship to suffering," an impression that established the basis for linking her star image with neurosis later on (4). As McLean explains, "even in the absence of the literal constriction of her body by the demands of M-G-M's ideals of feminine beauty or public awareness of the stresses of her offscreen life, we probably would still have tended to describe Garland subjectively in terms invoking vulnerability, insecurity, incongruity, ambivalence . . . someone whose stance and physique continued to embody the childlike and, at least partly therefore, the ambiguously feminine" (8). While McLean primarily looks at Garland's dancing in later musicals, *Ziegfeld Girl*'s glamour finale could readily be cited as additional evidence of how a Garland performance registers a "dichotomy" between a woman's experiencing her body as a culturally defined object and her experiencing her body as a capacity for being and doing (12).

Yet in staging that dichotomy, the finale highlights the reverse side of McLean's argument as well—the camp informing a Garland performance which mitigates the apparent evidence of suffering and neurosis. I am not alone in approaching Garland this way. Arguing for the compatibility of camp with feminist concerns, Pamela Robertson proposes that, historically, there is every reason to assume that "women may have liked Garland for many of the same reasons as gay men" (62). Mizejewski agrees with Robertson: "In contrast to dreamy Ziegfeld Girl gliding, Garland's performances make heterosexuality look difficult—explaining why straight women, as well as gay men, would find Garland appealing as camp" (199). When recognizing this camp appeal, however, it is imperative to recall the crucial distinction which Dyer makes about Garland: "She is not a star turned into camp, but a star who expresses camp attitudes" (*Heavenly Bodies*, 179).

A Garland number such as "Ziegfeld Girls" insists on that distinction because of the way it positions her *as* a camp. The number projects a performer who knowingly occupies the dichotomy McLean describes, and it does so by aligning Garland with a camp subjectivity finding humor, not pain, in the balancing act required of femininity, particularly when acting out its most idealized, hetero-sexualized, and incongruous cultural expression, glamour. From this perspective, the closing shot of Garland smiling, although some minutes after "Ziegfeld Girls," still leaves a residual impression of her secret bemusement, rather than inward suffering. Grinning just too emphatically, she joins in the singing of "You Never Looked So Beautiful Before" and seems pleased as punch by the irony that it is she, not Turner or Lamarr, who has landed in the top spot on the cake as number-one Ziegfeld girl.

Let me be clear. I am by no means trying to determine Garland's own state of mind while filming the finale but am describing the camp affect which the external evidence of her performance encourages through the distancing stance it takes toward glamour. The performance allows for, even invites, such inferences of a camp subject—Garland's playing of agency in the number—whose ironic engagement with the scene theatricalizes the reversible binary meanings of the Ziegfeld girl's glamour as opposed to being defined by them as a figure of abjection.

Nor do I mean to imply that Garland's own experience as a performer is inconsequential to the number's affect. There is no doubt from her many biographies that she suffered from (and later rebelled against) the studio's oppressive, demeaning treatment of her body. Even so, it seems equally clear and as significant that a number like "Ziegfeld Girls" was designed to take advantage of her considerable gift for mimicry, as crucial to her star turns as her intensity. When a very young teen, one biographer reports, Garland already had a keen sense of the ridiculous. "She was a clever and accurate mimic—no one was safe from her impersonations. You could not afford to feel pompous in her company because she would feed you your mannerisms back to you, heightened for the sake of effect" (Finch, 98). This skill held her in good stead when making numerous musicals a year; by all accounts, she ordinarily had to be shown how to do a number only once or twice because, with her mimic's careful eye and ear, she could then reproduce it on the set exactly as taught in rehearsal.

This is why Roger Edens's contribution in writing or arranging numbers for Garland along with his coaching of her vocal performances cannot be underestimated. Her biographers all emphasize his importance to her career at MGM in "refining her talent" and helping her "to gain poise and an assured sense of style," as Christopher Finch puts it (110–11). One continuing inflection of that style, and a fundamental source of Garland's growing poise and assurance on film, resulted from Edens's influence in shaping her mimicry skill and appreciation of the ridiculous with a camp's outlook. Ann Miller recalls, "Roger Edens *was* Judy Garland; he became Judy Garland: his songs, the way he wrote them, the dialogue that he did" (Fricke, *Judy Garland: A Portrait in Art and Anecdote*, 98). And Edens was not alone in recognizing how to use Garland's sense of the ridiculous as it combined with her talent for mimicry. When staging their first number together, the finale of *Presenting Lily Mars* (1943), Charles Walters got Garland past her insecurity as a dancer by instructing her to impersonate Tony DeMarco, and "she went into the dance without any trouble" (Frank, 175).

The glamour finale of *Ziegfeld Girl* seems particularly self-defining of Garland because of Edens's lyrics to start with. Her parodic delivery and gesturing then give his material a denser camp texture; she establishes disjunctions between the nostalgically recalled Ziegfeld Girl, her own difference in not measuring up to that standard, and her send-up of both as the number's star. The result is an impersonation of an impersonation which aligns Garland's performance with the camp's ironic stance toward the incongruities of glamour in its manufacturing of female authenticity. The very last image in the film disavows Garland's camp performance because the inserted footage from *Great Ziegfeld* erases her from view, substituting the long shot of Virginia Bruce in the star's place. Garland may get to smile but she is denied the last laugh, even though a viewer may still find camp humor in the substitution's own incongruity. What the closing moments cannot entirely recuperate, however, is the more developed camp understanding of *Ziegfeld Girl*'s recreation of glamour in Garland's earlier specialty number, "Minnie from Trinidad," also written by Edens. A subtle and nuanced star turn, "Minnie" deserves close analysis—if for no other reason than because it is the number which first gave Garland the opportunity to dance with the boys in the chorus as their camp star.

It takes a while before Garland appears in the "Trinidad" sequence, which consists of three discrete but related sections. In opening, "Trinidad" is another glamour tableau. At the steering wheel of a small yacht, Tony Martin sings of romance and moonlight to Hedy Lamarr, who reclines on a bench. The camera pans overhead for her close-up, moves down below her to a tropical fish tank, and presto!— the underwater creatures and vegetation become costumed showgirls. Here the fashions are less haute couture and more predictive of Bob Mackie and Cher. Wearing seaweed that decorously covers her breasts, pelvis, and hips, Lana Turner has flocks of birds nesting in clumps of branches on each outstretched arm as well as her head, and this is not the most ridiculous outfit by any means. One showgirl wears fish attached to her arms and waist, as if they are pulling her through the water; another wears a dying swan wound around her neck and shoulders, the feathers fanning up high behind her head.

Following the tableau, Tony Martin arrives at his destination. The American tourist is greeted by locals who sing along with him that it's carnival time, so "forget your troubles and worries in Trinidad!" The crowd disappears and a Spanish dance team, Antonio (Ruiz) and Rosario (Pérez), billed as "The Kids from Seville" (the English translation of their Latin American nickname), perform a torrid flamenco duet. Beginning with its traditional costuming—Rosario in twirling ruffled skirt, Antonio in billowing sleeves and tight pants—the highly stylized dance characterizes the couple as Spanish gypsies, and the lighting amplifies their non-Anglo features. The couple's marked ethnicity functions, as Mizejewski notes about the Ziegfeld shows' practice, to equate showgirl glamour with its exclusive whiteness as a means of elevating the desirability of the women previously on display. Still another distinction appears, though, because of the dance's choreographing of mutual heterosexual passion through the speed and precision of the couple's footwork as they twist and turn across the stage. In contrast with the tableau's fantasy of desirable but placid women deriving from Martin's song of romance on a moonlit sea, Busby Berkeley's camera angles and dramatic lighting heighten the heteroeroticism of Antonio and Rosario's interaction, equating their passion with their ethnicity.

Garland finally makes her entrance for "Minnie from Trinidad" after the flamenco dance, arriving on a cart and chanting "Aye! Aye! Aye!" from the distance. Her Caribbean getup seems inspired by Carmen Miranda's screen debut the previous year. The bodice is loudly patterned in inverted V's and has a bow over the breasts; the ruffled skirt is open in front and tied with a sash hanging below the waist; faux pearls are wound around her neck and coiled on each arm from the wrist halfway up to the elbow; the peasant headpiece has a striped stovepipe attached to the crown with a big bow (perhaps meant to be a little palm tree turned on its end? or a barber pole? Regardless, it looks like a little phallus). The finishing touch is an artificial parrot sewn to one shoulder, bobbing with Garland's movement as if it were alive. While in keeping with the costume design of the Trinidad crowd who greeted Martin and return for "Minnie," the lines and accessories of Garland's outfit "all cut across and break up her body shape," showing her up in comparison with her two costars, whose nautical array sexualizes their bodies, as in the example of Turner's strategically placed seaweed (Dyer, *Heavenly Bodies*, 167).[2]

Garland's appearance further highlights her marginalized status "as not-exactly-Ziegfeld Girl" because she wears café-au-lait blackface (Mizejewski, 177). This extra feature complicates her clownish look because the dark makeup implies more than a lack of glamour. Without doubt, blackface and its theatrical source in the minstrel show bring an intricate, overdetermined history to any movie musical, starting with *The Jazz Singer* (1927), as critics have analyzed.[3] Bookending Garland's solo blackface turn in *Ziegfeld Girl*, her minstrel numbers with Mickey Rooney in *Babes in Arms* and *Babes on Broadway* (1941) are inseparable from that history, and they help to clarify how the blackface in "Minnie from Trinidad" functions differently as an element in this number's camp send-up of glamour.

The two *Babes* musicals depict minstrelsy as a theatrical form —"something tried and true," to quote from *Babes on Broadway*— which represents an unbroken continuity from traditional American folk music to the contemporary popular entertainment personified by the Garland-Rooney teaming. To invest the minstrel show with this value, the two musicals "use blackface to claim whiteness as a clear and stable category and to marginalize blacks," while also rubbing out ethnicity (Knight, 85). For instance, in *Babes in Arms*, Rooney's character tells his parents, unemployed vaudevillians planning a comeback by returning to the road, that he has written a show with "a new slant on things" because he has his "finger right on the pulse of the public." Since his illustration is Garland's "Opera Versus Swing," it's fair to assume that his show incorporates the big band version of jazz into a vaudeville revue, timing it to the pulse of youth. However, when he first puts on his show in an open-air theater with the hope of getting funding for Broadway, the "slant" is far from new. The kids put on a minstrel show. Garland's "My Daddy Was a Minstrel Man," new material written by Edens, introduces the revue by recalling the lineage of minstrelsy. Since she is not in blackface and also plays a child of vaudevillians, what she recites easily passes as a brief history of white American popular music. As Arthur Knight points out, "Minstrel Man" can therefore discretely evade referencing African American songwriters such as Eubie Blake and Jewish blackface singers such as Eddie Cantor even though the medley that follows goes on to include tunes composed by or associated with them, Blake's "I'm Just Wild About Harry" and Cantor's "Ida," done in blackface by Garland and Rooney, respectively (84). In this way the minstrel number exploits blackface as a racialized trope for representing the Garland-Rooney teaming as youthful and exuberant, with the two stars addressing the moviegoing public from a long-standing stage tradition established as white.

The blackface in "Minnie from Trinidad" works toward other ends. Garland's café-au-lait coloring does suggest that "Minnie" pays tribute to Follies numbers such as "Miss Ginger from Jamaica," in which showgirls impersonated "the dusky belle" from all-black revues as "a reference to and a displacement of [their] black counterpart" (Mizejewski, 178). Light blackface in a Follies showgirl number theatricalized the stereotype of exotic African American women but safely contained its overtones of dangerous sexuality because of the whiteness beneath the mask: these were Ziegfeld girls, after all. It follows from the antecedent that one purpose of "Minnie" is to differentiate the white glamour of the nautical tableau from the racialized comedy of Garland's blackface and clownish costume; the café-au-lait mask refers back to the tableau's conflation of whiteness and

Judy Garland in café-au-lait makeup and a costume inspired by Carmen Miranda in "Minnie from Trinidad." *Ziegfeld Girl* (MGM, 1941).

PHOTOFEST

femininity as a combination impossible to beat, adding more visual evidence of Garland's "own paradoxical marginality as an MGM star" (177). At first glance, then, the blackface in "Minnie" reinforces the clownish costume to parody Garland by equating her nonglamour with nonwhiteness.

Garland's racially marked difference as a parodied impersonator of the Ziegfeld girl, however, is also mediated by the flamenco interlude, and the sequencing of the entire "Trinidad" segment prevents the blackface from functioning simply as an emblem of racial absence that stabilizes whiteness for the nautical tableau. In accord with the carnivalesque Trinidad setting, Garland's blackface makeup, lighter than in either of the two *Babes* musicals, identifies her as "Latina," which in the 1940s, as mentioned in the previous chapter, was a racially unstable ethnic category with respect to whiteness. Next to the Ziegfeld girl, Garland in "Minnie" does not signify whiteness, but next to the Kids from Seville, she does not signify blackness. Her light blackface appearance (and what an oxymoron that is!) is thus dark yet not-dark. And since Garland's spot comes right after

Antonio's and Rosario's, it is all the more obvious that the café-au-lait *is* a mask, underscoring the clownish artifice as well as the instability of her racial impersonation. Furthermore, because the flamenco equates heterosexuality and ethnicity, indirectly noting the absence of both in the nautical tableau, the placement of Antonio's and Rosario's dance between the tableau and "Minnie" calls greater attention to the way Garland's café-au-lait look, while referencing the "Miss Ginger from Jamaica" type of number from Ziegfeld's revues, fails to produce the source's conventionalized heteroerotic signification for this darkened showgirl. Watched in sequence, then, the three parts of "Trinidad" make it easier to see Garland's clownish café-au-lait appearance as contributing to a highly theatricalized performance of gender, sexuality, and race, one with the potential to turn Ziegfeld glamour on its feminine, straight, white head.

The last point relates to another key difference between this blackface number and those in the two *Babes* musicals. "Minnie from Trinidad" is a new composition that does not refer to minstrelsy or a mythic past of American popular music, but to glamour and movie stardom. In brief, the song recounts how Minnie Breeze, "the hottest thing in Trinidad" and with a "steady beau, Calypso Joe," wins a dance contest which results in her discovery by Hollywood. There she has her name changed to "Minnie Lamarr" and becomes "a star, the siren of the picture show." However, one day a guy gets fresh ("the cad!"), she realizes her heart still belongs to her "native lad," so she gives up "her dough and fame" and returns "to where she came"—only to discover "with shame" that Joe is dead from a broken heart. In despair, Minnie "takes a gun to try suicide." But as she starts to pull the trigger, she cries, " 'I think I'd rather live instead!' "

This ditty written by Edens for Garland to sing in the middle of *Ziegfeld Girl* is not quite the "bleached, Disney style ballad that justifies onstage donkeys, straw hats, and palm trees" that Mizejewski describes when comparing it with Ziegfeld numbers like "Miss Ginger" (177). For, with its explicit reference to *Ziegfeld Girl* costar Hedy Lamarr, Minnie's name change gives an immediate clue that something else is going on here. This detail draws out the equivalence of the Latina Minnie after her transformation into a screen siren and the comparably white but not-quite-white Eastern European Hedy Lamarr, who personified MGM's manufacturing of exotic female glamour out of ethnicity (Negra, 112). Through Lamarr, the song nods to the film's most elegant fashion mannequin as well, the fictive Sandra. From this reference it is easier to notice how additional details in Minnie's story pick up other threads from *Ziegfeld Girl*: discovered for her talent in a dance contest and turned into a star, Minnie recalls Susan/Garland at one moment; sacrificing true love to the temptations of fame and fortune, she parallels Sheila/Turner at another. By way of these condensed references, "Minnie" invites a reading of *Ziegfeld Girl* which understands the film's nostalgic recreation of the Follies setting as a metaphor of Hollywood glamour in its fullest industrial realization: female stardom.

To be sure, the song itself claims to lack seriousness, beginning with the breezy simplicity of its repeated rhymes (*lad* and *cad* with *Trinidad*, etc.). When beginning her tale, Garland cautions, "There is no moral to be made." Then she contradictorily adds, "but don't forget when you're dancing / That somehow / The piper must be paid." If Minnie's story genuinely has no moral then it *is* simply frivolous stuff. Yet if the story does show "the piper must be paid," isn't that also the point of the melodramatic Lana Turner/Sheila plot line in *Ziegfeld Girl*? It is not just coincidence that at the close of the "Trinidad" sequence this character drunkenly stumbles while posing onstage (though given the burden of holding up those birds and branches, who can blame her?). Dismissed from the Follies, she "pays the piper" in her downward spiral from gold digger to prostitute to victim of that nameless disease which is always so fatal to fallen women in Hollywood melodramas.

Minnie's own story then complicates the moral because it calls the inevitability of that melodramatic fatality into question. Throughout this jaunty tale of film stardom attained and then abandoned, one fact remains unquestioned: Minnie is a free agent and a survivor. Yes, she loves Joe and feels shamed by his death, but love and shame do not minimize her independence or her agency as a woman, since she is free to leave Joe and Trinidad, then to give up Hollywood and stardom, and finally, in the ironic twist of the song, to prefer to live instead of sentimentally pulling the trigger. The phrasing as well as the abrupt upbeat in the melody at this last point indicates that her high spirits remain intact and she does not dive headfirst into mourning according to formula. Even more relevant to *Ziegfeld Girl*, whereas "the Follies is life in one stiff jolt," as the director tells the new girls on their opening night, for Minnie Hollywood is *not* life. Her return to Trinidad is prompted by the realization that, despite the "dough and fame," being "the siren of the picture show" just isn't all it's cracked up to be.

Edens's song, in short, is a witty and playful reassessment of *Ziegfeld Girl*'s premises, providing a framework for watching this number as a camp star turn. The song's tongue-in-cheek allusions extend the film's view of Follies glamour to Hollywood stardom, turning it every which way, and the multiple elements of gender/sexual/racial masquerading suggested by Garland's outlandish getup then focus attention on how the filmed performance of the song amplifies a camp's understanding of stardom-as-glamour.

Garland herself does not play Minnie but tells the latter's story, and the clownish costume and café-au-lait makeup distinguish between the sexy siren and her overanimated interpreter, who sings the tune for its punch lines. She begins while standing in a giant seashell with satin lining, looking like the most unexpected pearl ever to be found in an oyster, and ends by recounting Joe's death and Minnie's life-affirming decision to a donkey (whose head Garland has to hold firmly in place since the animal keeps trying to turn away). Furthermore, Garland is followed throughout by Sergio Orta, a chubby Hispanic in a black top hat who is billed simply as "Native Dancer." Orta keeps disappearing from view only to return at the end of each verse, allowing Garland to punctuate the song's rhythm with varying looks of surprise, annoyance, but also interest. Though Orta seems to be chasing her, from Garland's facial expressions it's hard to tell just who is pursuing whom. He enters the number following her cart, but she spurs him on—for instance, she pokes him in the chest for emphasis when she sings that the piper must be paid—and while she eludes him each time she begins a new verse, she looks for him when she reaches its finish for the visual exclamation mark the two supply. Is this pair meant to represent Minnie and Calypso Joe? Hardly. Neither exhibits the heterosexual passion described by the song other than to play the roles in order to deliver the jokes, refracting that passion as a camp couple.

Garland's camp remoteness from the song's heterosexual content is even more pronounced because her audience onstage consists primarily of the boys in the chorus, who bring out the number's gaiety in all senses of the word. According to John Clum, the gay connotation of chorus boys on Broadway, particularly a show's dancers, goes back to the 1920s (8). The generic label "chorus boy" even records this presumption for "it brands them as male, but not quite men" (199). Like their female counterparts, chorus boys "exist to be looked at" (200) and for this reason are "usually the best looking men" (206). Historically, they have also been "allowed a freedom of expression and an overt sexiness denied the male star" (8) but without necessarily being heterosexualized by their display. As members of the ensemble, chorus boys do not perform as characters whose heterosexuality is secured by the narrative but are there just to dance, oftentimes with each other rather than chorus girls, as when backing up a female star. Dancing with each other as an ensemble, moreover, they commonly have to move, gesture, and hold their bodies in positions that, outside of a theatrical setting, would otherwise suggest effeminacy. Dyer mentions in an early piece that, while very much concerned with what it is to be a gay man, "camp is not masculine. By definition, camping about is not butch" ("It's Being So Camp," 110). When discussing how drag and the camp figure form a continuum, Newton similarly observes, "to be a feminine man is by definition incongruous" (105). In a musical number, when a whole chorus of boys acts this way in unison, appearing visibly male while not connoting conventional straight masculinity, their dancing compounds the camp impression of pretty young men who sashay together rhythmically.

The choreography of "Minnie," probably by an uncredited Danny Dare under Berkeley's direction, encourages this gay association with the chorus boys. Followed by Orta and a strolling band, Garland arrives onstage in a cart pulled by three chorus boys in sleeveless shirts, and more boys merrily greet her. The latter's costumes pick up the asymmetrical geometric design of hers—horizontally striped shirts with a low V-neck and vertically striped three-quarter trousers—and when they approach her in single file, their backs to the camera, wiggling their butts in unison, these boys look every bit like a queer's fantasy of a convict line. Lest we miss the point, after helping her out of the cart, the boys shake their booties once again to the cadence of Garland's repeated "Aye! Aye! Aye!"

The boys in stripes travel with Garland all the while she sings

22

23

25

24

26

27

Judy Garland sings the story of "Minnie from Trinidad" to her most appreciative audience, the boys in the chorus. *Ziegfeld Girl* (MGM, 1941). Frame captures.

"Minnie." Although showgirls in Trinidadian costume are at times visible in the background, the number is shot with Garland facing the camera directly. The chorus boys are almost always present, appearing either to the side or behind her; furthermore, she uses her eyes to keep attention drawn to them as well as to her. Moving in collaboration with Garland once she starts the song, the boys mime impressions of her camp distance from Minnie's feelings for Calypso Joe. She describes Joe and the camera pulls back to show the boys surrounding her, shimmying to the music and rolling one hand over the other. She sings that Minnie and Joe swore never to part and the boys bend to form a tableau behind her, each with a hand on the back of his neck in order to listen intently to the story's serious part. She recounts Joe's heartbreak on Minnie's departure for Hollywood and they arrange their bodies in staggered postures to frame hers. Moving on to the refrain, Garland then repeats their earlier hand-rolling gesture as the boys line up in single file behind her, swaying their hips to the song's rhythmic beat.

As the number continues, additional chorus boys, including those playing the strolling musicians, join the boys in stripes, with Garland wandering intimately among this gaily attentive crowd, touching a dancer's shoulder, pinching another's chin, comfortably bumping bodies with a third. The crowd gets so large and unmanageable, in fact, that at odd times a dancer gets pushed out of position or jumps to keep from colliding with another dancer, resulting in occasional moments of raucous interaction between these boys, albeit in the margins of the frame, as they race to make their marks in time with Garland. Midway through, when more of the mixed ensemble can be seen, the chorus boys' suggestive gay presence remains in full view. Showgirls appear in the crowd in order to be looked at, and so do the chorus boys, striding past Garland as mannequins in their own right; again, she acknowledges them with pronounced eye gestures, whereas she pays no mind to the showgirls. As Garland describes how Minnie became "the siren of the picture show," three chorus boys appear out of nowhere with bunches of bananas covering their arms from shoulder to waist; then a bare-chested buccaneer, holding a stuffed parrot in a hoop, which he displays for Garland, stands to her left, and from off-screen another bare-chested bucca-

28

29

30

31

Judy Garland moves through the crowd
in "Minnie from Trinidad." *Ziegfeld Girl*
(MGM, 1941). Frame captures.

neer with a parrot approaches as she moves to the right. A showgirl struts past Garland with a basket of flowers on her head, and a chorus boy with two baskets on his head follows on her heels. When more showgirls balancing flower baskets stand behind Garland, posing in typical Ziegfeld fashion, some half a dozen chorus boys sit cross-legged in a circle in front of her, stretching their arms outward in unison.

With a cut to a long shot during the song's final refrain, the chorus boys and girls, along with Garland and Orta, pair up as dancing couples, but the choreography's shift to a mixed ensemble does not heterosexualize all these boys following the star. The couples' dancing is awkward and childish, meant mainly for the overall effect of the long shot's view of the entire company. Duplicating each other's steps, dancers stand next to each other, touching palms, twisting hips, twirling, doing a hop step, and the boys leap over the girls like kids in a playground. Breaking up the coupling, some of the chorus boys in stripes team with the banana boys to place Garland on a decorated straw platform; joined by more members of the ensemble, they attach bamboo poles to the platform to raise her up and down several times, with the rest of the company dancing around them in a circle. Here, the motive seems primarily to achieve a Berkeley-esque patterning of angled light and dark shadows around the star. Finally, the dancers stand the poles upright, forming a giant birdcage around Garland (maybe because of the parrot on her shoulder?), and while the overhead shot momentarily suggests she is being confined by their adoration, she easily pushes the poles aside for her close-up as the number finishes.

Garland wears the same open-eyed expression of sincerity and innocence as in all her close-ups with Rooney at the end of their production numbers, so this close-up breaks with the number's camp persona, in effect allowing her to take leave from "Minnie" as "Little Judy." But she goes on to drop this second persona in her curtain call, when she resumes her fictional character of Susan and smiles more humbly before the applauding audience. Because she has dropped two personae in succession, the curtain call reminds me of that closing moment in a blackface number when, if there has not been a blacking-up scene beforehand, the performer reveals her or his white identity—for example, Joan Crawford pulling off her wig and scowling after her blackface turn in *Torch Song* (1953). But isn't it also like the moment when a female impersonator lets slip his feminine mask to reveal his male gender?

The two comparable revelations come to mind during the curtain call, I think, not because Garland has been turned into the facsimile of a drag queen, but because "Minnie from Trinidad" ultimately uses her blackface as a form of straightface. Robertson comments that the category of "black" often marks the whiteness of camp because "tropes of blackness operate . . . as an authenticating discourse that enables the performance of sex and gender roles" (20). What seems so striking about "Minnie from Trinidad" is that, while deploying blackface as part of Garland's clownish getup, the number does not work to authenticate her whiteness, certainly not in the way the minstrel show in *Babes in Arms* does; yet neither does "Minnie" make any moves to turn her ethnic imposture into an authenticating ground for all the camp play with sex and gender roles in the choreography of the chorus boys, Garland's interaction with them while singing the song, and the song itself. Rather, the ethnic masquerading is one factor in the number's camp interrogation of the binaries (masculine/feminine, white/black, heteroerotic/homoerotic, normative/deviant) that structure what glamour is supposed to mean throughout *Ziegfeld Girl* as a whole.

Admittedly, Garland's standing as a teen star at MGM when she made *Ziegfeld Girl* may well account for why this number, like the finale, takes pains to distance her visually from the sexuality implied by the glamour of her costars, Turner and Lamarr. When her costume and makeup refer directly to Ziegfeld glamour, the clownish getup signifies a girl impersonating womanhood; but because the song's parody of Ziegfeldness redirects this reference toward the context of Hollywood, Garland's outfit acquires added meaning as a camp's masquerade, sending up MGM's cookie-cutter reproduction of glamour. Whereas Minnie is "the hottest thing in Trinidad," a sexy dancer turned into a sexy star, Garland herself voices the camp's recognition of the incongruities underlying stardom-as-glamour, and the choreography stages how this star and her cohorts in the chorus are in on the joke together.

"Minnie from Trinidad" was an important number for Garland's career at MGM because it set the pattern for a distinctive camp star
turn with the boys in the chorus that has since become indelibly associated with her. The emotional ballad remained a centerpiece of
every Garland musical, just as her problematic fit with the glamour
mill determined her on-screen characterization (even the entire plot,
as in the case of *Easter Parade*). But after *Ziegfeld Girl* the dance number with the boys supplied a format for numbers which comment on
her difference from the sexy sirens of the picture show at MGM by
positioning her in camp fellowship with a corps of male dancers who,
in their look and movement, connote another kind of difference.
"Get Happy" in Charles Walters's *Summer Stock* (1950) is the now famous example, establishing the iconic imagery of Garland dancing
in a tuxedo jacket and fedora as "one of the boys" (Dyer, *Heavenly
Bodies*, 175). Edens and Walters then used the song and its staging to
introduce Garland's vaudeville act at the Palace in 1951, where she
was billed with her "boys" to make the first of her legendary comebacks, which immediately crystallized this number's importance for
her post-MGM career.

"Get Happy" is the last of several numbers organized around Garland and the boys in the chorus, choreographed either by Walters
("Embraceable You" in *Girl Crazy* [1944] and "The Great Lady Has
'an Interview'" in *Ziegfeld Follies*), or Robert Alton ("Who?" in *Till
the Clouds Roll By* [1946] and "Mack the Black" in *The Pirate* [1948]).
These numbers give Garland a more glamorous, even sexier appearance befitting her maturity and stature as a top box-office draw, but
they still work out of the same camp perspective staged in "Minnie."
Alton, in fact, appears to borrow openly from that earlier number for
"Mack the Black." As Garland's character lets her hair down, literally
and figuratively, to sing of the virile Mack's exploits to a mixed ensemble, the chorus boys—a visual contrast with the song's depiction
of the legendary pirate—follow the star through the crowd, framing
her in camp tableaus, miming her gestures, accompanying her when
she jumps on the stage, finally sitting on the floor before her in preparation for a tremulous close-up toward the end of the song.

That such Garland numbers were conceived of as a distinctive *camp* star turn stands out all the more when her version can be compared with another performer's. "The Great Lady has 'an Interview'" in *Ziegfeld Follies* is arguably the most self-conscious of the camp numbers featuring Garland; with delicious wit, it combines the parodic stance toward glamour in "Ziegfeld Girls" and her fellowship with the chorus boys in "Minnie from Trinidad." Roger Edens and Kay Thompson wrote the piece for Greer Garson, expecting Metro's leading dramatic actress to have fun sending up her serious and matronly star image. Unamused by their audition at her home, she declined, citing her mother's advice ("No, it's not for you, dear"), so the pair thought it would be "great for Judy," twenty years Garson's junior but "a good mimic" who could imitate Thompson's performance of the Lady down to the letter (Fordin, 140).

As it happens, "Great Lady" was used again for another MGM star. On Ed Sullivan's television show saluting the studio's thirtieth anniversary in 1954, Lana Turner performed a condensed reproduction of the number for the program's finale. In 1944, when Garland filmed the number for *Ziegfeld Follies*, the collaboration of choreographer Walters, director Vincente Minnelli, and composers-arrangers Edens and Thompson found a compatible fit between the number's camp wit and their understanding of Garland's talent as it distinguished her in MGM's musicals. A comparison of Garland's version to Turner's brings this into bolder relief. In particular, Garland's number builds off the premise, already noted in chapter 1, that she is a star able to bond effortlessly and enthusiastically with her "camp followers" on and off the screen (Tinkcom, *Working Like a Homosexual*, 59). As importantly, collaborating with the camp partnership of Edens and Thompson for the first time, in this number Garland "found herself doing things she had never done before and that would become incorporated in her later work" (Frank, 208).

"Great Lady" is not a traditionally structured song but a self-contained musical sketch which segues back and forth between patter and singing. Although it flows seamlessly, the number has five movements: the journalists' arrival for the interview, the Lady's self-theatricalizing entrance, her revelation of a dilemma in wanting to make a career change, her description of her next dramatic film, and her dance with the journalists occurring spontaneously out of that account. The chorus boys direct the number's progress, and they offer the most unlikely characterization of the press one can imagine, especially when recalling how journalists were ordinarily portrayed by Hollywood at this time.

Arriving at the star's mansion in sets of threes and fours, the boys are freshly groomed and uniformly dressed in formal black suits, polka dot bow ties, and gray waistcoats. From their clean, youthful appearance, they look rather like naive undergraduates all spruced up for a big dance—but going with fraternity buddies instead of dates. As the group increases in number, with boys singing of their admiration for the Great Lady while skipping arm-in-arm into the room, they become freer with camp mannerisms and language, suggesting they belong to another type of fraternity. For instance, a trio stands in the doorway, turned away from the camera; as the boys rotate forward in succession, leaning backward with their arms crossed, they announce to the butler they have come to see the "fabulous, dabulous Lady." The starstruck boys explain: "We don't mean Greta and we don't mean Betta / or Loretta or the Song of Bernadetta." With the last "in" reference to Jennifer Jones, they mime a spiritual vision, first elevating their eyes and hands toward the sky, then wrapping their arms around their shoulders and bending to the knees. Each new group arrives in this fashion, professing their adoration of the Great Lady as if in attendance at an official meeting of her fan club. When everyone is present, they sing in unison, "She's stupendious, commendious, collossical, terrifical! / She's got it! But definitely!"

The boys' linguistic flamboyance identifies them as members of the tribe and indicates that they assemble to honor a star whom they value for her camp. In going on to represent Garland as this "terrifical" star who has "it," "Great Lady" asks a viewer to hold together two perspectives of what happens during the course of the number: finding humor in the parodied movie star being interviewed by her entourage of fans, which evokes one set of references to Hollywood's veneration of Garson-like divas, while appreciating as well the witty enactment of this parody by another type of star who works in a different genre and takes obvious pleasure in performing with her not-so-straight comrades in the chorus.

Garland's own mannerisms and speech indicate a separation between her performance and the character of the Great Lady, all the while retaining Garson as the number's discernible target. For ex-

32

33

34

35

The gentlemen from the press arrive
for their interview with the Great Lady.
Ziegfeld Follies (MGM, 1946).
Frame captures.

ample, Garland deflates the Lady's pretensions of high seriousness with a caricature of Garson's recognizable diction. When reciting the patter, she often gives equal stress to the syllables of words so that her speech has a halting, overenunciated, and unnatural cadence. "The glamorous, amorous lady," as the reporters refer to her throughout, is also quite aware of her standing as first lady of the screen. Dressed in a long, silky white gown, Garland makes a regal entrance from a hallway, framing her figure against a glowing crimson backdrop. Promenading into the room, she stops before her portrait, narcissistically mirrors the pose in the painting, then turns, looks around, and inquires of her butler with feigned surprise, "What is all this?" After she informs the reporters, who all kneel worshipfully, that they have caught her "pitifully unaware," she greets them, shaking hands or patting shoulders, while pushing down one fellow when he attempts to stand prematurely. Sitting dramatically on a marble desk, she signals for the butler to aim a spotlight and, once properly backlit, tells the adoring journalists that they "may rise" to get on with the interview, though she has to repeat the command several times because they are so enthralled.

Given how regularly her musicals negatively compare her with glamour girls of the sort featured elsewhere in *Ziegfeld Follies*, Garland's elegant, stylish appearance here adds another dimension to the parody. She belies that convention of her own star image, but also sends up glamour since it is wrapped up in the Great Lady's haughty self-importance. As the interviewers sing of their intent to pry into her private life—which amounts to their asking, "What is your next ve-ee-ee-hicle to be?"—the Great Lady assumes various reclining positions on the desk to pose for glamour shots, imitating the kind of publicity photographs Garland herself had to do at that time along with every other female star at MGM.

The Lady's career dilemma references Garland as well. When the flashbulbs cease, she stops the choral singing of these "adorable, dear, dear boys" in order to speak "confidentially, off the record," of her "curious problem," namely, that she wants to make a musical. Protesting that "the cinema *must* exhibit me in roles that *so* inhibit me," she longs "to do what I adore so, do my acting with my torso, and give all the natives a start!" After all, she continues, "What is Ginger Rogers that I am not? / And what has Betty Grable got that I haven't

The Great Lady poses for photographs. *Ziegfeld Follies* (MGM, 1946).

got?" (Surely rhetorical questions when Judy Garland, but not Greer Garson, asks them.) As she explains that she would "like to be a pinup girl, a cheesecake girl, too," Garland uses the Lady's Oscar to undercut her condescension, holding the statuette by the head and waving it in the air, rocking it back and forth between her legs, tossing it in the air and catching it. But although the Lady wonders if her public would forgive her if "I tried to show the world I'm really hep," her next picture, which she cannot remember at first, promises to be "dramatic" and "full of Oscar-winning magic" like all her others. In an obvious nod to Garson's *Madame Curie* (1943), "Madame Cremetone" will be a "monumental biographical tribute to a monumental biographical woman," whose "magnificent discovery" has benefited the world. And what was that invention? The safety pin!

Describing this next project, the Great Lady goes on to give a performance of Madame Cremetone's "poverty," "toil," and "suffering" and seems moved to tears herself by all this drama, since she takes a green scarf from her desk and blows her nose after finishing. As the boys applaud the star's "monumental" performance, their clapping becomes rhythmic, establishing a beat for the patter. Garland continues with an account of the safety pin's invention, and the boys to her left cease taking notes and start doing dance steps, first offhandedly, then noticeably. The three boys to her right continue to scribble, but from off-screen a trio leaps over them to join in the others' high stepping. Now the patter becomes dialogic in the manner of a revival meeting. The boys reunite as a chorus, repeating or replying to what the Lady says and regulating their cadence with the percussive tempo of their feet, until, with dancers circling behind her, she gets caught up in the beat too. They sway to the left and the right, and she does the same, motioning for everyone to follow her as she takes over and shows just how "hep" she can be: she puts one hand to the top of her head, waves the green scarf with the other, rolls her eyes, and exclaims, "hoop-tee-doody! Madame Cremetone did!" Matching her steps with her entourage's in order to follow the rhythm of their dialogic patter, she reaches the story's conclusion and announces, with overwrought drama, "for on that cold and frosty morn the safety pin was born!" The dancers bend on one knee to chant "hallelujah!" and Garland adapts their idiom, singing with the boys for the first time in the number: "Shout hallelujah and a big amen / for the lady with the safety pin!"

The star's shift to patter and then full singing indicates how the chorus boys, celebrating something as trivial as the safety pin, release her inhibitions and allow her to be herself, the "hep" Judy Garland. She knows how to swing with these camp boys, and that, this number intimates, is what Garland has that Rogers and Grable do not. The chorus boys, in the meantime, sing, "Who cares what it's all about?" when the safety pin gives them an excuse to dance together. In fact, when repeating "hallelujah" for "the big invent" they get so carried away by their infectious enthusiasm that Garland has trouble keeping up with them. She starts to sit on one dancer's knee, but he stands up to follow his mates and she momentarily stumbles forward; the dancers move in one direction and she faces the other way, seemingly out-of-sync with their choreography, though another group soon joins her from off-screen; when all the dancers encircle her, she seems exasperated by their camaraderie, because it now exceeds their admiration of her, so she jokingly hits one boy with her flowing green scarf. For the big finish, still honoring "the lady with the big invent," the camera moves back for an angled perspective of Garland stand-

37

38

41

39

42

40

43

The Great Lady shows she's "really hep"—but has trouble keeping up with the boys. *Ziegfeld Follies* (MGM, 1946). Frame captures.

44

45

The big finish of the Great Lady's interview. *Ziegfeld Follies* (MGM, 1946).

ing with arms upraised in front of the portrait and the desk, rhyming with her entrance. Predicting the opening of "Get Happy," the chorus boys line up in profile on both sides of the star, their gyrating hands framing her as she holds her last notes against a frantic drum beat. A final close-up on Garland displays a rapid change in facial expressions which summarize her camp performance: smug satisfaction, a kittenish smile, a big, hearty laugh.

The layered camp viewpoint of Garland's "Great Lady" disappeared when Lana Turner performed it on the Sullivan show. Obviously lacking a film's production budget and rehearsal time, and needing to accommodate the program's hour-long time spot, the number was reduced by half and presented as a straight diva turn. The cuts are significant because they amplify how this version suppresses the number's camp intent, fully realized on-screen with Garland and the chorus boys. The journalists' introductions are gone, the patter simplified, the "hallelujah for the lady with the big invent" dropped, and the dancing refocused, all to center attention on—as studio head Dore Schary puts it in his introduction—"That glamorous, that talented, that magnificent . . . Miss Lana Turner!" Lacking the timely target of parody in Greer Garson which Garland had, the number now celebrates the Great Lady and the star performing her, merging their two personae. Thus the segment opens with a close-up of Turner's feet and the hem of her floor-length, black-and-white fur stole. The journalists are already assembled and the Lady appears on a staircase (which, remembering *Ziegfeld Girl*, Turner well knows how to negotiate with finesse). Professing to be caught unprepared, she drops her wrap, tosses it aside, and arranges herself seductively for her waiting admirers.

As soon as the butler spotlights her correctly so she can pose for photographs, Turner gets right to the interview, recounting her secret yearning to do a musical. Her patter, however, is somewhat changed from Garland's. To be sure, this Great Lady still wants to shock the natives by acting with her torso to show the world she's "really hep." Instead of comparing herself to Ginger Rogers and Betty Grable, however, she vows, "I'll always act in Shakespeare / I'll never let him down," then coyly adds that just once she'd like to play Juliet to Fred Astaire's Romeo. Lana Turner in Shakespeare? Surely, this lady does project too much! For all her considerable screen charisma, Turner's stardom was in fact geared to acting with her torso, not only as a manufactured glamour object but in her performance style. She typically delivers dialogue in her films by turning away from a costar and "adopting a posture, head-on to camera although not actually looking into the camera" (Dyer, "Four Films," 94). For this reason, when Turner confesses that she would "like to be a pinup girl, a cheesecake girl, too," this revelation, not her fidelity to the Bard, seems more fitting because it recontextualizes "Great Lady" in her own film career, going back to her star-making role in *Ziegfeld Girl*.

The self-referentiality here is circumstantial, the result of Turner's star image as MGM's glamour girl being brought to lines that Garland, with a very different image, had performed a decade earlier. That the number's application to Turner does not engage a parodic intent either on her part or that of the uncredited director is evident in the narcissistic shading of her performance, which accounts for the close alignment of her persona with the Great Lady's. Whereas Garland undercuts the Lady's self-important posturing, Turner indulges in it, frequently caressing herself or gesturing toward her body as her way of reinforcing lines. Moreover, lacking Garland's comic timing and

Lana Turner in her version of "The Great Lady Has 'an Interview'" on Ed Sullivan's 1954 salute to MGM's thirtieth anniversary.

delivery, Turner does not try to exaggerate her rendition of Madame Crematone's "monumental" biography, but instead speaks the patter breathlessly with a flat, unvarying rhythm.

Turner's uninflected recitation is underscored by the subordination of the chorus boys, who no longer direct the dialogic patter toward their sung proclamation of "hallelujah," which prompts Garland to begin singing and then initiates the final segment when their camp dancing brings her out as a "hep" star. For Turner the chorus of boys is divided hierarchically to feature, as Schary says, "four fellows and a girl," an indication before the number begins of how this version of "Great Lady" removes the camp staged with Garland and her entourage of admirers by heterosexualizing the Lady's interaction with the all-male ensemble. The "four fellows" are MGM contract players: Richard Anderson, John Ericson, Steve Forrest, and Edmund Purdom. These male starlets—for that's what they are—stand out from the corps of dancers, both in terms of how they look (their black suits in contrast with the others' white ones) and what they do (not much, since they don't dance). Basically, the four starlets are here for Turner to direct her patter to and touch flirtatiously, as when Ericson hands her a cigarette in a holder, thereby confirming her glamour; such stage business further distinguishes the starlets as her main focus of attention, reducing the rest of the ensemble to a uniform chorus line.

With the boys pushed to the background, the number's staging, though modeled on Walters's choreography for the Garland version, pays serious homage to the Great Lady's glamour, and this defining characteristic of her stardom keeps her aloof from the dancers. When their applause for her rendition of Madame Crematone turns into rhythmic clapping, the boys wait for Turner's signal before they begin dancing—and she holds her eye contact with them for too many beats, as if making sure her timing is correct. In the rear the four male starlets clap but do not otherwise move, and the chorus boys form a line with Turner in the center. They do not have to coax this star into dancing through their camp rapport; instead, she immediately takes center stage and they repeat her gestures and steps, even the way she angles her body. Furthermore, the dancing abruptly stops when Turner reaches her account of the safety pin's invention, allowing for a new conclusion that characterizes this staging of "Great Lady" as the baby-boomer edition addressing a Sunday night television audience. Everyone sings, "And the next time your baby starts to chafe, / you can thank Madame Crematone, bless Madame Crematone, love Madame Crematone / for the safety pin!" Anderson and Ericson lift Turner on their shoulders and she blows a kiss to her audience, acknowledging that she has just done a bravura star turn.

Redefined to suit Turner's limited musical talent and to uphold her glamorous image, this version of "Great Lady Has 'an Interview' " never establishes a camp perspective of the Lady or the star, whether with parodic reference to the construction of mature female stardom as glamorously aloof or to Turner's fading status at MGM in 1954, since by this point Ava Gardner had succeeded her at the studio as resident siren of the picture show. True, doing a routine associated with Judy Garland on television takes nerve and shows Turner has chutzpah; but because she never drops the diva act, remaining in character even with that final kiss, her appearance in the number is presented straightforwardly as if she were in the same league as

Katherine Cornell or Helen Hayes, doing light comedy for a relaxing change of pace. From this view, Turner's taking the chance to show the world she's "hep," simplified in execution because the chorus boys' participation has been so drastically reduced and straightened up, does amount to professional slumming, just as the Lady's patter outwardly declares. On the other hand, Turner's own reputation as a star who made good on the basis of her looks and not her talent warps this frame of reference, so the number turns against her pretense of having achieved dramatic heights in her film career while secretly pining to do a musical. From this view, "Great Lady" almost appears to make *her* the parodic target, though it cannot sustain the parody as camp because of Turner's stature as a glamour queen, which the number's amended staging respects.

By contrast, Garland's performance of the number in *Ziegfeld Follies* sustains its camp intent from every angle. This version folds in on itself doubly, parodying its ostensible target of Greer Garson together with Garland's own nonglamorous persona, but it then goes further to validate the latter's stardom, albeit not in the expected terms. As depicted here, Garland's star value derives not from being more authentic and intense than the norm (or than her sexier rivals in musicals at other studios, like her era's most famous pinup girl Betty Grable), but from rendering a camp sensibility musically with the chorus boys; moreover, unlike Garson (and Turner when she does the number), Garland is the same age as her ensemble, which adds to the impression of their rapport as it unfolds through the camp patter and choreography. On their end the boys determine the musical structure of the piece with their singing and dancing, which entice the Great Lady into letting go so she can show the world that she is "really hep." While her being hep alludes to the patter's hip jive style, it also resonates with the camp hipster's ironic wit. Through her performance Garland shows from the start that she is hep to the number's layered, self-reflexive parody of the supposedly straight orientation of musicals, their makers, and their fans. When she and her chorus boys sing and dance together, the idea of thanking Madame Cremetone for solving the problem of chafed baby bottoms seems the furthest thing from their minds.

ABSOLUTELY CAMPABULOUS!

There is an obvious reason why Judy Garland, the female star most identified with MGM's production of musicals and a performer with her own wry appreciation of the incongruous, best exemplifies the camp turn. Her long-standing, close working relations with Edens, Walters, and Alton developed and then sustained a performance style defined through recognizable camp elements, a factor contributing to her by-now legendary gay following. When analyzing the basis of that cult value in her star text, Dyer distinguishes Garland's "camp attitudes" from two other major contributing elements: the essential yet problematic "ordinariness" of her screen persona (her lack of glamour, her excessive peppiness and intense emotional energy, her youthful characterization as a moviegoing fan rather than a star) and the repeated imagery of or reference to her "androgyny" in her numbers (her adolescent "in-between" status as a teen, her tramp, clown, or tuxedo outfits as an adult) (*Heavenly Bodies*, 145). These two components of the image manufactured for her at MGM—both of which, Dyer notes in passing, valued Garland as "one of the boys" (167, 175)— were then given their special resonance by the camp attitudes (hers, Edens's, Walters's, Alton's) shaping her star turns.

The three attributes singled out by Dyer did not appear in isolation from each other. Garland's normality-as-difference and gender in-betweenness worked in combination with the attitudes conveyed by her performance, down to her inflected reading of lines for their ironic incongruity, to make her stand out as a knowing camp subject. In *Meet Me in St. Louis* (1944), for instance, Garland's character, Esther Smith, reluctantly has to put on a corset for the first time in order to attend the Christmas ball looking as "elegant" as a lady from the East, even though it makes her feel "like the ossified woman in the sideshow." Earlier in the musical, when Esther announces that she intends to let the boy next-door kiss her, her sister advises her that men do not like such forwardness since they "don't want the bloom rubbed off." Esther replies that she thinks she has "too much bloom," confessing, "Maybe that's the trouble with me."

The corseted girl with "too much bloom" summarizes how Garland personified a gender problem ready-made for camp in her num-

THE LADY IS A CAMP ~ 133

bers: her talent made her extraordinary, perfectly suitable for the musical genre, yet did not translate into the "pinup girl" or "cheesecake girl" movie-star standard, to quote from "Great Lady." Particularly when she was paired with a male lead who did not sing or dance with her—that is, when she didn't appear opposite Mickey Rooney, Gene Kelly, or Fred Astaire—Garland's numbers gave greater license for her to enact, as a camp's performance of "ordinariness," the excess radiating from her girlish "in-between" persona—too much intensity, too much physicality, too little glamour, too little heterosexual rapport with the dancing boys. It is therefore easy to see why, as the studio attempted to shape her body through costumes, efforts in the romance plots of her musicals to corset the problematic sexuality and spirited independence of her persona could so readily bend to a camp inflection when she performed a number like "Great Lady" or "Minnie." These camp turns enabled Garland to come out of glamour's closet, so to speak, and let herself go with the help of the chorus boys.

All the same, the obvious debt of Debbie Reynolds's "Lady Loves" to "Great Lady" points out that camp star turns, while a specialty of Garland, were not confined to her. Reynolds's early MGM musicals indicate that she was being developed into a star personality in terms reminiscent of Garland's screen persona, so something of the same dynamic which I have just described shaped Reynolds's persona as well. She typically plays roles characterized by a problematic relation to glamour, excessive peppiness, an androgynous quality in her tomboyish demeanor and athletic dancing, even at times a fan's devotion to the movies. *Singin' in the Rain* builds her character off this persona, and *I Love Melvin* most completely depicts its camp intimations. In addition to "Lady Loves," Reynolds has a second dream of stardom in *Melvin* which again parodies the glamorous movie star. Attending a premiere, she and her preteen sister wear matching mink coats and walk matching poodles (standard size for Debbie, miniature size for kid sis, natch). This dream number goes on to have Reynolds dance with six chorus boys wearing Gene Kelly and Fred Astaire masks; noting the absence of these two major MGM stars from *I Love Melvin*, the chorus boys give Reynolds more choreographic freedom and more mocking distance from glamour than if she were to dance opposite either star. She goes on to win an Oscar in this dream, paying parodic homage to the first *Star is Born* but without the troublesome drunken husband to disrupt the ceremony—the chorus boys applaud her win instead. Then there is Reynolds's frantic show number, which takes advantage of her gymnastic training. She plays a football vied for by two teams of athletes who throw her in the air and across the stage, but who also don't seem very butch and are just a tad more interested in huddling together at the scrimmage line than in hurrying to catch her.

As additional evidence of how the studio saw Reynolds at this time, her appearance on the Sullivan salute in a new staging of "Applause," the finale of *Give a Girl a Break* (1953), offers a very different impression of a star turn from Turner's. The filmed rendition of the number pairs Reynolds with Gower Champion as two entertainers celebrating show biz pizzazz and Technicolor, with Reynolds achieving overnight stardom as a last-minute replacement for the missing Marge Champion, Gower's on-screen love interest and former dance partner (and off-screen wife, as their joint billing records). In the television routine Reynolds dances with several chorus boys. Dressed just like them in overalls in order to paint a theatrical set, she clowns around as one of the boys. She slaps their backs and butts with her wet brush, until they turn the tables on her at the end by holding her down and dousing her with a full bucket. The choreography here epitomizes how Reynolds is most often used in her musicals as a tomboyish ingenue most at ease with the chorus because she can match their playful shenanigans and be thrown around the stage a lot, without worrying about maintaining a glamorous heterosexual image. No surprise, then, that Russ Tamblyn's first number with Reynolds in *Hit the Deck* (1956) has him joining three chorus boys during a rehearsal in order to meet her, and in "Lulu," Tamblyn and his sailor pals, Tony Martin and Vic Damone, avoid detection from shore patrol by sneaking on-stage to blend in with Reynolds and her naval ensemble.

Delivering a different sort of camp star turn, Garland's and Reynolds's contemporary at MGM, Ann Miller, represents their opposite as a character type but still sends up glamour. If nothing else, an Ann Miller number relishes the sexual exchange motivating showgirl glamour and makes no bones about it. In *Easter Parade*, her first film at MGM, she replaced Cyd Charisse to play a straightforward glamour girl who goes on to headline the Follies, but thereafter Miller's usual character is a modernized variation of the soubrette, the brassy lady

of the chorus who loves the men, the money, and the merchandise—
she can even juggle more than one sugar daddy at a time. Miller's solo
numbers, always performed in her function as the second-string costar of a musical, derive from this unpretentious persona. Her chorus
boys, furthermore, register its impact: no staid showgirl she, when
Miller performs the explosive effect of her tapping is, as her cowgirl
number in *Texas Carnival* (1950) puts it, like "dynamite."

"It's Dynamite," staged by Hermes Pan, compares love with the
powerful explosive, but as soon as Miller strips off her cowgirl skirt
and, guns in hand, blasts away with her feet, she shows that the song
is really about her tapping, which allows her to express an overzeal-
ous female sexuality while simultaneously distancing herself from it
as a performer because of her technical virtuosity. The chorus boys
have to jump out of Miller's way more often than they dance with
her, else she just breezily taps around them. When, toward the end of
this number, she leaps from table to table, not stopping or hesitating
as a dancer pulls tablecloths out from under her feet, the boys stand
back warily to watch, while she never waivers in her confidence or
her tapping. Even the band is not exempt. Miller dances on some of
their instruments when she begins and for the finish jumps atop the
piano to tap, blaring her guns, while the chorus whoops behind her,
mimicking wild Indians on the run, and costar Red Skelton, to whom
Miller addresses the number as far as concerns the plot, shakes uncontrollably as if he were really near dynamite.

This number is typical Ann Miller. Her rapid-fire tapping stages a
correlative of a camp's sexual innuendo. She does not need the help
of Cole Porter's lyrics, as she has in *Kiss Me Kate* (1953), when, for
instance, she sings of wanting any "Tom, Dick, or Harry," but most
of all "a Dick." In "Dynamite," her dancing around the boys of the
chorus serves the same purpose as a naughty pun by Porter; it redirects what the lyrics overtly state so that the number more logically refers to her own perfectly executed, perfectly repeated time
steps, which turns inside out the masculine/feminine dualism underwriting glamour. The chorus boys appear intimidated by Miller's explosive motion because it confirms her aggressive female sexuality.
Another of her numbers staged by Pan, "I'll be Hard to Handle" in
Lovely to Look At (1952), dresses the chorus in wolves masks to show
how they pursue her with predatory glee, albeit in the manner of a

Tex Avery cartoon, but her tapping demonstrates exactly why she is too much for them. The choreography suggests that the boys are indeed better off hanging back together in a pack, because, despite her showgirl appearance, Miller's dominance gives the impression that they lose their heterosexuality (or at least their superiority as wolfish males) through their admiration of her empowerment when dancing. This implication is hard to ignore since Busby Berkeley made it his main conceit when staging "I've Gotta Hear that Beat" for *Small Town Girl* (1953). The surreal design of this number reduces the male chorus to an unseen orchestra, with only their hands and instruments visible through holes in the tiered set. Once Miller hears the beat of her heart, so she sings, we hear and watch the beat of her feet as she spins tirelessly yet precisely around the chorus' instruments for the duration of the number. Her camp turn here is quite literally a series of untoppable *and* unstoppable turns.

As central as Garland and, to a lesser extent, Reynolds and Miller are to what I have been arguing about the camp star turn, before they were prominent at the studio, MGM's understanding of a star's unconventional value with respect to both showgirl glamour and the male chorus could already be seen in the musicals of Eleanor Powell. *Ziegfeld Girl*, in fact, was originally intended for Powell, until her diminishing box-office appeal caused this musical to be redesigned for the up-and-coming Garland, who had made her debut in support of Powell in *Broadway Melody of 1938* (1937). In that film as well as its predecessor, *Broadway Melody of 1936* (1935), Powell plays a talented dancer who comes to New York determined to make good if she can only get the chance. The plots of both musicals set her character in a triangle with an ex-showgirl who bankrolls the producer (Robert Taylor). The rivalry is more professional than romantic insofar as it temporarily forces Powell out of the show, but the rival's hold on the producer, with her promiscuity attributed to a showgirl background, indirectly characterizes Powell's femininity as more wholesome if nonetheless more problematic due to her lack of glamour.

Powell's nonconformity with the glamorous protocols of female stardom was exaggerated by her dancing style but also brought extrafilmically to her screen persona. According to Shari Roberts, MGM saw Powell much as it did Garland, considering the dancer to be "too 'unfeminine'" and so forcing her "to undergo a series of beauty treatments" (76). Further, Powell's dancing, which she herself usually choreographed, was sometimes called "unfeminine" by the press because it was not ballroom and used "steps, positions, and movements usually reserved for men" (77). Encouraging this view was "the trademark tuxedo" that Powell frequently wore in dance numbers (64). Hence, Roberts notes, Metro's inability to find a suitable male dance partner for Powell who could also function as her leading man, that is, until she costarred with Fred Astaire in *Broadway Melody of 1940* (1940) in a teaming that generated little sexual spark but a lot of heavyweight challenge dancing.

What Roberts calls "Powell's masculinity" (77) was expressed both in the male costuming of her tap numbers and in the plot machinations requiring her to cross-dress, whether as a stable boy in *Broadway Melody of 1938* or a cadet in *Rosalie* (1937) or, more interestingly, as a glamour girl in *Broadway Melody of 1936*. To finagle her chance in Taylor's show, Powell's character, Irene Foster from Albany, pretends to be "Mlle. Arlette," actually an invention of an unscrupulous gossip columnist (Jack Benny) wanting to humiliate the producer by tricking him into signing a star who does not exist. "Arlette," named after a cigar brand, is at first impersonated by the columnist's sidekick (Sid Silver), and he plays her in full drag even though his task is just to answer the phone. After discovering this ruse and appropriating the persona, Powell-as-Irene-as-"Arlette" signs with the producer. She shows up at rehearsal in the drag costume—with a curly blonde wig and large beauty mark pasted to her cheek, and speaking thee French accent very theeckly—and her accompanist is none other than Roger Edens.

Roberts observes that Powell's character takes on a double masquerade: "She imitates a man in drag who impersonates a nonexistent woman," which foregrounds "the artificiality of the concept of femininity" (78). But the artifice of femininity being mimicked is also quite specific in its reference to Ziegfeld glamour. The flurry of reports in the newspapers and on the radio about the producer's questionable ability to sign "Arlette," which the columnist engineers, recalls Ziegfeld's publicity angle for Anna Held when he brought that star to New York from Paris. Ziegfeld kept the public guessing about whether or not Held would come, when she would arrive, and if he could sign her (Mizejewski, 47), a detail repeated in *Great Zieg-*

feld. The manufactured glamour girl, her femininity easily appropriated for drag comedy, establishes the comparative framework that heightens the value of Powell's dancing as a camp gender performance when she dons her tuxedo to dance in the finale, "Broadway Rhythm."

Before then, however, Powell's first big production number in *Broadway Melody of 1936* evinces signs of MGM's uncertainty about how to showcase its new star because of her nonconformity with the types of female stars then dominating musicals. At MGM itself, Jeannette MacDonald was just beginning her series of operettas opposite Nelson Eddy, and Joan Crawford had personified the gold-digging dancer in *Dancing Lady* (1933); at RKO, Ginger Rogers was partnered complementarily with Fred Astaire; at Warners, Ruby Keeler hoofed her way out of the chorus repeatedly only to disappear each time in a Busby Berkeley kaleidoscopic spectacle. Midway through *Broadway Melody of 1936*, Powell's character fantasizes about stardom in "You Are My Lucky Star," and this number tries to make the star's dancing conform to a femininity more consistent with star glamour, a mistake MGM did not repeat again on so grand a scale.

Seated alone in an empty theater, Powell sings the lyrics (with Marjorie Lane's voice dubbed in), but it is not clear who the "you" of the title is, so the number's internal logic is incoherent to begin with.[4] Powell starts by noting, "My hero sings these words to me," which means she is standing in for an absent Robert Taylor, who does have a musical duet earlier in the film, sung with her rival, June Knight (who then dances to it but, oddly, with Nick Long Jr. instead of Taylor). Once Powell imagines her alter ego on the bare stage, she more openly sings to herself about herself, until a reverse shot discloses that a formally dressed phantom audience files into the empty theater, in effect taking her place there. A cut back to the stage shows a male chorus in white tuxedos serenading Powell; using her lyrics, they conventionalize the star's femininity by making her an object of heterosexual male veneration, their lucky star. Rather than go on to have Powell dance with this chorus, however, "Lucky Star" unexpectedly puts her in a ballet staged by Albertina Rasch. This part of the number has little to do with the song's content, Powell's known expertise on Broadway as a great tap dancer (why MGM signed her, after all), or her character's talent, previously established when she hoofed with Buddy and Vilma Ebsen on the rooftop of their boarding house; but this shift in "Lucky Star" does ask an audience to imagine Powell's stardom through a choreographic style that aims, by drawing on balletic convention, to glamorize as well as heterosexualize her. However, dancing en pointe with a female corps de ballet, who repeat her twirls, reigns Powell in considerably. Like her successor as MGM's queen of taps, Ann Miller, Powell is a very physical solo tap dancer whose steps enact the liberated energy of a female body moving rapidly yet rhythmically in space, unfettered by the gender conventions of classical ballet.

Powell's later rehearsal with Edens as "Arlette," performed to a reprise of "Lucky Star," makes this very point about her dancing. She asks Edens to play "something with rhythm, n'est-ce pas?" Soon complaining he is doing it wrong, she stops him and taps vibrantly without musical accompaniment, allowing her feet to do all the work in setting the rhythm. When Powell dances in "Broadway Rhythm," she gets to do this kind of footwork too. She appears at the end of this number, following appearances by the film's other musical performers (Frances Langford who sings the song, a dance duet with the Ebsens, then another one with June Knight and Nick Long Jr.). Dressed in a sparkling top hot, tails, and white pants with a glittering racing strike to match the jacket, Powell goes solo with the freedom denied to her in "Lucky Star," while the male chorus surrounds her in a circle, holding their hats upraised on their canes, much in the manner of Astaire and his chorus in the title number of *Top Hat* (1935). As the counterpoint to her "Arlette" pose at the rehearsal, here her various "masculine" physical moves—from her backbend to the way she holds her arms—disrupt the heterosexual binary otherwise structuring the number's repeated placement of showgirls and chorus boys in visually contrasting but paralleled lines. By the end, the showgirls disappear from view entirely, and Powell finds her fitting ensemble with the male dancers who most resemble her in movement as well as appearance.

The finale of *Broadway Melody of 1938* virtually recreates "Broadway Rhythm" but with the camp stance of Powell's "in-between" status given even more emphasis. This does not seem to be the case when "Your Broadway and My Broadway" begins, however. Powell dances with George Murphy in a ballroom style that makes her look

Eleanor Powell in the finale of *Broadway Melody of 1936* (MGM, 1935).

mighty uncomfortable; while he grins, her face is stern, forsaking her usual big toothy smile. What is more disconcerting, her long gown conceals her legs, which amounts to hiding her dancing from view. Their duet imitates Astaire and Rogers but without that team's metaphoric implications of seduction and consummation; rather, Murphy directs Powell's movement, Svengali-like, and lifts her several times, constraining her individual movement. Their choreographed pairing makes Powell's glamorous demeanor register as an artifice imposed on her body, despite the effort to link her, as the feminine half of the ballroom duo, with the elegantly dressed showgirls who stand on steps behind the couple, lined up in diagonal patterns according to their black or white costumes.

Following the example of "Broadway Rhythm," this finale is put together as a mini-revue to spotlight the musical's stars. After the Powell-Murphy ballroom duet, Buddy Ebsen comes out to do his rubbery footwork with a very young Judy Garland, and Sophie Tucker sings the lyrics of "Your Broadway and My Broadway," recalling the continuity between vaudeville and the theater. Between these spots, as in "Broadway Rhythm," the male and female choruses dance together in parallel lines, a visual representation of the heterosexual nature of everyone's Broadway. But when Powell reappears with Murphy and Ebsen for the number's closing section, the great dancer overturns that premise by exchanging one gendered costume for another. She wears a plain black tuxedo and top hat just like her partners and the ensemble of chorus boys who line up on both sides of the trio across the stage. What is more, she holds her body, moves her arms, and does turns exactly as all the men do, not allowing the dance to differentiate her from them. Unlike in "Broadway Rhythm," Powell's tuxedo here lacks even a single sparkle to distinguish her from the male ensemble in the long shot capturing this sequence. The costume goes beyond the stage convention of the female entertainer who appropriates formal male attire but wears it in a way that outlines her femininity, usually by forsaking the trousers to show off her legs—Garland in "Get Happy," say, or Powell herself in the toreador number from *Ship Ahoy* (1942). Rather, Powell's appearance in the tuxedo amounts to a female's passing as male. She quite visibly dances as one of the boys, and does so effortlessly.

When Murphy, Ebsen, and the chorus defer to her solo spot, Powell performs a soft-shoe to a slower arrangement of the music. She mimes the masculine gestures that go with her clothing, but with more attention to these details than when she did the same in "Broadway Rhythm." She adjusts her bow tie, touches the brim of her hat, puts her hands in her pants pocket and pushes her pelvis out, while also gesturing to accent the line of her body, not its curves, as she moves and raps the floor with her feet. Returning to salute her as the music quickens, the chorus boys repeat the tag refrains of "Broadway Rhythm" and "You Are My Lucky Star," incorporating the previous *Broadway Melody* into this number as a frame of reference for Powell's cross-dressed star turn. This finale then tops that previous one by using the male ensemble to enable Powell to dispense with the dance conventions regulating femininity, as shown in the opening ballroom duet with Murphy. For instance, chorus boys lift Powell so that she can do a split when she lands, and they toss her in the air, after which, as if dizzy from the throw, she makes her body more gangly, mimicking costar Ebsen's loose-limbed style. Close-ups of her smiling face, hands under her chin, hair stuffed into her hat, give her the air of a clown—in fact, she looks a bit like Harpo Marx in these shots—and

48

Eleanor Powell in the finale of *Broadway Melody of 1938* (MGM, 1937).

the editing of her dancing at this point focuses on her carefree, androgynous pose by momentarily freezing her movement as an image several times.

Finally, when the female chorus, dressed in what look like bridal gowns, comes out to preen, the return of a showgirl line makes more inescapable Powell's difference from these other women as a camp star dancing with the boys. Her difference is visualized through her physical comfort with the chorus boys; like no one else in the number, Powell openly straddles the masculine/feminine dualism that superficially organizes the number's staging of the full ensemble. To finish the number, she does her backbend and then a somersault and comes to rest with her legs wide apart—a confident stance considered male because of its violation of feminine decorum—and holds this authoritative position as "Broadway Melody" comes up in electric lights behind her.

Powell's cross-dressing in the finales of the two *Broadway Melody* musicals is of apiece with the later glamour parodies in the numbers

I have examined that feature Garland, Reynolds, and Miller. Taken together, all of this chapter's examples distinguish the female performer by setting her stardom off against glamour. It is through this camp dialectic that the numbers revise the star's value for an MGM musical to appreciate her difference, which they reinforce through her nonerotic rapport with the chorus boys, themselves weighing in with a different value than her leading man. Although the star's alignment with camp agency is most completely worked out in the Garland numbers, "Great Lady Has 'an Interview" and "Minnie from Trinidad" offer a blueprint for seeing the camp in other star turns parodying glamour as well. When Powell, Miller, or Reynolds perform with the boys in the chorus and, in one way or another, resist the norms of glamorous stardom to imply a stance which recognizes its incongruities as a mechanism of gender regulation, their numbers rely on the camp strategies more fully articulated in "Great Lady" and "Minnie."

It is crucial to recognize, however, that with the exception of "Minnie" these camp star turns also take for granted the whiteness of both glamour as their target of parody and the star's difference from the glamour mill, which positions her in alignment with the camp figure. Lena Horne's career at MGM makes the racial boundaries of the camp star turn all too evident. Although she worked with the same people as Garland, and was also discovered by Roger Edens for the Freed unit, Horne's numbers elevated her to stardom precisely through the trope of glamour that Garland's numbers sent up.

Elegantly costumed, coifed, and lit in order to refute the stereotypes of African American performers then working in the white film industry, Horne is frequently immobile as well as isolated while performing a number. Shifts in camera angles and colored filters, or the presence of mirrors in the mise-en-scène to multiply her image, simulate the movement within the frame taken for granted when Garland sings or dances. For example, in her set of two numbers for *Words and Music* (1948), Garland (playing herself) leaves a crowd of partygoers to perform "I Wish I Were in Love Again" with Mickey Rooney (playing Lorenz Hart). When pushed by her cheering audience for an encore, before she begins "Johnny One Note," Garland brings some of the orchestra members off the bandstand so they can interact with her more intimately. Horne also performs two back-to-back numbers in this musical but, in contrast with Garland's guest spot at Larry Hart's party, is spatially detached from a white audience in a nightclub setting, and there is no additional context in the narrative for her sudden appearance. Horne's first number, "Where or When," follows the glamorously aloof style of her solo appearances in other films, and while her second, "The Lady is a Tramp," lets her dance a bit to underscore the lively and clever wit of this song's lyrics, her jaunty steps seem designed to direct the flow of her whirling white skirt so that the ever varying contrast with its bright red lining serves as the source of visual interest. After performing her set, Horne drops the vivacious, expressive persona displayed for "Lady is a Tramp" by taking her bow stiffly, her face shutting down any sign of emotion other than an enforced humility.

The *Words and Music* set illustrates how, as Roberts explains, Horne's glamorously aloof screen presence was central to her crossover success in the 1940s because it enabled two contrasting racialized responses on the part of viewers, neither drawing on camp. Black audiences could read Horne's "stylized, distant, inaccessible performance style . . . as masquerade, and therefore as a parody of the racist expectations of Hollywood audiences" (136–37), while the same pose simultaneously offered "a blank screen for white audiences" by appearing to efface racial concerns so that her nonwhite body was visible yet invisible, there but not there (141). With the visual coding of her numbers typically encouraging this polarized view, Horne's rare camp star turn at MGM therefore stands out for the way it fills up the racially "blank screen" she was ordinarily made to embody.

In Alton's staging of Hugh Martin and Ralph Blane's "Brazilian Boogie" for *Broadway Rhythm* (1944), Horne gets a chance to forgo her customary glamorous demeanor and even to be "hep" with boys in the chorus. The song caters to the 1940s craze for Latin American music but, reflecting how the star and her ensemble are African American, it trades on racial hybridity: this new "boogie," Horne sings, was born as a "half-breed, because its mammy was a samba and its pappy was swing"—while its authors, one cannot forget, were white. Dyer comments that "the degree to which black and Hispanic music and dance founded US popular music cannot be acknowledged —they are incorporated so far in MGM musicals as to disappear from view" ("Colour of Entertainment," 29), so it is worth appreciating

Lena Horne sings and
dances in "Brazilian
Boogie." *Broadway
Rhythm* (MGM, 1944).

PHOTOFEST

how this number at least glimpses that origin. From the setting and
costumes, which combine Latin carnival with African primitivism, to
the chorus boys' blending of South American dance moves with African American tap steps, to the staging's melding of the movie musical's conventional Caribbean and Harlem show numbers, to black
diva Lena Horne's performance of this "brand new kind of hotcha,"
"Brazilian Boogie" mixes together signs of race and ethnicity to prevent either from being stabilized against its binary opposite in whiteness. What makes this number a camp turn in line with the others
I have examined is the way it places race and ethnicity in dialectic tension so that neither has an absolute physical referent in the
star's body.

Whereas Garland's star image defined her through gender, as her
camp turns bring out, Horne's star image defined her through race.
This number makes an effort to destabilize that image by crossing
black Americanness with Latin American ethnicity, which the star
and her ensemble then darken. Because the hybrid boogie has "the
style and spirit of Miranda, which makes for perfect propaganda,"
the number nods to the black sources of Carmen Miranda's Brazil-

ian persona, whitened for American consumption. The dark-skinned chorus boys—placed in contrast with the lighter complexions of the chorus girls and Horne herself to mark gender differentiation in the staging—help to visualize this. But another point of the number is its expression of how Horne's own blackness, segregating her as the sole bronze siren of the picture show at MGM, can function as a camp masquerade, a form of racial-ethnic passing turned inside out. Horne not only gets to move more freely than usual here, but her dancing with the chorus boys—who wrap arms or legs around hers, wave at her with gloved hands extending from the edges of the frame, and boogie with her side by side—accentuate her embodiment of the hybrid beat, which "makes you tingle" and "wish you were single." A bit like Garland's blackface in "Minnie," Horne's somewhat Latinized appearance calls into question the authenticity of her raced image, yet without granting a superior status to Latinness. She does not impersonate a Latina but wears a Latin costume and undulates to a Latin beat, showing up the exchangeability of race and ethnicity in the cultural idiom. Their equivalent value for whites dancing to the samba and swing, "Brazilian Boogie" suggests—if only as the unstated corollary of the hybridity driving the number—is what allows Latinness to cover up while also marking the film musical's marginalization of African American entertainers.

Lena Horne and "Brazilian Boogie" expose the ideological limits of the camp turn, which, in parodying glamour, could acutely see through its regulation of gender and yet be blinded by its whiteness. That limitation, however, should not distract from what the camp turn does make visible. The numbers I have looked at recognize, albeit with varying degrees of self-reflective parody, the female's act of passing as "genuinely, intimately feminine"—to quote one more time from "A Lady Loves"—which was required of a star in the name of glamour. Particularly when heightened by the star's interaction with her chorus boys, these numbers knowingly recognize the affinity of women and queer men, identifying their comparable positions in the culture with respect to the oppressive mechanisms of heterosexual normality. Hence my claim that, although the camp fascination with female stars may have resulted in cross-gendered identification on the part of some gay fans, inspiring a repertoire of amateur and professional drag acts, the camp star turn is not reducible to drag. Rather, this type of number addressed a minority segment of the mainstream audience through the mediation of a camp outlook, which the stars displayed on screen even to those not "in the know."

To be sure, the camp star turn, ordinarily detached from the narrative as a show number to account for its heightened theatricality, did not dominate the studio's customary bill of fare in its musicals. They more regularly featured ballads, duets, and big production numbers, and, more often than not, simultaneously sought to promote glamour, trading on the Ziegfeld example even while debunking it. The incoherences of *Ziegfeld Girl* testify to that, and so do the many other MGM musicals that feature showgirl tableaux or chorus lines. *Easter Parade* leads Astaire to appreciate Garland's difference from his former showgirl partner, Ann Miller, but this does not stop the film from recreating Ziegfeld glamour in "The Girl on a Magazine Cover" with Miller as the lead showgirl—and to do so immediately after Garland and Astaire perform "A Couple of Swells" in hobo costumes. Nonetheless, even if a musical was, like *Easter Parade*, set at the turn of the century, MGM's citation of Ziegfeld glamour in films released during the Depression or the war years or the postwar boom found a different extrafilmic referent; the obsolescence of that glamour was already written into the showgirl's appearance. Thus while the idea of glamour continued to function for MGM musicals as a standard measuring femininity and equating it with a woman's consumption of fashion, by invoking Ziegfeldness as a production value, the musicals also circulated imagery of glamour that was already out-of-sync with the lives of their audiences, whether they saw its nostalgic sheen as fodder for escapism or for camp amusement. The star turns discussed here indicate that the lady who performed "glamour" with the camp's parodic eye showed viewers how to be more hep to the latter possibility.

Chapter Three

*I*n "Why Am I So Gone About That Gal?" from *Les Girls* (1957), Gene Kelly performs a show number which parodies Marlon Brando's biker character in *The Wild One* (1953). Accompanied by his motorcycle gang, a leather-clad Kelly strides into a diner where he catches sight of Mitzi Gaynor, the lone waitress. In a mumbling voice, he sings of being unaccountably drawn to the waitress, although all he gets is a black eye whenever he tries to kiss her. Gaynor ignores Kelly's song, but after finishing it, he harasses her until she finally joins him in a dance.

At first the choreography positions them as sexual antagonists. Dropping a coin in the jukebox, Gaynor turns her back on Kelly yet shakes her body in rhythm with the music, while he removes her apron and teases her with it to gain attention. In response, she pushes him onto a table, which he somersaults over. As he rises, she circles as if preparing to attack, so he defensively holds her off with a chair, suggesting that she, not he, is the true "wild one." They parry back and forth like this until Kelly draws his resistant partner into a romantic pas de deux. With the choreography transforming the two opponents into a couple, the number closes with Gaynor's willingness to be kissed, but the embrace is interrupted by a gang member signaling that it is time to go. Kelly's biker shrugs and leaves, choosing his pals over the gal he was "so gone about."

Les Girls was the last musical Kelly starred in for MGM as a contract player, and this number, the final one in the film, is a fitting coda to his tenure as a leading man at the studio. Jack Cole is credited with the choreography of *Les Girls*, but the ideas behind "Why Am I So Gone About That Gal?"—the playful impersonation of Brando, the recuperation of a confident heterosexual masculinity through dance, the homosocial bonds reinforcing that masculinity—are in keeping with Kelly's athletic, sexually aggressive dancing style and the virile star image it reinforced.

After all, it was Kelly himself who once declared that he was "the Marlon Brando of dancers" as compared to Fred Astaire's "Cary Grant." Kelly made this comparison to describe their singular approaches as "two highly individual dancers," ranging from their dissimilar styles to their different signature costumes (Hirschhorn, 116). By invoking Grant and Brando as his touchstones, Kelly's comparison also acknowledged how his dancing—in contrast with Astaire's, as in "Sunday Jumps," say—drew on recognizable gender tropes to make it appear more legible as an authentic masculine activity. "He was not a very good dancer at all," commented Jack Cole, "but he was interesting as a phenomenon. It's a cultural thing that he happened to succeed—which is always the way with popular art. There is always the establishment attitude about dancing, and men dancing in the right way" (Delamater, 197).

Obviously not a fan, Cole criticized Kelly for using dance to project a reassuring image of "men dancing in the right way." What this "right way" required of Kelly was vividly recalled by his collaborator, Stanley Donen:

> And I remember being impressed by Gene as soon as I saw him on the stage. He had a cockiness, a confidence in himself, and a ruthlessness in the way he went about things that, to someone as young and green as myself, was astonishing. I also found him cold, egotistical and very rough. And, of course, wildly talented. He was the only song and dance man to come out of that period who had balls. There were good dancers around, like Don Loper, Jack Cole, Gower Champion, Charles Walters, Dan Dailey—even Van Johnson. But they somehow weren't as dynamic as Gene. No one was. That's why he was such an explosion on the scene. It was the athlete in him that gave him his uniqueness. (Hirschhorn, 74)

Donen's comment that Kelly stood out as "the only song and dance man to come out of that period who had balls" assumes that a male dancer cannot prove his manliness unless, as in Kelly's case, he makes a spectacle of attributes that testify to his inherent masculinity: confidence, athleticism, egotism, ruthlessness, in short, "cockiness" in all senses of the word. If "the athlete in him" made Kelly unique, moreover, it also associated him with a working-class inflection of masculinity. "What I wanted to do," Kelly explained, "was dance . . . for the common man. The way a truckdriver would dance when he would dance, or a bricklayer, or a clerk, or a postman . . . I grew up with all these kind of peoples, you know" (*Reflections on the Silver Screen*). After his death in 1996 the obituaries evoked the same virile image. According to the headlines, the star was the "he-man dancer [who] perfected the filmusical [*sic*]" (Howard); he "imbued dance with blue collar style" (Wolk); and he was "the athlete who danced our dreams" (Matthews). Choreographer Twyla Tharp made the same point in a *Los Angeles Times* memorial, claiming that "Gene Kelly is rightly credited with bringing a massive and much needed dose of vitality, masculinity and athleticism to American dance."

That colleagues and admirers still remember Kelly in these terms is not surprising. On the face of it, the insistence on the dancer's normality seems unrelenting enough to deserve John McCullough's critique that the Kelly image was "simplistically dogmatic and not complex enough to embody the inherent contradictions and conflicts of the period" except symptomatically as "an image of hysteria and anxiety" about patriarchal masculinity (44, 46).

Historically, however, what Kelly signified as a male dancer during his years at MGM was more complicated, less stable and coherent, than McCullough recognizes or retrospective accounts now recall. Far from being fixed early on and all of apiece, the Kelly image made for an incongruous picture with a strong potential for camp affect: the eroticized spectacle of a male performer whose dancing "with balls" exceeded heterosexual regulation yet without his ceasing to appear manly. The extrafilmic commentary about Kelly at that time reacted by mediating his star image through the anxiety that he might really be a "sissy dancer," but what his possible effeminacy connoted was indeterminate because the category of effeminacy itself was a variable one at midcentury. Kelly's musicals display this same indeterminacy. They craft a homosocial persona for him through the prominence given to his buddy pairing with a male costar such as Frank Sinatra, and the exhibitionist solo numbers, usually choreographed by Kelly or in collaboration with Donen or Robert Alton, dwell on the dancer's body as the primary source of erotic energy and viewer interest. The musicals and extrafilmic commentary worked together to establish the ground for viewing Kelly from a camp perspective, bringing out how his dancing on screen crossed the gendered and sexual coordinates of the era's understanding of heteronormative masculinity.

Unlike the house style and female star turns discussed in the last chapter, Gene Kelly is ordinarily not thought of as a source of camp in MGM's musicals. I therefore shift my attention somewhat from camp production to its cultural legibility. The ambiguity of Kelly's star image is the basis for recognizing the camp affect of his dancing, and his 1940s musicals, *Anchors Aweigh* (1945) and *The Pirate* (1948) in particular, make textually evident the same semantic indeterminacy condensed into the extrafilmic question, is he a sissy dancer or not? In large part because it puts masculinity rather than femininity under scrutiny, this question brings to his screen performances a different, less defiant, yet perhaps more unsettling element of camp than I have discussed so far. That baiting question also informs *Singin' in the Rain* (1952). For in offering a revisionist account of Kelly's stardom which tries to settle the matter once and for all, *Singin' in the Rain* has to disavow the camp in his dancing "with balls" so memorably on view in his musicals of the 1940s.

WHO'S A SISSY DANCER?

Throughout Kelly's career, the extrafilmic commentary approached his dancing as a problem by implying that his profession undermined his outwardly virile physical appearance. For instance, a short magazine piece about Kelly recounted the following off-screen incident in 1946:

> It was lunchtime, and he was hungry, so he ducked into one of the thousands of hamburger joints that dot New York's sidestreets, slid onto a stool at the counter, and ordered one medium

rare, please—and don't spare the onions. "Coming up," said the waitress briskly, "right away, sir—*oooooooh!*" and down went the burger on the floor and up went a pair of large, believe-it-or-not looking eyes. "*Pardon* me," she breathed, "but aren't you Gene Kelly?" The sailor glared, and shoved his cap further over his bright brown eyes, very tough-like. "What?" snorted Gene. "Me, a sissy dancer? I should say not! *I'm* a sailor!" "Well, I'm sorry," the waitress muttered, "I didn't think *he'd* eat *here*, anyway!" Which goes to show how wrong a gal can be.[1]

Referring to Kelly's leave of absence from Hollywood when he joined the navy toward the end of World War II, this anecdote has the ostensible purpose of showing that he is not "a sissy dancer," and it gives the star himself the opportunity of voicing the disclaimer. This end is achieved, though, by having Kelly undertake a rather self-conscious imitation of virility—when he glares and lowers his cap "very tough-like"—so the story layers one mask on another. Which is the pose and which is not, sissy dancer or tough sailor? It's not easy to tell. The disbelieving waitress loses her bearings as soon as she recognizes the star—becoming breathless, dropping the food, fixing her eyes on him, clearly responding to his "charisma"—and she does not perceive his ordinariness as just another sailor until he denies he is Gene Kelly, "sissy dancer." For this reason, while the anecdote "show[s] how wrong a gal can be," the cause of her error is ambiguous. The waitress mistakenly agrees with Kelly that dancers cannot be sailors and that movie stars are too pretentious to eat at lunch counters like everyone else, but she also errs when she no longer sees "Gene Kelly" seated in front of her, and may even be most "wrong" when she no longer sees him as "a sissy dancer." The anecdote follows a strategy of defining the sailor as the manly opposite of the dancer, yet its comedy of misrecognition depends on knowledge that Kelly is both, a dancer in a sailor suit and a sailor who dances.

This story typifies how extrafilmic commentary about Kelly placed "effeminacy" and "manliness" in opposition to reinforce the impression of his virility, but the ambiguity in the piece is also symptomatic of how his star image compromised the opposition structuring it. Because he was a virile movie star who danced, the dualism had the ultimate effect of representing him as manly *and* effeminate simultaneously. In another example, this time from later in Kelly's career, the same antithesis determined how Richard Griffith phrased his introductory comments in the program published for the Museum of Modern Art's 1962 tribute. "Gene," Griffith wrote, "a superb specimen of manly beauty, doomed, you'd say, to matinee idolatry, has neatly escaped from the trap by dancing and miming in such a way that you would never mistake him for anybody but an ordinary Joe" (3).

The economy with which Griffith offers this appraisal compacts rival cultural frameworks for evaluating Kelly's masculinity in relation to dance, placing him at their intersection. The critic concedes that Kelly's "dancing and miming" put his "manly beauty" on display, allowing his body to be appreciated as "a superb specimen." The remark that the dancer could, as a consequence, have been "doomed . . . to matinee idolatry" refers to a journalistic bias from the Jazz Age, which dismissed as unmanly those male stage stars like John Barrymore with a large and visible female following. That era's matinee idols were perceived as "woman-made men" and, hence, as "ambiguously gendered" because their striking good looks focused undue attention on the male body (Studlar, 111). With his dancing raising comparable suspicion, for Kelly this negative connotation translated into his potential for being viewed as the "sissy dancer" of the lunch counter incident. Alluding to this doubt, Griffith insists that Kelly avoids the matinee idol's "trap" of emasculation because this dancer is "unmistakable" as just another guy, an "ordinary Joe" who fully conforms to the status quo. By calling Kelly an "ordinary Joe," Griffith links the star with another instantly recognizable cultural stereotype while casting this normalizing epithet in direct opposition to the more pejorative "matinee idol."

More or less framing the time span of his career at MGM, these two accounts protest too much, raising suspicion that Kelly is "a sissy dancer" even while rigorously asserting the contrary. Kelly himself repeated this defensiveness in interviews. "I'm just Joe Average," he declared to *Photoplay* in 1943 as his Hollywood career began to gain momentum. "I've got a wife, a kid, a car and a house. There are a million guys like me." After this quotation, the article immediately notes that "bloody noses and blacked eyes were Gene's earliest memories of life in his hometown," adding, "the same dancing that brought him fame [later on] was responsible." Kelly explains, "The road to [danc-ing] school was lined with kids . . . I had to do battle on each of six corners to prove I was no sissy" (Proctor, 37). A 1954 interview in Sidney Skolsky's daily column likewise begins by noting right away that "dancing gave him a black eye . . . He got the black eye when the neighborhood kids thought any one who studied dancing was a sissy." Kelly adds parenthetically, "('I proved otherwise to them')," inserting his own voice into the article's indirect discourse.

The defensive tone about his dancing was not limited to fan maga-zine articles and newspaper interviews. In 1958 Kelly hosted an epi-sode of NBC's *Omnibus* which was designed to support the star's oft-repeated assertion, as biographer Clive Hirschhorn reports, that "any man . . . who looks sissy while dancing is just a lousy dancer" (225). Titled "Dancing: A Man's Game," the program draws explicit paral-lels between competitive sports and dance, showing how dance in-corporates the same movements as boxing, tennis, baseball, and foot-ball, and how sports depend on similar uses of the long, unbroken line of the male body in rhythmic, disciplined action. The opening segment, for instance, initially counterpoints athletes and men in ballet tights exercising at the bar, and then goes on to demonstrate how the agility of Mickey Mantle sliding to first base, to mention just one of the many sports figures featured, can be effortlessly translated into dance conventions.[2] The dancers performing the sports-inspired choreography, *Dance* magazine commented afterward, "were uncon-troversially virile. No one had to point it out" (Barzel, 30).

Although "Dancing: A Man's Game" spoke to public assumptions about the effeminacy of male dance, ballet in particular, Kelly's star-dom gave the show's thesis its defensive, self-reflective stance. The program draws on sports to normalize the sight of men dancing through the same manly/effeminate dualism that structured his star image. Nearly two decades after the *Omnibus* special, the goal of normalizing Kelly's dancing still set the agenda of Hirschhorn's au-thorized biography, published the same year as the first installment of *That's Entertainment!* (1974). In describing the star's impact as a dancer on-screen, Hirschhorn emphasizes Kelly's great success in *On the Town* (1949), remarking that "the big test" of the dream ballet in this film "was whether Gene, personally, would be able to make the transition from wise-cracking sailor to ballet-dancer without jarring the audience . . . His problem in *On the Town* was to retain his sailor-boy characterisation in the ballet and convince audiences that what they were watching rang true and was in no way incongruous" (155). According to Hirschhorn, this "test" proved easy enough to pass because of Kelly's athleticism, which countered any inference of his being a sissy dancer in a sailor suit:

> And instead of alienating his male audiences, which he feared he might do, he made them identify with him and won them over by the virility of his dancing. There was nothing sissy or effeminate about him, and they relaxed completely in his presence. Gene was "safe." "Like a guy in their bowling team—only classier," as Bob Fosse put it. Women found his smile and the cockiness of his personality most attractive and responded to his sex appeal. (157)

Carefully wording his appreciation of Kelly's skill in masculinizing ballet, Hirschhorn goes out of his way to insist that, as a male dancer, the star is *not* "effeminate" or a "sissy," but "safe." The biographer's remarks nonetheless indicate what could have made Kelly's dancing seem "incongruous" enough to test his masculine mettle: not the transition from sailor to ballet dancer, but the fact that men as well as women watched him dance, and did so with pleasure. After admitting that audiences of both genders found Kelly appealing to look at, presumably why men would have trouble relaxing in his presence, Hirschhorn then explicitly heterosexualizes the dualism structuring his account. The biographer concedes that women "responded to his sex appeal," seeing the eroticized matinee idol in the dancer, but declares that men identified with "the virility of Kelly's dancing," recognizing the normative masculinity they shared with this ordinary Joe. That Kelly's dancing does not easily accommodate Hirschhorn's neat gender categorization, however, is signaled by the odd phrasing of the Bob Fosse quotation, included to authenticate the star's normality by comparing it to working-class masculinity. Fosse notes that the dancer's style makes him "like a guy on a bowling team," but then immediately throws the affiliation awry by adding, "only classier." Kelly is just like them, yet he's not, and this uncertainty makes his dancing a troubling spectacle. Virile *and* sexy, his dancing has an erotic potential that disturbs the manly/effeminate antithesis imposed on it.

In an interview in *Dance* magazine promoting *That's Entertainment, Part 2* (1976), as Kelly looked back on his career, he reiterated this problematic ground of his dancing when he explained the purpose of his signature costume, the sailor suit worn in *On the Town* and before that, *Anchors Aweigh*, the same outfit that also provided the premise of the lunch counter anecdote. For audiences in the 1940s, the sailor suit instantly linked his dancer persona with normative masculinity, identifying him as an ordinary Joe, but that is not Kelly's point here.[3] "A sailor costume . . . is the *best* . . . for a man to dance in if he's playing a role," he observed. "It is one way to avoid the balletic convention of the tights" (Stoop, 71). He then went on to joke:

> The greatest contribution Gene Kelly made to the American dance . . . is that he's finally shown the male dancer how to dress! You can't play a *part* and come out in ballet slippers, and you can't come out in regular shoes, so I sort of invented the wearing of moccasins (which bend like ballet shoes) and white socks, and made sure that the pants were very tight and rolled up a bit, and wore a shirt or a sweatshirt or something that would show the figure. Like I said, a sailor suit was ideal because you outline the body, practically like a pair of tights, except for the flare at the bottom; so you could get by and still be real. (73)

To defend the "realism" of his dancing, Kelly claims that his sailor costume worked against the outright objectification of his body. Wearing tights, the costume associated with the female chorus as well as the corps de ballet, would have diminished his masculine presence, so his great contribution was his remasculinization of male dancers, even though, in another gender reversal, that amounted to his showing them "how to dress." Behind the self-deprecating irony one can sense discomfort with the dancer's need to let the movement and musculature of his body be visible. The sailor suit served him as more than a manly compromise with "the balletic convention of the tights" because the costume did not obscure his value as a spectacle. On the contrary, as Kelly points out, the costume was close-fitting enough to "outline the body," so when he struts, flexes, leaps, even wiggles his buttocks while dancing in the sailor suit—all common moves of his on screen—he might just as well have been wearing tights. Indeed, even when performing in casual dress, Kelly notes, his pants were "very tight," his shirt chosen to "show the figure." Associated closely enough with his dancing to continue serving as a metonymy of it in the 1970s, the sailor suit epitomized the cultural incongruity of Kelly's star image. The suit condensed the effeminate/manly dualism that made his virility legible, but in functioning as a theatrical costume as well, it gave him an erotic significance when he danced on screen that exceeded those binary terms.

Well after he starred at MGM, then, and in contrast with the way that Cole remembers it, extrafilmic accounts of Kelly continued to be mediated by uncertainty as to whether or not he was "dancing in the right way." The rhetorical strategy of making him appear "safe," as Hirschhorn puts it, by measuring Kelly's virility against the suspicious effeminacy of the "sissy dancer," constructed his star image in response to the presumption that a man dancing immediately troubles normative masculinity, even if he does it in a sailor suit. No doubt as far as Kelly himself was concerned, defensiveness about being a sissy because he danced had an autobiographical source; as his interviews stated, with dancing shoes in hand, he gave taunting kids a black eye to prove he could give better than he got, and he often said, as reported at his 1985 American Film Institute tribute, that what he had really wanted to do was play professional baseball, not dance for a living. For Kelly's star image when he made musicals, though, the ambiguity about what to see when he danced—the ordinary Joe or matinee idol? the sailor or the sissy? the athlete or the dancer in tights?—was more ideologically loaded.

To return to Donen's appreciation of his collaborator's uniqueness, if Kelly were indeed "the only song and dance man to come out of that period who had balls," then the remark also means that, as a rule, male dancers are emasculated men. There is a literal as well as figurative sense to Donen's insistence that Kelly was the "ballsy" exception, suggesting that a male dancer's sexuality and his gender are equally in doubt. As Ramsay Burt explains in his book on masculinity and ballet, the prejudicial dismissal of a male dancer for being a sissy not only assumes that dancing is an emasculating activity, but perceives it this way through the secondary postulate that " 'effeminate' is a code word for homosexual" (12). In Kelly's case, the extrafilmic commentary refers to that assumption by being obliged to declare, in one way or another, that he is *not* a sissy dancer. However, during his movie career, the cultural coding of the "sissy dancer" as both effeminate and homosexual was not as clear-cut. "Effeminacy" was an indeterminate category; when invoked as a means of establishing his normality by describing what he was *not*, the term made Kelly's image much less stable than is now readily apparent. Although signs of it remain in the defensive rhetoric which the early and later commentary share, the retrospective accounts of his masculinity efface both the historical specificity of the sissy-dancer question and the significance of camp as its answer.

THE INDETERMINATE SISSY

According to Burt, the prejudice against men dancing theatrically did not exist until the early twentieth century, when professional dance began to give prominence to men. This view "did not . . . arise because of any actual belief that male dancers were homosexual," but from a cultural need to "police any infringement of heterosexual norms" occurring through the visual objectification of the male dancer (28). Presumptions of the male ballet dancer's effeminacy and homosexuality, like the comparable connotations of his Broadway cousins, the boys in the chorus, worked to safeguard heteronormality by equating gender and sexuality, obscuring how each were ideological categories with uneven cultural histories. As Alan Sinfield points out, "Effeminacy preceded the category of the homosexual, overlapped with and influenced the period of its development, and has continued in potent interaction with it. To run the two together prematurely is to miss the specificity of their relation, both in historical sequence and as they overlap" (78). Sinfield analyzes the history of the effeminate homosexual—the dandy—in British culture prior to and following the publicized trial of Oscar Wilde, but his cautionary observation has relevance for a parallel development in the United States, where the equivalence of "effeminacy" and "homosexuality" has had a comparable uneven history.

In his documentation of gay social life in New York City during the first four decades of the twentieth century, George Chauncey records how the ideological weight of sexuality and gender as mutually informing categories of identity varied according to class location. The category of "gender" did not correspond to or determine sexual practices for urban working-class culture, as was already the case for the middle class (48). Effeminacy or manliness, not homosexual or heterosexual activity, served to make visible differences among working men, dividing them according to which ones were "fairies" and which were "normal." Focusing on the feminization or masculinization of male bodies as the ground on which a man based his identity, this gender system allowed for a range of accepted sexual practices even while marking the fairy as deviant.[4] A "manly" man could have sex with other men as well as women without impugning his virility so long as he took the so-called active role and appeared masculine in his outward demeanor (66). The fairy's effeminacy was thus socially tolerated in urban working culture as the gender inversion authenticating the inherent masculinity of his opposite.

Whereas the manly identities of working men hinged on their displaying virility in contrast with the fairy's show of effeminacy, prewar middle-class culture privileged object choice over demeanor, equating "manliness" with "exclusive desire for women" (117). This ideology transformed the event of same-sex relations "into a language of personal identity" to the point where "the homosexual male and the man who was insufficiently manly were understood in the same figure of speech" (Rotundo, 275, 278). The middle class's sexualized understanding of manhood was then given legitimacy by the emergent disciplines of psychiatry and the social sciences. In this new discursive setting the homosexual and heterosexual were treated as complete opposites: the middle-class "queer" male, as distinct from the working-class "fairy," defined his homosexual identity and lost his masculinity through his "deviant" sexual desire for other men, just as his "straight" counterpart secured his heterosexual identity and found his masculinity through his "natural" attraction to women.

Throughout the first half of the twentieth century, then, "effeminacy" and "manliness" were far from stable cultural categories. What either meant as a reference to gender demeanor or sexual practice shifted according to its class location. Their instability was powerfully evident in the contradictory reasoning of official military policy regarding exclusion of homosexuals during World War II. A groundbreaking 1942 regulation instructed examiners at induction centers to look for outward signs of gender deviance (Bérubé, 15). This policy, concerned with a man's ability to fight in combat, was "based on exaggerated stereotypes of both the combat soldier and the sissy 'queer.' " (176). Dancer—like interior decorator and window dresser —was considered an effeminate profession, instantly signaling men who had "difficulty with their 'acceptance of the male pattern' " (20). The "sissy queer," set in opposition to the "combat soldier," provided the index through which the army screened homosexuals under the assumption that they were visibly different because of their gender demeanor. Soon after the 1942 regulation, however, the military incorporated into its screening methods the medical establishment's psychological view that "effeminacy" was a personality trait identifying homosexuals absolutely (and pathologically) as "pseudo men who did not fit the profile of the masculine, aggressive soldier" (157).

Predictably, the screening process produced contradictory results. The policy governing it conformed to middle-class ideology in theory, treating gender and sexuality as equivalent identity categories, but the procedure itself followed working-class ideology in practice, determining who was fit and who was not according to whether they appeared manly or effeminate. The screening process could therefore target "sissy" men who happened to be heterosexual while passing over "masculine, aggressive" homosexuals whose physical appearance belied the psychosexual profile and who went on to serve the military as capable soldiers. According to one of the veterans that Charles Kaiser interviewed for his history of modern gay culture, many homosexual men enlisted just to prove their "manhood" in the face of the prevailing belief that "all homosexuals are effeminate." When these men enlisted, Kaiser reports, "despite the elaborate new regulations developed to discriminate against gays in the army, the only obstacle many of them encountered at the induction center was the 'Do you like girls?' question" (32). Certainly, the need to maintain a sizable armed forces during the war accounted for the expediency with which many officials handled the screening process, "turn[ing] a blind eye to almost anyone who was willing to put up the right front for the three minutes or less that the standard interview took" (Loughery, 137). But while filling quotas may have been the motive, the lack of a uniform cultural agreement about "effeminacy" and "manliness" made each an indeterminate sign, capable of blurring rather than equating the categories of gender and sexuality, which enabled the military's scrutinizing if hypocritical eye to be so easily blinded.

Within the same-sex environment of military life, furthermore, the effeminate/manly dualism that structured wartime masculine culture enabled just as much as it regulated gender and sexual irregularities. The military had to depend on many of the same professions that supposedly signaled a homosexual personality. Routine duties such as "secretary, typist, or stenographer" labeled "a man as gay" but were nevertheless crucial to the bureaucratic infrastructure, so the men who performed these jobs were tolerated, even valued for their work, despite the sissy identification (Bérubé, 61). This tolerance also extended to civilian professions like dancing. One inducted gay stage performer, C. Tyler Carpenter, remembers that the proportion of show-business personnel drafted into the army "far exceeded all other professions" (45). Whatever the veracity of his claim, it reflects the importance given to all-male army shows organized by local talent like Carpenter, which encouraged a visible drag subculture, often attracting "heterosexual men who loved to entertain" even when that meant impersonating Gypsy Rose Lee (46).

On the other side of the coin, the proper gender demeanor was no surer an index of a GI's sexual behavior. Despite occasional purges (the numbers increased in severity after the war), it was recognized that military life fostered "deprivation" or "situational" homosexuality (Costello, 106; Loughery, 141). Recalling canteen dances on Friday nights, where no liquor was served and the local women in attendance were forbidden to socialize with GIs after hours, Carpenter observes: "There were 50 guys for each girl and the stag lines were lengthy. Gay and bi-sexual soldiers soon discovered that the stag lines were an excellent opportunity to make contact with guys who wanted some action" (68). In this setting thousands of men confronted their homosexuality and found a sense of community they had not imagined. But, as importantly, some men had sex with each other without necessarily thinking of themselves as homosexual afterward. Carpenter, for instance, recalls several trysts with a lieutenant who "preferred to cheat with men instead of women. There were many GIs like Buck—married soldiers who sought sex with other soldiers rather than the available whores" (131). Another way in which military culture gave primacy to same-sex bonds was the "buddy system," which "formally organized men into pairs" (Bérubé, 188). This official practice encouraged close male friendships which, in their emotional intensity as well as official status, could rival, as well as substitute for, heterosexual activity, even when physical intimacy did not occur as a result.

The contradictions circumscribing military life as an unstable gendered institution and equally unstable sexualized environment were extreme, perhaps, a product of wartime; but these contradictions were not exceptional insofar as they manifested the lack of cultural consensus about perceptions of male normality more generally at midcentury. Kelly's star image, itself linked to the military through film roles that cast him as a sailor, soldier, or veteran, registered comparable uneven overlapping of a gendered understanding of "manliness" and "effeminacy" and a sexualized one of "heterosexuality" and "homosexuality," and the sissy dancer encoded this indeterminacy in the extrafilmic commentary.

The lunch counter incident from 1945 is again exemplary and for this reason worth a second look. The anecdote demonstrates that the real Kelly is more proletariat sailor than elitist movie star, authenticating his masculine identity in terms of gender. When the star claims he cannot be "Gene Kelly" because he is obviously not a sissy dancer, he means that he has a manly demeanor like that of any other enlisted man. He proves his manliness through his cocky performance, not his heterosexual orientation, which is taken for granted. But as already stated, because the waitress only perceives his ordinariness when she fails to see the actual star standing before her, the anecdote does not liberate "dancer" from its pairing with "sissy." On the contrary, it leaves the loaded phrase *sissy dancer* in place and attached to Kelly, whose appearance in the sailor suit remains juxtaposed to his professional identity as a movie star. In the story being recounted, Kelly and the waitress "meet cute" around the same kind of misunderstanding that was a convention of musicals, his included. The story's premise, moreover, is that Kelly is already well-known enough from *Thousands Cheer* (1943), *Cover Girl* (1943), and *Anchors Aweigh* for him to be recognized as a star of musicals, so it calls on awareness of the athletic, muscular body which those films feature in his dance numbers. On-screen the star does not have an effeminate-looking body, so why should the question of his being a sissy dancer even arise? Unlike Kelly the sailor, Kelly the star troubles the gendered logic by which the waitress becomes convinced of his authenticity, raising suspicion that deviation from sexual norms may be the real issue. The anecdote does not automatically intimate homosexuality when it invokes the sissy dancer, but neither does it *not* do so. The anecdote can allow for either reading because "sissy dancer" was not yet fixed to a single referent in the culture's thinking. In this indeterminacy, furthermore, the sissy dancer functioned for Kelly much as the Ziegfeld showgirl did for female star turns: as the basis of camp engagement.

THE WOLF AND THE MOUSE

Kelly's musicals directly contributed to the gender-sexual indeterminacy of his star image through the screen persona they constructed for him. When analyzing the persona, critics emphasize the same characteristics, by and large evoking the way the actor himself was portrayed through his extrafilmic star image: egoism and cockiness, athleticism and physicality, all-Americanness and ordinariness.[5] The musicals shape this persona by giving it a standardized narrative trajectory. As Jerome Delamater observes, "The Kelly character is often a city character, though one with a small town soul . . . [which suggests] that there is a more personal and friendly nature hiding behind the outward appearance of the city" (147). The disclosure that a decent ordinary Joe lurks inside the pompous, hustling wise guy occurs in almost every one of Kelly's films as an ongoing revision of the much edgier role in *Pal Joey* that brought him Broadway stardom and a movie contract in 1940. This pattern begins with his first film, *For Me and My Gal* (1942), where the role of Harry Palmer is closer to Joey Evans than any of Kelly's later parts; thereafter, his characters can be as arrogant and self-centered as Harry or Joey, but with each film their egoism is more directly linked to gender posturing and sexual insecurity than to unbridled ambition. Repeatedly, as the musicals reveal the "small town soul" concealed by the "city character," they dramatize Kelly's ordinariness much as the lunch counter incident does, distinguishing between a "true" and "false" masculine appearance in order to locate his "authentic" identity in a more convincing gender performance. Once his character's gender pretenses are deflated, a successful heterosexual romance is then overlaid on his ordinary identity, so the musicals have the effect of placing a gendered understanding of Kelly's masculinity in an uneven relation to a sexualized one.

Crucial to this narrative pattern is the buddy pairing which supports Kelly's meaning as an ordinary Joe and is usually represented in musical terms, prompting Gerald Mast's remark that "dancing is something Kelly does with his buddies" (249). A male sidekick—not only Frank Sinatra in *Anchors Aweigh*, *Take Me Out to the Ball Game* (1949), and *On the Town*, but also Phil Silvers in *Summer Stock* (1950) (as well as in Columbia's *Cover Girl*), Oscar Levant in *An American in Paris*, Donald O'Connor in *Singin' in the Rain*, Van Johnson in *Brigadoon* (1954)—figures as importantly as the female costar in the casting of a Kelly musical. The buddy pairing teams Kelly with "a meek and mild guy," as Donen described Sinatra's portrayal of this role (Hillier, 27). In their three films together, Sinatra's more effete demeanor, like that of the other screen sidekicks, is set against Kelly's muscular physique, athletic manner, and heterosexual self-confidence. "Why do you have to run after girls all the time," Sinatra's Chip asks Kelly's Gabey in *On the Town*. "I'll tell you when your voice changes, Junior," Gabey snaps back. These asymmetrical male friendships give Kelly's masculine persona its distinct social inflection as a working-class man: ethnically identified as Irish, psychologized by his dependence on postadolescent male friendships, and manifested in an overexaggerated display of sexual bravado that stands out in comparison with the sidekick's more effeminate demeanor.

According to the scenarios routinely fabricated for these musicals, the Kelly character's normality is initially confirmed by the contrast between his brash personality and the sissy pal's, but then that brashness is exposed as a false front in order to show that the more authentic ordinary Joe is only masquerading as a mug. Thus the pattern repeated in his musicals is his character's movement from male bonding with a sidekick like Sinatra, which identifies Kelly's ordinary-Joe persona with a working-class ideology of gender normality, to romance with Kathryn Grayson, Esther Williams, or Vera-Ellen, which relocates the persona in a middle-class ideology of exclusive heterosexual orientation. As a result, Kelly's screen persona appears to erase the gender-sexuality slippage given his star image by the extrafilmic specter of the sissy dancer, which is in its turn displaced onto the effeminate buddy. But while comparison of Kelly's virile hero and his sissy sidekick may allow a male viewer to identify more easily with the star's dancing as a "safe" representation of virility, producing the kind of effect Hirschhorn describes, the unequal gender dynamic of a buddy pairing still determines the narrative trajectory of his musicals. As inevitably happens in the plots constructed around Kelly's persona, his macho posturing attracts the meek buddy but initially turns off the female, so a tacit homoerotic admiration underlies the buddy bond. The homoeroticism is brought out all the more by the plots' ideological realignment of the persona through heterosexual romance and the homosocial rivalry that usually obstructs it until the finale. Because the gendered differentiation of the two buddies as manly/effeminate implies their possible asymmetrical sexualities, too, a tension between two sources of erotic affect is not fully resolved—insofar as it is not completely exhausted—when the narrative closes with the successful formation of a heterosexual couple.

The Kelly musical from the 1940s that fully dramatizes this tension is *Anchors Aweigh*. It established the protocols of the musicals he would go on to make at MGM during the next decade after his return from the navy, just as it supplied the iconography of his star image for the 1940s: the dancer in the sailor suit whose normative masculinity is not a foregone conclusion. As *Anchors Aweigh* draws on that ambiguity, it makes both Kelly's persona and his dancing more legible as a camp performance of masculinity which dialectically crosses the categories of gender and sexuality.

Anchors Aweigh opens with two navy buddies, Joe Brady (Kelly) and Clarence Dolittle (Sinatra), departing on a three-day pass. The pair mockingly sing "We Hate to Leave" to their shipmates and then go off together, intending to separate in pursuit of dates once they reach shore. Having been away at sea for eight months, Joe anticipates an evening with his old flame, Lola. (When asked if she is different, he replies, "If you like dames, what's the point of getting one who's different?") Once they arrive in Hollywood, however, Clarence dogs his friend's heels. Each time Joe senses someone is behind him and turns around, he catches sight of Clarence, who smiles self-consciously and shyly waves. Joe finally confronts Clarence to ask about this shadowing act. It appears that Clarence, unlike his pal, is still a virgin—"Even in Brooklyn," he confesses, "things can go wrong"—so he implores Joe, "the best wolf in the navy," to help him out by "getting him started."

Reluctant at first, Joe finally agrees. He poses as a "dame" on the street in order to sample Clarence's technique then and there. Broadly wiggling his body as he walks, with one hand on his hip and the other limp-wristed and poised in midair, Joe overacts the woman's part.[6] He looks like a swishy fairy picking up a sailor for trade, which is just what a passerby thinks, causing the two friends to make a hasty retreat. "Listen, Brooklyn," Joe advises afterward, "when you're going hunting it's how you feel that counts. You'll be looking for cheese and that's what you'll get. But if you feel like a wolf, nothing can go wrong." While Joe gives mousy Clarence a lesson in how to perform as a wolfish male—"You gotta feel manly"—it turns out that Joe himself is only passing as a wolf. He never does meet up with Lola, but instead spends the entire evening with Clarence. Together they tend to young Donald (Guy Stockwell), a runaway boy who wants to be a sailor, and later they meet his aunt and guardian, Susie (Kathryn Grayson). The next morning, when the sailors perform "I Begged Her" to an audience of impressed servicemen, wolf and mouse alike are bragging about heterosexual conquests the night before that did *not* take place.

While this early scene on the street initially establishes a clear difference between Kelly's manly sailor and Sinatra's effeminate one, it ends up displaying much the same indeterminacy as the lunch counter incident. As the mouse to the other's wolf, Clarence at first enacts how the sissy functioned with respect to his manlier opposite. This "pickup" scene stages the same kind of situation that Alan Bérubé describes when he reports how effeminate GIs frequently modeled their behavior on "the roughest, toughest guy[s]," copying everything they did in order not to be labeled a "sissy" or a "fruit" (54). Here, Clarence is the one seeking instruction on how to meet a woman, which, in Joe's view, amounts to teaching the virgin how to appear manly. When that passerby observes the two sailors on the street, though, his glance calls attention to the queerness which the buddies suggest as a couple. Despite their gendered difference as wolf and mouse, all the stranger sees is sexual sameness. As medi-

Joe the Wolf (Gene Kelly) teaches Clarence the Mouse (Frank Sinatra) how to pick up "dames" while a stranger walks by. *Anchors Aweigh* (MGM, 1945). Frame captures.

ated by the perspective of this onlooker, the scene alludes to homosexual gossip about sailors, how they have long been part of a "sexual
folklore about men in uniform, because they were out at sea without women for long stretches of time, they were younger than men
in the other branches and their tight uniforms looked boyish, revealing and sexy" (Bérubé, 110–11). Because the passerby presumably sees
the gender role-playing of the two sailors as a homosexual pickup,
the scene raises the possibility that even Joe's wolfish virility may be
more a matter of his only appearing to be straight—in fact, as far as
the observer is concerned, Joe is the sissy sailor soliciting Clarence.

The scene consequently alludes to an ambiguous cultural context
for representing the virility of Kelly's character in contrast with that
of Sinatra's. It depicts the teaming of wolf and mouse in such a way
as to intimate a confusion of gender (with sissy behavior characterizing a meek and mild effeminate guy who illuminates the wolf's
virility) and sexuality (with the same sissy behavior implying homoerotic desire that implicates the wolf, despite his virility). This confusion makes the sailors' close friendship hard to read except as camp
because it can simultaneously be viewed in sexual or gendered terms.
Whereas Joe himself stages the pickup as a lesson for Clarence in
proper manly behavior, the passerby sees their encounter as a bud-
ding sexual transgression. More to the point, the film's spectator has
to perceive the gap between the sailor's intention and the observer's
interpretation in order to get the gag that ends the scene. Although
the scene seems to be making a joke at the sissy's expense, its variable
logic exceeds the manly/effeminate duality ostensibly characterizing
the two sailors, and the slippage in reference invites a camp perspective of Kelly's wolfish character and Sinatra's mousy one together,
which is to say, as a couple.

"You're a strange team," Susie later observes to Joe. "Clarence is so
shy—you're a sea wolf!" The pickup scene shows just how "strange"
their teaming can appear, and it further establishes why *their* coupling drives the narrative's romantic entanglements. Kelly's ordinary Joe teaches Sinatra's sissy Clarence how to behave more aggressively with women only to become transformed himself into "a nice
guy" willing to make an emotional commitment to Kathryn Grayson's Susie. Susie is the one who first excites Clarence's interest in
women, yet her presence as a source of rivalry between the two bud-

dies sustains their close relation, since Joe's desire for her makes him feel guilty about betraying his best friend. Kelly's ordinary-Joe persona depends on such a homosocial triangulation of masculinity; it authenticates his character's normality through the comparison of manly/effeminate buddies, which the romantic rivalry heterosexualizes. However, because the outwardly virile Kelly persona derives its attractiveness from both male bonding with Clarence and heterosexual romance with Susie, Joe's wolf functions in *Anchors Aweigh* much as the sissy dancer operates in the extrafilmic commentary.

As *Anchors Aweigh* characterizes it, the virile Kelly persona, not the meek Sinatra one, runs the risk of eroticizing the homosocial bond. This risk makes the buddy pairing stand out as camp commentary on the formulaic heterosexual romance which the plot privileges but which the musical's numbers do not—Kelly's dancing undercuts Joe's outwardly safe position as the virile wolf in contrast with Clarence's sissified mouse. Once Susie triangulates the buddy relation, *Anchors Aweigh* goes on to differentiate the two male stars in musical terms. Whereas formerly they sang and danced together in three numbers, Sinatra, the idol of forties bobbysoxers, now croons of romance to turn into the film's straight man, while Kelly dances to express the childishness, vulnerability, and dreaminess previously exhibited by Sinatra's character, turning into the film's not-so-straight man.

In the most famous of these numbers, "The Worry Song," Jerry the Mouse succeeds Sinatra as Kelly's dance partner. Young Donald asks his idol Joe for an account of his Silver Medal (really awarded for saving Clarence's life at sea), and Joe gives a fanciful version, telling Donald and Donald's classmates to close their eyes and imagine what he narrates. A dissolve on the boy's face, suggesting that Donald is fantasizing what the sailor recounts, marks the transition to the number's animated setting, where Joe discovers he is not allowed to sing or dance because, a squirrel informs him, "There's a law, there's a law, there's a law!" "I'll sing and dance where 'ere I will, / No law on earth can keep me still," the sailor defiantly exclaims. Since King Jerry has banned music from his kingdom because he himself cannot sing or dance, Joe helps the mouse by getting him started, much as he helps Clarence at the beginning of the film.

With its mixing of cartoon and live action, "The Worry Song" redefines what dancing means for Kelly's wolf in *Anchors Aweigh*. This number eroticizes Kelly as none of the previous duets with Sinatra have done. Forsaking the black sailor uniform he sports at other times in the film, Kelly wears a brightly colored, striped T-shirt that displays his muscular build and white sailor pants that stretch tightly across his crotch, thighs, and buttocks. The choreography then features Kelly's eroticized body as the object of spectacle, dominating the animation. He performs a number of gymnastic steps which push him forward and backward in space; he bounces Jerry from bicep to bicep, slides the mouse down his leg, swings him in the air and under his legs, dances over him. The camp in the choreography derives from its eroticization of Kelly. Although "The Worry Song" means to visualize how his dancing liberates him from gravity and other earthly constraints much as pen and ink do for a cartoon mouse, the number's eroticization of the dancer's liberated and lawless body is not heterosexualized in its aim or energy; after all, Kelly *is* dancing with a male mouse and the number *is* being imagined by a boy. Far from making Kelly seem effeminate when turned into such a spectacular object, "The Worry Song" celebrates his virility and directs appreciation of it to viewers of any gender, since this number's use of space and camera angles is not in any way reflective of or bound to the heterosexualized gaze of a female spectator.

Kelly's other two dance numbers have comparable impact. His next one, "The Mexican Hat Dance," partners him with a young girl who watches more than dances with him. In this number Kelly turns a deserted plaza into a theatrical stage, using ordinary objects, such as candlesticks and clay pots, as his props. As the number alternates between duet and solo, fast and slow tempos, traditional and swing arrangements, folk and theatrical dance styles, Kelly travels around the plaza, enacting the narcissistic pleasure his character takes in his manic energy as compensation for losing the woman he secretly loves to his best buddy—or as guilt for desiring her and breaking the bond of friendship (the dance's narrative motivation allows for either interpretation). Disrupting the still setting, Kelly's dancing turns noise into a percussive beat and his own frantic motion into rhythm. His most consistently used prop throughout is thus his own body.

Later, when Joe confesses to Susie that words fail him, a third number, danced to "La Camparsita" and set on a Hollywood soundstage, allows him to enact what he feels. Borrowing from swashbuck-

56

57

60

58

61

59

62

Gene Kelly teaches Jerry the Mouse
how to dance in "The Worry Song."
Anchors Aweigh (MGM, 1945).
Frame captures.

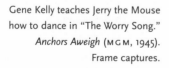

63

ling movies, he imagines her as a princess and himself as a bandit risking his life to see her. Dressed like a matinee idol in scarlet-and-black cape and a ruffled canary yellow blouse, his eyes masked like Zorro's and his tight black pants accentuating the taut line of his body, Kelly twirls, taps, does a flamenco; he climbs, jumps, swings, slides, all to get to the balcony of his beloved, who is unseen for most of the number. This fantasy ballet collapses the distinction between performance and authenticity that otherwise structures the Kelly persona in *Anchors Aweigh*. The number's premise is that the wolfish Joe can display his genuine feeling for a woman not through words, which seem unbelievable to him, but by performing it through a dance that engages him in an alternative male masquerade.

These three solo numbers in *Anchors Aweigh*, all choreographed by Kelly with Donen's assistance, show how his dancing achieves a provocative intersection of gender and sexual content which allows his personification of virility to be viewed as a spectacle of camp masculinity. The dancing self-consciously draws on the cultural tropes constituting virility, plays with the manly/effeminate opposition that naturalizes virility, and uses the male body to sexualize virility but in a way that is potentially as queer as it is straight. Confirming the gender performativity first dramatized in that scene on the street with Sinatra, the three numbers give Kelly an erotic value that is not determinately heterosexual in its aim or energy but is instead invested in his body's motion, its liberating energy, rhythm, and coordination. This may be why the three numbers align Kelly with outlawry; by dancing, he breaks the law, disturbs the peace, impersonates a bandit. Most importantly, far from making him seem effeminate, these numbers eroticize his virility, and herein lies the camp dialectic which the three solos display: Kelly is not a sissy dancer but a very sexy one. When dancing, he can as easily lose as perform his heterosexuality, yet signify maleness nonetheless.

CAMPING WITH BALLS

At one point in *Anchors Aweigh*, a group of women catch sight of Joe Brady. Ogling his butt in his tight-fitting sailor uniform, they turn the tables on this wolf and whistle at *him*, and he smiles back in acknowledgment. The athleticism of Kelly's dancing, like the aggression in his screen persona, is a means of compensating for the spectatorial attention to his body which his solo numbers not only require but actively solicit by making his body the main focus of attention. "Slaughter on Tenth Avenue," the *Words and Music* (1948) specialty ballet, has Kelly making his appearance lying on a bed, arms at his side, one knee bent, the shot emphasizing his body as defined by his tight costume. He turns over, stretches, returns to the first position, kicks up a leg and raises his arms over his head, lies back, jumps up, and so forth, until he climbs down a fire escape to the street below and meets Vera-Ellen. In contrast with her introduction in the ballet's previous segment, which immediately places her in the story line, the introduction of Kelly does not give him a narrative purpose but instead dwells on his well-developed body and its movement as the only object of visual interest. This focus then determines Kelly's erotic value when he pairs with Vera-Ellen for the rest of the ballet.

Even when his dance numbers are more firmly bound to a character whose shift from narrative to number is motivated by the plot, they still make Kelly's body the main source of attention. The numbers often overemphasize his gender demeanor as a "manly" performer and match his steps to the exaggeration. In "Fido and Me" from *Living in a Big Way* (1947), Kelly dances with a statue of a woman twice his size. He mimes seduction of this unresponsive, immobile "female" by doing versions of French apache, Spanish flamenco, and American swing that parody the masculine persona identified with each style. The more the choreography brings out this contrast between "male" and "female," human and statue, dancer and prop, the more it openly locates the number's sexual valence entirely in Kelly's body because his is the one that moves. The heavy reliance on mime throughout underlines his difference from the statue, and the finish testifies to it when he jumps atop the statue's leg to mock its frozen pose.

Later in this film, "The Construction Dance" begins as Kelly's character attempts to show the neighborhood boys that girls' games are as interesting and athletic as softball. He turns those games into a gendered dance, sashaying with a hand on each hip as he skips or plays hopscotch. By the number's end Kelly has made the setting—a construction site—into his own playground; using the narrow wooden beams of the unfinished building as parallel bars on which to do a handstand and a tightrope on which to walk in midair, he continues to mime gender stereotypes, even to mix them. Thus when he stands high atop a ladder careening from one part of the construction site to another, he waves his handkerchief flirtatiously. The gesture allows a viewer to locate his body in the long shot, shows that he is not using a double, and links the stunt to the "feminine" miming he earlier indulges in when playing with the girls.

As commentators have remarked numerous times, Kelly's solos stand apart from his romantic duets or big ballets because of their greater physical demands and technical conceits. The two numbers in *Living in a Big Way* summarize a lot of what he does with his solos. As if to go out of his way to prove he is not a sissy dancer, Kelly's choreography overemphasizes his gendered demeanor in accordance with what Stephan Prock describes as the dancer's "developing 'masculine' aesthetic" of "extreme male subjectivity" (315, 317). Hence the costumes which accentuate Kelly's torso, starting with the sailor suit; the mixture of formal dance moves (tap, ballroom, ballet) with athletic stunt work or ordinary physical movement in order to give the precision of dance weightier connotations of muscularity and strength; the medley of contrasting orchestral arrangements of the music to keep redirecting the rhythm of his motion and establish his body as an expressive tool; the exaggeration of stereotypical masculine gestures that calls as much attention to his arms and face as his feet. In film after film, his solos display all the conventional tropes of manliness, so that Donen's retrospective description of his collaborator as a dancer with balls seems quite apt and Kelly's choreography is legible as a masculine aesthetic cast in a heterosexual matrix. But the numbers also take their choreographic conceits from those tropes, redefining their value as camp through the eroticization of his body. Donen's description then seems all the more fitting, though with a somewhat different implication. Indeed, that Prock sees Kelly's dancing *resisting* objectification while I see the dancing *performing* it well catches the camp dynamic of passing at work in the choreography.[7]

Other male dancers in musicals, such as Michael Kidd and James Cagney, draw on the same cultural tropes of manliness, but Kelly deploys them in a way that allows for both camp and noncamp readings. Because, as Rick Altman puts it, the most memorable dancing in his musicals is "not a Gene Kelly *making love* but a Gene Kelly *showing off*" (55), the solo numbers work as straightforward exhibitionist displays. As they underscore the dancer's awareness of being watched, however, they make more visible the choreography's camp inflection of Kelly's "showing off" as a self-conscious performance of manliness that teeters between exhibitionism and parody in the erotic display. Most often, in fact, Kelly's dance solos are not show numbers like "Slaughter on Tenth Avenue" but still have an on-screen audience: the young girl in the plaza or Susie on the balcony in *Anchors Aweigh*; the children at the construction site in *Living in a Big Way*; the servicemen watching him do "Let Me Call You Sweetheart" in *Thousands Cheer*; the clambake revelers when he does "It's the Hat My Dear Old Father Wore" in *Take Me Out to the Ball Game*. Whether Kelly is miming seduction with a prop, mugging before children, or leaping and climbing tall ladders and high buildings as easily as he taps or spins, the solos in his forties musicals engage him in so much gender hyperbole, while investing his body with equally pronounced erotic value for a viewer, that it is tempting to see Kelly as MGM's male version of their other major star of camp musical spectacle, Esther Williams. (Was it just coincidence that she was the only other performer at the studio to pair with Jerry the Mouse in a live-action/animated sequence?) Like Williams's musicals, Kelly's are built around big numbers that exploit his physique and coordination as well as his technical skills for camp effect.

Of all his 1940s films, the one which most famously capitalizes on Kelly's value as a spectacle is *The Pirate* (1948). It still surprises and delights many viewers today for its blatant but always playful objectification of Kelly's body, particularly in the musical's big ballet number. Although its reputation has always been linked more to costar Judy Garland than to Kelly (as the film whose production was besieged by her emotional troubles and as the one whose over-the-top approach was before its time but consistent with what was later praised as her camp style), *The Pirate* is of great significance for his career, too: it was an expensive failure which signaled Garland's imminent decline as the studio's major star of musicals, while also predicting his ascent as her successor. The rare Kelly musical that does not team him with a buddy in the plot, *The Pirate* dispenses with the homosocial masculine persona of his other films and makes no effort to normalize the star as an ordinary Joe. Instead, it lets loose the gender-sexual indeterminacy of his dancing. As a result, *The Pirate* most completely and most provocatively realizes the camp informing Kelly's performing style as well as Garland's.

"A FLAMING TRAIL OF MASCULINITY"

In *The Pirate*, Manuela (Judy Garland), a dreamy, repressed young woman, is infatuated with the legendary pirate Macoco, who leaves behind him "a flaming trail of masculinity," as she sings in "Mack the Black." But Macoco's impressive manliness, recorded in the books she reads about his great exploits on the open seas, turns out to be bogus as well as oppressive, and this discovery ultimately leads her to greater appreciation of Serafin (Kelly), an actor who wants her to join his band of players. As an actor, Serafin's own masculinity is grounded entirely in gender performance and erotic spectacle, establishing a contrast with the legendary pirate's. Manuela is at first unimpressed with Serafin precisely because he is an actor, and a conceited one at that. For his part, what excites him most is her singing. "You know, it isn't essential for you to love me to be in the troupe," he admits, when she turns him down. "It helps, but it isn't essential." Serafin is more interested in finding a costar than a lover because his erotic energy is entirely invested in performing. On discovering that Manuela's "namby-pamby" betrothed, Don Pedro (Walter Slezak), is the real Macoco in disguise, Serafin therefore does not reveal the secret but instead poses as the notorious pirate himself.

"The Pirate Ballet," occurring midway through the film, is Manuela's fantasy of Serafin-as-Macoco come to life. The ballet evokes Douglas Fairbanks's *The Black Pirate* (1926), as when Kelly slides down a rope from a crow's nest, but gives swashbuckling a decided and witty Freudian edge, what with its phallic imagery of pillage, rape, even castration. This "wild, exploding, sexy number," as Richard Dyer describes it, is at once a "turn-on," in the eroticization of Kelly's body, costumed in black vest and cut-offs, and photographed primarily in full or three-quarter shots, and a "send-up," in the equally obvious parody of heterosexual machismo which the ballet puts on display (*Heavenly Bodies*, 185).

Adding to the double sense of "The Pirate Ballet" as erotic turn-on/parodic send-up, the editing of the sequence does not make per-

Gene Kelly dances macho but in cut-offs in "The Pirate Ballet." *The Pirate* (MGM, 1948).

fectly clear if the dance derives from Manuela's fantasy of the pirate's "flaming trail of masculinity" or from Serafin's knowing performance of what he assumes is her fantasy.[8] The sequence leading into the dance begins with a point-of-view shot of Manuela at her window, but the editing pairs that shot with one of Serafin looking back at her from the ground below. After acknowledging his awareness of being watched, Serafin vanquishes the guards sent to apprehend him: he throws one over his shoulder, kicks a second, tumbles with a third, flips a fourth, then wrestles all four to the ground until they flee from the scene. Throughout, the editing alternates between Manuela at the window and the scene below. Brandishing a broken pole and screaming "Macoco" in triumph, Serafin circles around a mule, quickly glancing upward at Manuela to indicate again that he is doing this as a performance to gain her interest. A return to her viewpoint dissolves to the ballet, with Serafin now in the same position but dressed as Mack the Black, swinging a cutlass instead of the broken pole, and dancing around a woman (Manuela's stand-in) in place of the mule. He repeats the action that happened prior to the dissolve, this time defeating four soldiers, then another four, then four pirates.

With the ballet's Mack the Black overcoming soldiers and rival pirates alike in order to keep the booty and kidnapped women all to himself, the number refers to Serafin as well as to Macoco. The story it choreographs takes cues from what Manuela has earlier described as "the ego, the conceit" of the actor as much as it reproduces her books recounting the exploits of the legendary pirate. Regardless of how its content is construed and its subjective viewpoint interpreted—whether as Manuela's erotic fantasy of the pirate's manliness or as Serafin's—the thrill of the number is still in the erotic spectacle of Kelly's scantily clothed body as he twirls and leaps against a fiery red backdrop. This camp display of hypermasculinity is so exciting yet parodic that, judging from the close-up of Manuela which reestablishes her character's point of view after the number concludes, it appears to intoxicate her—or to give her a headache, one is never entirely sure from the expression on Garland's face.

Commenting on *The Pirate*, Jane Feuer agrees that Kelly's Serafin is "highly eroticized" in this number but goes on to mention that he is "also coded as effeminate." In explanation, she states that he fails to be the "fully phallic male," which the pirate represents in the fantasy of Garland's character, Manuela, and that he is simultaneously made the sexual object of her desire in the ballet. Serafin's masquerade as the notorious pirate, Macoco, Feuer goes on to say, results in a feminine reformulation of heterosexual masculinity, which has the residual effect of allowing Serafin to be readable as "a gay icon" (*Hollywood Musical*, 143). This does not make him a sissy dancer, however, but destabilizes the manly/effeminate dualism through a camp performance of both sides of the antithesis. Whether impersonating Macoco, performing as an actor, or wooing Manuela, Serafin exaggerates feminine as well as masculine characteristics, just as Kelly's dancing is choreographed to achieve homo- and heteroerotic affect. Feuer thus can see in Kelly's Serafin an eroticized, effeminate male, even a gay icon, just as Dyer can view Kelly's dancing as half turn-on, half send-up, because, in both characterization and performance, the figure's references to gender and sexuality do not fall into alignment, resulting in the ambiguity that the two critics describe. Male yet not entirely manly, heterosexual yet not fully heterosexualized, eroticized yet parodic, Serafin's own "flaming trail of masculinity" cannot be fixed to a determinate meaning one way or the other.

Kelly's first solo number, "Niña," makes perfectly clear that Serafin's masculinity can, in camp parlance, be "flaming" without ceasing to represent him as male. The number begins with Serafin's celebration of his voyeurism in song. "When I arrive in any town," he boasts, "I look the ladies up and down." The virtuoso dance that follows choreographs his heterosexual arrogance as an act of male exhibitionism. He climbs up a balcony to serenade one woman, turns away when he catches the eye of another, stretches his body backward, one leg in the air, as he makes love to this one, and continues in this same manner from woman to woman, throwing his body around the town square with great bravado, and much wiggling of hips and buttocks. At one point Kelly even takes a cigarette from a woman, rolls it inside his mouth before kissing her, and then exhales afterward! The female dancers, in turn, far from serving as objects of his desire, as the Cole Porter lyrics seem to avow, are instruments of the dance, directing his movement from one to the other and appropriating his gaze.

As a result, Brett Farmer observes, Serafin "assumes a 'feminine' position of erotic objectification," so a "position of desire for any one gender is thoroughly undermined." But if the shifting specular dy-

65

Serafin (Gene Kelly) climbs onto a balcony in "Niña" to serenade a woman and to show off his form. *The Pirate* (MGM, 1948).

Serafin (Gene Kelly) as
the object of spectacle
in "Niña." *The Pirate*
(MGM, 1948).

PHOTOFEST

namic of the choreography "unleashes a wild eruption of communal desire" (108), that is because Kelly's dancing in "Niña" visually
draws the men of the village into its orbit along with the women
with whom he partners, registering what Matthew Tinkcom calls the
camp homoeroticism staged by "the pleasure of Serafin in the spectacle of his own movement" (*Working Like a Homosexual*, 67). Serafin
initially addresses the number to the men as his means of explaining why every woman is the same to him, justifying his calling them
all "Niña." Throughout the number, when Kelly uses his eyes, face,
arms, or torso to draw the other dancers toward him through mime,
his movement continually directs the attention of everyone watching—men and women, on-screen and off—to his body as a source of
ambiguous sexuality: is Serafin performing for the women, the men,
or himself?

The answer is all of the above. "Niña" characterizes Serafin as
an arrogant, insincere, narcissistic seducer more interested in the
game (and the gaze) than its outcome, which is why, at the num-

ber's conclusion, he poses before a banner advertising his troupe. The dance can then immediately be reread as his self-conscious enactment of male posturing, a form of advertising meant to promote the actor himself as the spectacle worth watching: Serafin's goal may have been to solicit an audience of men and women for that evening's performance of his show. Viewing "Niña" as a camp exhibition of ambiguous male eroticism embedded in a gender masquerade of machismo—each put in quotation marks, so to speak, by the number's purpose as advertising for the theatrical troupe—is in perfect accord with *The Pirate*'s plot, which never relieves Serafin from the need to perform his masculinity in some outrageous fashion. As the plot plays itself out, his multilayered masculine impersonations (performer as womanizer as pirate as performer) do not lead to his final disclosure of a more authentic male concealed by the macho mask, as happens in other Kelly musicals.

As importantly, Serafin's various impersonations of masculinity liberate Manuela from the rigid gender-sexual categories that initially define her femininity and desire in opposition to a fantasized male figure such as Macoco. The actor's send-up of the pirate results in Manuela's own turn to camp impersonations of femininity: she pleads not to be delivered to "Macoco" on her wedding day while secretly primping and making herself up as a virgin sacrifice; she pretends she has not learned the truth about Serafin's imposture in order to deflate his "ego" and "conceit" by sarcastically dismissing his talents as an actor (and what she describes as the "real" man beneath the actor's mask recounts "The Pirate Ballet"); in the climax, she feigns being hypnotized in order to save Serafin's neck by making Don Pedro jealous enough to reveal that he is the real Macoco. Unlike most musicals, *The Pirate* fittingly ends, not with a kiss, but with Serafin and Manuela teamed on-stage in wigs, painted faces, and baggy pants, boisterously performing "Be a Clown" and laughing hysterically as if taking shared pleasure in the number's camp send-up of both proper gender roles and proper heterosexual passions.

The Pirate achieves the fullest coordination of a narrative with the camp affect of the gender-sexual ambiguity structuring Kelly's dancing, but the musical's exhilarating flamboyance is on view in his other films of that era. In acknowledging his spectacular value as camp for its contrast with his ordinary-Joe persona, many of these films also find a correlative for Kelly's dancing in the tradition of swash-buckling action stars such as Douglas Fairbanks: as well as playing Serafin and a Zorro-styled bandit in the fantasy number in *Anchors Aweigh*, Kelly is a former circus trapeze artist in *Thousands Cheer*; Black Arrow, another Zorro type, in the long fantasy segment of *Du-Barry Was a Lady* (1943); and finally, D'Artagnan in the nonmusical remake of Fairbanks's *Three Musketeers* (1948). Although *The Pirate* contributed most to Kelly's "reputation as the Douglas Fairbanks of dance" (S. Harris), the other films also draw on the swashbuckler as-sociation to show how his acrobatic style allows his body to blaze "a flaming trail of masculinity" which appears to be half turn-on, half send-up, so they similarly presume awareness that Kelly was per-ceived as a forties-styled "matinee idol" because of his dancing, and that he could be read straight or otherwise.

The script of *Singin' in the Rain* (1952) follows this thinking as well with Kelly playing a silent movie star, Don Lockwood, modeled after Fairbanks. A scene from Kelly's *Three Musketeers* is even included to represent Lockwood's silent epic, *The Royal Rascal*. However, this use of the clip turns the camp inflection of Kelly's 1940s star image to pseudo-camp, epitomizing Kelly/Lockwood's hammy overacting rather than his ambiguous eroticism. In this context, the clip mocks the fictional star for being a "matinee idol"—the very trap into which, a decade after the release of *Singin' in the Rain*, Richard Griffith said Kelly himself would have fallen had he not been just another "ordi-nary Joe."

DANCING IN THE RIGHT WAY

At first glance, *Singin' in the Rain* does not appear to question the authenticity of Kelly's filmic counterpart, Don Lockwood, all that much. In recounting the transition from the silent era to the talkies, the plot complications of *Singin' in the Rain* arise from movie star Lina Lamont (Jean Hagen), not her screen partner. He has the talent needed to adjust to the new technology's requirements whereas she does not. As Don's best friend, Cosmo Brown (Donald O'Connor), observes, "She can't act, she can't sing, and she can't dance—a triple threat!" For that matter, *Singin' in the Rain* explicitly takes Kelly's own star value for granted. Right after the MGM logo, the film introduces its three leading players *as* stars, their names superimposed over their bodies, and this trio—Kelly, Donald O'Connor, and Debbie Reynolds—then go into a spirited chorus of the title song before the credits roll. The final credit, moreover, identifies Kelly as the film's codirector, leading to Peter Wollen's interpretation of *Singin' in the Rain* as "a summation of Gene Kelly's own work up to that point, echoing and developing numbers he had done in earlier films, crystallizing the principles and ideas about dance and film which he had been forming, consciously or unconsciously, since early childhood, more intensely still since his arrival in Hollywood" (29).

Wollen notes the many allusions to prior numbers in Kelly's choreography, interpreting the dancing as a career "summation," but the allusions—motifs repeated from numbers in *Cover Girl, Anchors Aweigh, On the Town*—can as easily be seen as citations of past Kelly efforts much like that inclusion of a clip from his *Three Musketeers*, reminding audiences that they are watching Kelly the star. Despite Betty Comden's and Adolph Green's contention that they did not originally plan the script with Kelly in mind—a claim that Donen and Kelly both dispute—the film's reference to Kelly's star image through Don Lockwood is impossible to ignore. After all, the screenplay makes a conscious effort to reinvent the fictional star as a song-and-dance man in the mold of "Gene Kelly."[9]

This agenda is disclosed right away. At the premiere of *Royal Rascal*, Don's posturing as a glamorous male movie star before his screaming, swooning fans equates this strutting matinee idol with his equally glamorous and inauthentic female costar. Don is arrogant and egotistical, as invested in performing to a crowd as Serafin, but this time the point is to send up what makes the star a turn-on for his fans. When asked by gossip columnist Dora Baily to share his life story with her radio audience, Don gives a fictionalized account that exposes a manufactured star image. Summarized by the pretentious motto "Dignity, always dignity," he supplies an elitist upbringing: dancing school, performing before his parents' society friends, exposure to classical theater, training at the Conservatory of Fine Arts and a dramatic academy, then a concert tour at symphonic halls around the country, finally a career in motion pictures playing "urbane," "sophisticated," and "suave" leading men. Throughout the visual flashback accompanying Don's spoken narration, the editing

67

Don Lockwood (Gene Kelly) and Lina Lamont (Jean Hagen) greet their fans while Cosmo Brown (Donald O'Connor) looks on. *Singin' in the Rain* (MGM, 1952).

returns to close-ups of Kelly's grinning face, his perfect teeth gleaming as white as his glamorous evening clothes. At the same time, what the film shows in the flashback montage differs considerably from what Don describes, revealing a more ordinary, working-class Joe as the person behind the fabrication of movie stardom. As youths, Don and Cosmo dance for pennies in a poolroom and sneak into a nickelodeon to see a movie serial; as adults, the two friends entertain in a tavern, do a comic act on amateur night, and perform "Fit as a Fiddle" in a third-rate vaudeville hall, until they find themselves in Hollywood, where Don accidentally gets a job as a stuntman.

Don's encounter with Kathy Selden (Debbie Reynolds) after the premiere continues the demystification of his stardom. Escaping from a crowd of zealous fans, he leaps onto the top of a streetcar and jumps into her convertible with the same kind of athleticism that characterizes his overacting in *Royal Rascal*. Then, in trying to impress her, Don carries over the egotistical persona that he displayed for his public at the premiere. Unimpressed when she learns his identity, Kathy dismisses Don's acting for its inauthenticity. "The personalities on the screen just don't impress me," she declares. "I mean, they don't talk, they don't act, they just make a lot of dumb show . . . You're nothing but a shadow on film. A shadow." This scene concludes with a joke at Don's expense—when he catches the tail of his jacket in the car door and the cloth rips across his back—again puncturing his claim to "dignity, always dignity," so Kathy's comments can be taken at face value. Despite her own pretensions in professing to aspire to the legitimate stage (she will soon be exposed as a showgirl and later as a fan), her criticism predicts the future direction of the movies, which, with the advent of sound technology, will put together voice and body in Don's singing and dancing, authenticating his stardom over Lina's by making him more than just "a shadow": namely, the star of movie musicals.

Since these opening scenes satirize Don's star image, highlighting its fabrication along with Lina's, in order subsequently to validate his transformation into a song-and-dance-man just like Gene Kelly, *Singin' in the Rain* must also depict the greater authenticity of that other kind of stardom. As Prock observes, despite the visual demystification of "Don's revisionist and misleading narrative" when he recounts his biography at the premiere, "the film becomes increasingly caught up in revealing the falseness, the very constructedness, of the 'feminine' and the inability of women in the film to present or control their own representation" (300). The many dance numbers in *Singin' in the Rain* reinforce this theme. As the plot becomes increasingly concerned with the new sound technology and its ability to counterfeit female stardom through dubbing, the numbers represent Don's spontaneous expressions of joyful emotion and native star talent. They directly contrast with the contrivance of physical action in his silent films on one hand and with the insincerity of his speech when not acting on the other.

For instance, when he and Kathy meet again several weeks later, Don reveals that he cannot tell her how he genuinely feels. "I'm such a ham," he confesses. "I'm not able to without the proper setting." So he goes into the number "You Were Meant for Me," which measures the sincerity of his singing and dancing against the insincerity of his phony speech and hammy acrobatics. The setup of this number borrows from the similar one on a soundstage in *Anchors Aweigh*, but whereas the swashbuckler fantasy ballet in that earlier film shows the dancing matinee idol beneath the inarticulate ordinary Joe, this time out it proves just the opposite. Don introduces his love song by calling attention to its theatricalized setting on a soundstage, using studio technology to simulate a suitable romantic atmosphere copied from the movies he stars in with Lina. He initially highlights the artifice of his lovemaking and its inspiration in the movies in order for his lyric declaration of love to express a more genuine emotion.

The other, more exuberant numbers in the film—"Moses Supposes," "Good Mornin'" and the title song—work even more transparently to authenticate Don's talent, repudiating his matinee-idol image by returning him to his vaudeville roots. These numbers make no overt reference to the industrial technology that complicates film production and exposes the fraudulence of movie stardom in the narrative, all of which gets concentrated on Lina, the one character who cannot perform musically. They deserve closer examination, however, because their impact as numbers exceeds the thematic purpose of linking Don to masculine authenticity through his body in contrast with the plot's connection of Lina with feminine inauthenticity through her problematic voice.

What is immediately striking is how the Kelly numbers in *Singin' in the Rain* differ from those in his other musicals. Absent are the spectacular solos for the star that serve as camp highpoints: there is no equivalent of "The Worry Song" or "Niña." The title number, while Kelly's most famous, is perhaps the least innovative solo of his entire career, an unabashed declaration of joy more unified in style, and much simpler in its execution (as Kelly himself commented), than any others that come to mind. Further distinguishing *Singin' in the Rain* from the 1940s musicals is the greater extent to which Kelly is partnered in his dances. This may be due to the fact that co-stars O'Connor and Reynolds could keep up with him, but it also has an important consequence. Their dancing with Kelly helps to dislocate the gender-sexual indeterminacy on display in his solos of the 1940s. As a result, *Singin' in the Rain* effaces that indeterminacy from the spectacle of Kelly's body only to disperse it throughout the many dance numbers featuring the three stars in one combination or another.

The contrast between the first and last numbers, each a throwaway of sorts, illustrates how the film's musical elements bear a more specific relation to Kelly's star image than may first seem apparent. The version of the title song performed before the credits, as Patricia Mellencamp notices, includes all three stars singing and dancing together, unlike the finale at the end, which briefly pairs Kelly and Reynolds in "You Are My Lucky Star," the lyric punning on their characters' future coupling, professional as well as romantic. *Singin' in the Rain* achieves its closure, Mellencamp points out, by pushing O'Connor's character, Cosmo, out of the story along with Lina (6). Always marginalized as Don's best friend who has no private life or professional ambition of his own (which he jokes about), Cosmo moves into the orchestra pit to conduct the musical accompaniment of "You Are My Lucky Star" when Don and Kathy reunite and then disappears. Underscored by a heavenly chorus continuing the song, the final shot shows Don and Kathy beneath a billboard advertising their teaming in a new *Singin' in the Rain* which, unlike the *Singin' in the Rain* we have been watching for nearly the past two hours, does not feature a star trio.

Mellencamp supposes that generic convention encourages a spectator to accept without further thought Cosmo's marginality and final elimination. Kelly's star image makes Cosmo's shifting status much more noteworthy, however, since this best buddy also triangulates the couple until the very end. From the view offered by the number that precedes the credits, the romantic duo of *Singin' in the Rain* is not achieved by heterosexually combining man and woman but by subtracting the extra male from the initial equation. "The interchangeability of Kathy and Cosmo," Mellencamp observes, is made clear when he uses her to demonstrate how Lina can be dubbed, and repeated in the film's climax when Cosmo takes Kathy's place at the concealed microphone and causes Lina's humiliating exposure in front of a live audience (6). The teaming of Don and Lina before Kathy enters the picture has the same resonance, since Lina treats Cosmo as if he were her rival, and vice versa. Much like *Anchors Aweigh*, in short, *Singin' in the Rain* begins with Don *already* coupled—and "fit as a fiddle," thank you—with his life-long friend, constant companion, first dance partner, and collaborator: Cosmo. The buddy, more than Lina, poses the serious obstacle to the normative heterosexual masculinity that Don comes to represent in the film's closure when he and Kathy star in their own version of *Singin' in the Rain*.

The many dance numbers evoke the disturbance to heteronormality that Don's close bond with Cosmo intimates. Retaining the ambiguous eroticism of Kelly's dancing, though without centering it as explicitly or solely on his body as in *The Pirate* and *Anchors Aweigh*, the numbers choreograph multiple possibilities of sexual combination. With the exception of Don and Kathy's final duet, which is not a dance, only one of the numbers involving the main characters ("You Were Meant for Me") directly celebrates the heterosexual couple, and this one begins with Don setting the stage—with his enacting heterosexual desire as a self-conscious performance. The title number does not express Don's heterosexual desire so much as his auto-erotic pleasure in singing and dancing and, finally, splashing in the rain. Kelly called this type of number "dancing happy," suggesting its purpose not to recount the motive for joy but to express the emotion alone, in excess of its narrative motivation—one reason why "Singin' in the Rain" is so easily excerpted.

Don's sexual interest in Kathy, in fact, is more evident, even though only implied from his position off-screen, when he watches her and a female chorus line perform "All I Do Is Dream of You" at the post-premiere party. But Don watches in something of the same way, also off-screen, when Cosmo dances for his pal's amusement in "Make 'Em Laugh," a number whose conceit of performing, though not its broad vaudeville style, is more in keeping with Kelly's solos from past films. Here it is the buddy, not Kelly, who turns himself into a spectacle of energetic, even maniacal movement, as Cosmo tries to make Don forget the blow to his self-esteem resulting from that first encounter with Kathy. Cosmo's athletic clowning, not encoded as "sissy" dancing by any means, problematizes Don's perspective, leading to Alex Doty's passing comment about the difficulty of responding to O'Connor's solo "as anything but a case of overwrought, displaced gay desire" (*Making Things Perfectly Queer*, 11). That response is not out of line when O'Connor does a bit of sexual play with the headless, genderless dummy; he puts his hand on the dummy's knee suggestively and gets hit in the face for making a pass.[10] The placement of Kathy's and Cosmo's numbers in quick succession, with Don as their primary audience (according to the narrative introductions of the numbers), further encourages this inference. The sequencing parallels the male best friend and prospective female lover as competitors for Don's attention, anticipating the later moments in the plot when their interchangeability is more openly dramatized. The intimation that dance stages homoerotic desire resurfaces when Don and Cosmo, glancing at each other throughout as they keep their steps and bodies aligned, synchronize their movement as a challenge dance in "Moses Supposes." Satirizing the pretentious speech lessons of the diction coach, who watches their dance, they proceed to tear up the room. Much more so than in their frantic "Fit as a Fiddle," the vigorous tap dancing of Kelly and O'Connor breaks down spatial boundaries with a liberating sense of physical anarchy, displaying their obvious pleasure in performing with each other as a matched team. The apparent spontaneity of their choreographed hijinks contrasts with the self-conscious artifice of Don's one romantic number with Kathy, "You Were Meant for Me," which "Moses Supposes" almost immediately follows, counterpointing one kind of dance coupling with another.

And if, as Kelly commented about his choreography of *On the Town*, "the idea of three men dancing together seems to be a very effective masculine way to approach things" (Stoop, 71), what about two men and one woman dancing together? Three men dancing together is no more effectively masculine than two men dancing together, except that a same-sex trio may not as readily imply a queer ménage.[11] When Don and Cosmo perform "Good Mornin'" with Kathy in celebration of their plan to revitalize the star's doomed career by turning the disastrous first talkie, *Dueling Cavalier*, into a musical, the choreography positions Kathy between the two men every step of the way. "Fellas," Don says to Cosmo and Kathy right before the number begins, "I feel this is my lucky day." The three "fellas" never vary from their side-by-side tapping except in the middle of the number. At that point, each dancer grabs someone else's hat and raincoat, using the costume as a prop for a solo that is specifically inflected as a performance of gender: with Kathy's coat, Cosmo dances a Charleston; with Don's, Kathy dances a hula; with Cosmo's, Don dances a flamenco. This interlude enhances the number's high-spirited disruption of any presumed correspondence between gender and dancing as a performance of fixed sexual identities. In fact, right after this number Cosmo comes up with his proposal to dub Lina as a means of circumventing her lack of talent. Standing in front of Kathy while she sings the opening lyrics of "Good Mornin,'" he mouths the words and a female voice appears to issue from his lips.

The numbers, in short, do not restate *Singin' in the Rain*'s otherwise strong narrative investment in the romantic coupling of Don and Kathy and the male/female asymmetry supporting the heterosexual framework through which the film revises Kelly's star image. On the contrary, these great dancing sequences reverberate with the gender-sexual ambiguity more pronounced in Kelly's solo dancing in his 1940s films. At the same time, it is as important to recognize that *Singin' in the Rain* actively distances Kelly from that ambiguity and its camp valences; except for the title number, these are not his solos, as in past musicals. The film, moreover, formally contains all this dancing with two key moments that stand out because of their parallelism: Don's account of his rise to stardom at the start, which deflates his star image, and "The Broadway Ballet" toward the end, which reinvents it.

Introducing "The Broadway Ballet," Don explains to studio head R. F. Simpson (Millard Mitchell) that there is one number left to shoot for the musical revision of the disastrous *Duelling Cavalier*. It will recount "the story of the young hoofer who comes to New York," and Don proceeds to describe it: "First, we set the stage with a song. It goes like this." An immediate cut to the number shows Don in straw hat, black tie, and cane, illuminated by a spotlight, singing the first lines of "Broadway Melody." The camera moves back until his body is barely visible, the Times Square setting lights up behind him, and the young hoofer arrives from the sticks, making the rounds of agents as he proclaims, "Gotta dance," punctuating each repetition of the phrase with his tapping. After the number's conclusion, Simpson remarks, "I can't quite visualize it. I'll have to see it on film first." While that line gets the big laugh, Cosmo's retort is more telling: "On film, it'll be better yet." The framing dialogue establishes a gap between what is shown and what Simpson hears, rhyming "Broadway Ballet" with the undercutting of Don's voiceover by the biographical montage at the start of the film. The ballet's own "star-is-born" narrative parallels the story the montage tells at the premiere of *Royal*

Gene Kelly's hoofer finds an agent in "The Broadway Ballet." *Singin' in the Rain* (MGM, 1952).

Rascal—the hoofer rises from speakeasy, to burlesque, to vaudeville, to the Ziegfeld Follies—but the number reverses that earlier demystification of his stardom. Whereas Don's athleticism is initially a sign of his inauthenticity on screen, with the change in genres, his physical movement is set to music in "The Broadway Ballet" and becomes visible proof of his authenticity as a star—and of Gene Kelly's.

It is revealing of the number's implicit connection to Kelly's stardom that the published screenplay by Comden and Green adds after Don's introduction: "This is a big production number shown as it will appear in *The Dancing Cavalier*" (64). That is not quite the case, however. For while set in the 1920s, the number takes full advantage of 1950s technology—with a mobile camera, vivid Technicolor, numerous set changes, and back-screen projection in its big finish—so it in no way duplicates what it would have looked like in 1927 and consequently has as much relevance for Kelly's star image in 1952 as it does for Don's. Without such implied reference to Kelly, "Broadway Ballet" would seem even more out of place in *Singin' in the Rain* than it already does. This number makes no effort to simulate period filmmaking, in contrast with the other times a film featuring Don

Gene Kelly's hoofer meets Cyd Charisse's vamp in "The Broadway Ballet." *Singin' in the Rain* (MGM, 1952).

Lockwood is shown; it has nothing to do with Hollywood; and it does not pair Kelly with his leading lady. Even codirector Donen thought it did not fit perfectly, remarking, "The ballet was always too long. I thought it at the time and still do" (Silverman, 164).

The inclusion of the ballet follows the formula of successful Kelly musicals made right before *Singin' in the Rain*. *On the Town* and *An American in Paris* also feature an elaborately produced and expensive ballet, and this type of number became closely associated with the star. It incorporates more classical ballet than his solos, duets, or threesomes; as a set piece that characterizes the quintessential "Gene Kelly musical," moreover, it openly heterosexualizes his dancing by pairing him with an equally expert female dancer trained in classical ballet: Vera-Ellen in *On the Town*, Leslie Caron in *American in Paris*, Cyd Charisse in *Singin' in the Rain*. But in each film this number just as repeatedly depicts heterosexual loss, recounting an inner narrative of Kelly's losing the woman with whom he dances. In "Broadway Ballet," the hoofer fails to sustain his erotic rapport with the seductive vamp played by Cyd Charisse; both times they meet in this number, after they dance up a storm, the vamp leaves the hoofer for her gangster-lover. When the vamp rebuffs him, all the hoofer has to console him at the ballet's end is his success as a dancer, but that success is considerable since he is now a bona fide star. The cycle starts anew when a new young man arrives from the sticks, dressed exactly as Kelly was in the number's opening and just as determined to make good on Broadway. The arrival of this youthful counterpart awakens Kelly's hoofer from a reverie, suggesting that the entire ballet may be a flashback. With a shrug, Kelly repeats, "Gotta dance!" and, returning to the number's opening, sings "Broadway Melody" against the backdrop of the Great White Way and a chorus cheering him on. The number concludes with a shot of Kelly's face slowly filling the entire screen.

Despite the way its star-is-born narrative is placed in counterpoint to the vamp's seduction and betrayal, "Broadway Ballet" gives every impression of completely heterosexualizing Kelly's dancing. While not related to the plot or its setting, the ballet closely follows the rest of *Singin' in the Rain* in opposing the authenticity of masculinity to the inauthenticity of femininity. The narrative views women as disruptive, the source of all of Don's troubles, because of their voices. Lina throws the studio into crisis when her shrill voice does not match her lovely body, and her lack of talent motivates her replacement by Kathy, who becomes Don's partner on and off the screen. But Kathy's outspoken criticism of Don's acting for its reliance on mime and dumb show also jeopardizes his on-screen impersonation of masculinity and off-screen confidence. Consequently, before she can be successfully teamed with Don in their own version of *Singin' in the Rain*, the very vocal Kathy is replaced as his partner in the ballet by Cyd Charisse's distinctly *mute* dancer. Not accidentally, these women also carry the burden of obvious camp for this film—Lina as the preening, conniving, and not-too-bright blonde diva, Kathy as the feisty chorus girl who pops out of a cake, Charisse as a Louise Brooks–styled gangster's moll—but the camp inflections of the actresses' performances are the unflattering proof of their characters' antagonism to the Kelly figure. Unlike *The Pirate*, say, which allows Garland/Manuela to challenge Kelly/Serafin, to get away with it, and most importantly, to be an attractive camp figure right alongside him from their first meeting to the clown finale, *Singin' in the Rain* turns against its challenging camp women: the film embarrasses Lina time and again, transforms Kathy into a docile ingenue, characterizes the moll as a heartless vamp.

Cyd Charisse may have been needed for "Broadway Ballet" because Reynolds was not a trained classical dancer, but the substitution only makes the pattern clearer: whereas the camp female figure is punished (Lina) and redeemed (Kathy) in the plot, she is completely silenced and eroticized as pure spectacle in the ballet (Charisse). Prior to Charisse's entrance, the first part of "Broadway Ballet" is actually more in keeping with Kelly's camp solos from the 1940s musicals. Arriving in New York, his bespectacled young hoofer is decked out as the primary object of visual interest in his own right, what with his straw hat, yellow vest, reddish tie, and pink-and-blue checked jacket. As he travels up Broadway, an assortment of Times Square types pass by on a moving sidewalk behind him, directing attention to his body's motion in the foreground. When he gets an agent, the first thing the agent does is take off the hoofer's glasses and remove his jacket, leading him, now in rolled-up shirtsleeves, to his first job in a speakeasy. There the hoofer finds the correlative for his song, "Broadway Rhythm," in his shimmying movement; making use of arms and torso as well as legs, he dances with his entire body. While performing a variety of different tap steps to show off his footwork, he also spins, leaps, kicks his feet together in the air—until he is stopped by the sight of the vamp's outstretched leg, his hat perched on the end of her shoe. Beginning with the first shot introducing her by way of her long legs, the choreography and camerawork then focus on Charisse's body, distracting attention from Kelly's, a shift made all the more noticeable because of her silence. The hoofer's ability to sing as well as dance, by comparison, shows that he can synchronize language with movement, the song lyric that drives the number: "Gotta dance!" His wholeness, carrying out the sound/image dualism that structures the film in so many other ways, is epitomized by the shots of Kelly's face that frame the number; the close-ups here contrast with and so revise what his grinning face initially represented about the fabrication of male stardom during the opening sequence at the Hollywood premiere.

Don's stardom as a song-and-dance man in *Singin' in the Rain*, this is all to say, is not fully authenticated until his dancing is overtly heterosexualized in "Broadway Ballet" through the duet with Charisse, which engenders it as a more traditionally masculine activity. Why else would this number need to digress from its Times Square setting for that inserted fantasy sequence, when the choreography shifts from tap and jazz to classical ballet? With Charisse's long, trailing veil blowing in the air by way of the same kind of wind machine that "You Were Meant for Me" earlier mocked, Kelly (clad all in black) and Charisse (in white) dance a conventional pas de deux which, in its arty seriousness, belies the jauntier tempo and wittier tone of the number as a whole but more firmly establishes the gender asymmetry of their duet. Unlike their first meeting in the speakeasy, this time Kelly lifts Charisse a lot more and, instead of wrapping her legs around him seductively or leaping into his arms, she falls passively to his feet; he also keeps his back to the camera during much of their dancing, and when he faces front, the veil wrapping around the two of them obscures his body, but not hers, because of his dark clothing. Thus, even though the hoofer loses the vamp, at the finish of "Broadway Ballet" Kelly's close-up confirms the authenticity of the star who knows he's "gotta dance!"—and can do it in the right way.

REMEMBERING THE ORDINARY JOE

The ballet's transformation of matinee idol into hoofer anchors *Singin' in the Rain*'s revision of Kelly's 1940s camp star image, solidifying the more normative one recalled five decades later in the actor's obituaries. Ironically enough, though, *Singin' in the Rain* proved to be more of a valediction to Kelly's career than a benediction. It was the last of his big hits, and at the time of its release was eclipsed by the greater prestige of *An American in Paris*. That situation has of course been reversed with the growing reputation of *Singin' in the Rain* as the greatest movie musical of all time. This is the Kelly film almost everyone still sees at some point, so it is not surprising that *Singin' in the Rain* now determines how he is most remembered.

The ongoing mediation of Kelly by *Singin' in the Rain* is nevertheless more than the result of circumstance. It is in perfect accord with the film's revisionist view of what his star image ought to represent: not the matinee idol's gender-sexual indeterminacy, but the ordinary Joe's heterosexual normality. When *Singin' in the Rain* was made a number of industrial factors no doubt converged with postwar cultural influences to determine (or more likely, overdetermine) the film's strong investment in normalizing Kelly's star image: his greater star power after *On the Town* and *American in Paris*, which made him the most important musical star still under contract at MGM and a more valuable commodity to protect; his political harassment by the House Committee on Un-American Activities (HUAC) and the FBI for his and wife Betsy Drake's left-wing affiliations in the 1940s, which resulted in their departure for Europe after he completed this film; his own partial authorship of *Singin' in the Rain*, which gave him greater leave to insert his views of dance as a "man's game"; Comden's and Green's more heterosexualized understanding of the Kelly persona, already evident in *On the Town*; the studio's effort to retain a mainstream audience in the face of television by conforming their product to the more conservative values of the postwar blockbuster Broadway musical. One reason cannot be singled out, but the effect is noticeable all the same. Some twenty years after its release, and without appearing to do the film any injustice, a BBC interview with Kelly could simply treat *Singin' in the Rain* as if it *were* telling his life story.

"Much of the film *Singin' in the Rain* is drawn from incidents in Kelly's own life or known to him," the interviewer, Gavin Millar, says in voiceover. "And the image of the small town boy looking for both success and culture runs through most of his films." As Kelly's voice describes his background—mentioning, for instance, how he and brother Fred first did a dancing act together—the documentary shows "Fit as a Fiddle," the vaudeville number Kelly performs with Donald O'Connor in the biographical montage. "The Broadway Ballet" is likewise shown to portray Kelly's later career. This number "says it all. An eager young hoofer from out of town. The first job in a speakeasy. In his dreams he will advance from vaudeville to modern dance; and like Gene Kelly, and the image of dance itself in America, he's going up in the world" (*Evening with Gene Kelly*). That except as an example of his work neither number corresponds factually to Kelly's life does not appear to matter, and why should it? These two segments from *Singin' in the Rain* can function as evidence of "Gene Kelly" for the interview because they carry that same value in the film itself.

Although the BBC program's account of Kelly misrepresents his biography, simply reproducing his screen persona, it reflects how *Singin' in the Rain* not only encapsulated the history of his star image but effectively reconstituted it as well. In contrast with his 1940s musicals, this film revises Kelly's image according to the alignment of gender and sexuality that became hegemonic in the 1950s, defining normative masculinity according to a stricter binary of male versus female, heterosexual versus homosexual. Indeed, "The Broadway Ballet" works so convincingly to heterosexualize Kelly and Don Lockwood alike because it characterizes the hoofer and the vamp through the narrow view of sexual difference consistent with that ideology. But as importantly, the film's other dance numbers retain disruptive traces of Kelly's provocative 1940s image, an image of camp masculinity still resonant in the biker number from *Les Girls* and still powerful enough to continue shaping the extrafilmic commentary after his MGM career in the repeated insistence that he is not and has never been a sissy dancer.

"More than any star, I think," Fred Astaire states in *That's Entertainment!* when introducing clips of his colleague's career, "Gene Kelly became the symbol of the MGM musical of the 1950s." This symbolic association is still entrenched in the popular imagination in large part because the media kept it in place following renewal of interest in the studio's musicals after the success of *That's Entertainment!* Until his death, interviews in print and television, newspaper and magazine articles, and documentary programs confirmed Kelly's role as elder statesman of the MGM musical; this role became more prominent with each issue of the *That's Entertainment!* franchise, and it was further validated by the critical canonization of *Singin' in the Rain*. Today, when inserted in a documentary about the studio era or used to promote Turner Classic Movies on cable, a shot of Kelly dancing in the rain or Times Square stands for "MGM musical" as readily as it evokes his own star image. Kelly's stardom *in* musicals was another matter altogether. The camp dialectic of his screen presence as a dancer "with balls" at the height of his film career stands out in bold contrast with what he came to symbolize decades afterward as the MGM poster boy. *Singin' in the Rain* still registers that dialectic but covers it over by using Don Lockwood, that ersatz Gene Kelly, as its camp alibi. Furthermore, that is not all this film does with its recycling of the MGM musical's history, as the next chapter discusses. There I shall examine, as the historical counterpoint to what I have been arguing about Kelly and *Singin' in the Rain* so far, why this most celebrated of the studio's many musicals well deserves its popular reputation as "the first camp picture."

Chapter Four

*I*t is an understatement to say that the various owners of the MGM library during the past half century have done well by *Singin' in the Rain*. One of eight musicals which the studio released in 1952, *Singin' in the Rain* was built around songs written for MGM in the late 1920s and 1930s by lyricist Arthur Freed in collaboration with composer Nacio Herb Brown. Freed's intent when initiating the project as a producer was to showcase his own song catalogue in much the way that his unit had previously done with the catalogues of Jerome Kern in *Till the Clouds Roll By* (1946), Richard Rodgers and Lorenz Hart in *Words and Music* (1948), and George and Ira Gershwin in *An American in Paris* (1951). Today, most everyone agrees that, transcending this initial purpose, *Singin' in the Rain* epitomizes the Freed unit's and Gene Kelly's artistry in perfecting the movie musical. It was ranked the fourth-best movie of all time in *Sight & Sound*'s 1982 polling of critics and tenth in the British magazine's 2002 tally, was among the first twenty-five titles to be listed by the U.S. National Film Registry in 1989, and placed tenth in the American Film Institute's "100 Greatest American Movies" in 2000.

The critical elevation of *Singin' in the Rain* apparently began when it was brought back into circulation in 1958 as part of an MGM package of studio classics. Then in 1962, before being handed over to television, *Singin' in the Rain* returned to theaters as a single reissue and the year following was included in another MGM series. During this time it was also discovered by film societies and was a standard item in revival houses. Viking Press published the screenplay by Betty Comden and Adolph Green in 1972, giving the text the imprint of an MGM classic, and shortly afterward the compilation tribute, *That's Entertainment!* (1974), drew attention back to the old musicals, this one in particular, so *Singin' in the Rain* was revived in theaters yet again. Since then, the film continues to show up with regularity in an eclectic assortment of venues, some not anticipated by its creators: in old downtown movie palaces and revival houses, museums, college classrooms, even the Hollywood Bowl with a live orchestral accompaniment in 1990. Although a vault fire destroyed the original negative, *Singin' in the Rain* now looks better than ever, too. The print was restored for theatrical exhibition on the occasion of its fortieth anniversary and redone in even more pristine condition with the aid of digital technology to mark its fiftieth.

This theatrical resilience is remarkable because, along with its dependable presence on television during the past four decades, *Singin' in the Rain* has been a staple of the home video market for classics. Aside from its continued availability on VHS, several editions were released on laser disc, including the high-end Criterion Collection series in 1988, immediately placing this musical alongside the cinema of Bergman, Fellini, and Hitchcock, and in the nineties the two remastered prints were each put out on DVD. The fiftieth-anniversary restoration in that format, appearing after the latest theatrical revival, reinforces the film's reputation. Distributed by Warner Home Video, which now controls the MGM library from the studio era, the two-disc set includes separate documentaries on the Freed unit and the making of the film, voiceover commentaries by people involved in the production (Debbie Reynolds, Donald O'Connor, Cyd Charisse, Kathleen Freeman, Stanley Donen, Comden and Green) as well as film historian Rudy Behlmer and director Baz Luhrmann, visual annotations of the history inspiring the story's setting in the industry's transition from silents to talkies, prerecorded tracks (some with alternate lyrics or arrangements), and numbers from the older MGM musicals which *Singin' in the Rain* references through its previously used Freed-Brown songs.[1] Paralleling the long shelf life on home video, the soundtrack of *Singin' in the Rain* has been issued on various labels following the recording industry's format changes during the past half century from 45s to LPs to cassettes to CDs. These have been produced in increasingly more complete versions, with a two-disc fiftieth-anniversary CD edition released in 2002 by Rhino Records, another Time-Warner subsidiary, to complement the DVD.

The prestige of *Singin' in the Rain* as "the ultimate MGM musical," as Behlmer calls it on the DVD's commentary track, remains undiminished, so much so that fifty years after its release Kelly's rendition of the title song is, if not "the single most memorable dance number on film" (Wollen, 9), then certainly the most instantly recognizable one. Whether watched in the film or as an excerpt, Behlmer concludes, this number has "never worn out its welcome . . . It works, and it works for everybody." The same applies to *Singin' in the Rain* in its entirety. New viewers, particularly those who do not enjoy musicals, always seem taken by surprise that this one still delivers on its advertising tag, "What a Glorious Feeling." Peter M. Bracke, editor and founder of DVDFile.com, began his review of the fiftieth-anniversary DVD (his first viewing of the film), by noting that *Singin' in the Rain* "actually lives up to all the hype." It is "that true gem, a feel-good, Technicolor concoction of a movie that for once doesn't result in sugar shock. It left me feeling good, footloose and fancy free." This is much the same spirit in which Steve Martin offered his suggestion, quoted in Army Archerd's *Daily Variety* column on 20 March 2003, that putting George W. Bush and Saddam Hussein together in a room to watch *Singin' in the Rain* would prevent the imminent invasion of Iraq by the United States, an event with the potential to disrupt the coming weekend's Academy Awards ceremony. "I don't think we'd have much of a problem," Martin explained, "because the nature of that movie is to celebrate joy and fun and silliness. So how could two men, even those who have vast ideological differences such as when and how much to bomb the living daylights out of each other, hate one another after seeing 'Singin' in the Rain'?" (As it happened, the column ran on the very day when the Pentagon announced it would hold off on its planned "Shock and Awe attack" but began it that evening anyway; the Oscars went on as scheduled the following Sunday with Martin as emcee; and a screening of *Singin' in the Rain* was not made a high priority in Washington or Baghdad.)

Singin' in the Rain stands out as "the ultimate MGM musical" because it can simultaneously be appreciated as one of the best films ever made *and* as feel-good escapism from a bygone era that still works its movie magic. "What makes *Singin' in the Rain* so special?" Debbie Reynolds asks when introducing *What a Glorious Feeling*, the making-of documentary on the DVD. To answer, she notes that film historians, analyzing the film's "tightly woven story, spectacular musical numbers, and wonderful performances," all reach the same conclusion: "It's just a fabulous movie." All the more curious, isn't it then, to hear Kelly remarking in his 1974 BBC interview, "A lot of people have called it the first camp picture." Even though he immediately added his own uncertainty about the camp label, muttering, "I don't know," Kelly said he had in mind the film's send-up of recognizable Hollywood types, such as the gossip columnist and studio head who were based on actual persons, Louella Parsons and "our own Arthur Freed," respectively (*Evening with Gene Kelly*). To this example one can add the send-ups of Roaring Twenties glamour, silent film acting, the industry's frantic and inept conversion to sound, the manufacturing of Hollywood stardom, and so forth.

But is this parody the stuff of camp? Not as Comden and Green tell it in their introduction to the published screenplay. In this account, reprinted in the pamphlets for the two most recent CDs, the send-up of the silent era's demise more simply reflects how they were taking "the dramatic upheavals of that period, when great careers were wrecked," and fitting "the stuff of tragedy" into "a lighthearted satirical comedy that featured fifteen or twenty Freed-Brown songs along the way" (5). Their "lighthearted" comedy is achieved by way of a retrospective look at the movie musical's beginnings which takes for granted the superior modernity of the present, knowing what is outdated and what is not. The send-up of the travails with which, as the trailer for *Singin' in the Rain* puts it, "the screen learned to talk . . . and the talkies started to sing," is premised on an understanding shared with viewers that the conversion to sound began the inevitable, beneficial progression for both the industry and audiences of laughable silent film genres and bad acting into the more sophisticated, pleasurable dance musicals which the Freed unit specialized in making and which Kelly personified for the moviegoing public after *American in Paris*. In hindsight those musicals were themselves approaching obsolescence, just like the silent era's historical melodramas being parodied. Writing two decades after the release of *Singin' in the Rain*, Comden and Green observed in 1972 that a number of the great Freed musicals "survive, not as 'camp' or sociological curiosa, but as films to be enjoyed, admired, and even wondered at— expressions of a form that has all but vanished" (2).

Reinforcing what I argued in the previous chapter, the screen-writers' defensiveness about the Freed musicals' survival "as 'camp' or sociological curiosa" makes it difficult to see how *Singin' in the Rain* can be called a camp picture let alone be considered the first one. Kelly's own remark notwithstanding, camp rarely supplies the criterion for *Singin' in the Rain*'s unquestioned renown as an American classic. Yet the connection Kelly offered in passing does make some sense historically, deserving further examination.

Singin' in the Rain can indeed be thought of as "the first camp picture" insofar as it participated early on in the migration of camp toward the mainstream. Thus even though I have already looked at this film rather closely through its revisionist treatment of Kelly's camp masculinity, I now want to view it more directly in the light of what happened during the past half century, when, as already noted in the introduction, camp became more democratized as "mass camp": a nonqueer and ahistorical "sensibility that views past Holly-wood films as inadvertent campy send-ups" (Klinger, 133). An audi-ence finding a mass-camp value in old films watches from a posi-tion of historical as well as aesthetic disengagement; it forgets "the fact that such forms had been shaped by their own industrial and social conditions of production" and laughs instead at conventions that seem hokey, artificial, or quaintly anachronistic "in comparison to present representational systems that appear to have greater veri-similitude" (141). Although she traces this phenomenon back to the sixties and seventies, and does not mention *Singin' in the Rain*, Barbara Klinger could well be describing how this musical represents old Hollywood from a perspective that is now more recognizable as the characteristic stance of mass camp. In both its "lighthearted" screen-play and recycling of the Freed-Brown song catalogue, *Singin' in the Rain* imposes a Pop-styled modernity over the past in order to por-tray the obsolescence of old musicals as hokey artifice manufactured by Hollywood during an earlier, more naive and technically primi-tive era; this strategy for investing the genre with new value, more-over, is consistent with the way the film revises Kelly's star image by sending up his alter ego, Don Lockwood. The parodic self-reflexivity of *Singin' in the Rain*, in short—why this film routinely gets singled out as *the* classic musical from the studio era, why it appears to have been ready-made for that present-day veneration, and why it remains the one musical from the studio era that still seems perfectly accessible to *contemporary* audiences, even those who ordinarily dislike the genre—openly makes itself legible to viewers as "camp," and it does so without appearing to have any queer signification whatsoever.

CINEPHILES, CULTISM, AND CAMP

Accounts of *Singin' in the Rain*'s reception in the commentaries on the high-end video product mention that, before being universally recognized as a classic, it first found a cult audience through the repeated showings in revival houses and on television during the decades following the film's theatrical release in 1952. On the anniversary DVD, Reynolds closes the making-of documentary by referring to the film's "rebirth when it developed a cult following"; in the audio commentary, Behlmer calls the first renewal of interest "this cult thing"; and in both the audio and documentary, Donald O'Connor describes the musical's fame as "like a cult movie." Kelly was alluding to this "cult" rediscovery of his musical when he mentioned in 1974 that some people consider *Singin' in the Rain* "the first camp picture."

The cult reputation of *Singin' in the Rain* never elevated it to the pantheon of mass cultural icons like *The Wizard of Oz* (1939), which also saw an audience revival through television at this same time but on a much larger scale, all the while remaining a gay cult film. Rather, the cult forming around *Singin' in the Rain* was driven by cinephiles: industry professionals, film reviewers, die-hard movie fans. Disagreeing with the high culture/mass culture debates of the fifties which dismissed film as passive or harmful escapism, they defended this musical as a perfect attainment of unpretentious, popular art by the Hollywood factory system. In his audio-essay on the Criterion laser disc, Ronald Haver—the same archivist who spearheaded the restoration of *A Star is Born* (1954)—begins by warning listeners that his remarks will not offer "a heavy analysis" because *Singin' in the Rain* "doesn't bear heavy analysis." Yet the film does appear to hold up to repeated viewings by film aficionados like Haver. Quoting early on a Lina Lamont malapropism (her declaration that she makes more money than "Calvin Coolidge—put together"), a chuck-ling Haver justifies remembering the joke out of sequence by describ-ing it as one of those "lines that run through every cinephile's head." Revealing the same kind of fascination with *Singin' in the Rain*, Roger Ebert confesses in a retrospective review that he has watched the musical "at least once a year" after first seeing it at the old Clark repertory theater in downtown Chicago. And Comden and Green re-call being approached in the late sixties by "a breathless and awe-struck" François Truffaut who rapturously confessed "that he had seen the film many times, knew every frame of it, felt it was a classic, and that he and Alain Resnais, among others, went to see it regularly at a little theater called the Pagode, where it was even at that moment in the middle of a several-month run" (10).

The film curator at the Los Angeles County Art Museum (Haver), a widely quoted newspaper and television reviewer (Ebert), and an esteemed French director (Truffaut)—*Singin' in the Rain* does not seem the kind of film likely to attract the dedication described by these cinephiles. To be sure, the musical was scripted by writers who placed themselves in this category: "We both knew the period [in which *Singin' in the Rain* is set] intimately and were amateur authori-ties on silent films and early talkies," Comden and Green declare, "long before Cinema 1 and 2 was a subject taught in every kinder-garten in the country" (5). Even so, the Donen-Kelly musical does not meet the profile of the more typical cult classic such as *Vertigo* (1958), to mention another film from the fifties which acquired a comparable reputation among cinephiles a decade or so after its initial release and also made its way to the *Sight & Sound* ten best list. *Singin' in the Rain* was not the work of a high-profile auteur director; it did not get disappointing box-office returns and meet with a lackluster, dis-missive critical reception warranting reappraisal. Nor is *Singin' in the Rain* like the B movies also rediscovered by cinephiles, such as *Kiss Me Deadly* (1955), which made no claim whatsoever to middlebrow sig-nificance because of its irreverent pulp energy and low budget. *Singin' in the Rain* came to revival houses bearing all too respectable studio credentials—MGM, Arthur Freed, Gene Kelly—and should therefore have been written off as lavishly produced yet lightweight escapism, not watched over and over again until cinephiles remembered every line and knew every frame.

For that matter, the cult following of *Singin' in the Rain* does not seem immediately reconcilable with the direction of cinephile film criticism as Greg Taylor charts its emergence in his study of Manny Farber and Parker Tyler, two influential reviewers of the 1940s and fifties. Analyzing their different approaches, Taylor distinguishes between Farber's "cultism," which "identifies and refuses 'mass' taste by developing a resistant cult taste for more obscure and less clearly commodified cultural objects" (15), and Tyler's "camp," which is "more process-oriented than cultism . . . it demonstrates that potentially *any* mass culture object can be re-created aesthetically" (16). Although his discussion of Farber and Tyler maintains their polarity, "both traditions," Taylor mentions in his concluding remarks, were "skillfully mainstream[ed]" in the sixties by Pauline Kael (122)—who happened to be one of the first to champion *Singin' in the Rain* in print, referring to it as "just about the best Hollywood musical of all time" in a 1962 review criticizing the deadening high art pretensions of *West Side Story* (1961) (Kael, 128). Keeping in mind the eventual union of "cultism" and "camp" in journalistic writing like Kael's, *Singin' in the Rain* may have been a more logical choice for cinephile reappraisal than is first apparent: the film aesthetically recreates the movie musical's past, sending it up as "camp," in order to promote a "cultist" taste for the genre in the present as a self-reflective yet entertaining popular art form, thereby giving the two opposing critical approaches laid out by Taylor an opportunity to merge.

Baz Luhrmann's contemporary response as part of the DVD commentary illustrates my point. Referring to the opening montage when Don Lockwood narrates his life story in contradiction with what is being shown, Luhrmann remarks: "It sets up the rules, and that is, is that we're going to wink at you all the way through this thing, right? So, it allows you to accept the fact that, every now and then, you're reminded, really clearly, that you're watching a movie." Likewise, during "You Were Meant for Me" he observes of the number's self-conscious use of its locale on an empty soundstage, "every now and then you're reminded you're watching a movie. Some people just see that as a lovely musical number. Others will perceive that they're being winked at yet again." In effect, *Singin' in the Rain* says to Lurhmann, "Don't take me seriously because I am just 'a movie,' and I am serious about being that." Describing the musical's self-reflexivity as a wink, Lurhmann shows that he's hep to *Singin' in the Rain*'s display of camp—that is, camp as "a vision of the world in terms of style"; camp as "the love of the exaggerated, the 'off,' of things-being-what-they-are-not"; camp as seeing "everything in quotation marks" (Sontag, 56). The self-reflexive winks and their acknowledgment by this director—chosen for inclusion in the DVD's ensemble of commentators because of his own contemporary "winking" musical, *Moulin Rouge* (2001)—distinguish between an ordinary viewer consuming pleasures manufactured for him or her and the more knowing "cultist" cinephile able to see a "camp" alternative in the film's self-mocking send-up of its genre, its conventions, and its apparatus. However, there is nothing particularly queer about this cultist-camp wink, either on the part of Luhrmann or the film's own self-reflexive imposition of artifice over illusionism.

I don't mean to conflate Lurhmann's contemporary appreciation of *Singin' in the Rain* with the cult animating its reputation decades earlier but rather to place them together in order to indicate where the cult following was headed because of when it began. It is no accident that a cinephile cult forming around *Singin' in the Rain* started in the late fifties and sixties. For this was also the period when the Pop movement appropriated camp as, and so reduced it to, a visual style deriving from the throwaway mass-produced artifacts of popular culture, including movies and their stars. Andrew Ross dates the corollary emergence of "Pop Camp" as a category of taste during these same years, which "saw the recirculation of classic Hollywood films on television, giving rise to the first wave of revivalist nostalgia, and to the cult of Hollywoodiania" (56). The camp effect of that type of cult revival, Ross claims, is created when commodities from "a much earlier mode of production, which has lost its power to produce and dominate cultural meanings, become available, in the present, for redefinition according to contemporary codes of taste" (58). Perhaps something of the same can be attributed to nostalgia. However, Pop Camp differed from nostalgia in recognizing that all mass-culture commodities face obsolescence, their cultural worth following a logic of perishable surplus values—the sense in which Ross describes camp as "a rediscovery of history's waste" (66).

The Pop movement began camp's entry into the mainstream. Not long after Susan Sontag's "Notes on Camp" appeared in *Partisan Re-*

view, the television series *Batman* (1966–68) then indelibly linked camp and Pop together, with the media frequently quoting from Sontag to explain the TV show's hugely popular reception and its stylistic intentions (Torres). Despite the source material's own queer subtext, *Batman* was instrumental in further broadening and heterosexualizing the term's meaning in general usage until, as Moe Meyer contends, "camp" became "confused and conflated with rhetorical strategies such as irony, satire, burlesque, and travesty: and with cultural movements such as Pop" (7). With its queer intentions obscured, camp was also depoliticized, misrecognized as "a dominant performative gesture of incorporation meant to muzzle an opposing voice by substituting the act of appropriation itself as the referent of camp" (14). The residual persistence of camp's historical source in queer social practices remained somewhat visible—in this regard, camp was "outed" by Pop—but was neutralized as the "harmless reassignment of values to junk store items that Pop theorists have convinced themselves is 'camp' " (15).

Emptying camp of its history and its politics, the Pop version enabled straight-identified audiences to enjoy what had originated in queer tastes as a cultish vanguard (for instance, of fashion, decor, music, films) while disavowing any connection to sexual dissidence. Thus, even while it continued to be recognized as the social coding of "gay," often with homophobic and stigmatizing connotations (as in the media coverage), camp was detached from queer practices—and even, eventually, from Pop. In the wake of Sontag and *Batman*, as Pop Camp morphed into mass camp, "oblig[ing] a certain annulment of a text's historicity" (Klinger, 141), a camp label could account for almost any kind of audience formation around artifacts of popular culture which made no claim to seriousness, authenticity, originality— or queerness. Camp Lite, as it were.

According to Ross, Pop Camp contradictorily put together the marginality carried over from camp's history as a queer practice with the egalitarian but flattened values evident in the wide appeal of mass culture as a means of negotiating how "this most democratic of cultures could be partially 'recognized' by intellectuals" (66). The cinephiles repeatedly watching *Singin' in the Rain* at this same time never related their revaluation of its merits and pleasures to camp (Pop, mass, or otherwise), but they were engaged in a negotiation of

film tastes similar to the one Ross describes occurring among intellectuals. Cinephiles defended their passionate commitment to film
as a popular art by distinguishing their judgments from elitist standards on the one hand and Hollywood nostalgia on the other, following an aesthetic "sensibility" modeled on camp but as reinflected
through the Pop movement's dismissal of high culture. Further, the
rise of academic film courses in the postwar university along with
the "explosion of media recycling" by Hollywood and on television
in the 1960s and 1970s created "an audience schooled in convention
and primed by parodies to discover the inherent artifice of the more
'naïve' products of the film industry," fostering the "savvy" mass-
camp response to classic Hollywood product (Klinger, 139).

That *Singin' in the Rain* played a role in this development, however minor, indicates the proximity of the cinephiles' defense of
popular film to Pop and mass camp in the continuum of new dis-
courses through which studio-era Hollywood was being reassessed
according to the tastes of a burgeoning new film culture. Hence my
earlier claim that *Singin' in the Rain* invited a merger of cultist and
camp approaches to popular film. This musical was ripe for cult reappraisal via mass camp because, in its retelling of the genre's origin
and recycling of the Freed-Brown song catalogue, *Singin' in the Rain* is
itself appropriating from "a much earlier mode of production, which
has lost its power to produce and dominate cultural meanings." In
other words, the operation of mass camp in renewing obsolete forms
of "*discursive value* production, not *industrial object* production," as
Meyer helpfully qualifies Ross's phrasing (14), applies equally well to
Singin' in the Rain's account of silent film's demise with the coming of
sound in 1927, to its own status as an MGM musical in 1952 when the
genre's popularity was about to wane in response to changes in industry practices and audience tastes, and to the film's new currency
for the cinephiles rediscovering it later on.

THE SCREEN STARTS TO SING

Singin' in the Rain is "first" among musicals, as Ebert puts it, "because
it is not only from Hollywood, it is about Hollywood"—yet as far
as *Singin' in the Rain* is concerned, "Hollywood" is the MGM musical. Jane Feuer points out that musicals about the creation of popular

entertainment tend to represent "the history of the *genre* as the story of a continuing cycle of conservation within innovation, or, to put it in a more radical perspective, of innovation *as* conservation" (*Hollywood Musical*, 91). *Singin' in the Rain* inverts this pattern; it cites the MGM musical's history as its central frame of reference in order to depict generic conservation as a trajectory toward innovation. Comden's and Green's screenplay works hand-in-hand with Kelly's and Donen's staging of the Freed-Brown song catalogue to celebrate the MGM musical's history but also to send it up. With this double move *Singin' in the Rain* invites a mass-camp viewership; although obviously that audience formation was not the overt target in 1952, the film encourages a viewer to wink *with* rather than *at* its representation of old Hollywood, which is why, two decades later, it could be considered "the first camp picture."

But with this overview I am also getting ahead of myself. Keeping in mind what Klinger states about the ahistoricism of mass-camp appreciations of old movies, I first need to demonstrate how the account of the talkies' arrival in *Singin' in the Rain* supplies the ground for the mass-camp recycling I go on to look at in the rest of this chapter. The Comden-Green screenplay mythicizes the MGM musical's status in the present day by selectively remembering and as selectively forgetting the genre's own industrial history as a mode of production, starting from its origin in the conversion to sound technology and extending toward its uncertain future in the early 1950s. As made evident by the many anachronisms that arise through the course of the film's account of sound's impact, the affectionate send-up of the early talkies era effectively removes historicity from the picture.

To be sure, while watching *Singin' in the Rain*'s recreation of 1927 as the year dividing the silent and sound eras, it seems perfectly reasonable to agree with its premise that the movie musical was introduced with a bang. It was the genre that best surprised, then delighted audiences with the new Vitaphone technology heralded by Al Jolson's breaking into song several times and speaking some impromptu lines in the otherwise silent Warner Bros. film, *The Jazz Singer* (1927). Film historian Richard Barrios notes that, despite "some elisions and oversimplifications" when depicting the industry's conversion to sound, "*Singin' in the Rain* remains true to the spirit of its sources" (5). Similarly, Haver observes on the Criterion LD: "the elements of the story of *Singin' in the Rain* were all grounded pretty much on actualities," and Kelly also declared, "Everything in *Singin' in the Rain* is true" (*Evening with Gene Kelly*). As evidence of this historical authenticity, it is frequently pointed out that Comden, Green, Donen, and Kelly took pains to incorporate oldtimers' recollections about the coming of sound, even to hunt down and use the cumbersome old equipment from that era as props, such as the noisy, stationary camera fitted inside a booth for soundproofing (Wollen, 54).

Yet for all its fidelity to details, *Singin' in the Rain* noticeably glosses over the slower, more deliberated course by which the various studios converted to sound as an industry standard (Crafton, 1–22). From the start there were two technologies in competition, Warners's Vitaphone sound-on-disc process, the one shown in *Singin' in the Rain*, and Fox's more flexible Movietone sound-on-film process, which all the other studios, including MGM, used in one form or another. Both Vitaphone and Movietone were initially tried out in musical shorts or newsreels and presented as novelty attractions before being applied to feature-length movies, a more expensive and much riskier undertaking. The first features to use sound, moreover, were not all-talking pictures, let alone musicals like *Singin' in the Rain*, but part-talkies like *The Jazz Singer*, silent films with snatches of dialogue, sound effects, musical scores, perhaps some numbers. Although *Jazz Singer* still gets full credit for prompting an industry-wide rush to make talkies, Warners's follow-up hits in 1928, *The Lights of New York* and Jolson's *The Singing Fool*, convinced the other studios to convert to sound (Crafton, 275). Nearly two years after *Jazz Singer*, MGM's *The Broadway Melody* (1929)—advertised with the slogan, "ALL TALKING, ALL SINGING, ALL DANCING"—was "the first true musical film . . . The work that established movie musicals as potent and viable entertainment" not because of "what it did first, but what it did *right*" (Barrios, 59). With the popular and critical success of *Broadway Melody*, the bandwagon started to roll for musicals at full speed.[2]

No doubt the Comden-Green screenplay condenses this history for reasons of narrative economy, but it does not do so innocently. According to its retelling, *The Jazz Singer*'s unexpected impact brings silent film production to an abrupt halt, requiring the industry's immediate conversion to sound recording while causing artistic chaos as filmmakers and performers struggle to adapt the techniques of silent films to talkies. By way of this temporal condensation, it also appears that, despite the chaos, musicals begin to be produced almost the day after *Jazz Singer* premieres—or at least the montage recording the immediate impact of the "first" talkie depicts it happening this way. A series of undated *Variety* headlines announce in quick succession, "Revolution in Hollywood," "Studios Convert to Talkies," and "Musical Pictures Sweep Nation." Following this seamless continuity of events, "bits of typical musical numbers in the style of vintage 1929–1930 film musicals" (Comden and Green, 41) imply the impact not of *Jazz Singer*, but of *Broadway Melody* and MGM's second all-singing, all-dancing hit, the all-star *Hollywood Revue of 1929* (1929), notable now for introducing the song "Singin' in the Rain." The four "typical" Freed-Brown numbers, not all from 1929–30 pictures, briefly appear in sequence as a parodic homage to the genre overtaking the country, then are rapidly cut together in a kind of generic frenzy, only to segue into a fifth "vintage" song, "Beautiful Girl," done as a full-scale production number, complete with a fashion show of twenties glamour.

Comden's and Green's description of the talkies montage acknowledges that it compiles anachronisms since the story so definitively takes place during a relatively short time span in 1927. Visually, the sequence refers backward in time as well as ahead. The mise-en-scène blends references to trends and styles from throughout the 1920s (Jazz Age flappers, the Charleston, a Rudy Vallee–type crooner) and the early 1930s (the mobile camerawork, overhead views, and kaleidoscopic arrangement of dancers' bodies exemplified by Busby Berkeley's Warner Bros. musicals beginning with *42nd Street* in 1933, a cinematic style achieved only after modification of early sound technology allowed for tracking crane shots). Nor does the montage as a whole aim to reproduce the look and sound of the earliest musicals. It is shot in Technicolor, the dancers wear makeup designed for that color process, the sequence uses some animation and matte effects, and the arrangements and orchestrations of the songs are new. For that matter, the fashion show in "Beautiful Girl" may have "vintage" antecedents but it follows a convention still operative at MGM, as in *Lovely to Look At* (1952), released the same year as *Singin in the Rain.*

Of all the numbers in the talkies montage, "Beautiful Girl" is particularly anachronistic. It is shown being filmed at Monumental Pictures, the fictional version of MGM, right after *Jazz Singer* causes the studio to convert immediately to sound; yet as Haver observes on the Criterion LD, the number's production within the film includes technology inaccurate for the 1927 setting, such as an unenclosed camera and a microphone hanging overhead. Furthermore, no orchestra is present to record the music live, as was the practice before 1929, and despite the visible presence of a microphone for the singing, the scene also appears to follow the later protocol of using a prerecorded track for musical numbers, since while watching "Beautiful Girl" being filmed, the director and studio head chat about Kathy Selden, one of the dancers in the number, in earshot of Cosmo Brown.[3] In these small but observable details, "Beautiful Girl" unaccountably belies the very cumbersome technological elements of making an early talkie in 1927 which, very soon after the montage, will supply fodder for the comedy of Lina Lamont's inability to cope with sound recording when *Duelling Cavalier* is started anew as a Vitaphone talkie.

The thinking behind the talkies montage may well have been that for a 1952 audience the twenties and thirties were all the same in connoting "old-fashioned" as opposed to "modern," sufficient enough to convey the "vintage" impression despite the intrusion of contemporary technology, so the anachronisms didn't matter. But they do signal how, by foreshortening the time in which "the screen learned to talk . . . and the talkies started to sing," the sequence from the *Variety* headlines through "Beautiful Girl" makes the arrival of sound hinge on the industry's conversion not just to talkies but to musicals in particular. The compression determines that the successful teaming of Lamont and Lockwood in historical melodramas is doomed from the moment Jolson opens his mouth. As a result, the somewhat longer historical view which the montage condenses supplies the informing context for the subsequent parody of *Duelling Cavalier* as obsolete even with Vitaphone; and what this does is shift the focus from the historical development of sound, with its fatal impact on silent films, to the musical's emergence as the prime Hollywood genre of the modern sound era.

Ignoring the incongruities of "Beautiful Girl" as a number filmed

70

The "Beautiful Girl" number in *Singin' in the Rain* (MGM, 1952).

within the film, *Singin' in the Rain* thus builds its satiric look back to 1927 on the problems resulting from the industry's first approaching sound as if it were a little something extra merely embellishing the visual image. "You do what you always do. You just add talking to it," studio head R. F. Simpson declares just before the talkies montage begins. Following this dictum, Monumental Pictures stumbles into the talkies era with disastrous results: Lamont's and Lockwood's *Duelling Cavalier* uses the new technology crudely, if hilariously, simply adding hokey, impromptu dialogue and overamplified sound effects to the pantomime acting style carried over from silent film. Saving the day, to rescue both the studio's future and the career of its leading male star, is this turkey's transformation into a full-fledged musical, the all-talking and now all-singing, all-dancing *Dancing Cavalier*. The generic metamorphosis, moreover, occurs during the short time elapsing between the sneak preview and the prearranged release date set for six weeks later. The ineptly made talkie, which caused audiences to laugh with derision at its first showing, is reshot and redubbed as an extended song-filled dream sequence that, in turn, is placed in a newly written modern backstage narrative represented in

Singin' in the Rain by "The Broadway Ballet." As a recreation of *Broadway Melody*'s title song (Don Lockwood refers to the number by this name when describing it), the ballet makes full use of the hitherto untapped singing and dancing talents of its leading man, honed through his background in vaudeville—and audiences wildly cheer the result. Shout hallelujah and a big amen, the movie musical is born!

With this condensed account of the musical's beginnings, *Singin' in the Rain* invests the genre with special importance for the economic future of Hollywood: as a form unimaginable without the addition of sound, the movie musical takes the film industry forward in the evolution of popular entertainment through modern technology. For a point of comparison consider how differently *Babes in Arms* (1939) represents the same events. The first MGM musical to credit Arthur Freed as a producer, *Babes in Arms* also features a montage recounting the period of sound's arrival and the subsequent boom in musicals, but here sound wields the death blow to vaudeville, "the greatest entertainment in the world," as Joe Moran (Charles Winninger) proclaims in 1921 when toasting the backstage birth of his son, Mickey (Mickey Rooney). A prescient friend, Maddox (Henry Hull), offers a note of caution, warning, "There's a shadow coming up—it may change things a lot. It's getting taller, that shadow, wider, very fast. The motion picture." Moran dismisses the threat with laughter, anticipating Kathy Selden's criticism of Don Lockwood's silent film acting in *Singin' in the Rain* as "a lot of dumb show . . . nothing but a shadow on film." "Shadow is right," the vaudevillian counters. "Making faces! A flash in the pan. Motion pictures change things? Not until the Hudson catches fire!" "I hope you're right," Maddox replies, adding, "Here's to forty weeks—may it last forever."

Reiterating the dramatic irony behind this exchange, a 1923 *Variety* headline trumpets, "Vaudeville Booms!" The header introduces a montage of Moran and his wife on tour across the nation during the next several years, with little Mickey joining the act. The New Year's celebration ushering in 1927 casts the ominous shadow of what is to come, but it is a 1929 headline of *Variety* that exclaims, "Talkies Arrive! Film Grosses 100G's in Record Week," followed by a brief clip from *Broadway Melody* to identify this record-breaking film. Then a 1930 *Variety* headline announces the full impact of that arrival, "Film Songs Sweep Nation—'Singing in the Rain' Sweeps Country," and a snippet of that number in *Hollywood Revue of 1929* illustrates. Successive headlines from the trade newspaper go on to record the industry's full conversion to sound in 1932: "Garbo Talks! All Key Houses Wired for Sound" and "Talkies Top Vaudeville! Vaudeville Hits Abnormal Slump," until the inevitable outcome happens, "Vaudeville Doomed!"

This montage explicitly incorporates references to MGM's first two musicals as touchstones of the talking picture's influence (record grosses and hit songs), but *Babes in Arms* nonetheless looks back nostalgically to vaudeville as a sort of prelapsarian state of popular culture's technological innocence, regretting the talkies' destructive impact on "that happy yesteryear of entertainment which was called vaudeville," as the opening title card describes it. *Babes in Arms* goes on to recreate this lost tradition through a grassroots revival by the talented children of unemployed vaudevillians, thereby giving "the greatest entertainment in the world" a new, more contemporary demographic appeal. Mickey Moran partners with Patsy Barton (Judy Garland) in a backyard production of a minstrel show, which leads to a full stage production of "God's Country," financed by the always sagacious Maddox.

True, the sleight of hand is inescapable: *Babes in Arms* uses the movie musical, which supposedly killed vaudeville, to reinvigorate the latter's democratic spirit as the people's entertainment. But this should not detract from the significance of how *Babes in Arms* represents the arrival of talkies to make the case for perpetuating vaudeville as an entertainment tradition in defiance of Hollywood's alteration of popular tastes through innovations in its technology. Unlike the montage in *Singin' in the Rain*, this one more carefully delineates the process by which musicals appeared and theaters nationwide became wired during the years 1929–32, resulting in the elimination of live acts from the vaudeville palaces' bill as they switched over to movies full-time. The *Babes in Arms* montage records the older tradition's erosion in the face of the movie musical's improvement of the film medium, while also bypassing the Depression as a causal factor acting on the entertainment industry as a whole. By recording the asymmetrical histories of one form's growing popularity and the other's diminishing appeal, the montage can then substantiate vaudeville's existence *beyond* film, motivating the nostalgic value later attributed to its revival *on* film when Rooney and Garland get all the kids together to put on a show.

Singin' in the Rain draws on the same conventions which *Babes in Arms* uses to synopsize the talkies' stimulation of a musicals boom, even including *Variety* headlines. The latter is a timeworn device in musicals, but with the two montages placed side-by-side, *Singin' in the Rain* appears to be playfully rhyming its account with the one in the earlier film (not surprising, perhaps, since *Babes in Arms* is the source of "Good Mornin' " and, according to Behlmer on the DVD, Donen, Comden, and Green watched old MGM films for source material and inspiration in preparing their film). But as well as condensing the time frame and attributing causality solely to *The Jazz Singer*, the 1952 musical awards a different value to the genre created instantaneously once sound is added to the image. By equating the conversion to sound with the full-blown birth of the movie musical, *Singin' in the Rain* shows that the new genre is superior to both silent film and live performance because it makes full use of modern technology, as demonstrated initially by the talkies montage and then more completely by the ballet, a number more technically ambitious than anything imaginable in 1927. Consequently, as *Singin' in the Rain* goes on to depict 1927 as the transitional moment in film history, vaudeville does not end with the arrival of talkies but is happily incorporated into the new genre, which carries on its tradition but does it better. As the title suggests, "The Broadway Ballet" has nothing to do with Hollywood. This important number—meant to illustrate how *Dancing Cavalier* builds on Lockwood's former career in vaudeville—follows the logic of the montage's historical condensation and anachronisms. The ballet represents the modern-day film musical's development out of both its MGM past, i.e., *Broadway Melody*, and the tradition of live performing—the hoofer rises to stardom through burlesque, vaudeville, and the Ziegfeld Follies—that preceded the talkies and inspired the first "true" musical two years after *The Jazz Singer*.

Somewhat uncannily paralleling *Babes in Arms*'s account of the economic demise and nostalgic revival of vaudeville, however, *Singin' in the Rain*'s re-creation of the musical's origin is itself framed by a nervous glance at the genre's uncertain present, which motivates the celebratory view of its value in the past. When *Singin' in the Rain* was released in 1952, a rival technology which also put together sound and image—namely, television—was already being perceived as strong competition for film audiences. The TV variety show, which featured live musical performances in a format drawing on vaudeville, offered home viewers an alternative venue for the entertainment associated with musicals, even without the technical sophistication and production values that television would later acquire. In fact, broadcast live in black and white, featuring performers not yet accustomed to the new medium, and with staging often awkwardly geared to the requirements of its technology, the variety shows of this era resembled the first musicals, as Barrios notes when comparing *Hollywood Revue* to "early television," and the resemblance is even stronger when one recalls how audiences were "awed" by both innovative media, despite their apparent shortcomings (163).

Television was not the only challenge to the film musical's claims of being "the greatest entertainment in the world." The studio system controlling production, distribution, and exhibition of films in the United States, a monopoly which the introduction of sound technology in the late 1920s helped to implement for some companies (like Warners) and solidify for others (like MGM), was being dismantled as a result of the federal antitrust suit brought against the five major companies. The landmark case was successfully resolved in 1948 with the Paramount consent decree forcing divestiture of the studios' theater chains. For MGM the vertical integration had been especially important to its production of musicals; theater ownership supplied the incentive for producing a large number of films annually, and theater profits maintained the studio's physical plant, specialized departments, large roster of contract players and technicians, and investment in stars—all indispensable elements in making a musical like *Singin' in the Rain*.

Loew's, MGM's corporate parent, waited longer than the other majors to spin off its theater chain into a separate entity. The year when Kelly, Donen, and company made *Singin' in the Rain*, the company was also flush with profits from *Show Boat* (1951) and *An American in Paris*, both huge hits. *Singin' in the Rain* performed almost as well at the box office, so these successes seemed to promise a rosy future for the studio's musicals. All the same, the economic structure enabling the genre's regularized production was already showing its vulnerability because of the consent decree, predicting how the MGM musical would soon be as "doomed" as *Variety* declares vaudeville is after the talkies achieve their dominance in *Babes in Arms*. Not many people saw the situation this way until a bit later in the decade, but the signs were already in evidence. Coupled with the rival attraction of television, the huge fall-off in movie attendance starting in 1948, the same year as the federal decree breaking up the studios, sounded a crisis which the industry did hear—and to which *Singin' in the Rain* is also responding in its condensed account of 1927 as a comparable moment of upheaval in the film industry. Although not too long afterward musicals would begin displaying a lack of confidence in the genre's underlying "belief in Hollywood itself as the great inheritor of musical entertainment" (Feuer, *Hollywood Musical*, 87), *Singin' in the Rain* still clings to that belief, with the "lighthearted" account of the talkies' arrival mythicizing the MGM musical's longevity as proof of its currency. Anchoring this myth, the recycled Freed-Brown catalogue of standards then slants it more toward the way mass camp operates.

MGM'S MUSICAL TREASURE

The many anachronisms in Comden's and Green's parodic account of the film industry's conversion to sound emphasize the MGM musical's importance as the cornerstone of that event, preparing the way for a mass-camp renewal of the genre's value as entertainment for the 1950s. Referentially speaking, *Singin' in the Rain* therefore keeps leading us right back to Culver City. The recycled song catalogue of Freed and Brown further solidifies this circumscribed referential field and keeps it steadily in view through the numbers' modern reshaping of their historical sources. In contrast with the songs of Kern, Rogers and Hart, and the Gershwins featured in the other Freed catalogue musicals, the old tunes dusted off for *Singin' in the Rain* have antecedents specifically identifying them with MGM, going back to the studio's first "all-talking, all-singing, all-dancing" musicals, *Broadway Melody* and *Hollywood Revue*. Comden and Green note that their decision to place the story of *Singin' in the Rain* "during the painful transition from silence to sound" had everything to do with the song catalogue: "Many of these songs had been written by Freed and Brown for the earliest musical pictures made, between 1929 and 1931 . . . and it occurred to us that . . . they would bloom at their happiest in something that took place in the very period in which they had been written" (4-5). Given the witty film they went on to script, the writers clearly made a wise decision, even though their premise was a bit fuzzy. The Freed-Brown catalogue is not exclusively from that period of "earliest musical pictures" since many famous ones, such as "Broadway Rhythm," were written in the thirties. Nor does this catalogue comprise just any set of old standards firmly bound to their moment of composition. MGM's exploitation of these songs enhanced their identification with the studio as its own set of "greatest hits." The main theatrical poster for *Singin' in the Rain* calls it "M-G-M's Technicolor Musical Treasure," and the slogan refers to the catalogue's long-standing value for the studio just as much as it describes the film in its own right.

Following an industry-wide practice, studio-owned standards like the ones written by Freed and Brown for MGM were routinely used again after their first outing had made them known, often as underscoring because their familiarity could expeditiously make a musical point, or for a nightclub performance in a drama. What's distinctive about the Freed-Brown songs chosen for *Singin' in the Rain* is that so many of these compositions had already been recycled in other MGM musicals. While a few—"Would You" from *San Francisco* (1936) and "Good Mornin'" from *Babes in Arms*—did not have such an afterlife before their reappearance in 1952, as near as I can tell, most had been used over again. "You Were Meant for Me" was written for *Broadway Melody*, then a few months later featured in *Hollywood Revue of 1929*. "Should I?" in the talkies montage originated in *Lord Byron of Broadway* (1929) and was revived for *Thousands Cheer* (1943). Eleanor Powell danced to and Frances Langford sang "Broadway Rhythm" in *Broadway Melody of 1936* (1935), after which the number was briefly incorporated into *Broadway Melody of 1938* (1937) and later sung by Judy Garland twice, first in the "Opera Versus Swing" sequence of *Babes in Arms*, then again in the finale of *Presenting Lily Mars* (1943). Garland also performed "Singin' in the Rain," the hit song from *Hollywood Revue*, in *Little Nelly Kelly* (1940), as did Jimmy Durante in *Speak*

Easily (1932). "You Are My Lucky Star" from *Broadway Melody of 1936* returned, albeit for just a moment, in the follow-up and also figured in the "Opera Versus Swing" sequence of *Babes in Arms*.

Through this prior recycling, the Freed-Brown catalogue brings to *Singin' in the Rain* long-standing associations with the MGM musical, a surplus value which gives added texture to the film's retrospective view so that the history of the genre's production at the studio seems to occur logically, inevitably, and immediately after the arrival of sound in 1927. Which is also to say that, by following the lineage supplied by the recycled songs, as far as *Singin' in the Rain* recreates this past, 1927 cannot be conceived of without thinking ahead to what had become MGM's signature genre by 1952. Although not every song from this MGM treasure chest contributes equally, the catalogue marks out three memorable stages of progress characterizing the genre's history at the studio: (1) the first all-talking, all-singing, all-dancing *Broadway Melody* and *Hollywood Revue* in 1929; (2) the former musical's reinvention as a franchise showcasing the studio's thirties star, Eleanor Powell; and (3) the Rooney-Garland backyard musicals that began with *Babes in Arms*, which established Freed as an MGM producer and clinched Garland's importance for his future productions as the studio's reigning star of the genre during the forties. *Babes in Arms* itself already recognizes this lineage by repeating two songs from Powell's first musical at Metro and excerpting from *Broadway Melody* and *Hollywood Revue*, all within the first half hour or so.

More than just alluding to the past—the usual function of recycled standards in fixing the nostalgic character of a period musical—the Freed-Brown catalogue establishes the MGM musical as the primary historical referent of *Singin' in the Rain*: as Comden and Green stated, the songs are what determined their decision to set the story in 1927. Consequently, it is the catalogue which gives significance to the screenplay's recounting of the coming of sound, rather than the other way around. The sequence before the credits immediately signals that the catalogue's recycling will assume its own referential weight with the appearance of Kelly, O'Connor, and Reynolds performing "Singin' in the Rain" in yellow slickers, the same costumes worn for the number in *Hollywood Revue*. Kelly's later solo version of the song sans raincoat then adds the crucial phrase "and dancin'" to the original lyric's plainer "I'm singin' in the rain." The extra phrase sets in motion the choreography and justifies his version's spontaneity—because of the number's integration with his character's expression of joy and, hence, its greater illusionism as a street dance and not a show performance—to contrast with the song's 1929 appearance in the revue. The title number, in short, puts forward dancing as the singular modernizing element characterizing the MGM musical's development.

So does "The Broadway Ballet." Combining "Broadway Melody" and "Broadway Rhythm," the ballet projects Kelly's hoofer against the backdrop of the two films where the songs originated. "Broadway Ballet" opens with Kelly having traded in his usual sailor suit or baseball cap and loafers for a straw hat, tuxedo, and cane. The outfit recalls Charles King's performance in the dress rehearsal version of *Broadway Melody*'s title number, and the close-up of Kelly's grinning face at the end repeats the final shot of Powell's "Broadway Rhythm" in *Broadway Melody of 1936*. The rhyming shots anchor the ballet in the tradition of MGM backstage musicals, but Kelly's likeness to King as fellow entertainers in the music-hall tradition of singing and, correspondingly, his difference from Powell as a dancer in terms of their style and gender also subordinate the MGM musical's historical reliance on female stars in the interest of advancing Kelly's stature as a dancer-choreographer (Prock, 308–309). In "Broadway Rhythm," Powell's dancing emphasizes her dazzling technique, with her taps often sounding louder than the orchestra. Kelly's dancing in "Broadway Ballet," on the other hand, emphasizes his fusion of ballet, jazz, and tap; the fluid mixture of styles in the choreography serves the progression of the hoofer's story while visualizing how Kelly has taken the genre forward from the days of *Broadway Melody* and its successors with Powell (Chumo).

Other songs recycled in *Singin' in the Rain* refer to their antecedents less directly than the title tune and the ballet, but they make the same point. "Good Mornin'" parallels its first appearance in 1939's *Babes in Arm* because in both musicals the number marks a "Hey, let's put on a show" turn in the plot. In *Babes in Arms*, Mrs. Moran comes up with the inspired idea of staging a vaudeville comeback by forming a road company of all the old unemployed troupers, cheering up her depressed, debt-ridden husband whose career is over because of talkies.

71

72

Top: Charles King sings the title song in *Broadway Melody* (MGM, 1929). **Bottom:** Gene Kelly dances to "Broadway Melody" in *Singin' in the Rain* (MGM, 1952).

A cut follows Moran's excitement to answer his earlier question, "Where's Mickey?" Well, Mickey and Patsy are auditioning "Good Mornin' " for a song publisher. The number features Garland's peppy singing as she stands by Rooney at the piano, with her movement primarily confined to hand gestures—waving arms, snapping fingers—which makes her energetic voice the focal point of the song's exuberance. "Sell it, Ma, sell it!" Mickey shouts at the number's finish, showing that the newcomers have the same instincts for a rousing vaudeville performance style as their parents and thereby predicting that the young generation will succeed in reviving the tradition of "the show" when the older generation fails. Told that there's "nothing very new there," Mickey replies, "Oh, what good is new? It's the same old rose you see every year. But it's just a little fresher, but it's the same thing, isn't it?"—and the publisher buys the song.

As redone in *Singin' in the Rain*, "Good Mornin' " expresses the excitement generated by Cosmo's inspired idea of turning *Duelling Cavalier* into a musical, cheering up a depressed Don, who thinks his career will end after that talkie is released. But more than freshening up the "same old rose" that sells Garland's voice in *Babes in Arms*, in *Singin' in the Rain* the number builds off the lyrics to set the momentum for the high-spirited, rapidly paced, and complexly structured dance with Kelly, Reynolds, and O'Connor. When the three sing "Good Mornin' " to start with, their tapping is made part of the song's content, subordinating the cadence of the lyrics to the beat of their feet. The lyrics become completely incidental once the number pulls out all the stops, choreographically and cinematically, to propel the three dancers across space from room to room, up and down furniture, their tapping synchronized in a show of incredible physical stamina and technical virtuosity unmatched by *Babes in Arms*.

The self-reflexive approach to "You Were Meant for Me" also refers to its vintage sources. In *Broadway Melody* and *Hollywood Revue*, the song is performed without dancing by Charles King and Conrad Nagel, respectively. The one number in *Broadway Melody* not staged as part of a show, "You Were Meant for Me" arises out of suppressed sexual desire, enabling Eddie Kern (King) to confess his love to Queenie Maloney (Anita Page), who feels the same way but resists his declaration out of loyalty to her sister, Hank (Bessie Love), Eddie's fiancée and Queenie's stage partner. A medium shot keeps King and Page together in the frame while each sits on opposite arms of a chair, he singing plaintively and she looking away. The number does not unite the couple at this point in the film but complicates their emotions. Reused in *Hollywood Revue*, the same song is done as a theatrical performance of seduction by Nagel (with King's singing voice dubbed in) to the same Anita Page, with the couple seated at a piano. After the song, Nagel gets the kiss that Page denies to King in *Broadway Melody* and—all the while knowing this number has been staged as a performance for the revue format—we are persuaded by the emcee's expression to infer that the song results in even more hanky panky for this couple, since Nagel takes Page's hand and leads her off-stage as if they were heading for the privacy of a dressing room.

Kelly's "You Were Meant for Me" synthesizes the authenticity and theatricality of the two 1929 versions: his rendition is at once sincerely heartfelt like King's in *Broadway Melody* and suavely, self-consciously seductive like Nagel's in *Hollywood Revue*. As mentioned previously, Kelly/Don leads Reynolds/Kathy onto a studio soundstage, "the proper setting" for his song, in order to liberate himself from his constructed screen persona so that he can reveal his genuine feelings to her. He consequently strips the veil away from movie technology, by showing, for instance, how a burning sunset, blurry mist, and starry sky are effects of filtered lighting. Having turned on all this equipment to demonstrate, Don uses the technology to woo Kathy, and it does indeed create "the proper setting" in which to make a romantic declaration. The machinery drenches the huge soundstage in luminous pools of red and blue filtered lighting, visibly uniting the two as a couple in silhouette when they dance in and out of the colored shadows. Far from breaking with the number's illusionism, the self-reflexive highlighting of cinematic technology in the mise-en-scène enhances it (Feuer, *Hollywood Musical*, 46–47). This paradox, in fact, is the wink that Luhrmann describes on the DVD.

As crucial to the number's significance in establishing Don and Kathy as a romantic couple, its incorporation of movie technology also points up the greater finesse with which Kelly choreographed and Donen filmed "You Were Meant for Me" in comparison with the song's static staging and editing when first done on screen. In *Broadway Melody*, King sings to Page in a single, uninterrupted shot without any movement by the camera. In *Singin' in the Rain*, the number consists of four shots, one for the song and three for the dance. Compared with "Good Mornin'," which has ten shots from the singing in the kitchen to the last flip over the sofa, "You Were Meant for Me" hardly seems to have been edited at all. The reduced amount of editing, however, places greater emphasis on the camera as "the recorder, the definer, and enhancer of the space" (Charness, 103), not a new style for filming dance in the 1950s by any means, but one which, in the context of *Singin' in the Rain*'s historical setting, depicts its modernity by virtue of the camera's liberation from the primitive technology of early talkies. Each of the four shots begins with the camera positioned at a different angle and distance from Kelly and Reynolds; as he first sings and then the two dance together, the camera dollies in, tracks around them, moves closer, or withdraws. This camera is not immobile—it soars, whereas the two dancers remain earthbound. Given the simple choreography, the camera appears to be doing the more intricate footwork, driving the dance with its energy and motion, and the number closes with a crane shot that pulls way back to locate the couple as two miniscule figures along with the props of cinematic technology on the vast soundstage.

Admittedly, although the recycled songs place these numbers in quotation marks, none warrants a mass-camp label from the perspective of parody—unlike the ones included in the talkies montage, these are not sending up their sources.[4] But parody is not the only sign of mass camp. The vintage Freed-Brown catalogue identifies MGM musicals as the point of reference for *Singin' in the Rain* in 1952, with the new versions of the old songs acquiring mass-camp value insofar as their currency has been enhanced through their recycling *and* it has been done with full awareness of how the surplus features of stylistic, choreographic, and generic innovations cancel out their obsolescence. After all, the songs themselves are not representative of early 1950s popular music, and the catalogue musical as a subgenre turned out by the Freed unit at this time contrasts with MGM's musicals of the 1940s, which more directly connected with that era's tastes in popular music through the regular appearances of big bands in the films, the composition of new songs that often topped the charts, and wide radio airplay for cross promotion. *Singin' in the Rain* aims to reconnect the Freed-Brown catalogue with popular tastes through markers of generic progress—dance, integration with the story, fluid camerawork—so that the songs are modernized while still kept referentially bound to their vintage antecedents by the story's Hollywood setting and historical era.

BROADWAY MELODY OF 1952

"Broadway Ballet" is particularly important in visualizing the mass-camp outlook underwriting *Singin' in the Rain*'s endorsement, via a story set in 1927, of the MGM musical's immediacy as "the greatest entertainment in the world" for a 1952 audience. A Broadway number was an afterthought, replacing a cowboy routine planned for Kelly and O'Connor. That idea had to be scrapped when the latter's obligation to do a television show required a change in thinking (Hirschhorn, 187, Silverman, 164n). The Broadway number then became more ambitious as a result of popular and critical acclaim for the ballet in *American in Paris*, which pushed the MGM musical toward high art by combining classical dance, Gershwin's jazz- and blues-inflected music from 1928, and European modernism in the form of French Impressionist and Post-Impressionist painting. The *Singin' in the Rain* ballet copies its predecessor's scale but not its high-art pretensions: instead of Gershwin's famous suite, this one uses a composite of Freed and Brown's two hymns to Broadway; in place of Renoir, Rousseau, Van Gogh and the like, it draws on Prohibition, the film *Scarface* (1932), and Louise Brooks (Cyd Charisse's vamp); and in lieu of the ex-GI artist residing in the City of Light, it features a hoofer finding success on the Great White Way.

That the *Paris* ballet represents a new standard for MGM, which *Singin' in the Rain* is sending up through its salute to Broadway, is noted by a joke more probably intended for the amusement of Freed unit insiders than anyone else. As mentioned in the previous chapter, Don begins to recount to Simpson the number called "Broadway Melody" yet to be shot, which provides the transition for the ballet to begin on-screen. Afterward, when Simpson states, "I can't quite visualize it," the gag is self-apparent but also recalls Dore Schary's response when Kelly and Vincente Minnelli described the projected *Paris* ballet at length in their pitch for final budgetary approval. Schary reportedly said, "Well, I don't understand what the hell you're driving at, but it sounds exciting and the sketches look great, so why not go ahead?" (Hirshhorn, 173–74). Kelly repeated this story during his BBC interview—the anecdote is also inserted in the Freed documentary appearing on the *Singin' in the Rain* DVD—but makes Schary sound even more like Simpson: "I don't understand one word that you're all talking about." Significantly, no one, not even Kelly, mentions the studio head's inability to follow the pitch in Donald Knox's oral history of *American in Paris*. There Schary recalls seeing the set and costume sketches by Irene Sharaff and the camera angles worked out by Minnelli, exclaiming, "I just fell in love with it" (145).

While Kelly's account may be a memory retrospectively determined by the gag in *Singin' in the Rain*, it nonetheless suggests how "Broadway Ballet" can be seen as a camp rebuttal to the *Paris* ballet's association of the MGM musical with high art. The difference between the two ballets is more immediately evident in the mise-en-scène visualizing the referent of the two recycled "Broadway" songs than in Kelly's choreography. The locale of *Singin' in the Rain*'s ballet is not the Broadway of legitimate theater but the Broadway represented in backstage movie musicals with Charles King and Eleanor Powell and, as much to the point, the Broadway exhibiting those films. After first revealing Kelly alone in complete darkness except for the spotlight on his figure, the camera pulls back and Broadway suddenly lights up all around him, recalling the backdrops of both "Broadway Melody" and "Broadway Rhythm" when first performed on film. Far from representing Shubert Alley or even the old legitimate theaters on Forty-Second Street, such as Ziegfeld's New Amsterdam, the marquees on view in the ballet are those of the movie palaces along the main stem itself: Loew's State, the Criterion, the Astor, the Strand, the Capitol, their luminescence generating the Great White Way as an enticing invitation to filmgoers in search of leisure amusement, not high culture.

To portray Broadway through its recognizable markers, the set design by Cedric Gibbons and Randall Duell uses a Pop style of illustration: sketchy, two-dimensional renderings of the street and a bold use of primary colors, often in lurid juxtaposition. As the narrative begins—with Kelly's hoofer arriving at Penn Station, making the rounds of theatrical agents, and getting his first job at a speakeasy—the interiors of these locales have even more of the flat surface of drawings; their details, shadows, and depth are indicated by rough, quick lines. In its design, the *Paris* ballet has a drawn quality as well, but its visual look is determined by famous painterly styles; the sets record more three-dimensional depth, in large part because the space for dancing is not as open and expansive as in "Broadway Ballet" but frequently representative of narrow, angled Parisian streets; and the locale of each section tends to be organized around three-dimensional objects, such as the Place de Concorde fountain or flower stalls in the market. By contrast, in "Broadway Ballet" the set design finds its perspectival referent for visualizing the street in those ubiquitous postcard photographs looking down at the Great White Way from Times Square. This is the camera's position in the opening and then again in the finale, which creates the impression that the hoofer is a human figure inhabiting a two-dimensional world reproducing the Pop look of children's book illustrations, advertising art, or cartoons.

The ballet's sets become more three-dimensional the closer the hoofer gets to success in the legitimate theater and, correspondingly, the further he moves away from that Great White Way. In the montage depicting his rise to stardom, the burlesque show occurs on a stage with three-dimensional effects painted onto a flat set; the vaudeville show takes place on a stage with red, white, and blue curtains draped over pillars to suggest depth; and the Ziegfeld Follies incarnation, with showgirls positioned around the hoofer on all sides in a tableau, most fully projects the three-dimensional expanse of a proscenium stage. In all three locales, the hoofer's act uses the same tune but the staging changes to reflect the theatrical setting, with his dancing becoming progressively stiffer until he is immobile in the Follies.

After this montage, the hoofer enters the casino, presumably to celebrate his success on the Ziegfeld stage. While the casino is located on Broadway where the street crosses Seventh Avenue, its interior is, in comparison with the bustling thoroughfare outside, a realistic set with chandeliers, gaming and dining tables, and curtains in the background. Here, too, Kelly's dancing with the vamp corresponds with the hoofer's progression to this upscale locale; the fantasy pas de deux lacks the more robust, frenetic energy and erotic heat of the hoofer's first encounter with the vamp in the speakeasy. When she rejects him a second time and he finds solace in the "Broadway Rhythm" refrain, "Gotta dance," the ballet returns him to that Great White Way dominated by movie palaces, where the crowd rushes to envelope him in the street's pulsating vitality, the true Broadway rhythm.

Although "Broadway Ballet" is usually judged and found wanting by the standard of *American in Paris*, because both starred Kelly, its Pop visualization of Broadway indicates that the number has more in common with "The Girl Hunt Ballet" in Minnelli's *The Band Wagon* (1953), another film based on a Comden-Green screenplay written for a Freed-unit catalogue musical. Obviously, "Girl Hunt" and "Broadway" differ in the motifs selected to represent popular culture. "Girl Hunt" sets its sights on best-selling author Mickey Spillane, his pulp thrillers, film noir women, and the restraints of classical dance: "It chortles over the fevered lust and sadism of the Spillane school of pop lit., while gleefully mocking the somber, formal body language of ballet," writes Stephen Harvey (*Directed by Vincente Minnelli*, 123–24). Whereas "Girl Hunt" takes aim at contemporary mass tastes, "Broadway"—set in the era of prohibition and borrowing the stock star-is-born narrative from backstage musicals—is more referentially fixed to mass entertainment from the past.

Nonetheless, when the Simpson joke alludes to the *Paris* ballet after the conclusion of "Broadway Ballet," the connection illuminates how, through its Times Square setting, this number sends up the high art of *American in Paris*, making "Broadway" more like "Girl Hunt" as a camp affirmation of the MGM musical's entertainment value for a general public losing interest in the genre. "Broadway Ballet" achieves this goal in its Pop visualization of the thoroughfare celebrated by "Broadway Melody" and "Broadway Rhythm," which enables the number, first, to refer to the MGM musical's history more directly than "Girl Hunt" can do, and second, to represent—stylistically as well as choreographically—a modernization of this tradition that is solely available to a 1952 audience. No wonder Simpson has trouble visualizing the number! His inability to "see" it signals a wink recognizing the historical condensation which the ballet performs: this pseudo-representation of the "modern" backstage narrative in *The Dancing Cavalier* of 1927 draws on the *Broadway Melody* musicals from the decade afterward yet can only be realized in a fifties-

73

74

77

75

78

76

79

The mise-en-scène depicting the
hoofer's rise to stardom and return
to the Great White Way in "The
Broadway Ballet." *Singin' in the Rain*
(MGM, 1952). Frame captures.

80

81

82

85

83

86

84

87

88

era MGM musical that brings the genre up to date by reimagining its mainstream appeal in terms that put Pop and camp together on a "Broadway" fabricated by Hollywood.

A PIRATED *PIRATE*, DUBBED DEBBIE, AND LINA LAMONT

The song catalogue is not only the vintage material that *Singin' in the Rain* recycles in the spirit of mass camp. According to Haver on the Criterion LD, Don's lavishly appointed mansion, the locale of "Good Mornin'," reuses the set design of *Flesh and the Devil* (1926); and both Haver and Behlmer observe that the fashion show in "Beautiful Girl" was an afterthought, inspired by Walter Plunkett's costumes. Many of these were gowns he had previously done for twenties film stars, when the fashion hyperbole of the designs connoted the height of chic rather than "tongue-in-cheek," as Debbie Reynolds now describes them in the DVD's making-of documentary.

Likewise, the film's revisionist depiction of Kelly's star image helps to shape a mass camp perspective for *Singin' in the Rain* by giving new purpose to borrowings from his career, beginning with the clip of *Three Musketeers* (1948), which is recontextualized to send up Don Lockwood's silent films. Cosmo's premise of making the revised *Duelling Cavalier* a dream within a modern Broadway narrative echoes the plot of *DuBarry was a Lady* (1943), one of Kelly's early MGM musicals; the policeman who stops Don's street dancing in "Singin' in the Rain" repeats the closure of "Make Way for Tomorrow"—a number whose choreographic conceits also return in "Good Mornin'"—in *Cover Girl* (1943); what Don describes to Kathy as the "proper setting" for a love song before beginning "You Were Meant for Me" recounts almost exactly what happens during the fantasy number with Kelly and Kathryn Grayson on a soundstage in *Anchors Aweigh* (1945); and the joke within "Broadway Ballet" of having the hoofer sing the same tune as he moves up the ladder from burlesque to vaudeville to the Follies comes from the nightclub montage in *On the Town* (1949).

Additionally, Haver considers one of the two new songs, "Moses Supposes" written by Comden and Green with Roger Edens, "almost a direct lift" from their "French Lesson" in *Good News* (1947) insofar as both use a tutoring lesson to inspire the playful, nonsensical lyrics. The other new song is more palpably a "direct lift" from a prior source. Needing a solo number for O'Connor and not finding an appropriate one in the Freed-Brown catalogue, Donen asked them to write a new upbeat song that would be like Cole Porter's "Be a Clown" in *The Pirate* (1948). What Freed and Brown composed, "Make 'Em Laugh," is too remarkably like "Be a Clown" to be anything but "100 per cent plagiarism," according to Donen (Fordin, 359). Their melodies are virtually identical. The plagiarism has now become accepted lore about the production of *Singin' in the Rain*. In the DVD documentaries as well as previous television interviews, Donen recalls Freed's discomfort when Irving Berlin visited the shoot of O'Connor's number, started to express his astonishment about the likeness to Porter's song, and before he could finish was whisked off the set by the producer.[5]

A more subtle instance of "direct lifting" occurs in *Singin' in the Rain* as another in-joke and, like the song plagiarized from *The Pirate*, it has become fully ingrained in the film's mystique (although this one goes unmentioned anywhere on the anniversary DVD). At the point when Kathy dubs Lina's singing and speaking, Debbie Reynolds's voice is itself dubbed by someone else (Betty Noyes for the song, Jean Hagen—who plays Lina—for the dialogue), yet elsewhere the young star's own voice is used, as in "Good Mornin'" and her reprise of the title song. Donen maintains that Reynolds was dubbed in these scenes because of her regional accent. The voice looped over Lina's "was supposed to be cultured speech—and Debbie had that terrible western noise" (Fordin, 358). Truth be told, you can hear the twang as well as her limited vocal range in Reynolds's deleted solo of "You Are My Lucky Star," part of the home video packages for the past decade.

Unlike the voice doubles MGM used for dancers Eleanor Powell and Cyd Charisse, the composite created for Reynolds was not engineered to approximate her speech or singing; the difference in timbre, accent, and vocal range is audible on the soundtrack whenever the doubling occurs, even though none of the characters appears to hear it. Furthermore, the dubbing is used selectively. Only at the points when *Singin' in the Rain* exposes the manufacturing of a performance through Kathy's dubbing of Lina is the off-screen engineering of the voice deployed and cleverly acknowledged by the use of Hagen herself to double for Reynolds's speech. With Hagen involved, the circularity detaches the voice from its referent in a body, putting the performance almost literally in quotation marks: the dubbing appropriates Hagen's voice, recycles it in place of Reynolds when the latter is shown dubbing Hagen's character's dialogue, and refers back to Hagen for the joke.

The self-referential dubbing suits the character of Lina, herself a composite of recycled legends, anecdotes, and stereotypes about or from the movies. Lina sends up "the dumb show" of silent film as soon as *Singin' in the Rain* lets her speak, revealing to all that her voice "is shrill, flat, and coarse, and a terrific shock coming out of that beautiful face" (Comden and Green, 21). John Gilbert, universally if inaccurately remembered as the most famous silent star unable to sustain a career in sound because of his high-pitched voice, is usually mentioned as the inspiration for Lina's misadventures with sound and failed film career. Gilbert supposedly caused laughter in his first talkie, *His Glorious Night* (1929), and the sneak preview of *Duelling Cavalier* refers to that anecdote. Although he went on to costar with Greta Garbo in *Queen Christina* (1933), Gilbert was gone from MGM by 1934, with gossip still speculating about other reasons for his departure. Norma Talmadge, remembered for being unable to make the move to talkies because of her thick Brooklyn accent, is another frequently mentioned referent for Lina.

To be fair to Lina, it's worth noting that her difficulties adjusting to sound are not entirely without basis nor are they peculiar to her larynx. Historically, the new Vitaphone sound-recording process was a technology unfavorable to female silent stars trying to make the transition to talkies because it recorded and reproduced men's voices with greater accuracy (Barrios, 43). Furthermore, although recourse to a voice double in 1927 may seem extraordinarily inventive on Cosmo's part in *Singin' in the Rain*, recall that Conrad Nagel sang in *Hollywood Revue* with Charles King's voice. In fact, off-screen dubbers were frequently employed on set during the early days of sound films, "singing into the mike while the star mouthed the lyrics" (Barrios, 141), just as Kathy sings "Singin' in the Rain" for Lina to lip-synch after the premiere of *Dancing Cavalier*.

In order to get around any suggestion of historical appropriateness for Lina's problems with early sound technology, which her costar suffers from as well (Don also causes laughter at the preview, remember), the characterization further refers to a parodic type from the early sound era: the wiseacre dumb blond who uses words incorrectly and mangles their pronunciation. Just as Reynolds's regional accent, "that terrible western noise," made her voice unusable when Kathy's speech needs to sound "cultured," Lina's "ugly" voice is "unusable" because of its uncultured, working-class connotations as well as its shrill and coarse tones. This element of the character draws on Jean Harlow's early 1930s sex comedies, such as *Bombshell* (1933), itself a send-up of Hollywood, in effect making Lina a recycling of a parodic construction of female stardom typifying Hollywood's golden age.

Strengthening this sense of Lina's being a copy of a parody, Comden and Green more or less wrote the part for their friend Judy Holliday, modeling the character after the dumb-blonde persona—with a shrill voice, uneducated diction, and insubordinate attitude much like Lina's—which they had helped Holliday perfect in their revue company some years before. Holliday herself had just adapted this persona to her Oscar-winning performance of Bille Dawn in *Born Yesterday* (1950), a role she had first done on Broadway. Because Holliday was under contract to Columbia by the time *Singin' in the Rain* went into production, and too big a star at that point to play a supporting role anyway, the part of Lina went to Hagen, an MGM contract player who, it turned out, had taken over for Holliday in the road company version of *Born Yesterday*. Hagen's performance, letter-perfect in its own right, was thus designed with the Holliday persona functioning as one more antecedent for Lina, resulting in an additional circular loop (Hagen as Holliday's "Billie" as Lina) that parallels the engineering of the dubbing.

When added on top of the character's various layers of referentiality, Lina's obstructionist role in the plot, which leads her to demand that Kathy's contribution to *Dancing Cavalier* go unacknowledged and results in another type of plagiarism, makes additional sense: it slyly raises a question about the resemblance of appropriations which recycle sources from the movies, the mode of representation characterizing *Singin' in the Rain* as mass camp, and those which result in an outright theft, as in the on-screen substitution of Kathy's voice for Lina's, the uncredited off-screen manufacturing of a voice

double whenever that occurs, and the behind-the-scenes plagiarism
of a Porter melody for "Make 'Em Laugh."

BUT WHO DO YOU SYOO?

Pointing to both the dubbing and the plagiarism, Carol Clover reasons that "*Singin' in the Rain*'s morality tale of stolen talent restored
is driven by a nervousness about just the opposite, about stolen
talent *un*restored" (725). According to Clover, the film is riddled
with anxiety about white performers' borrowings from the tradition of great African American tap dancers, rarely acknowledged by
the Hollywood musical. As a result, "black men's dancing bodies
haunt even the film's title number" (737). Its street setting and watchful policeman implicitly evoke the history in which "black tappers
learned their trade in the shadow of the law," competing for the
best street corners to practice and show off their steps until a cop
was spotted, when they "went back to work shining shoes . . . If we
in the nineties do not know the racial resonances of the trope of
the street-dance-interrupted-by-policeman, Kelly and his colleagues
surely did" (738).

The matter of that "stolen talent" and its recycling by a white
dancer actually came up at Kelly's AFI tribute in 1985. Gregory Hines
recounted an anecdote about "creating a step" while improvising on
stage, only to discover afterward when watching a Kelly musical on
TV that the dancer had "copied my step thirty years before." Hines
then confessed, "Over the years I've borrowed a couple of your steps.
More than a couple." Later in the evening, the Nicholas Brothers,
who had danced with Kelly in "Be a Clown," jokingly told Hines not
to worry about "stealing Gene Kelly's steps because he stole them
from us." This exchange recognizes that "stolen" choreographic influences cannot always be traced back to an origin, but they are re-
cyclable and, as Hines's phrasing implies when he joked that Kelly
"copied" his "new" steps some thirty years before their "invention,"
the recycling eventually supersedes an origin. In the industrial setting of Hollywood, where even dance steps are placed in circulation
as a product of commodified labor, thereby losing any relation to an
original pair of feet, it turns out to be more a matter of "right to copy"
than "copyright."

89

Kathy Selden (Debbie Reynolds) rewards Don Lockwood (Gene Kelly) with a kiss while Cosmo Brown (Donald O'Connor) looks on. *Singin' in the Rain* (MGM, 1952).

White anxiety about borrowing from a tradition of black dancing without due recognition is by no means the only ambiguity about credit which *Singin' in the Rain* raises. What about Cosmo? Is it just coincidence or is it symptomatic that his solo number is the plagiarized one? After all, it is Cosmo who comes up with the plan to turn *Duelling Cavalier* into a musical, who explains how to get around Lina's lack of talent by dubbing her, who invents the modern backstage plot and new title for the revamped talkie, and who goes on to supervise Kathy's looping of Lina's dialogue. Nevertheless, his invaluable contributions receive little notice. Following "Good Mornin'," when Don agrees to take Cosmo's scheme to Simpson, Kathy exclaims that Don is "a genius," and they kiss, while Cosmo looks on. "I'm glad *you* thought of it," he observes ironically to Don, so Kathy gives him a quick peck on the cheek, muttering, "Oh, Cosmo." In response, he pulls his hat over his face to feign embarrassment like a little boy.

Cosmo's exaggeration of blushing indicates that a peck on the cheek is disproportionate to his being the real genius behind the dubbing scheme, so he well knows Don is getting all the acknowledgment from Kathy without justification. As tellingly, Cosmo's bit of comic schtick in response to her obligatory, passionless kiss characterizes him as a neutered clown, making him rather like the headless, genderless dummy he "flirts" with in "Make 'Em Laugh." But to call Cosmo "neutered" is simply not to see him in the same heterosexual light as his best friend. In the original shooting script, when Cosmo stands in front of a singing Kathy to demonstrate how to dub Lina and Kathy's voice appears to come out of his mouth, Don fails to get the point, responding with a sissy joke reminiscent of Kelly's 1940s buddy musicals: "Great, what are you doing this evening?" The line was subsequently censored by the PCA because of its queer implications and replaced by the simpler "What?" (Haver on the Criterion LD).

Cosmo's asexuality may be what allows him to function as comic second banana, yet it also registers, however indirectly, the marginality of another invisible group whose labor on a musical went without open acknowledgment: the queer men working at MGM whose sexual identities were as publicly unacknowledged as the tradition of black tap dancing, but perhaps even more effaced because in many cases their contributions are still uncredited as the labor of homosexuals. Aside from its revision of Kelly's star image, much evidence of the genre's camp history at the studio is noticeably absent in *Singin' in the Rain*, even given the era's censorship of any suggestion of queer activity. Visually, the film reigns in the more outlandish, excessive, and camp style characteristic of MGM in the 1940s with "tighter narrative integration" organized around a heterosexual romance (Tinkcom, *Working Like a Homosexual*, 40). Thus the "Beautiful Girl" number is visually uninteresting, its parody relying on Plunkett's costumes, while "Broadway Ballet" redirects its visual extravagance into a Pop style. Yet as Plunkett's costumes remind us, a queer labor force was still at work behind the scenes on *Singin' in the Rain*, its contributions traceable in what I have been examining. To give the most notable example, Roger Edens received official credit for composing the music of "Moses Supposes," but various accounts indicate that he also had an uncredited hand in devising the fashion-show patter of "Beautiful Girl," the vamp for Kelly's "Singin' in the Rain," the new introductory verse for Reynolds's "You Are My Lucky

Star" (deleted after previews), and the multipart structures of "Good Mornin'" and "Broadway Ballet."

Singin' in the Rain gives these hints about the ethical dilemma arising from appropriation of someone else's hard work and originality, be he black or queer, but it contains them in a hierarchy centering on the straight white male star, Don Lockwood, and explicitly directs the charge of stealing credit at that insubordinate, undeserving, and parodied female star, Lina Lamont. More than just sending up her inability to adjust to talkies, *Singin' in the Rain* vilifies Lina because she crosses the line of power at the studio as determined by gender. When she bursts in on the looping session to find Kathy redoing her voice, then discovers that there will be a credit on the film acknowledging she has a voice double, the angered star defiantly exclaims, "They can't make a laughingstock out of Lina Lamont! What do they think I am—dumb or something? Why, I make more money than— than—Calvin Coolidge—put together!" The next day, after engineering her own publicity campaign to announce her new singing persona, she stands up to Simpson, demanding that Kathy continue to serve as her uncredited voice double for all future pictures. "Lina Lamont," the star points out, is a studio asset, and protection of that asset's value is guaranteed by her contract. She consequently expects Simpson to follow the terms of this document, which make Monumental Pictures responsible for safeguarding her reputation, or she will take legal remedy and "syoo" the studio. His shocked response indicates surprise that she should overstep her position and have the legal wherewithal to do so, just as his immediate capitulation to her demands confirms the subversion of corporate authority when a woman dares to recognize and then act on her economic value as a commodity.

This obsolete silent-screen star—constructed out of bits and pieces of recycled Hollywood lore, with the disparity between the artifice of her blonde glamour and her shrill "real" voice heightened by the gap between what she says and what she means—cannot simply be written off as the film's villain. Haver's commentary on the Criterion LD suggests how Lina may be made "a laughingstock" in a way that connects her back to the older camp tradition at MGM. He frequently points out and laughs at the jokes made at Lina's expense but usually with the sense of enjoying the doubled meaning in her mangled English or obtuse observations. For instance, when the studio starts *Duelling Cavalier* over again with sound, Lina can never remember where the microphone is hidden, requiring various strategies for bringing it closer to her mouth until finally it is sewn into her costume; the scene concludes with Simpson dragging away what he thinks is a stray cable, which causes a shrieking Lina to tumble headfirst off a bench and onto the floor. She is made the butt of every verbal and visual gag in this scene. Haver nonetheless sees resistance in her ineptitude, mentioning how much he "loves" her barely disguised "outrage at the whole idea of talkies." For Haver, Lina's character enables a camp's perspective of queerlike marginality that at least partially sees through *Singin' in the Rain*'s mythmaking and mass-camp recycling—perhaps that's why her malapropisms, appreciated for their double sense, are so quotable for cinephiles like himself. It perhaps explains, too, why, according to Haver, one early version of the screenplay ended by pairing Lina with Cosmo as a surprising but somehow rightly matched couple alongside Don and Kathy at another Hollywood premiere.

I mention the possibility of a resistant camp position occupied by Lina because her figure puts the most overt pressure on the appropriation of other people's talent within *Singin' in the Rain* and the equally dubious "theft" of the "original" sources comprising this film's extrafilmic referential field as the basis of its mass-camp recycling of the MGM musical's history. The Comden-Green screenplay, however, makes sure that Lina always gets her just desserts—public humiliation—beginning with a pie in her face meant by Kathy for Don early on. He, as an important contrast with his female costar, has leave to do whatever he wants at the studio, such as improvising his own dialogue and planning his own musical numbers. Even so, his freedom at Monumental Pictures is not achieved without its own appropriation of credit, namely, Cosmo's. Adding a bit of irony to his "theft," Don began his career at the studio by working as a stunt double, standing in for other actors who received the credit for his daredevil performances.

More interestingly, the intertwined professional collaboration and long-standing friendship of Don and Cosmo mirrors the Kelly-Donen collaboration creating *Singin' in the Rain*. Art director Randall Duell describes their partnership in terms which explicitly evoke Don and Cosmo's in the film: "Gene ran the show. Stan had some good ideas and worked with Gene, but he was still the 'office boy' to Gene, in a sense, although Gene had great respect for him. But they made a good team, because they were very compatible" (Delamater, 247). A former dancer himself, Donen often split directing chores with Kelly when filming, shooting different scenes and numbers on separate soundstages. This is not to suggest that Kelly directed the numbers and Donen the nonmusical portion. On the contrary, their collaboration was interactive at every point. "Even through rehearsing the numbers, when everything would really get complicated I would be with him," Donen said of working with Kelly. "When there was real pressure to get a lot done in terms of rehearsal, I would rehearse in one hall and he would rehearse another number, but then we would switch and I would go supervise his number and he would come to do mine. So it really was a collaboration. There was no question about it" (Harvey, "Stanley Donen," 5). In various television interviews many years afterward, however, Kelly still spoke of his collaborator as his apprentice, assistant, or protégé. Yet Donen was no "office boy," and his solo career—as director of *Royal Wedding* (1951), *Seven Brides for Seven Brothers* (1954), and *Funny Face* (1957), as well as the nonmusicals *Indiscreet* (1958) and *Charade* (1963)—turned out to be more distinguished than his former partner's.

Singin' in the Rain's concern with appropriated origins, symptomatically expressed in so many ways both within the film and in accounts of the film, keeps pointing toward the collaborative labor behind the production of a musical, which exposes traces of an industrial history which the mass-camp recycling "forgets." If this concern is more striking when watching *Singin' in the Rain* some fifty years later, that is because the film's account of the MGM musical's genesis in 1927, a response to the genre's potential obsolescence as mass entertainment in 1952, predicted the postmodern recycling of old Hollywood more prevalent today. I have in mind the compilation films such as *That's Entertainment!* and its sequels, the reuse of Kelly imagery from *Singin' in the Rain* to represent the MGM musical and the studio's golden age, the inclusion of scenes from this film or its trailer to illustrate the arrival of sound in TV documentaries, and, perhaps most of all, the controversial digital manipulation of imagery from old films in commercials—Gene Kelly in a sailor suit dancing with Paula Abdul in place of Frank Sinatra to sell Diet Coke or Fred Astaire dancing with a vacuum cleaner instead of a coat tree to sell Dirt Devil. Such reuse is the logical conclusion of mass camp's indifference to, even alienation from, the industrial history behind the imagery being appropriated and the latter's simultaneous reinvigoration with a new commercial value for the present day.

The digital form of recycling can generate considerable profit—the Astaire estate reportedly earned $750,000 from three Dirt Devil commercials (Lacher). It also muddies the issue of what in an old film is copyrightable and by whom. Owners of the MGM library retain rights to the films themselves so long as they can keep renewing the copyrights, but what about the extrafilmic value of the stars performing in them? What constitutes an origin for recycled imagery from old Hollywood, and who has the right to profit from its ongoing currency or to "syoo" when a star's likeness on film is appropriated for commercial reuse without proper consent? To settle the matter, in 1999 the California state legislature passed the Astaire Celebrity Image Protection Act, so called because of his widow's aggressive lobbying for it (Madigan). This law expanded the rights of a celebrity's heirs to his or her persona, understood to include the visual images rendering it, not to preserve its integrity so much as to assure proper compensation. While excluding instances where artistic license can apply, the law protects a star's likeness from the unauthorized poaching that characterizes the postmodern nature of today's popular culture through the influence of mass camp. Appreciating the extent to which old Hollywood is, in effect, never old but always renewable, the law echoes Lina's thinking, influenced by *her* attorneys, when she confronts Simpson and points out the studio's obligation to preserve the economic value of her image according to an ironclad contract that guarantees her credit, deserved or not.

As for *Singin' in the Rain*, its legibility as "the first camp picture" comes from the way its recycling so clearly anticipates what the Diet Coke and Dirt Devil commercials do when, detaching imagery from *Anchors Aweigh* and *Royal Wedding*, they digitally transform Kelly's and Astaire's dancing to invest it with new currency. Yet the many implications of theft which underlie *Singin' in the Rain*'s mass-camp slant on the myth of the MGM musical, filmically and extrafilmically, also suggest that when the act of recycling the past turns into out-right appropriation the result is no laughing matter, even though the Comden-Green screenplay works hard to insure that, on screen at least, the right person ultimately gets her proper credit. In this re-gard, the ultimate theft of an origin recorded by *Singin' in the Rain* may well be the appropriation of camp itself from its own history of queer referentiality. The recycling that renews the value of MGM's signature genre effaces that history in the name of mass camp, and this erasure accounts for why *Singin' in the Rain* is the single musical that still works for everybody five decades later.

Chapter Five

That's Entertainment! (1974) opens with a pre-credits sequence of clips demonstrating how "Singin' in the Rain" served as "a theme song of MGM" over the years: in the 1920s Cliff Edwards sang the tune while strumming his ukulele in *Hollywood Revue of 1929* (1929); in the 1930s Jimmy Durante gave it his customary panache in *Speak Easily* (1932); in the 1940s Judy Garland belted it "her way" in *Little Nelly Kelly* (1940). Then in the 1950s, narrator Frank Sinatra comments, "Gene Kelly, Donald O'Connor, and Debbie Reynolds put it all together in what many folks would call the best musical ever made," as illustrated by the first version of the song in *Singin' in the Rain* (1952). "If you're wondering what happened in between," Sinatra continues, "well, sit back and relax, you're about to find out." Actually, what happened *afterward* to the MGM musical has a history of its own just as much worth telling.

When *That's Entertainment!* appeared in 1974 to commemorate MGM's fiftieth anniversary, the nostalgic appeal of the studio's famed musicals, a consequence of their relative scarcity beyond big-city revival houses and unpredictable TV showings, defined a widening demographic split between young moviegoers and the older audiences schooled on studio-era films who now stayed home to watch TV for their entertainment. This gap in audience tastes was obvious, as *Mad* magazine pointed out in its parody of *That's Entertainment!* the year following that compilation's release: "That's right! They're singin' 'em again . . . in a successful new film . . . all them outdated songs from all them corny old MGM musicals! And what's even *more* amazing is: People are standing in line and paying good money to see this movie! And it hasn't even got a plot! Which makes us kinda wonder . . . What's entertainment?" (Jacobs, 5, ellipses in original). Rewriting the lyrics of "That's Entertainment," the *Mad* parody then answers its question right off the bat: "Or haven't you heard? / Nostalgia's the word—/ NOT en-ter-tain-ment!" (5).

Two decades later, when *That's Entertainment! III* (1994) revived the series as a tribute to the studio's seventieth anniversary, the cultural standing of the MGM musical was even more marginalized. Gay men, who had historically been considered an implicit but rarely acknowledged part of the audience, were now thought of as the musical's primary fan base. The presumption was that a love of camp makes gay men appreciate these old films more passionately and disproportionately than any other group of fans. That assessment is far from the case since the genre and its stars, notably Judy Garland, continue to attract a strong female following, too, as the next chapter discusses. Nonetheless, while the MGM musical still represented an outdated form of popular entertainment which could incite nostalgia, by the time of this third compilation in 1994, the films' appeal more unmistakably signified the niche market of gay consumers.

In the mid-1990s Turner Entertainment, the new owner of MGM's library, made efforts to commodify the musicals anew by exploiting that contemporary double valence of "Hollywood's Most Precious Jewels"—as promotional material now described the musicals when announcing the collaboration of Turner and Rhino Records on a series of remastered and expanded soundtracks in 1995. At this same time, a comparable exploitation of the studio library characterized Turner's partnership with MGM/UA on deluxe laser-disc editions of the musicals along with the two companies' revival of the compilation series. In contrast with the nostalgia permeating *That's Entertainment!* and epitomized by its opening use of "Singin' in the Rain," this more recent merchandising of new product derived from the old films sought to reinvent the MGM musical as a crossover commodity by reclaiming its nostalgic appeal for the present, all the while recognizing its camp value from the past.

In a TV promo for the Rhino soundtrack restorations, George Feltenstein, a Turner Entertainment executive, made another claim for the films' appeal: "When something is good, and it is exceptional, and it is of excellence, and it is of quality, it isn't nostalgia, it's still entertainment."[1] Feltenstein produced many of the laser-disc editions for MGM/UA and then, following Time Warner's purchase of Turner in 1996 and Rhino in 1998, moved with the library to serve in the same capacity for the CDs. Since 2002 a senior vice president of Warner Home Video and now supervising the classics division on DVD, he "holds the keys to a kingdom of Golden Age Treasures" (Krauss). An undeniable economic incentive clearly motivates Feltenstein's contention, "It's still entertainment." What makes his defensiveness so striking, though, is that his explanation of the MGM musical's enduring value links it to good taste, to a superior recognition of "excellence" and "quality" despite changing standards, even though, as in the case of the Turner/Rhino CDs, that timeless quality has been re-engineered with the help of contemporary technology.

The promo with Feltenstein summarizes how the Turner company's repackaging of the musicals on CD and home video tries to re-fashion them as an attractive product for contemporary consumers. Behind the defensive assertion "It's still entertainment" lies the inescapable recognition that, with the possible exception of *Singin' in the Rain*, the films and their soundtracks no longer have a guaranteed consumer base of any size or standing. For this reason, the re-packaging also emphasizes the musicals' historic importance as a lost popular art form—so isn't nostalgia the main attraction after all? The Turner/Rhino sampler CD announcing the new series of soundtracks characterizes it as "a journey through Hollywood's Golden Era." This trip back in time illuminates, to quote from the booklet included with the *Ziegfeld Follies* CD, "an invaluable record of a golden era of talent and achievement that will never again be equaled." Likewise, as *That's Entertainment! III* begins with Fred Astaire's "Here's to the Girls" number from *Ziegfeld Follies*, an anonymous voiceover comments that, when this musical was released in 1946, "MGM was at the height of its success in creating incredible fantasies and setting them to music." After a pause, the voice continues: "Here Lucille Ball tames a pack of exotic cat-women. It was imaginative, outlandish imagery, and audiences loved it! It was a time before television and VCRs, when on average ninety million Americans went to the movies each week, and the MGM musical was king of the box office, the most popular entertainment in the world!"

As in the Feltenstein promo for the CDs, the rhetoric here minimizes the MGM musical's commercial insignificance following the end of the studio era although that diminishment is what prompts the reminder of the genre's formerly majestic stature at the box office. The voiceover not only asserts that the MGM musical was once "the most popular entertainment in the world," but the commentary also disavows the camp in what appears on the screen in support of that claim: a mute, expressionless Lucille Ball—her flaming red hair set off by a pink gown embroidered with gems and a matching headdress piled high with ostrich feathers—standing inside a large cage against a blazing red backdrop. She cracks her whip, while the felines she is taming—clothed in revealing black costumes and sporting cat ears—snarl, writhe, and flash their clawlike red finger nails. The extravagant conceit of this scene works as parodic counterpoint to the previous display of those beautiful girls celebrated by Astaire in song, ersatz Ziegfeld showgirls draped in pink, jewels, and feathers like Ball and standing somewhat nervously atop real horses, the reigns held in place by female guards in white uniforms, all on a revolving pink and white carousel. As the two sections of this number, the merry-go-round and the circus ring, spatially connect on screen, at the left side of the frame Ball, snapping the whip one more time, stands along with her wild cat-women, while at the right side Cyd Charisse emerges in a fluffy pink tutu to dance on point in front of the mannequins on the carousel and inside a moving circle of still more showgirls. Then the soundtrack shifts to a stereo register, introducing the first notes of "That's Entertainment," and the compilation's title is superimposed over the entire unforgettable image. Despite the visual proof that this "imaginative, outlandish imagery" still delivers considerable camp pleasure for an audience watching it in 1994, the voiceover insists on the MGM musical's mainstream popularity as a means of normalizing the number's over-the-top spectacle. It's still entertainment, at least for those who know what to watch for.

The voiceover's accompanying commentary discounts what the compilation visually acknowledges when beginning with this particular clip: the MGM musical's historical relation to consumers

90

91

Superimposed over the "imaginative,
outlandish imagery" of *Ziegfeld Follies* is
the title card of *That's Entertainment! III*
(MGM-UA, 1994). Frame captures.

through its distinctive camp style. Given that the moviegoing public of the 1990s was much more conscious of the signifying role of camp in distinguishing gay consumer tastes from straighter ones, *That's Entertainment! III* appears to send a contradictory message when the opening proclaims the MGM musical's mass appeal as mainstream entertainment, "king of the box office," while displaying the "out-landish, imaginative imagery" of the studio's camp style in the *Zieg-feld Follies* excerpt of Lucille Ball, queen of the cat women. Compare this opening with that of the first compilation. *That's Entertainment!* introduces the MGM musical by equating it with studio talent, show-ing singing performers who are not part of the type of oversized spectacle on view in *Ziegfeld Follies* and *That's Entertainment! III*. The first compilation, moreover, goes further to identify the musicals' entertainment values with *Singin' in the Rain*, that greatest of all MGM musicals. The introductory sequence of *That's Entertainment! III*, by contrast, makes it seem as if this third compilation cannot exactly determine what audience it should be addressing because in 1994 the camp value of the MGM musical and all that it implies about gay fan formations around the films cannot be ignored as blithely as in the past.

This double address is less confused than a first impression sug-gests. In its appreciation of the MGM musical's over-the-top style, performances, and aggregate energies, an awareness of camp spec-tatorship thoroughly informs *That's Entertainment! III*. Whereas the 1974 compilation values the MGM musical for its nostalgic affect pure and simple, the 1994 edition more noticeably allows a viewer to nego-tiate between nostalgia and camp and to recognize their dialectical tension within *That's Entertainment! III* itself. This double address is even more pronounced in the lavish "collector's edition" of the compilation released on laser disc following its lackluster theatrical release. As supplemented by the making-of documentary produced for the deluxe boxed set edition, this third compilation reveals how the effort to attract both the gay niche market and a crossover audi-ence has the crucial effect of reversing the relation of camp to non-camp recognition from the studio era. With its camp now in plain sight, the new product has to make a more deliberate effort to pass as timeless, "quality" entertainment. *That's Entertainment! III* exem-plifies how the product line of the nineties on CDs and home video, which featured the musicals' technological and archival enhancement for a contemporary audience, self-consciously wraps these new editions of "Hollywood's Most Precious Jewels" in a discourse of nostalgia harking back to the first *That's Entertainment!* However, as this third compilation and its subsequent boxed set edition further illustrate, the merchandising aiming to reinvent the MGM musical as a commodity for the nineties is nonetheless resorting to camp as its alibi for reentering the mainstream.

"THE OLD MGM IS GONE"

In order to appreciate this turn of events, let me first review what happened to the legendary Metro-Goldwyn-Mayer and its film library. Both the 1974 and 1994 versions of *That's Entertainment!* stop short of pointing out the unhappy fate of MGM—namely, its complete collapse as a major Hollywood studio.

MGM's economic misfortunes began with events of the mid-1950s but extended through the entire second half of the past century. The company's troubles in the fifties were shared by all the major film companies, resulting from the economic transformation of the industry once the Paramount consent decree of 1948 separated the studios' production-distribution arms from their profitable theater chains. Generally speaking, in the first wave of change following the consent decree, the studios increasingly came to function as distribution venues for independent productions, and in the second, the studios themselves were absorbed by transglobal corporations, oftentimes, as when Transamerica purchased United Artists or Coca-Cola bought Columbia Pictures, with disastrous results. Once the dust settled in the 1990s, the studios functioned synergistically as manufacturers of "content" or "software" for gigantic media conglomerates, as Columbia now does for its new owner, Sony, and Warner Bros. for Time Warner. However, unlike other companies from the studio era, MGM was eventually reduced to just the famous logo—that roaring lion—with little behind it but the historical era covered by the series of *That's Entertainment!* compilations. This is the meaning, for instance, which Disney exploits by licensing MGM's name for its Hollywood theme park in Orlando, Florida.

The industry's economic transformation therefore had singular consequences for MGM, and these are etched into the waning fortunes of its signature genre. Although all the film companies continued to produce musicals in the 1960s and 1970s, primarily adaptations or imitations of established Broadway hits for road-show exhibition, the end of the studio system was detrimental to the kind of musicals represented in the *That's Entertainment!* series: original, star-driven productions turned out on a regular basis and using the same personnel over and over to maintain a consistent style identified as MGM's special brand. These films required the mode of industrialized production which the studio system had fostered. As it economically eroded during the 1950s, so did the musical's domination of MGM's annual output. On 16 June 1954, *Variety* reported, "Metro's leadership in the musical film field continues unabated. At least one third of the company's upcoming releases are slated for the musical treatment and it appears that the number of tuners for 1954 will top the ten (out of a total of 45) releases issued in 1953" ("Metro Shooting Lotsa Musicals"). In contrast with that prolific investment in the genre, MGM released just four musicals in 1956, five in 1957, four in 1958, and only one in 1959.[2] This abrupt shift in the studio's priorities resulted from the administration's responses to the economic crisis of the 1950s, since its decisions had the effect of dismantling the industrial support which the MGM musical required.

MGM immediately reacted to the industry-wide decline in attendance by doing away with unit production and gradually terminating contractual arrangements for the exclusive services of stars, writers, directors, and the like. Further lowering the company's profit margins, MGM dragged its heels for ten years before finally spinning off the Loew's theater chain as a separate entity; the last of the majors to comply with the Paramount consent decree, MGM had already reduced its annual output during the slow process by which it set up the independent theater holdings, but because of that delay, MGM also found it more difficult to rebound when it began to lose money for the first time in 1957 (Gomery, 75). While it sorted out the financial separation from Loew's theaters, the studio suffered from uncertain leadership. In New York, President Nicholas Schenck's elevation to board chairman in 1956 effectively ended thirty years of successful management continuity for the company. Earlier, at the Culver City studio in California, cofounder and production head

Louis B. Mayer had been forced out in 1951 after ongoing disagreements with second-in-command, Dore Schary, who then succeeded Mayer. Whereas Mayer had championed MGM's commitment to production of musicals and given Freed virtual autonomy at the studio, Schary did not like musicals, which he saw as trivial, escapist fare. He okayed their production only so long as the long-standing association of the studio with the genre continued to prove its economic worth (Schatz, *Boom and Bust*, 375).

Still MGM's signature product when Schary was at the helm, the musical's reliability was no longer as certain as it had been during Mayer's years. The genre was now contending with competition from television variety shows for family audiences on the one hand and from rock and roll's new importance for the youth market on the other. The studio had formed its own record label in 1944, reviving it commercially three years later primarily to release soundtracks of its musicals, and by the late 1950s MGM Records had a diverse roster of music genres on its list; but despite what was happening in the recording industry as a result of rock and roll's growing popularity with teens—and unlike competitor Twentieth Century-Fox, which jumped on the bandwagon by signing white teen idols Elvis Presley, Pat Boone, and Fabian for films—MGM made only one attempt to attract that audience with a musical, *Jailhouse Rock* (1957) featuring Presley. Rather, the studio looked to repeat past successes and did not develop new teen musicals around the likes of another young Mickey Rooney, Judy Garland, or Jane Powell until the mid-1960s. Then Presley returned to the lot to begin a string of yearly musicals, singer Connie Francis made three in succession, and "quickie" producer Sam Katzman moved over from Columbia to put together several low-budget films exploiting new dance crazes. Typical of the motley fare the studio now turned out was the Katzman remake of Garland's *Girl Crazy* (1943). Retitled *When the Boys Meet the Girls* (1965), it starred Connie Francis alongside guest artists Sam the Sham and The Pharoes, Herman's Hermits, Louis Armstrong—and Liberace!

Even the nine Oscars awarded to *Gigi* (1958) and its big success at the box office failed to resuscitate the studio's former commitment to releasing a full slate of expensive musicals each year. The few lackluster big-budget musicals that MGM continued to produce, such as

Bells Are Ringing (1960) with Judy Holliday and *Billy Rose's Jumbo* (1962) with Doris Day, only made more evident the corporate indecision and financial troubles besetting Loew's throughout the 1960s. In fact, with the costly but unsuccessful remakes of *Cimarron* (1960), *The Four Horsemen of the Apocalypse* (1961), and *Mutiny on the Bounty* (1962), the company seemed most interested in trying to replicate the block-buster success of *Ben-Hur* (1959). The profits of that expensive remake gave the financially unstable studio some breathing space at the start of the sixties, but the debt-ridden, mismanaged company became a prime target for a stockholder raid, which finally happened in 1969 when Kirk Kerkorian finessed control away from Loew's.

Kerkorian installed James Aubrey as head of production to give MGM a dramatically different direction, although not necessarily one any more appreciative of the changing marketplace for films. More ominously for the company's future, Kerkorian and Aubrey gutted the studio in order to reduce the company's heavy debt but also, as it would turn out, to finance construction of Kerkorian's MGM Grand Hotel in Las Vegas. There the history condensed in the famed studio logo was reified as a new style for Vegas hostelry, providing the inspi-ration for the Grand Hotel's decor, with suites and public rooms de-signed to evoke specific films or named after major MGM stars (Feuer, *Hollywood Musical*, 106).

In Culver City, on the other hand, MGM's famed past was dis-carded altogether. Once the Irving Thalberg Building was renamed the generic Administration Building, Aubrey announced, "I don't want to hear any more bullshit about the old MGM . . . The old MGM is gone" (Bart, 39). As evidence of its complete break with the past, the "new" MGM sold off part of the studio's backlot and reduced pro-duction of expensive films, canceling many high profile projects in development and alienating the rest of the industry as a result. The new management then went on to arrange for the world's greatest fire sale, an auction "of the countless treasures acquired from Metro-Goldwyn Mayer" by the David Weisz Company, which took place over a period of eighteen days in May 1970.[3] During the auction any-thing not hammered down to the Culver City lot—recall the four floors of the celebrated props department—became bankable mer-chandise for its tie to the studio, despite Kerkorian's and Aubrey's own indifference to this value. Wardrobe, furniture, carpets, figurines, musical instruments, paintings, genuine antiques, plants, an assortment of planes, trains, tanks, cars, wagons, and Roman chariots, even the "Cotton Blossom" paddle wheel steamer from *Show Boat* (1951), all went on the block. What did not go on auction, mostly annotated screenplays, publicity stills, and studio correspondence, ended up for sale as souvenirs in the Grand Hotel's gift shop the following year.

Although Aubrey resigned in 1973 after a string of box-office failures further reduced MGM's stature, the company's fortunes did not improve under succeeding administrations. MGM consequently closed down its distribution arm in 1974 and contracted with United Artists to release its new production schedule of six to eight films yearly, beginning with *That's Entertainment!* The old MGM may have been gone, ceasing to operate as a major film company with the release of *That's Entertainment!*, but as Aubrey's successors begrudgingly realized after the compilation's success, there were still profits to be accrued from remembering the studio's salad days. In 1976 the company produced a follow-up, *That's Entertainment, Part 2*, and in 1985 another compilation with a somewhat different theme, *That's Dancing!*, which included clips from other studios but gave special attention to MGM's former standing as the leading producer of musicals.

Of greater impact on the future commercial value of the MGM musical, ownership of the film library changed hands several times following Kerkorian's takeover. He split the film and hotel units into separate entities in 1978, and two years later MGM Film Corporation purchased a financially troubled United Artists from Transamerica, forming the MGM/UA Entertainment Company and swelling its library to include UA's own output as well as that of pre-1948 Warner Bros. and RKO, the rights to which United Artists owned. Primarily to obtain that sizeable catalogue for his developing cable networks, Ted Turner bought the merged company in 1986. As a means of reducing his debt, Turner immediately sold back to Kerkorian the United Artists name and MGM logo. Turner then let go of the studio lot, selling it to Lorimar-Telepictures, which tore down the MGM sign standing over the property, prominently featured in a panning shot to Sinatra after the opening credits of *That's Entertainment!* When Warners purchased Lorimar shortly afterward, the Culver City lot was traded to

Columbia in exchange for the latter's half ownership of Warners's Burbank studio, so the Culver City property eventually ended up in the hands of Sony Pictures.

Because these divestitures did not address Turner's entire debt, he had to sell back to Kerkorian what remained of MGM: the production, distribution, and home-video units—that is, everything save the film library. Kerkorian subsequently formed MGM/UA Communications Company. Moving to a suite of business offices in Santa Monica, this newest incarnation of MGM lacked both a library and production facilities, placing it at a considerable disadvantage in comparison with the other film companies, despite their own corporate takeovers. MGM/UA still retained an identifiable connection to its once glorious past, though, because it licensed home-video rights from Turner Entertainment, which now owned all existent footage in the MGM archive along with the films themselves.

Meanwhile, MGM itself continued to go in and out of Kerkorian's hands. In 1990 he sold the company yet again, this time to an international conglomerate, Pathé Communications. To help pay for the deal, Pathé arranged for Warners to distribute the home-video product under the MGM/UA label. With Pathé's own legal problems mounting from investigations of its questionable financial activities in Europe, Kerkorian bought back MGM in 1996, while Warner Bros., following its merger with Time-Life, absorbed Turner's company that same year. In 1999, MGM negotiated with Time Warner to terminate the home-video deal prematurely. As a result, the immense Turner library of studio-era films was split, with control of United Artists product reverting to Kerkorian's latest corporate version of MGM/UA, which by this point had purchased the defunct Polygram and Orion for their libraries, and Warners—now part of the AOL Time Warner media conglomerate—regaining ownership of its own classic line, RKO's, and everything the old MGM had made prior to 1986.[4]

UNLOCKING THE VAULTS

While Kerkorian continued to sell and buy back MGM/UA following the 1986 acquisition by Turner Entertainment, the latter company made full use of the old studio's archive—outtakes, trailers,

prerecordings, short subjects, production footage, promotional documentaries—to reinvigorate the film library's commercial value.[5]
What I want to emphasize is how the Turner company, while mindful
of the MGM musical's nostalgic appeal, exploited the vault material to
redefine that appeal as a specialized taste without acknowledging its
basis in camp, although elsewhere that connection is more evident.

To begin with, the MGM library supplied programming for a new
cable venture, Turner Network Television, which premiered in 1988.
Trying to give the library a more contemporary appeal, the Turner
Company engaged in a controversial project of colorizing black-and-
white films for showing on TNT and later distribution on VHS; these
were mostly dramas and comedies, so few of the musicals received
such mistreatment. Additionally, recognizing the currency of mass
camp as a mode of legibility for these films, not the least through
the exclamatory hype of their promotion, TNT ran a half hour of old
trailers on Sunday nights under the umbrella title "Trailer Camp."
As a first foray into producing new content, Turner's company then
drew on the archive for a three-part miniseries recounting the rise
and fall of MGM from its formation in 1924, its golden age in the 1930s
and 1940s, its troubles in the 1950s and 1960s, the auction in 1970, and
Turner's acquisition in 1986. With much fanfare and a pretentious
narration by Patrick Stewart, MGM: When the Lion Roars premiered
on TNT in March 1992. A hefty, well-illustrated book by Peter Hay
using the same title was published by Turner Publishing in conjunction with the miniseries. After the strategy of showing MGM classics
ran its course, TNT switched to more contemporary films and more
coverage of sports events featuring teams owned by the Turner company. The library then served as the basis of Turner Classic Movies,
which began in 1994 as a commercial-free showcase for studio-era
films competing on cable with American Movie Classics.

In contrast with AMC, which in 1999 moved away from emphasizing pre-1950s films, began running commercials, and downplayed
its classics identification, TCM still keeps its sights primarily focused
on the studio era (Dempsey). The network makes extensive use of
material in the MGM archive to supply imagery for self-promotion
on cable and its Web site, as filler for showing in between movies,
and as content of an ongoing series of new documentaries and interviews with stars such as Ann Miller, Jane Powell, and Esther Wil-

liams. Moreover, in 1993 the company began "The Turner Archival Project" which films interviews with studio-era old-timers for use in the network's documentaries; nearly three hundred of these had been recorded by 2003 (Krauss). Outtakes of numbers shot but cut from release prints of MGM musicals have also been shown on occasion. Each month, too, TCM features a salute to a star and director as well as a special theme, while slotting genres such as the musical at a regular time each week.

TCM's host and interviewer Robert Osborne amplifies the network's attention to the studio era. Unlike his counterpart at AMC —the original host there was Bob Dorian, a former minor actor— Osborne came to TCM with credentials as an industry insider, since he is a columnist for the trade paper *Hollywood Reporter*, and one of the first historians of the Academy Awards. On TCM he introduces and concludes the showing of a film with anecdotes taking viewers behind the scenes of its production. Likewise, in each issue of the TCM monthly program, a magazine titled *Now Playing*, Osborne writes a second-page column in which he recounts firsthand experience of the featured star.

All of these programming strategies on TCM work together to present MGM as the centerpiece of the studio era as well as the classics network, establishing the latter's brand, in effect, as the MGM museum with Osborne as the expert tour guide, taking his audience back to the soundstages of what he has called "the Rolls Royce of the movie studios." To be sure, TCM also shows the Warner Bros. and RKO films that were included in the MGM purchase, and the network licenses films made by other studios and from later decades; but the old MGM nonetheless gets pride of place in the network's discursive reconstruction of studio-era Hollywood, especially in Osborne's commentary and interviews, and despite the generic variety on the schedule, MGM musicals are well represented in the monthly lineup.

The Turner company's exploitation of the MGM catalogue did not stop with cable but went on to include soundtrack recordings, too. The most famous of the musicals had always been available on records. In the 1970s MGM Records, at this point no longer owned by the studio, produced a series of double-feature LPs with condensed soundtracks called "Those Glorious MGM Musicals," and in the 1980s Columbia/Sony released more complete versions of individual scores on CD and cassette. With the latter's rights expired, at the same time as the classics network began in 1994, Turner arranged for Rhino Records to issue digitally remastered CDs of the scores, this time from the prerecordings originally made for the films' production. Since almost everything "ever recorded at the studio" was still preserved in the archive (Burlingame), MGM's innovative practice of prerecording numbers with "stems," microphones set at various angles to the orchestra and performers, allowed many tracks to be remastered in stereo. Turner and Rhino announced their series to the press in 1995 with a promotional CD sampling the new soundtracks, most of them musicals such as *Ziegfeld Follies, Easter Parade* (1948), *Show Boat*, and the Mickey Rooney-Judy Garland series in a four-disc boxed set.[6] The sampler itself was housed in a black, faux leather jewel box with "Hollywood's Most Precious Jewels" embossed on the cover over a drawing of a glittering diamond ring. Inside, the accompanying pamphlet exclaimed, "Shining Brighter Than Ever!" Six titles appeared in the series during its first year of production and fifteen the year after.

The promotion of these crown jewels no longer in MGM's outright possession clearly signaled a readjustment of attitudes regarding the old product as a source of commercial value, and that readjustment extended to home video as well. The Turner-Rhino soundtrack series followed the theatrical release the previous year of *That's Entertainment! III*, coproduced by Turner Entertainment and MGM/UA. This newest installment in the compilation series contrasted with its two predecessors by taking advantage of archival material, including deleted or alternate versions of numbers in its mix of clips. Despite the commercial failure of *That's Entertainment! III* in theaters, it generated a lavish laser-disc release from MGM/UA Home Video in 1995. The boxed set featured a longer cut of the film, a making-of documentary, and assorted supplements—additional outtakes, trailers, lobby cards, prerecordings on an analog track—and it conformed to similar deluxe versions of musicals released by Turner and MGM/UA on the laser-disc format beginning in 1993. These included special editions of *The Wizard of Oz* (1939), *Ziegfeld Follies, Meet Me in St. Louis* (1944), *Show Boat*, and separate Judy Garland and Gene Kelly collections, all chock-full of their own supplementary material to identify each boxed set as archival editions of the films. A few even included the new CDs as part of the package. Also in this line was a 1996 edition of the entire compilation series, *That's Entertainment! The Ultimate Treasury*, which, along with its own assortment of supplements, added an "unofficial" fourth installment limited to video, *That's More Entertainment!* That same year Rhino issued a six-CD "Ultimate Edition" soundtrack recording of the *That's Entertainment!* series to complement the home-video collection.

At first glance, this ambitious repackaging of the MGM musicals on cable, CD, and home video is notable for how the archival setting establishes the films' stature as classics, distinguishing the new releases from older ones through the addition of previously unavailable supplementary material. The sampler CD's brochure describes an enhanced product now directed at a consumer who is more of the amateur collector than ordinary fan:

> The complete expertise of Turner and Rhino has brought these classic soundtracks to life as never before. All previous issues of these soundtracks have been taken off the shelves so that we could start from scratch and give these special releases the attention they deserve. Each release is painstakingly remastered from the original studio tapes to restore the music to its original glory and supplemented with added outtakes, rehearsals, and other previously unreleased performances. Booklets featuring extended historical essays, rare photos, and session credits complete the packages, giving the music new life and drama you never expected. More important, the Turner/Rhino union will see the premiere release of many soundtracks locked away in vaults for years.

The pamphlet's listing of the CDs' special features applies to the Turner-MGM/UA collaboration on laser disc equally well since the latter followed the same strategy of replacing earlier versions of the musicals with remastered editions or bringing out titles not yet released in that format, all distinguished by color restoration, stereo soundtracks whenever possible, and the inclusion of outtakes, trailers and promotional footage, and prerecordings. The archival versions of the musicals on laser and CD thus take on new valence as commodities by being unmoored from their prior history of commodification. Replacing all previous versions, these "special releases" begin anew, we are promised, since the engineers have "start[ed] from scratch" in recreating the original conditions of the musicals' production. But through contemporary technology the CDs and laser discs now sound or look better than ever, brought "to life as never before," which is also to say that the new versions improve on the originals in two ways: they are technologically updated, in contrast with their former lives as monaural theatrical releases and LPs, and they are now packaged for consumption by being contextualized in previously unreleased supplementary material and an account of their production. The promised "new life and drama" stands out more audibly or visibly in the new product because of the technological enhancement, but this element emerges just as strongly from the reconstruction of the musicals' industrial back story.

Allowing for a kind of archeological reconstruction of MGM's golden age through its musicals, the archive of film outtakes and prerecorded, alternate, deleted, and extended vocal tracks constitutes the only record of that famed era surviving the 1970 auction that decimated the studio's past. The new merchandising of the musicals on CD and laser disc follows TCM's presentation of the library on cable—the back story functions much like Osborne's insider's view albeit with a more scholarly tone—but goes further in mass-producing "singular" material—the archival supplements—in order to invest the new editions with their special aura not simply as classics, but as rarer and purer versions of the classics. As a product line, the archivally enhanced CDs and videos serve as facsimiles of the specialist's collection, which, as Susan Stewart points out, makes "magical" not the object being collected but its "mode of production." The collection, she explains, replaces the object's origin with "the scene of acquisition, its proper destination" (165). Here, the legerdemain of collecting represents the musicals' original moment of production but displaces their history through the supplements that bear evidence of it. The special editions thus equate the musicals' historical production with the act of acquiring signs of their origin in the past. The amplified CD soundtrack or supplemented LD boxed set includes recordings and outtakes which, before this point, had been unavailable to the ordinary fan, or at best (as in the case of the Garland footage from *Annie Get Your Gun*) obtainable only in incomplete and much less pristine bootleg versions privately sold by or traded among collectors with industry connections. However, with mass reproduction negating the historical rarity of the vault material, its value for a collector resides in the supplements' ability to be purchased by like-minded aficionados everywhere; as a result, amassing the entire set ultimately distinguishes the serious collector from the casual fan of the genre. What makes the new product collectible on CD and LD, in short, is not its exclusivity but its liberation from the vaults—and from history.

Let me postpone for the moment a question that probably comes immediately to mind from this targeting of the new product toward collectors, namely, isn't this group of consumers dominated by gay men who take the musicals seriously for their camp? Right now my point has to do with how the discursive framing of that target audience obscures this question through an underlying nostalgia that annuls the MGM musical's historicity in a manner paralleling mass camp's ahistoricism but with a very different purpose. According to the promotional spiel on the sampler CD, the archival enhancement updates the musicals for consumers seeking to experience the past in the present moment through an obsolete form of entertainment that, no longer dominant or widely valued, has been historically annotated and technologically improved, and this amplification has been achieved without sacrificing the films' timelessness and universality. Pitching the new product so that it can retain its nostalgic value as "still entertainment" even for collectors, the merchandising is of apiece with previous efforts to capitalize on an older generation's affection for the MGM musical, most notably in *That's Entertainment!*

IT'S STILL ENTERTAINMENT?

The *That's Entertainment!* series was not the first time that one of MGM's various owners had profited from the studio library. Loew's successfully reissued its musicals to theaters on a regular basis, both before and after selling them to television, and it did the same with the soundtracks on MGM Records, reformatting the first ones as the recording industry turned from 78s to LPs, keeping them in circulation through new editions, and reusing tracks in themed collections, such as those devoted to a studio anniversary or to stars such as Judy Garland, Kathryn Grayson, and Gene Kelly. The well-known black and yellow label of the LPs, in fact, was borrowed decades later for the laser discs to evoke nostalgic association with these old recordings, and the Rhino line now reproduces the old LP covers inside the plastic cases of its CDs.

Loew's turned to prime-time TV as well. In 1955–56, the studio's first foray into weekly programming was *The MGM Parade* on ABC, a behind-the-scenes look at studio product, present and past, which recycled "That's Entertainment" from *The Band Wagon* (1953) as its theme song and serialized films with no apparent reissue value, such as *The Pirate* (1948). In a sense this series, which did not make much of an impression, had been tried out the year before in the salute to MGM's thirtieth anniversary on Ed Sullivan's *Toast of the Town*. Titled "The MGM Story," the special hour-long program featured live appearances by stars associated exclusively with the musical (Fred Astaire, Gene Kelly, Esther Williams, Ann Miller, Jane Powell, Howard Keel, Debbie Reynolds) along with Lucille Ball and Desi Arnaz, showed clips from three decades of studio achievement, recreated numbers from new releases such as *The Student Prince* (1954), *Seven Brides for Seven Brothers* (1954), and *Give a Girl a Break* (1953), and closed with Lana Turner's TV debut as a musical performer in the streamlined version of Judy Garland's "Great Lady Has 'an Interview' " number from *Ziegfeld Follies*.

When the Sullivan tribute aired in 1954 the musical was still a viable commodity for MGM, generating a large family audience, so the salute presents all the numbers, selected to epitomize the diversity of the studio's musicals, as straightforward entertainment for mass viewership on a Sunday night. Two decades later, when *That's Entertainment!* celebrated MGM's fiftieth anniversary on a grander scale than the Sullivan show commemorated the thirtieth, the compilation had to remind audiences of a lost connection to entertainment values no longer in vogue. Marketing the old MGM musicals as a wholesome alternative to the R-rated fare coming to dominate the movie business, the G-rated *That's Entertainment!* openly capitalized on the "retro" in retrospective. "Musicals were the fantasy trips of their day," Sinatra comments in his segment, translating the genre's utopian appeal into seventies lingo. They may "not tell you where our heads were at, but they will tell you where our hearts were at." The advertising claims underlined this appeal: "It's more than a movie . . . It's a celebration!" and "Boy . . . Do we need it now!" exclaimed posters and newspaper ads (*TE* press book). A featurette promoting the compilation, now shown on TCM and included with the laser-disc boxed set of the entire series, ended by quoting Sinatra's wistful conclusion to his segment: "You know, you can wait around and hope, but I'll tell you, you'll never see the likes of this again."

That's Entertainment! makes MGM musicals objects of nostalgia not individually but by compiling excerpts from them into an anthology, a series of quotations from the old films—not unlike the Turner/Rhino sampler CD, in fact. The greatest-hits format represents for the audience memories of the era when MGM was an industry giant, "the studio that invented the movie musical," as the trailer puts it. In this sense, *That's Entertainment!* writes large what many MGM musicals themselves do when they set their plots in an earlier era of vaudeville, incorporate the familiar personas of a star in characterization, or recycle songs such as "Singin' in the Rain" from previous films. As Jane Feuer points out, the genre frequently quotes from earlier sources in order to establish the continuity of present-day entertainment with its past, as well as to minimize the industrial conditions of the movie musical's mass production as filmed entertainment. Quotation has much the same purpose in the 1954 Sullivan tribute to MGM, including the Lana Turner recreation of a Judy Garland number. Because the 1974 compilation is premised on acknowledging the divide between past and present tastes in entertainment, reminding us that "we'll never see the likes of it again," *That's Entertainment!* makes more apparent how the convention of quotation is able to cancel history altogether. "Entertainment," Feuer observes, when discussing the post–studio era's turn to nostalgia in compilation films like this one, "comes to exist in a perpetual present which is also a perpetual past" (*Hollywood Musical*, 94). Nostalgic quotation of the musicals truly makes them "still" entertainment: they are shown to endure over time because they are wrenched out of time.

The nostalgic cancellation of history determines how *That's Entertainment!* uses excerpts to develop its own narrative, which purports to tell the MGM story through its musicals. Although framed by the chronology of the studio's golden age, so that the first segment covers the introduction of sound and growing sophistication which characterized 1930s musicals and the final segment looks at the genre's last CinemaScope triumphs in the late 1950s, the compilation as a whole swings back and forth in time. As the pre-credits sequence illustrates with the song "Singin' in the Rain," *That's Entertainment!* edits short clips into montage sequences that give an impression of the numbers' coexisting in a timeless golden age. Including almost every number ever associated with an MGM musical, *That's Entertainment!* often abbreviates them to the point where one dissolves all too quickly into another, as in the Esther Williams and Judy and Mickey tributes, the abrupt jump from June Allyson's "Thou Swell" to the finale of her "Varsity Drag" (itself reduced through several internal ellipses), the sequence illustrating Gene Kelly's acrobatics, the bits and pieces of numbers from *Meet Me in St. Louis* followed by repetition of Garland imagery cut into her performance of "Get Happy," and so on. The sequel released two years later, *That's Entertainment, Part 2*, does not even bother with chronology but arranges clips in helter-skelter fashion, and it even goes so far, as Feuer observes, to incorporate "source and quotation," present and past, in a single frame: when hosts Gene Kelly and Fred Astaire make their entrance with ladder in hand as if emerging from the 1953 rendition of "That's Entertainment" in *The Band Wagon*, but in the guise of their "real," much older 1976 personas (*Hollywood Musical*, 104).

That's Entertainment! and its sequel are rather blatant in their commercial exploitation of the old musicals' nostalgic value, as *Mad* magazine's 1975 parody recognized. "What's Entertainment?" skillfully lays bare the first compilation's agenda in mythicizing the studio's past while also economically profiting from it. Furthermore, in adding its own lyrics to familiar MGM melodies, *Mad*'s spoof turns quotation against *That's Entertainment!* as a means of exposing its nostalgic cancellation of history. For instance, instead of singing the real lyrics to "I Can't Give You Anything but Love," a chorus of MGM stars exclaims, "We can't make a film that's true to life, baby" (Jacobs, 10), which enables the parody to point out the artifice of the MGM musical's heterosexual innocence in the face of the screen's supposed liberation by the new ratings system. Similarly, in order to show what the compilation effaces through nostalgia—the MGM musical's industrial origins as mass-produced entertainment—in one song (to the tune of "Ol' Man River") actors bemoan the studio's factory system, which placed them in servitude to L. B. Mayer (7), and in another ("The Trolley Song"), Judy Garland complains about being required everyday to get "To the spot / On that lot / Where each plot / Looked the same" (9). Additionally, the parody's caricatures emphasize the physical difference between the stars in the present and when toiling at MGM. At the same time, it notes why these aging stars accepted the task of returning to their former studio to serve as hosts: "It was done for a fee—/ Not entertainment!" (4). Nor does the parody ignore the commercial motive of the studio, its glory days of box-office dominance well behind it, in reaching into its vaults to put together an unexpected hit that was not expensive to make. To the tune of "Singin' in the Rain," that film's three stars remind us in the parody's own pre-credits sequence that these musicals "were paid for / A long time ago," so with even "bigger" profits in mind, "We're bringin' . . . / And singin' em again!" (4, ellipses in original).

More than just burlesquing the appeal to nostalgia radiating from *That's Entertainment*, the *Mad* parody calls attention to the first compilation's dislocation from the present moment of the mid-1970s and to its comparable historical blind spots with regard to the past. By contrast, the 1994 installment of the series is much less confident than the first; it recognizes that at least some of its hoped-for audience, those unfamiliar with the old musicals except perhaps by reputation, may ask the same question that *Mad* had posed two decades before: "What's entertainment?" In this case, however, the answer is another question: "Whose entertainment?"

Returning to a format of recounting the musical's history at MGM, *That's Entertainment! III* is a virtual remake of the first compilation, but, like the production back stories that anchor the Turner/Rhino CDs, it takes a more self-reflexive stance, even sharing some of the same demystifying emphases we saw in the *Mad* parody. As George Feltenstein concludes about the new installment in the making-of documentary produced for the LD boxed set: "I think if we've achieved anything with this film, it was being able to really bring the audience backstage, as it were . . . so they feel almost like they were there watching the films being made, because we've given them that little piece of extra information that they never had before."[7]

That's Entertainment! III cannot avoid taking a demystifying stance toward its subject matter. Opening with awareness of the historical distance between the era when Leo the Lion was "king of the box office" and the present day of cable television and VCRs, *TE! III* (as publicity material abbreviated it) immediately turns away from the first compilation's undisguised invitation to nostalgia, which filtered everything shown through Sinatra's remark that "you'll never see the likes of it again." Because of the availability of the old musicals on video and cable in 1994, this compilation's audience *can* see the likes of it again, and again, and then still again, at least if they wish to. *TE! III* thus distinguishes itself by adding "that little piece of extra information," taking advantage of studio archives to include rare behind-the-scenes footage, outtakes, and alternate versions of numbers.

As a result, the presentation of clips is more outwardly informed by recognition of their historical setting in an industrial past which cannot be entirely collapsed into the present through nostalgic quotation or, alternatively, through mass-camp laughter. For instance, *TE! III* uses split-screen displays at several points as part of the backstage view described by Feltenstein: to contrast the apparent visual seamlessness of Eleanor Powell dancing to "Fascinating Rhythm" in *Lady Be Good* (1941) with a documentary record of the hard physical labor of anonymous studio employees behind the scenes during filming; to acknowledge the studio's economical recycling of a voice double's prerecorded track, from its initial use by Cyd Charisse in a number dropped from *The Band Wagon* to Joan Crawford's reuse of it in *Torch Song* (1953); and to compare the exactness of Astaire's dancing in two versions of "I Wanna Be a Dancin' Man" from *Belle of New York* (1952) as demonstration of his perfectionism, the result of much rehearsal and preplanning. The compilation similarly restores Ava Gardner's voice in place of the dubbed version used in the release print of "Can't Help Loving that Man" in *Show Boat*, removes the title credits obscuring Astaire and Ginger Rogers in *The Barkleys of Broadway* (1949), and exhibits footage from the aborted Garland version of *Annie Get Your Gun* and "March of the Doagies," the big production number once meant to lead into the climax of *The Harvey Girls* (1946).

From its backstage view, too, while the narrative about the MGM musical follows the same thematic division of the first *That's Entertainment!* (spots on Astaire, Kelly, Garland, Williams, the MGM "look," development of new stars, the 1930s beginnings, the 1950s grand finale, and so forth), *TE! III* revisits these topics with fuller knowledge of what, during the intervening two decades, the demystifying biographies about MGM stars from the studio era had revealed to a moviegoing public. The commentary dwells on the racism that stunted Lena Horne's development into a full-fledged star, alludes to the labor troubles that complicated Judy Garland's last years at MGM as revealed by the *Annie Get Your Gun* outtake, and documents the studio's operation as a "dream factory" under Mayer's firm patriarchal hand. The compilation likewise places its hosts at specific points on the studio lot: Esther Williams at her swimming pool set, Lena Horne in the recording studio, Debbie Reynolds outside the wardrobe department, Ann Miller in a dance rehearsal hall, Cyd Charisse on MGM stage 15 before a still-existent backdrop used in *Brigadoon* (1954). The first compilation did that as well, with Fred Astaire walking on a dilapidated set once used in *The Band Wagon*, but by 1994 the passage of time is more evident: in the lined faces, hoarse voices, and stiff bodies of the studio's former stars—those still alive and, for the most part, now in their seventies—but just as much in the locations, since the hosts return to what the publicity material and making-of documentary refer to only as "the former MGM lot," never mentioning its new corporate owner, Sony. If nothing else, MGM's minor role in the contemporary film industry resulting from the Kerkorian and Turner buyouts forces *TE! III* to keep the studio's musicals more grounded in their past.

The backstage perspective does not mean that the stars' commentaries are not frequently as banal as in the first compilation or that this one does not do some historical effacement of its own. It still invites a nostalgic appreciation of the musicals. The studio's past has passed but it was nonetheless "a time when dreams really did come true." And "what a time it was!" Gene Kelly opines at the end. "Life was simpler then, and so was the movie business. MGM's dream factory created a rich, romantic, compelling world of illusion. And although we may not see anything like it again, we're blessed with memories, and miles and miles of film. In the words of Irving Berlin, 'The song is ended, but the melody lingers on.'"

From this vantage point, *That's Entertainment! III* follows the same pattern of demystification/remystification which, as Feuer shows, underlies a backstage musical, especially when made by MGM.[8] This third entry in the series therefore does not entirely demystify its subject matter—the making of entertainment at MGM—by historicizing it. The compilation takes an audience backstage for a privileged view of the industrial setting but ultimately reasserts the MGM musical's mythic stature before the lights go back on. The closing moments of *TE! III* repeat fleeting but immediately recognizable clips from numbers featured in the first two installments of the series in order to end with a visual reminder of the MGM musical's timeless quality, its continuity as a source of pleasure for audiences with long memories—or with home-video equipment. The end credits do not stop rolling until this final message is delivered to audiences: "The MGM musical classics excerpted in this film are available in their entirety on videocassette and laser disc from MGM/UA Home Video."

For all this remystification of the MGM musical, which recommodifies it as "still entertainment," *That's Entertainment! III* nonetheless uses its backstage view to establish a camp perspective on the ahistorical nostalgia carried over from the other installments in the series. *TE! III* promises "The Return of the MGM Musical!"—as advance advertising on MGM/UA home-video products announced—but after watching it, one has to ask, just what entertainment values of the MGM musical are coming back after all this time? From its backstage view of the studio's operation, the compilation unabashedly celebrates the spectacular qualities of numbers' "outlandish, imaginative imagery," even when the clips involve solo turns or duets. As a reviewer of the LD boxed set observed about this "amusing, somewhat campy take on the genre," "like some of the lost footage, many of the clips in *TEIII* [*sic*] are far more enjoyable in their isolated form than in the context of the complete films" (Parke, 34).

Being a compilation, of course, *TE! III*, like the entire series, is the most aggregate of forms, so it has to divorce numbers from their original narrative contexts. But the effect is different this time out due to the prominence given to outtakes, alternate versions, and split-screen views. Outtakes and alternate versions of numbers, for that matter, never appeared in a narrative setting to begin with. The commercial imperative not to repeat selections from previous compilations, moreover, means that *TE! III* has to go deeper into the MGM library to excerpt from much less well-known and aesthetically valued musicals, such as *I Love Melvin* (1953) and *The Kissing Bandit* (1948), and these selections even more readily stand apart from their

original purposes in a film narrative, for who in the audience can remember them, or has even seen them? Perhaps most importantly, in
contrast with the breakneck speed of the first compilation as it cuts
down many famous numbers into montages and then reinserts them
all in a narrative of the MGM musical's golden age, *TE! III* excerpts
more generously. The new compilation showcases fewer pieces and
consequently allows an audience to pay more attention to how the
numbers work on their own terms *as* numbers, even when cut down.

The 1994 compilation's greater respect for the coherence of numbers as self-contained moments of spectacle, with a star's singing and
dancing all part of the overall "outlandish, imaginative imagery," is
shaped by the backstage view to encourage what Brett Farmer theorizes is the typical gay reading practice when it comes to musicals. To
restate what I discussed in the introduction, Farmer argues that a gay
spectator finds much pleasure in a musical despite its heterosexual
narratives by making an alternate investment with the film: "latching
on to certain moments or features that are marginal or oblique," in
effect he reads any musical by rearranging it into an aggregate form,
giving more weight to numbers and less importance to their narrative containment (81). Although not describing it as such, as I also
suggested, what Farmer points out is how gay spectators watch musicals for their camp. The backstage view in *That's Entertainment! III*
invites this type of spectatorial engagement with the MGM musical; the compilation itself focuses on marginal and nonnarrative moments of spectacle, and it rearranges the emphases with which the
first installment in the series recounted the MGM story. In this recontextualization of the films, *TE! III* not only acknowledges the camp
values evident in their characteristic style, but it formally licenses
camp spectatorship as an authoritative interpretation and legitimate
source of pleasure.

IT'S MORE THAN A MOVIE . . .
IT'S A BOXED-SET EDITION!

Once again, comparing the first and third compilations—in this
case, examining their approaches to MGM's distinctive house style—
heightens a sense of what the 1994 version does differently in addressing a camp spectator alongside a nostalgic one. The featurette

promoting *That's Entertainment!* claims that its purpose is "to capture the essence of the MGM musical." Asking what made it unique, the anonymous narrator points out the experimentation, professional discipline, and lavish style, quoting Debbie Reynolds's comment in her segment that the MGM motto was, "Do it big. Do it right. Give it class." *That's Entertainment!* itself gives over the question of the MGM musical's "essence" to Peter Lawford, who hosts a segment devoted to the 1940s. He comments: "When I first came to MGM, the world was at war. For the GIs overseas and the audiences here at home, the musicals were a very special kind of escape, both during the war and afterward. The films we made here had a certain style, a look that was unmistakable, whether it was the directing, or the lighting—I don't really know. But somehow you could always tell it was an MGM movie, especially the musicals."

The segment, however, makes no effort to explain how one *could* tell. After making this statement, Lawford turns to the studio's show-casing of new talent in postwar musicals, as if that accounts for it. Yet cut into his commentary at the point when he refers to the "certain style" of MGM fare is one of the few uncredited clips in *That's Entertainment!* An excerpt from *On an Island with You* (1948) shows Lawford playing a character who watches a musical number being shot within that Esther Williams film. The cut to a quotation of this scene as Lawford speaks about the MGM style indicates it is there to visualize what he cannot describe. Called "the pagan number" by the fictive director of the film being made in *On an Island with You*, the choreography is strictly Cecil B. DeMille set to music, a camp tossed salad of Technicolor, Orientalism, oversized scale, jungle rhythms, and feverish movement, with barely clad white dancers posing as "natives," their dancing enacting some kind of ritualized worship or sacrifice in front of a South Seas temple. There are apparently no words to describe the "certain style" of MGM musicals in the 1940s, just as the clip illustrating that style is not identified but treated as if it were found footage of Lawford. What the segment nevertheless displays at this moment is the camp style of the "unmistakable" look of MGM musicals: too outlandishly spectacular to be taken at face value as simple escapism, and also too campy to name as such.

The glamour segment hosted by Debbie Reynolds in *That's Entertainment! III* likewise covers the studio's distinct look, this time by attributing it to the MGM glamour mill, the various departments devoted to costume, makeup, hair styling, and lighting. Working together, these artisans, Reynolds comments, made all the studio's leading ladies "appear on screen as images of unsurpassed beauty." A montage of close-ups of MGM female stars, set against the vocal track of Tony Martin singing "You Stepped Out of a Dream" from *Ziegfeld Girl* (1941), illustrates, followed by a cut to the number's finale, which, according to Reynolds, epitomizes how "in 1941, the glamour age had reached its zenith." As he sings, Martin escorts Lana Turner, strutting the famous Ziegfeld walk down a staircase and across the stage. With the unnaturalness of her posture and silliness of her costume, starting with a headdress that makes it look as if a miniature metallic Christmas tree is sprouting out of her hair, this extravagant number offers camp commentary enough.

Despite the seriousness with which it first approaches the MGM look of "unsurpassed beauty," the segment appears to take its cue from the *Ziegfeld Girl* clip, for the numbers afterward all parody female glamour.[9] In the next excerpt, Reynolds herself does an exaggerated impersonation of a movie glamour queen in "A Lady Loves" from *I Love Melvin*, set in contrast with an unused version of her doing the number with a similarly mannered performance style but in a barnyard setting, and this is followed by Dolores Gray using "glamour as a weapon to spoof the power of the devastating female over the hapless male" in "Thanks a Lot, But No Thanks" from *It's Always Fair Weather* (1955). The third clip in this triptych also brings with it a famous camp following of its own: Joan Crawford appears in "tropical makeup" and with India Adams's voice to perform "Two-Faced Woman" in *Torch Song*. As the Crawford number is intercut with Cyd Charisse's lip-synching of the same track in the *Band Wagon* outtake, Reynolds comments with studied understatement, "It has been suggested that they may have dropped the wrong version."

More unexpectedly, although this segment is described in all accompanying material as just the glamour spot, at this point Reynolds abruptly shifts attention to the 1940s' "fascination with things tropical and south of the border." "Exotic rhythms and costumes," she comments, echoing the sentiment of Lawford's remarks in the first compilation, "transported audiences away from cold climates and the troubled times of a world war." The numbers in this second half of her segment now represent the MGM camp style even more directly. The theatrical version of *That's Entertainment! III* has Reynolds continuing with a brief reference to the prominence in 1940s MGM musicals of Latin bands like Xavier Cugat's, "recruited to lend an authentic sound to these films." The longer version in the LD boxed set adds an excerpt of Cugat's orchestra playing "Jungle Rumba/Jungle Fantasy," a nightclub floor show in *Neptune's Daughter* (1949) which visualizes Cugot's "exotic rhythms" as a spectacle of masked and barefoot dancers swaying to the beat of jungle drums. The excerpt, which camps the notion of ethnic authenticity through its exaggeration, is of apiece with the uncredited performance of "exotic" jungle dancers in the first compilation's illustration of the forties style.

The remaining numbers in the Reynolds sequence display the interaction of the Latin-inspired choreography, star performance, and MGM's camp style. Cyd Charisse and Ann Miller tap dance flamenco style in a ménage à trois with Ricardo Montalban from *Kissing Bandit*, causing Reynolds to interject, her voice inflected to recall the Mae West impersonation of her nightclub act, "there doesn't seem enough Ricardo to go around!" Camp icon Carmen Miranda, sporting a headdress made of tiny umbrellas, cavorts with two clowns, all three dressed in complementary primary colors, as they perform "Cha Bomm Pa Pa" in *Nancy Goes to Rio* (1949). Reynolds observes, "Carmen of course had her imitators. But none like Mickey Rooney." And the glamour sequence, which began with close-ups of the MGM roster and *Ziegfeld Girl*, ends with Rooney's drag impersonation of the Brazilian star in *Babes on Broadway* (1942).

Reynolds's glamour segment is the most thoroughly sustained camp sequence in *That's Entertainment! III*, but it connects back to the introductory use of *Ziegfeld Follies*, itself a camping of female glamour quoted to epitomize the MGM style, and it highlights additional moments of camp engagement in the compilation before and afterward. During her underwater swimming sequence with Tom and Jerry in *Dangerous When Wet* (1953), Esther Williams mutters, "You know, they were more animated than some of my leading men" (so much for Ricardo's sex appeal, Debbie!). As often, an interjection of camp commentary is not verbalized but results from a visible disjunction between the clip and its commentary. June Allyson refers to novelty acts "that just didn't catch on, no matter how hard they

Debbie Reynolds and the glamour
segment of *That's Entertainment! III*
(MGM-UA, 1994). Frame captures.

tried," and the illustration is a trio of female contortionists, the Ross sisters in *Broadway Rhythm* (1944). Their specialty as dancers is so bizarre, particularly when the number choreographs the twisting and misshaping of their individual bodies in a threesome, that it goes far beyond a question of their simply trying hard but not catching on.

Sometimes the disjunction is not made obvious but arises from an ellipses in the commentary. Gene Kelly introduces Eleanor Powell's numbers by noting, "even the biggest production numbers needed stars," without mentioning that the examples from *Broadway Melody of 1938* and *Lady Be Good* (1941) show the great dancer in her usual costume for a big production number, the tuxedo and top hat which visually set her apart from both men and women in the dancing ensemble to give her solo turns prominence as female drag. Similarly, one of the first excerpts in the compilation, the Dodge Sisters in "The Lock Step" from the unfinished *March of Time* (1930), uses what, in retrospect, is the same prison setting and choreographic conceit as Elvis Presley's "Jailhouse Rock," shown toward the end. The older number seems funny now because of the female dancers' awkwardness, made more apparent by the static camerawork, but the parallelism—not mentioned in the commentary—suggests the camp gender masquerades informing both the dancing female jail birds and Presley's wriggling hips and curled lips.

The turn in Reynolds's segment to "things south of the border," implicitly prepared for by the clip of Crawford performing in "tropical makeup," also calls attention to the whiteness of the preceding illustrations of female glamour, so this sequence provides a critical perspective by way of camp for the segment on Lena Horne and racism immediately following. The camp style highlighted in the Reynolds segment foregrounds how female beauty, whether personified by the glamour poses of MGM stars or Rooney's drag version of Carmen Miranda, is a form of racial and gender impersonation which privileges the desirability of a femininity as much white as it is heterosexual. As Horne subsequently talks about her inability to do more than guest appearances in MGM's musicals, leading up to her great disappointment in not being cast as Julie in the remake of *Show Boat*, her sequence points back to the ideological imperative of the glamour mill, namely, the MGM style's preoccupation with naturalizing whiteness through the artifice of "beauty." The spectacle of "a black girl in a bubble bath"—Horne's solo number in *Cabin in the Sky* (1943), cut by PCA censors, we are told, for being too dangerously erotic for the time because of her race—epitomizes the impassable limit covered over by the tropical blackface of 1940s Latin rhythms but also by the Anglo whiteface of the strutting Ziegfeld girl. Both are cultural tropes reinforcing racial and gender hierarchies. The camp brought out by the glamour segment has thus already begun to signal awareness of what Richard Dyer points out is the impact of Horne's commentary in making an audience realize the overwhelming whiteness of the MGM musical ("Colour of Entertainment," 23–24).

There is, to be sure, enough straightforward commentary in *TE! III* to allow for a nostalgic recuperation of the camp style as affection for the outlandishness of the old musicals, which is also to say that the style can still pass as noncamp. But the camp perspective which the Reynolds segment focuses for the compilation is given even greater texture and emphasis by the LD boxed set's supplementary material, so it is harder to ignore there. The longer version of the compilation includes several additional numbers cut from the theatrical print. The Astaire segment retains "Coffee Time," a number from *Yolanda and the Thief* (1945) in which he and Lucille Bremer dance on a floor with a swirling pattern that competes with the pair for the viewer's attention. The Garland tribute adds a second *Annie* outtake and "Minnie from Trinidad" from *Ziegfeld Girl*. Introducing the latter, Mickey Rooney remarks that in the late 1930s Garland was an "in-between," meaning no longer a child player but not yet an adult, and this number, he continues—with Garland in tropical blackface, what looks like a stovepipe on her head, and a stuffed parrot on her shoulder—illustrates how, once she grew up, the studio "gave her the full glamour treatment." Uh huh, sure it does.

Along with these extra numbers in the compilation, the boxed set features complete versions of Garland's "Mr. Monotony" cut from *Easter Parade* (in it she wears the tuxedo jacket and fedora later made famous by "Get Happy"), the deleted reprise of "Lady Loves," and "The Lock Step." More never-before-seen numbers appear in a separate "Collector's Treasury" comprising ten full-length outtakes not in the extended version of the compilation. For audiophiles, complete prerecordings of many numbers, some longer than in the form finally used on film (originally and in the compilation), can be accessed on a separate analog track. These numbers' supplementary standing outside of the compilation equates their value for the boxed set with an excess of excess, either because the supplementary version of a visual or audio outtake is fuller than in the compilation or because it is twice left over, unused originally and then unused again by the compilation.

Of all the supplements in the boxed set, the making-of documentary, *That's Entertainment! III: Behind the Screen*, most complexly enhances the compilation's camp address. As its subtitle indicates, the documentary doubles the view behind the scenes of the MGM musical by taking a viewer backstage during the compilation's production, going behind the screen of the numbers, so to speak, to inscribe a position of authorship for the camp perspective focusing *TE! III*. True, noticeably absent from the compilation itself is much reference to the MGM musical's authorship. Rather, the nine former MGM stars provide the exclusive point of entry into the backstage narrative, with commentary written for them that purports to represent their own firsthand experience. The use of stars as hosts authoring the commentaries is a device which speaks directly to a fan. In the making-of documentary, periodic shots of the hosts reading their commentaries from cue cards or teleprompters, not to mention a reference to Reynolds being the only one able to do hers in a single take, call into question the authenticity of these firsthand remembrances. As the stars offer additional remarks about their segments in interviews, their spontaneity then reestablishes their authenticity, in many cases through a camp inflection.

Esther Williams, for instance, recounts how each morning prior to doing an underwater number the makeup people "took a sloppy thing of Vaseline and a sloppy thing of baby oil," rubbing the mixture together in her hair. "And as you see," she points out, "I still have lots of hair so it was a perfect oil treatment. They made me like a duck. I was waterproofed." Ann Miller appears at several points to exclaim it was a lot of hard work, but everyday was like a party. Debbie Reynolds, we learn, was chosen for her segment because of her well-known efforts to preserve Hollywood history. "She has an incredible perspective on this material and what MGM was," Feltenstein comments. Reynolds's "incredible perspective" reinforces the camp viewpoint of her segment. She notes how "glamour was something we all had to learn . . . We were taught how to dress, what colors go together, . . . how to work with your hair, how to do your own makeup. It's just sort of a code. Esther Williams, all the girls, June Allyson, everyone always looked nice when they [went] out." The documentary then cuts to Allyson remarking that she didn't have "an MGM look" but her own look as "the plain one . . . the girl next door," as if to renaturalize the "code," but then immediately Reynolds returns for the camp punch line. She remarks, alluding to what everyone now knows from the tell-all biographies, "You can't have glamour if you don't light right. I mean, uh, these women, uh, drank and came in and they looked beautiful because they were lit right." Lena Horne, too, while described as still "angry" about her mistreatment by the studio, is shown laughing many times while filming her spot, cutting up with the tech people. She concludes her screen narration by saying, "Thank heavens things have changed." Although the shoot is done, Horne follows an incongruous association suggested by her scripted line and begins trilling, "Thank heaven for little girls." With somber, pained expression she comments to an interviewer that she was scolded for not being more grateful—after all, they *did* allow her to eat in the commissary—and then breaks up in laughter at the hypocrisy and its absurdity, evoking, as Dyer describes this affect with reference to Garland, "the knife edge between camp and hurt" (*Heavenly Bodies*, 180).

These moments of ironic or parodic punctuation are more derivative of camp attitudes than direct expressions of them, certainly, and the examples mentioned all involve female stars who carry a camp following to the documentary; Gene Kelly and Howard Keel play it very straight in their interviews, and Mickey Rooney, well, is Mickey Rooney. But the camp punctuation of the contemporary backstage view is reinforced by the documentary's interweaving of the star interviews with running commentary by the men who authored this new compilation: Feltenstein, Peter Fitzgerald (executive producer), and Bud Friedgen and Michael J. Sheridan (who wrote, edited, directed, and produced). Shown in talking-head shots either individually (Feltenstein, Fitzgerald) or paired (Friedgen and Sheridan), each man refers to his long-standing investment in the MGM musical as a source of pleasure; each, in short, comes off as an unabashed fan before anything else. Feltenstein enthuses, "It was really incredible to listen to Mickey Rooney or Gene Kelly talk about Arthur Freed. It was incredible." Friedgen similarly raves that it was "really wonderful to be back on the MGM lot and directing these people. It was quite a thrill." Fitzgerald informs us that Esther Williams was "the most vivacious person in the cast," "a joy to be around," and gushes, "I wish that everyone could have been there just to see her come back to the lot."

In offering their own revelations alongside those of the stars, the various authors of *TE! III* represent "everyone," as Fitzgerald indicates, insofar as they are the points of mediation between the stars and the less privileged audience who couldn't be "there." The compilation's authors are fans themselves, experts on the genre and awestruck by its stars, but they also have what fans lack and, in being fans, desire most: access to those stars, to the footage, and to the vaults where the most prized and "precious jewels" such as the rare outtakes are preserved. The four authors are, as Feltenstein notes, the "keepers of the archive." This envious status puts them in a more privileged relation with the MGM musical than that of mere fan. Sheridan recalls that preparing the compilation meant "literally crawling on [their] hands and knees through the vaults," and the first rough cut resulting from their research ran "a little over four hours." These men, though, are also more than keepers of the archive because they then went on to turn the archive into the compilation, rearranging the MGM musical into *That's Entertainment! III*. Compiler, archivist, and fan, in short, fold together as a single position of "authorship" for *TE! III*'s contemporary camp appreciation of the musicals. The press kit recognizes this composite positioning when it credits Feltenstein with originating *TE! III* as a fan spectator since, after watching the second *That's Entertainment!* in a theater when just a teenager, he went home and jotted down a list of sixty numbers not included in parts 1 or 2, thereby already envisioning the third compilation yet to come.

Collectively, these authors mark out an affective as well as economic investment in the MGM musical in the present which, as it evolves through the course of the documentary, approximates that of the contemporary gay spectator addressed by the compilation's camp perspective, indeed serves as a surrogate for him. These men are by no means characterized as gay themselves (Sheridan's wedding ring is clearly visible in his footage, for instance), but they nonetheless articulate a special relation to the MGM musical as, in effect, its camp re-producers decades after the fact of the genre's original moment of production during the studio era. In this way, the documentary brings out an authorial perspective on the compilation which makes more visible what Matthew Tinkcom calls the camp traces of gay labor in cultural objects like the old MGM musicals. The supplementary effects of their over-the-top camp style invite "some consumers to wonder at the commodity's production ('did a gay have some hand in its making?') and, simultaneously, for others not to have to engage in any such speculation" ("Warhol's Camp," 345). The effect of the supplements as a comparable form of camp excess in the boxed set edition of *That's Entertainment! III* invites the same speculation, even if not grounded in biographical fact about the filmmakers, of *possible* contemporary gay authorship in producing the compilation specifically for a gay spectator, and this trace epitomizes the process by which the MGM musical has been renewed as a camp commodity through the compilation.

The camp trace of authorship in the making-of documentary does not factually refer back to the actual persons making *TE! III* but instead marks how the renewed commodity, dislocated from its historical moment of production during the studio era, receives a contemporary value displacing its former one while simultaneously seeking to restore it. In recognizing the MGM musical's camp while nonetheless appealing to its timeless quality as "still entertainment," the compilation itself, particularly when dressed up in the boxed-set edition, refers to an inescapable historical disjuncture: the temporal gap between the musicals' bearing their double value as camp or noncamp during the studio era and their doing so again nearly half a century later. It is therefore crucial to appreciate that the camp address of *That's Entertainment! III* is itself a historicized view of the MGM musical, bound up in the tensions defining contemporary attitudes toward camp as both the residue of the closet and as a critical relation to the commodification of gay tastes in the present.

Camp may still saturate gay culture, as some critics maintain, but it is also symptomatic of a generational divide, as writers like Daniel Harris have argued. Post-Stonewall liberation, he comments, has had the consequence not only of mainstreaming gay culture but of bringing camp out of the closet and into the mall, turning "the aestheticism of art and culture into the aestheticism of products, the commodities that spill out of the Macy's bags" (37). The heavily supplemented boxed set simulates the authors' privileged access by commodifying the archive for a consumer, but the steep price of this edition, as well as the special equipment needed to watch it, also identifies a consumer of a particular age and class, one with considerable disposable income. Fixed to its own historical location in 1995, the boxed set speaks to a nostalgia less for the old entertainment than for pre-Stonewall camp: that doubly valent excessive style which characterized the MGM musical in its golden age, traced the gay labor force manufacturing and inspiring it, and is now being recommodified as a "new" product.

WHOSE ENTERTAINMENT?

Echoing the compilation's final credit directing viewers to the MGM/ UA home-video catalogue, the documentary closes with Esther Williams musing: "It's a time that has gone by . . . So when people say to me why don't they make movies like they used to, I just feel like holding their hands and telling them to go buy the video because they probably won't ever do it again." After watching the documentary, one has to wonder about which particular audience for the old musicals Williams really has in mind: the people who want to recreate the days when MGM was king of the box office, or those who want to watch Lucille Ball with her cat-women one more time?

Even then, what *TE! III* makes most evident through its camp address is the compilation project's own estrangement from younger gay as well as straight consumers, since neither group necessarily finds the MGM musical a source of camp or nostalgic affect anymore. The combined merchandising efforts of Turner, MGM/UA, and Rhino for their enhanced home-video and CD releases therefore seem ambiguous about the intended audience of these new classics because they aim to attract consumers without making the product noticeably gay, while still banking on the dependability of the gay niche market by selling a camp product to the most loyal audience for "Hollywood's Most Precious Jewels." The widespread recognition that these are also Hollywood's Camp Jewels helps to explain why the various archival lines failed to achieve crossover success on any sizable scale. Not only did *That's Entertainment! III* receive limited theatrical distribution after its premieres in New York and Los Angeles, but the Turner/Rhino soundtrack CDs also had weak sales, causing the company to reduce production of additional titles almost immediately after the first ones appeared. The output in 1995 and 1996 included numerous soundtracks and star salutes to Judy Garland, Gene Kelly, and Lena Horne, but Rhino released only a few of those each year thereafter, instead choosing to amplify its Turner lineup with occasional compilations organized around a more mainstreamed theme (romantic duets), well-known composer (the Gershwins), or recognizable musical style (big bands, Latin rhythms), as if to dissociate the content of the CDs from its source in the MGM musical as a body of individual films with a recognizable camp appeal and gay cult following in the present.

Explaining Rhino's reduced output, John Fricke, a Judy Garland specialist who served as consultant, writer, and/or producer on many of the CD and laser-disc products, has commented in a webpage column, somewhat elliptically: "During my association w/Rhino, my personal 'take' was that their marketing department didn't have a clue as to how to push such specialized material . . . nor did they take the time or make the effort to learn."[10] In fact, Rhino was planning not to renew its contract with Turner Entertainment in 1997 when Time Warner's purchase of the record company the following year assured its continuation as the corporation's outlet for exploiting the library on CD, albeit still with a much slower pacing of releases from the MGM archives than when the series began. With Feltenstein's production team at the helm, Rhino brought out a handful of new soundtracks in 2000 with releases of *Hit the Deck* (1955), *Unsinkable Molly Brown* (1964) and a long-awaited version of *Annie Get Your Gun* (1950) containing both the Betty Hutton and Judy Garland tracks. Recognizing the niche audience for the CDs, though, at the same time the company made some of these—such as *Athena* (1953), a *Summer Stock* (1950)/*In the Good Old Summertime* (1949) double feature, *It's Always Fair Weather* (1955), *The Pirate, Broadway Melody of 1940* (1940), and *Born to Dance* (1936)—available only as limited numbered editions for sale exclusively at its Rhino Handmade website.

Deluxe treatment of MGM musicals on home video, on the other hand, was another matter. Without a sizeable contemporary film library of its own, MGM/UA released a large number of musicals on laser disc along with other MGM and Warners classic titles throughout the late 1980s and early 1990s, culminating in the big, supplemented boxed-set editions, but the company stopped production when laser-disc technology gave way to DVD as the home-video industry's new high-end format. At that point MGM/UA and Turner began issuing some single titles on DVD, the usual suspects such as *Singin' in the Rain*, *The Wizard of Oz*, *Show Boat*, and *Brigadoon*. By contrast, after Time Warner gained full control of the MGM library, its home-video unit kept much of the catalogue alive on VHS but manufactured relatively few musicals on DVD, reissuing the MGM/UA titles under its own brand, and adding some additional Gene Kelly titles, a DVD version of the *Oz* laser-disc boxed set, and then a few others, such as *Annie Get Your Gun* (with the Garland outtakes included) in 2000 and *The Harvey Girls* in 2001. Unlike Turner Entertainment's arrangement with MGM/UA Home Video, the Time Warner units did not make an immediate effort to achieve synergy between the DVD and CD uses of the Turner holdings. The corporation's lack of commitment to its studio-era catalogue as a whole during the first decade of DVD's existence indicates a decision to wait based on recognition of the product's marginal appeal, not too surprising given Warner Home Video's publicized ambition to make DVD a broad-based format as soon as it was introduced. (Time Warner is a partner in all royalties received from any use of the DVD format.) Things began to change when Feltenstein moved over to the classics division, and the rollout of MGM library titles became more prolific in 2003-04. Through Internet-based venues such as The Home Theater Forum, officials claim the slow release pattern resulted from a need to restore the films to a condition befitting the DVD format; while that may be a factor, the surging popularity as well as imminent obsolescence of DVD once the high-definition format succeeds it in a few years may have also spurred the accelerated pace of classic releases, as it did at Disney.

The years 1994-96, then, which saw the launching of TCM, the Rhino CD series, the MGM/UA laser-disc boxed sets, and the release of *That's Entertainment! III*, stand out as the high-water mark in contemporary efforts to market the MGM musical on a somewhat wide scale. Nonetheless, despite apparent uncertainty as to how best to merchandise the MGM musical during that period, and for all the product's inability to achieve crossover success as a result, the people responsible for promoting this "specialized product," to borrow Fricke's ambiguous phrase, did in fact seem to know that the older, affluent gay market was always its best bet. Indeed, aiming *That's Entertainment! III* at this consumer group may have been a very deliberate business decision since the mid-nineties saw many large corporations and their advertisers explicitly identifying (if overvaluing) the demographic profile of professional gay men as an attractive, upscale, and as yet untapped market.[11]

MGM/UA and Turner give the impression of following this strategy after the box-office failure of *TE! III*. Whereas the theatrical poster and advertising art featured a stylized drawing evocative of Fred Astaire and Ginger Rogers to define the MGM musical as heterosexual in its appeal, the laser-disc boxed set substituted a drawing suggestive of Judy Garland in her signature costume of fedora and tuxedo jacket. The new image, also on the VHS version, refers to the "Mr. Monotony" outtake from *Easter Parade* featured in the compilation, but, as a more instantly recognizable reference to her famous "Get Happy" number in *Summer Stock*, this image is just as packed with allusions to her history as a camp icon of gay fandom.

The switching of "Fred and Ginger" to "Judy" as advertising art for *That's Entertainment! III* well summarizes the mid-nineties packaging of the MGM musical in general. As in *TE! III*, the MGM musical's historical relation to camp production and reception is put on display or at least alluded to, yet disavowed by the rhetorical mainstreaming of the genre in the accompanying merchandising discourse. These are, after all, "Hollywood's Most Precious Jewels." The doubled message about the MGM musical is less uncertain than first appears for it allows recognition of the musicals' camp to address gay consumers directly, but without being named as such, that address can pass by without as much notice by other consumers who happen on the product, too. The archival trappings work to enhance rather than detract from this camp "passing" of the renewed commodity.

Of all this product, a camp address is most fully realized in the 1994 compilation but it informs the rest in one way or another, since the more "Hollywood's Most Precious Jewels" are cast in new settings, the campier they inevitably seem as commodities because of their historical dislocation. The new archival setting for "Hollywood's Most Precious Jewels" still testifies to the MGM musical's marginal status, as the theatrical failure of *That's Entertainment! III* confirmed. The classics network on cable has been the most successful because it sells a site devoted to the studio era more than a specific, culturally inflected product per se like the musical, which is what the laser-disc boxed sets and CDs did. Their inability to achieve crossover success beyond the niche market of diehard fans was to be expected. After all, the pseudo-jewel case housing the Turner/Rhino sampler CD was itself a camp object: it was not made of leather but plastic; the CD, while colored gold and with a picture of a diamond ring on its label, was an artifact of contemporary technology; and the MGM musical remains a product that still primarily appeals to a marginalized demographic. In recognizing the musicals' camp, the revived product positions its audiences in opposition to mainstream tastes. When all is said and done, that may be the MGM musical's most distinctive value as niche entertainment in today's marketplace.

Chapter Six

*I*t is a truth almost universally acknowledged that a single man in possession of a Judy Garland CD must *not* be in want of a wife. However little known the feelings or views of such a man may be on his first entering a record store, this truth is so well fixed in the minds of the surrounding public that Garland is considered the rightful property of some one or other of Dorothy's friends. "It was no secret," Michael Bronski observes, "that her most dedicated fans were gay men" (103).

Their dedication was in full force at San Francisco's Castro Theatre on the evening of 17 December 1999. "A Judy Garland Christmas," produced by local promoter Marc Huestis, comprised three sections: a live show starring Connie Champagne, a female drag artist impersonating Garland—her banter, gestures, and inflections copied from the Carnegie Hall concert—with support provided by Mathew Martin as Katharine Hepburn doing a bawdy reading of "The Night Before Christmas"; special guest Lorna Luft, Garland's daughter, interviewed by gushing hostess Jan Wahl, a Bay Area television personality; and a screening of *Meet Me in St. Louis* (1944). Huestis sells the video of the Garland tribute on eBay along with tapes of other annual camp-star salutes he has organized at the Castro, also featuring drag shows with Champagne and Martin. According to the video, this particular evening was indeed a gay gala affair devoted to a star whose camp value has not diminished. Klieg lights flooded the sky outside the Castro as Luft arrived in a limousine, was cheered by a waiting crowd (and hawkers selling Garland souvenirs such as glittery Dorothy masks), and then escorted into the theater by the Castro District's "mayor." Inside, as the sellout audience of 1,600 took their seats, clips of Garland films flashed onto the screen and her voice played on the theater's sound system. The crowd was predominantly male, a mixture of young and old men in couples or small groups, all in good cheer and all ready to celebrate Garland through the camp mediation of drag, the daughter surrogate, and an MGM musical.

On this December night at least, the Castro's audience belied Michael Joseph Gross's claim seven months later in the *Atlantic Monthly* that, as his title puts it, "The Queen is Dead." He observes that the history of gay culture since Stonewall has dramatically revised the conditions which had previously invested Garland with her iconic value for gay men. She had acquired that special status because of her ability to voice a sense of suffering muted by resilience. "Garland embodied many of the paradoxical emotional states that gay men commonly experience while coming out: vulnerability and strength, sincerity and duplicity, self-consciousness and abandon, adolescence and maturity" (66). Her emotionally intense performance style thus spoke directly to her audience's own "earnest but imperfect effort to heal the anger and fear that coming out forced on them." Furthermore, whether on stage or screen, Garland could represent "the success in passionate emotional failure" because of "the purifying power of camp" (70). Gross's point is that Garland and the history she stands for are now an embarrassment for a younger generation of gay men who, seeking to assimilate more easily into heteronormative culture, "just want to be regular guys—with better-than-average bodies" (64). Garland's remaining fans, in the meantime, are looked down on with ridicule as "Judy queens" (66).

Gross's account of why Garland became a legendary gay icon is consistent with Richard Dyer's explanation in *Heavenly Bodies*. Dyer examines how the Garland star text, arising from her attempted suicide in 1950 and subsequent departure from MGM, structured "much of the gay reading" (143) in the fifties and sixties because the disclosures of her troubles at the studio heightened "the disparity between the [screen] image and the imputed real person" (156). Drawing on Dyer's analysis, Janet Staiger further demonstrates how, prior to the revelations of Garland's professional and personal turmoil in 1950, the basis for that gay reading was already present during the MGM years in the fan-magazine discourse, which promoted a "star image [that] was already at odds with her film roles" (Staiger, 165). With the release of her 1954 comeback vehicle, *A Star is Born*, Garland's star text was fixed enough in the public imagination to determine the reception of both her image and her work through what Staiger calls "alternate readings" of this film that reframed its significance through the biography.

Writing almost four decades after *Star is Born*, Wade Jennings simply takes for granted the centrality of that post-1950s reading when he uses Garland to exemplify the formation of cult stardom. Jennings argues that two related factors distinguish Garland from other stars of her generation. Because of "recorded performance, visual and aural," he first points out, ". . . virtually the whole career is preserved as a whole, an established canon of images and sounds that can be known and shared . . . Even when the career of a performer stretches over a long period and encompasses as many changes as Garland's, all the individual recorded performances interconnect and comment upon one another" (92). At the same time, he continues, her cult standing is dependent on fans realizing the incongruities of the life and the work, "find[ing] part of their identity in their de-tailed and considerable knowledge of the contradictions, the differ-ences between the publicized career and the reality . . . In the case of every star who becomes a cult figure, there is some variation of the notion of 'the suffering artist'" (93). No star, he remarks, referring to what has become a truism about her biography and career as they interacted, "more completely embodied" this abrasive confrontation with and triumphant overcoming of "personal defeat and despair" than Judy Garland (94).

By now, Garland's star text appears to have stabilized around the image of the doomed diva riding a roller coaster of suffering and buoyancy. The media keeps this impression firmly in place with every recounting of her life and career on television or in print. What was formerly an alternate reading of Garland has therefore become the preferred reading, dominating accounts of her stardom and her fans. For whether venerated, as at the Castro theater, or repudiated, as by the muscle boys on Fire Island referenced by Gross, Garland re-mains linked with gay cult fandom, itself characterized by a pre-

Stonewall ethos of camp abjection. Yet her star text is no more coherent or stable today than it was during her lifetime, and neither is
her fan following, which tends to be divided according to different
aspects of her career, focusing on the Garland of MGM musicals, the
Garland of the concert years, the Garland of the CBS television series,
the Garland of the Decca and Capitol recordings, or the Garland of
the annual telecasting of *The Wizard of Oz* (1939). These multiple fan
formations may interconnect, as Jennings proposes, but, far from
cohering around an agreed-upon object, a shared understanding of
Garland's stardom and what it represents, they mark fractured points
of resistance to a totalized reading.

The heterogeneity of contemporary Garland fandom is amply evident in the many webpages devoted to her on the Internet, which
provide a valuable opportunity for further inquiry into the ongoing
reception of her star text, albeit with some obvious limitations, since
whatever demographic picture results includes only those people
who have access to the Web and an inclination—not to say education, leisure time, and income—to use it. Nevertheless, this resource
allows us to witness how contemporary fans actively understood and
tried to reread Garland's stardom at a time more or less concurrent
with the commercial revival of the MGM musical discussed in the previous chapter. Her significance for fans is not fixed to the view that
dominates the journalistic and critical accounts but, on the contrary,
requires their continual, often defensive negotiation of the contradictory meanings Garland is still taken to embody.

This final chapter, then, moves beyond the attention to film which
has dominated this book so far in order to examine the present-day
reception of the star still most closely identified with the MGM musical, its history, and its camp reception. Focusing in particular on ambivalence about her status as a gay icon in the conflicted efforts of fans
to articulate Garland's value as a star, I look at the two sites that were
most central to the fan community with access to the Internet in the
1990s: "The Judy Garland DataBase" the most comprehensive effort
of all the webpages to document her career, and "The Judy List," a
daily e-mail discussion about her stardom which also had its own
webpage, where, among other features such as a bulletin-board chat
and audio files, the daily digests were archived as a public record until
the list's demise in 2001.[1]

As in the other fan pages devoted to Garland, the DataBase makes every effort to reconcile the contradictions between life and work, past and present, which Jennings sees as essential to her cult status; and to do so, it practically removes all traces of the features that Dyer argues were central to her association with a "gay sensibility" (154): an androgynous image, camp attitudes, and a persona that projects a "special relationship with ordinariness" because it is "saturated" with connotations of normality without being normative (156, 159). In contrast with the DataBase, the prominence on the listserv of debates about "the gay thing," as one poster called it, stands out all the more as a major focal point of fan negotiations. The controversial question of whether or not Garland's gay following was and continues to be a significant factor in her stardom repeatedly generated sharp disagreements among list subscribers. Raising homophobic anxiety in the list's debates about the queerness of Garland fandom, "the gay thing" often functioned to encode fans' resistance to, as well as recognition of, their idol's strong identification with camp. These discussions call attention to the ways that contemporary fans actively and self-consciously read Garland's stardom as a text, often interpreting it with a high degree of critical sophistication—and a determined agenda. In their differing ways, both the DataBase and the Judy List manifest fans' conscious efforts to replace the present dominant reading of Garland, itself originally an alternative account that privileged the biography, with a new, more recuperative interpretation that aims to read the life through the career as a means of closing the gap between her marginality as a cultural figure, symbolized by "the gay thing," and their own close identification with the heteronormality of mainstream consumer culture. All the same, the camp valences of Garland's stardom continue to linger, as that Christmas show at the Castro theater should remind us.

DOCUMENTING THE LEGEND

In 1998 there was enough Garland fan activity on the Internet to attract the notice of an Associated Press reporter, who, referring to "the 15 core sites," observed: "the number of elaborate, fan-generated Web sites dedicated to Garland so many years after her death is somewhat remarkable. Her Web presence dwarfs that of many contemporary artists" (Sampey). A year later, that number had doubled. Some notable sites in 1999 included "The Judy Garland Media Storage," containing sound files of songs and dialogues from her films; "The Judy Garland Photographic Page," featuring, along with the many images, a special Memorial Wall on which visitors inscribed testimonials and tributes; and a fan's memorabilia-filled "Judy Room," with photos of the contents that could be sent as electronic postcards. Another site specialized in her live performances and CBS television series; there were two different pages on *A Star is Born*; and the British-based Judy Garland fan club had a link to the president's own pages recording the star's various appearances in London. Still other sites were devoted to more avowed fan worship, offering photos, trivia games, polls, film- and discographies, magazine and newspaper clippings, and so forth. Even these were specialized in one form or other. "Young Judy Garland," devoted to her child stardom, offered "an alternative perspective on this natural artist who's [*sic*] precocious behavior and beautiful (divine) voice won the hearts of an entire nation"; and "Judy Garland: Forever Beautiful" had, among its many other features, a section titled "Judy's Guardians," offering fans a chance "to 'own' a certain part of Judy history (only in cyberspace)" by claiming a song, movie, character, concert, or TV appearance as their own (both downloaded 9 September 1999).

Other fan pages devoted to Hollywood stars of the studio era have similar ambitions, but the Garland pages surpass them in the sheer density of their archival documentation. Becoming increasingly "notable for their sophisticated design, breadth of information and intricate multimedia links" (Sampey), the Garland pages combine fan worship and collecting with an encyclopedic intent that exceeds mere dedication to the star, complicating notions of what such strong attachments on the part of fans reveal about their relation to her stardom. This phenomenon is amply evident in Jim Johnson's "Judy Garland DataBase," which served as the gold standard for the websites just mentioned.

The Garland DataBase began in 1995 and grew to the point where, four years later, it comprised "more than 800 pages and nearly 4000 files of information and pictures, occupying 80MB of disk space" ("Introduction," downloaded 18 September 1999). Devoted primarily to Garland's MGM years, while still covering her entire career, the Data-

Base underwent continual revision and expansion until 2001, when Johnson contracted its size and the site became dormant. Despite its many additions and subtractions, though, the structure has remained relatively the same, with its main contents organized around the obvious topics of Garland's music, films, radio, TV, and videos. These sections are then liberally subdivided to facilitate access to the information Johnson has collated, all elaborately illustrated, documented, and linked to each other. The DataBase, moreover, does not stop here. It features a large section devoted to Garland photos, and another one concerned with her presence in magazines. Johnson does not ignore his passion for collecting Garland memorabilia either, subdividing this section according to type, each with links to online dealers, and featuring a separate page displaying his own "Judy Room" dedicated exclusively to his vast collection, with seven photos arranged so as to simulate a panoramic 360-degree tour of the space. There are still more sections: a Garland biography; a categorized bibliography; a page about the Internet fan community; an album of fans' personal remembrances; an irregularly updated column by author John Fricke (considered by many fans to be the definitive historian of Garland's life); trivia games centering on the star; an archived list of updates; a search engine; a guest book; and the requisite links to other Garland pages and celebrity Web rings.

Johnson explains that he developed the DataBase, dedicated to "a major star . . . considered a legend in her own time," as a "serious hobby . . . I *hope* that it is a place that people can find information pertaining to Judy's career—people who are not particularly Judy's fans, but who are interested in, or curious about, her work" ("Introduction," downloaded 26 April 1997). By 1999 this project had achieved such an indisputable authority for fans that Johnson presented it as an evolving "reference volume . . . [where] the serious student can find the facts pertaining to Judy's work" ("Introduction," downloaded 18 September 1999). For all this professing of scholarship, the voluminous DataBase reinforces a position of fandom constructed by, rather than reflective on, movie culture. The contents do not historicize Garland's career but instead try to recover the terms by which MGM regulated her star image during her tenure at the studio in the late 1930s and 1940s. Moreover, addressing Garland fans as consumers of her talent through its ongoing commodification by the home-video and music industries, the DataBase assumes that the most dedicated of fans are those committed to preserving her studio-produced image in the name of its historical authenticity.

The DataBase acquires its authority from the manner in which Johnson's archival record of Garland's career equates fan dedication with amateur scholarship. This may be why, as the site became more comprehensive with each month's updating, he ended up removing all personal information in 1999. He eliminated not only his biographical profile but also a section devoted to his participation in Garland fandom. For instance, he had formerly included an account of his 1996 trip to Hollywood with his wife and their friend, the chair of the welcoming committee of the now defunct Garland Internet fan club. Johnson described how the trio stayed in Hollywood, visited the famous forecourt of Mann's Chinese Theatre to put their feet in you-know-whose footprints, photographed the Capitol Records Building (Garland's label in the 1950s and 1960s), shopped in various movie memorabilia stores, met with author John Fricke, and visited another Garland collector in West Hollywood ("Krista, Jim & Kellie Go Hollywood," downloaded 27 March 1997). Nevertheless, even with these omissions, traces of the DataBase's fan orientation remain in the attention paid to collecting Garland memorabilia, beginning with the presentation of Johnson's Judy Room, as well as in the fan album, magazine section, and photo gallery.

The gallery photos, although removed from the site at some point after 2000, offer a good example. They chronicle a range of Garland imagery, from chubby adolescent to girl next door to svelte star to Al Hirschfield's caricature, but they epitomize how the DataBase as a whole resists what Dyer points out was the ambivalent relation to Hollywood glamour that informed Garland's star image while working at MGM, primarily as focused around her body's lack of conformity with the regimen of female stardom. The gallery's cover page features a 1944 pinup from *Esquire* magazine, which displays the star in a negligee, lying upside down in a seductive pose ("Judy Garland Photo Gallery," downloaded 12 October 1999). The photo is the sort of glamorous publicity shot that MGM routinely used for Lana Turner and Hedy Lamarr but more rarely for Garland.

The DataBase's visual treatment of Garland works to normalize her persona by representing it in more conventional movie-star terms consistent with an overriding nostalgia for the presumed stability of the studio era. This view of her stardom effaces reference to the nonconformity of her studio work, which, along with the gay fans that responded to it most famously, functions as a crucial structuring absence of Johnson's archival documentation of her history.

Toward this end, the biographical section of the DataBase, unchanged in content despite the site's stylistic renovations, shies away from the victimization narrative that typically structures accounts of Garland's life. Johnson represents her well-documented personal and professional turbulence according to mainstream perceptions of star labor under the old studio system so that it does not readily connote the kind of "emotional difference born within normality" which Dyer refers to when analyzing the Garland star text and which summarizes its queer signification for gay fans (*Heavenly Bodies*, 162). Nor does the DataBase mention Garland's professional debt to and close friendships with the gay men in the Freed unit at MGM, who mentored, directed, choreographed, and costumed her, in effect, shaping her distinct performing style to achieve its camp register. In fact, like many diehard Garland fans, Johnson pretty much ignores the perspective taken by David Shipman's biography, *Judy Garland: The Secret Life of an American Legend*—a book that is explicit in drawing out the queer culture in which Garland worked and lived, but criticized by other Garland authors for its sensationalizing treatment— and follows *Judy Garland: World's Greatest Entertainer*, John Fricke's chronicle of the hardworking trouper whose love of performing and special affinity with her fans always transcended her private demons and conflicts with her studio.

What the DataBase tries to rewrite is the post-MGM impression of Garland as the "crazy victim," which Allen Larson points out was the star's dominant portrayal by the press after Metro fired her from *Annie Get Your Gun* in 1949 (192). From that point on, reportage of her professional and personal turmoil was routinely organized around "narrative themes of victimization and psychological illness" (194), with accounts of her mistreatment at the studio's hands and professional misconduct working in combination with disclosures of her neurotic crises and excessive insecurity. Garland's characterization as a "crazy victim" was complicit in a dramatic transformation of the discourse about female stardom occurring at this same time, made noticeable by a cycle of films "in which the very nature of female stardom was treated, in varying ways, as inherently problematic"—and, more often than not, as inherently pathological (198).

Depicting fictionalized female stars struggling to retain their careers while exposing their neurotic instability as "crazy victims" of the entertainment industry, these films figure high on what Larson calls the gay-camp pantheon: Gloria Swanson as Norma Desmond in *Sunset Boulevard* (1950), Bette Davis as Margo Channing in *All About Eve* (1950) and Margaret Elliot in *The Star* (1952), Joan Crawford as Jenny Stewart in *Torch Song* (1953), and by virtue of the ease with which it was immediately read in terms of her career, Garland in *A Star is Born*. "Why not say, then," Larson asks, "that gay camp is that which recognizes and remembers (even if only in the form of momentary affective pleasures) the alienated subject within stardom's dizzying fusion of sexual and laboring desires?" (355). In his view, the camp appreciation of the star as a "crazy victim" is attuned to the commodity fetishism of stardom, the way it covers over a story of the female star as an industrial as well as cultural product while smuggling evidence of her labor back into the scenarios of Hollywood's own self-representation (356). The camp affinity for the pathologized female star thus derives from the way her figure represents labor and gender in dialectical terms while depicting both as states of pathologized alienation.

As the ultimate "crazy victim" of the studio system, the legendary Garland fired from MGM only to make comeback after comeback actively encourages such a camp reading, with her well-publicized turmoil simultaneously viewable as expressions of resistant labor within the studio system and of emotional instability outside of it. Professionally, by the late 1940s Garland had become a star who, in essence, refused to conform to the production-line practice demanded by the film industry as it adjusted its working conditions to meet major shifts in its economical base and its audience after World War II. Her own psychological fragility factored in here, to be sure. But with her weight drastically going up and down as if in rebellion against studio regulation of her body in the name of "glamour," and her refusal to work when she could not deliver the goods 100 percent, she presented MGM with a case of insubordinate and, hence, "abnormal" industrial labor which needed to be reigned in as inexplicable and self-indulgent star behavior.

For all its efforts to erase the "crazy victim" from Garland's star image, traces remain etched into the DataBase's biography page. Johnson begins with a long quotation from Fricke's book that emphasizes her triumphs in "work[ing] for nearly forty-five of her forty-seven years." The first page recounts the life story in a pseudo-dialogic form as answers to a series of questions, from "Where and when was Judy born?" and "How did Judy get her start in show business?" to "Is it true that Judy was a drug addict?" and "Is it true that Judy was mentally ill?" Regarding her drug use, Johnson replies that, like other performers of her era, she took Benzedrine, which was not understood as addictive but considered "the new miracle appetite suppressor of the period," and resorted to sleeping pills in the evening to counteract the drug's effects. Furthermore, he reports, "she did manage to break her habit many times, but often started up again when the pressures of a new film came along." Was she mentally ill? No, she "had emotional problems, possibly including depression . . . Such is often the case with truly gifted people . . . However, it may be that Judy's emotional problems were caused by the drugs that she used." Likewise, in Johnson's account Garland and L. B. Mayer mutually agreed that she should leave the studio after her difficulties caused several suspensions by unsympathetic MGM executives. Omitted is any reference to Garland's 1950 suicide attempt, although mention is made of her explanatory letter to fans afterward, published in *Modern Screen*, where she disclosed that she had "suffered from a mild sort of inferiority complex," and the full text is included in the magazine section. Most triumphantly, Garland's "one last comeback" was her funeral, which drew a crowd of "more than 22,000 people" ("Judy Garland Biography," downloaded 26 March 1998).

In succeeding pages, Johnson chronicles Garland's career at MGM with a year-by-year account of her work, contracts, salary, production starts and delays, and so on. However, this attention to the material details of her work life indirectly points out how Garland's star text raises questions about the studio system as it operated to regulate star labor by personalizing it as "behavior" even while glamorizing and financially rewarding it. According to Fricke, after firing her from *Royal Wedding*, MGM still wanted to retain her services: "They considered revising her contract for a single picture with options for two more. But president Nick Schenck was afraid the stockholders would claim the studio was running its business on sympathy and not intelligence," and cited her "increased weight" as the reason for letting her go, since she was now "unrecognizable." As Fricke puts it, she "was no longer cost-effective" (*Judy Garland: World's Greatest Entertainer*, 123). By contrast, the DataBase's effort to dispel "a legend [that] has grown around Judy which shrouds much of the truth about her" ("Biography," downloaded 26 March 1998) effaces even these nonnormative resonances of her star text, revising the alternate reading that has come to dominate public perceptions of Garland since 1950. The detailed chronology underscores the sheer output of her work (vaudeville, films, recordings, radio, and TV), to be sure, and refers to the industrial conditions under which she labored as a contracted performer, but in letting the "facts" speak for themselves, Johnson's DataBase mediates them through a new "legend."

Turner Entertainment, the subsidiary of Time Warner which now controls most Garland merchandising related to her MGM career, has apparently not protested the inclusion of so many stills, posters, and video or CD covers on the DataBase. It is doubtful if Johnson has any direct connection with the corporate owners of Garland's MGM image, although there may well be some mediation by way of Fricke. Author of two books on *The Wizard of Oz* and two on the star's career, Fricke has had a hand in much of the recent Garland merchandise, writing liner notes for the MGM material on laser disc and Rhino CDs, and coproducing the Arts & Entertainment biography special, *Judy Garland: Beyond the Rainbow*. The DataBase's normalization of Garland is consistent with the merchandising of her musicals on home video and CD which, aiming for crossover appeal but without ignoring her camp following, revises her star image with the similar intent, as Johnson puts it, of enshrining "a true living legend" in terms that outwardly evoke the conventions of mainstream stardom. The cover photo of Rhino's double-CD, *Judy Garland: Collectors' Gems from the MGM Films* (released in 1996) features a glamour shot from the 1940s similar to the Esquire pinup. The publicity shoot from which that still was taken also provided the illustration of Garland in the 1997 special issue of *Entertainment Weekly*—a Time Warner publication—on 100 Greatest Stars. Johnson includes several stills from this series at the top of his gallery, too.

Nonetheless, as discussed in the previous chapter, the people responsible for merchandising the new Garland product seem well aware of her gay fan base and capitalize on it. As I pointed out, the laser-disc boxed set of *That's Entertainment! III* (1994) substituted a drawing evoking Garland in her signature tuxedo jacket and fedora in place of the image suggesting Astaire and Rogers used for the unsuccessful theatrical release of the compilation. Likewise, the liner notes for the LD boxed set of *Ziegfeld Follies* (1946) explicitly describe Garland's number, "A Great Lady Has 'an Interview,'" filmed in 1944, as "a campy novelty" featuring the star dancing with "sixteen anxious 'boys' of the press." Furthermore, this number achieves its camp import by parodying the glamorous posing in those publicity photos of Garland appearing in magazines such as *Esquire* at that same time. Contradicting the recognition of her camp value in the marketing, these photos are also now being recycled by Turner Entertainment and Johnson as emblems of Garland's golden days at MGM (the title of the LD boxed set of her films), that era prior to her legendary renown as a "crazy victim."

Again, the person overseeing the restoration and release of the MGM vault material on CD and home video has been George Feltenstein. In the making-of documentary included in the LD boxed set of *That's Entertainment! III*, he introduces the sequence featuring the outtakes from Garland's aborted *Annie Get Your Gun*. Feltenstein states how glad he is to have the opportunity to share the footage with her fans, adding, "As one of the keepers of the archives, I've always searched for a way to present all of this material . . . in a way that would finally release it to the people such as myself who are really crazy about Judy Garland." As Fricke comments in his Data-Base column, "George Feltenstein . . . is 'one of us'—a Judy fan, too" ("John's Page," June 1996, downloaded 26 April 1997). Just who comprises that "us"—and whether being a Judy fan is euphemistic of or just coincidental to her gay following—is neither self-evident nor free of controversy, at least not on the Judy List.

Inaugurated in October 1996 and ending abruptly (if somewhat riotously) in May 2001, the listserv devoted to Judy Garland fandom was owned and moderated by its founder, Mark Harris of North Carolina.[2] From remarks made at times by Harris in his posts and to the press, by 1999 the Judy List had a subscription base of over 250 members, a few of whom figured prominently (if silently on the list) in the entertainment industry. Two years later this number had increased to well over 300. The list immediately attracted many gay Garland fans of the era Dyer writes about, but the membership was by no means homogenous in its age, gender, sexual orientation, occupation—or opinions. Furthermore, what appears to have united the Judy List's readers from the start was not camp but a shared recognition of Garland's emotional intensity when performing and a hunger for finding a community of like-minded fans as a means of overcoming what they begrudgingly recognized as her insignificance for mainstream audiences.

During the first months of its existence, the list was quickly joined by professional Garland authors Fricke, Coyne Steven Sanders (*Rainbow's End*), and Al DiOrio (*Little Girl Lost*), and several producers of Garland material, such as Feltenstein and Scott Schechter (editor of the U.S. Garland fanzine, *Garlands for Judy*, publicity consultant for Pioneer's DVD release of the Garland TV series, and a CD producer and author). At once biographers and unabashed fans, these specialists represent a crucial interaction between reading and writing the text of Garland's stardom, so their authority tended to dominate the list's contents, particularly when it came to debating how—or if—her life and career cohere into a legible and transcendent personality. In writing to the list, that is to say, nonprofessional Garland fans similarly put themselves in the position of producing while consuming an authoritative star image, which sometimes resulted in heated conflicts and testy public exchanges between the professional and amateur authorities. This conflict would ultimately lead to the list's termination five years after it began.

One poster from San Diego, who could always be counted on to generate controversy, claimed this agenda as an important aspect of his fandom when he wrote in 1998:

One of my goals for the Judy List is to come up with a 'politically' correct view of talking about Judy's life, troubles, and attitudes. The 'politically' correct point of view may or may not be all the facts. However, it would reflect what most people think is the best 'spin' to put on Judy for the enhancement of her legend in the future. As we know, anyone can be made to look good or bad. We have the challenge to be fair and respect Judy's talent and life. I don't believe the truth will ever hurt Judy's legacy. However, errors in stories and false reports could be destructive. (Judy List daily digest, 18 February 1998)

What's so striking about this post—and exemplary for the list's discussions as a whole—is the writer's self-consciousness of fandom as an interested reading of Garland, one motivated by both ambivalence toward and respect for the authentifying status of facts. In this poster's mind, Garland fans must take an active role in the continual reconstitution of her star text, correcting the dominant readings promoted by the various media and accepted by the general public as "factual." By the same token, the terms for enhancing Garland's legacy from a " 'politically' correct point of view" are not identified, but that is not surprising. For as this goal plays itself out in the correspondence on the listserv, such a viewpoint has to obscure how the position from which fans read with or against dominant readings responds to the market value of Garland product for mainstream audiences, so their readings also reveal their own strong investment in commodity culture as the index of a "politically correct" normativity.

This is well illustrated by the list's major debates about Garland's status as a gay icon over the course of its five-year history. The topic was initially raised as a question by a female graduate student in October 1996, and it resulted in a relatively sympathetic discussion. The list manager cited identification with Garland's "always-evident emotion and indestructible talent," and alluded to her camp, saying, "Judy always came across as a FUN person, and what self-respecting gay man doesn't like to have fun?? <grin>" (9 October 1996). Another poster referred to the artistic stereotype of gay men and then historicized it: "Particularly in the fifties and sixties when Judy was alive, who had the time to develop a cult? Very young people without jobs and families and gays who weren't going in that direction"

(15 October 1996). My post, in which I talked about the resistance to gender norms in her film persona (13 October 1996), led someone else to read *Life* magazine's 1954 photo coverage of Garland on the set of *A Star is Born* in contrast with all the other photos in the issue that feature "women as objects used to advertise TVs and other products." Garland, he commented, comes off as "a powerful, action oriented, hard driving person, doing her best to make the movie terrific . . . In a sense," he speculated, "maybe she was blacklisted because she wouldn't be a docile, deferential lady" (28 October 1996). This was followed by someone writing in detail about Dyer's book, "a very good explanation of why Judy appeals to gay men" (8 December 1996). After someone else announced that he had put up on his own website Vito Russo's explanation of the gay Garland cult (13 October 1996), another poster offered to share a piece he had written about Garland's gay fan following for the *Washington Blade* (26 December 1996). This initial conversation, which ran on and off for over several months, was clearly dominated by agreement that Garland was and continues to be a gay icon. The posters were not only cognizant that their understanding of her star value amounted to a queer reading— and that their appreciation of her affinity with camp contributed to it—but they were well aware, too, of the mediation of their interpretations by academic and journalistic readings of Garland, which they incorporated into their own accounts.

The topic of Garland's gay following came up again in March 1997. That poster from San Diego began by announcing, after watching the Denmark TV interview sent to him by a collector: "Contrary to what people say, I believe the last six months of Judy's life were very happy." Then, almost without skipping a beat, this poster added: "In regards to a question about gays being attracted to her concerts, she almost went berserk with anger." After saying more about that, he reasoned:

> In real life, Judy was good friends with many gay people. Thus, I think she was more upset for her fans than she was for herself. Now, I don't think Judy's fans are upset about the association to gays. Of course, I never did or never will believe that a majority of her fans are gay. Nevertheless, the perception persists and is probably true to some extent. In the recent movie "American Presi-

dents" [*My Fellow Americans?*], they have a gay parade that features men dressed as Dorothy. How do people feel about this? Do you think it helps or hurts Judy's legacy? (14 March 1997)

How to interpret this question was immediately addressed by a twenty-something self-proclaimed straight man on the staff of a large midwestern university. "Well, I don't think it helps Judy's legacy, that's for sure." After decrying the appropriation of Garland's image by gay pride in the form of drag queens, he then stated that, if straight people were confronted by that camp spectacle in real life, "They might never want to buy a Judy Garland CD or watch 'The Wizard of Oz' again. Judy would not have wanted that, and it's not a good thing for us either." Citing the need to increase the Garland audience in order "to see more Garland material released by the CD and video companies," he continued, "I also feel, since Judy herself did not target her work to a specifically gay audience, it isn't compromising her image to let that association quietly fade away into non-existence" (15 March 1997). In a follow-up post, he clarified his point:

> I don't think it's good for Judy Garland fandom to be perceived as a 'gay thing' by the general public . . . See, you have to think about the other side. If the straight guy down the street thinks he's buying into a homosexual-oriented fetish by purchasing a Judy Garland CD, he's going to be a lot less likely to buy one. And that's a pretty critical issue. I'm somewhat of an exception to that—if someone wants to raise their eyebrows at me 'cause I like Judy Garland, let 'em. But an awfully lot of my heterosexual cohorts would not feel that way. To them it would make the difference between buying one of her CDs and not buying it. "I don't want anyone to think I am gay" is a powerful incentive, folks. To be honest, it is even for me (to a limited extent), although that's not going to stop me from being a Garland fan, or from having gay friends if I want to. (16 March 1997)

Both posters were in essence repeating what they had written before in the previous discussion of Garland's strong association with gay fandom, when their remarks had gone by without much comment, but by this time the list membership was larger and more diverse in its demographics—and the list erupted in a heated debate. However, at this point, because inflammatory posts were being returned for self-censorship, the discussion did not try to address the homophobia of the two threads, except obliquely through camp irony (one poster staged a mock outing) and symptomatically (by the lack of personal revelation). Most of the respondents accepted the recontextualization of the "gay thing" in what appeared to be the more pressing question of merchandising Garland to a mainstream audience. To be sure, the list manager was still quick to point out "that easily 50% on this list are [gay]—certainly a greater proportion than in the general population" (15 March 1997). Others wrote to applaud that reminder, and to explain, in some thoughtful detail, how "this 'Judy myth' is part of our collective culture—it's not something we gay folks have been, for lack of a better term, 'flaunting'" (16 March 1997). But more interesting at this point was how the discussion now generated, from both men and women, so many cautious, contradictory disavowals of homophobic panic about Garland fandom, and how that anxiety became embedded in a need to identify their fandom with mainstream culture, as if they could reclaim Garland's mass appeal from the 1940s. On one hand, this controversy was resolved by everyone agreeing that "not everyone likes Judy, just people with good taste; gay, straight, whatever" (18 March 1997). On the other hand, it was punctuated by daily posts from the chair of the Internet fan club's welcoming committee, telling list members how they could order the A&E biography in advance of its premiere on 23 March 1997.

The mounting excitement about the biography at the time this second debate occurred clearly resulted from expectations that the show would be presenting two hours of film and TV clips featuring Garland, some possibly never seen before. But it was also due to hopes that the program, scheduled on a Sunday evening when television viewing is at its highest, would provide a means of reconnecting Garland fandom to mass culture. Enthusiasm about the biography was so high that it seemed almost like the handiwork of a Hollywood screenwriter when a system crash silenced the Judy List for seventy-two hours that weekend, unexpectedly deferring the discussion that had been anticipated for several weeks, in some large part around the gay issue.

Immediately after the cablecast, John Fricke posted his promised behind-the-scenes commentary, disclosing a disagreement with coproducer Peter Jones over how to end the biography, whether it would feature the tragic or triumphant Judy. His intention, Fricke confided, was always to tell "the story of Judy Garland [as] that of a woman who came back from oblivion three major times: 1951, 1961, and since her death." In other words, he wanted to give evidence "of the impact Judy has had over the last three decades." At the last minute, Jones, seemingly in conjunction with A&E, presented Fricke with a "fait accompli scripted final act comprising a horrifically negative, downbeat ending." A compromise was reached, as Fricke argued "the finale back from negative to reflective" (23 March 1997).

The list's discussion was subsequently structured by Fricke's commentary and authorial role. Posters debated the biography's concentration on the life over the work, attacked or defended the treatment of Garland's drug use, and raised the "gay thing" again by complaining about the program's outing of her father Frank Gumm, second husband Vincente Minnelli, and former son-in-law Peter Allen, since they are not alive to "defend themselves," and since it invoked that gay orientation of Garland's star text, also acknowledged by the program with its account of her gay following. A contract dancer's reference to Minnelli's "green eyeshadows, and the purple lipstick, and the tam," as illustration of why no one at the studio ever expected him to marry anyone, particularly rankled. Fricke vigorously defended these revelations, writing:

> The statements we included about Vincente were used as such because—while all the MGM associates were free in discussing it off-camera (remind me in Grand Rapids to quote a little Ann Miller for you!)—that generation doesn't have the contemporary "take" on gay or bisexual lifestyles—i.e. the casualness of admission that is certainly more prevalent today. It WAS important to include in the show if only to demonstrate that, once again, Judy's life (like anyone else's) was NOT black and white—and that, although virtually every other book and commentary "blames" HER for the failure of that marriage, the difficulties and problems certainly did NOT all stem from her. (27 March 1997)

Fricke's friend, Al DiOrio, responded similarly, outing Garland's fourth husband, Mark Herron, for good measure (29 March 1997).

Fallout from the documentary was almost as immediate beyond the confines of the list too. Originally scheduled as a star attraction at the upcoming annual Judy Garland Festival held in her birthplace, Grand Rapids, Minnesota, to which he refers, Fricke was summarily uninvited because "the Luft family was unhappy with [him] (purportedly over the A&E 'Biography' comments about Frank Gumm and Vincente Minnelli)," and had delivered an " 'either Fricke or us' ultimatum" to the Festival director (23 May 1997).

The ambiguity resulting from the documentary's divided viewpoint—not only over *which* biographical narrative to tell but also *how* to situate Garland's legendary talent in the light of a contemporary musical audience (so that her final comeback in the A&E biography was now not her funeral, as in the DataBase, but her lasting hold on fans), and *what* to make of the lingering gay connection in both the life and the fans—all of this ultimately worked against normalizing Garland through her life story. That became perfectly clear in two long, detailed and quite extraordinary posts two weeks after the special aired.

Both posts reopened the problem of how to negotiate the star text in view of the biographical personality and its inescapable intimations of cultural marginality. One writer, a friend of Mark Herron, professed his longtime admiration of Garland's unique talent but added, "I have always regarded her with an objective, critical eye." For several pages he then stressed the point that he had "been interested and quite disturbed by the reaction to the discussion of Judy's drug addiction in the Biography special"—since it *was* about her life, and she *was* a drug addict, totally "responsible for her addiction"—and added that, contrary to that previous post about her being "happy," the last interview in Denmark showed the full extent of her decline. As the final means of authorizing this position, the poster signed his name, adding, "and I am an alcoholic" (5 April 1997). The next night another long post appeared, arguing against this viewpoint. Citing his authority as a clinical therapist, this writer diagnosed Garland as "probably Cyclothymic with depressive features. In layperson's terms, she cycled rapidly between up periods and down periods . . . there was more to Judy's drug use than someone that wants to get a rush or a high. This was someone who wanted to try to feel normal, happy, and productive . . . and was unable to do so herself because of a PRE-EXISTING emotional disorder" (6 April 1997). And he ended with the inscription of a diva snap. From either perspective, the Garland star text remained queer in the sense that it was still resistant to normalization, and as the latter post's camp salutation suggests, the gay issue brought to the surface the inability of fans to identify with mainstream culture through their fascination with Judy.

While list contributors did not immediately return to the "gay thing" once the debate about the A&E biography died down, in early 1998 equally contentious discussions began again over issues that feature comparably in Dyer's reading of Garland: the medical or cultural transgressiveness implied by her unstable body; a new Garland revue in New York City featuring a drag impersonator in the star part; and a show sensationalizing her life in E! Entertainment's series, "Hollywood Scandals and Mysteries," which apparently disregarded any efforts on the part of biographers Fricke and Steve Sanders to correct errors. The docudrama, in fact, hired list member Beverly Shields, a professional female Garland imitator, to play the aged star, complete with death scene on the toilet. So much accusation and blame were aimed at Shields for participating in the project that she eventually unsubscribed from the list, not with a diva snap, but not with a whimper either.

These moments of heated debate in the history of the Judy List should not give the impression that the "gay thing" was a continual preoccupation of writers. Daily posts concentrated more routinely on collecting and hunting down Garland music and videos, recounting reminiscences or anecdotal information, proposing what should be included in the multi-CD that Capital Records had once been planning or who should play Garland on TV or in the movies, posting reviews of books, reporting news of impending DVD releases, recounting personal feelings about Garland, analyzing the source of her appeal or her beauty, polling for her worst costume or hair style, and so on. Inevitably, though, such threads could often turn into discussions about the relation of Garland's biography to her stage or screen persona, the need to promote her to a mainstream audience, and the constitution of her fan following. These issues are ultimately related, symptomatically brought together for the list in resistance to the dominant reading of Garland and "the gay thing."

On the day of the A&E biography's cablecast, a female college student, who had complained more than once about her marginal status as a Garland fan among her friends and family, wrote:

> Now I know it's old but I want to put my point of view in on the gay thing. For one thing not all gays like Judy. My cousin and best friend Robert is not a fan of hers. And I didn't even know that she was considered a gay icon until this summer. My cousin's cousin on his side of the family is gay, and Rob, me, and his cousin Tom and Tom's husband Gary were at Six Flags in Texas. And they kept talking about Dorothy and the Wizard of Oz. Finally I asked why? And they said that most gay men think of Dorothy going over the rainbow into Oz is like gay men coming out of the closet. And I kind of can see their point. So I think it's OK. Like I said, just because you like Judy doesn't automatically mean you're labeled GAY. My ex-boyfriend Chris liked Judy, but than again we think he might be. That's another story. (23 March 1997)

The Judy List illustrates how Garland's perceived gay following still structures her star text as an account of her post-MGM stardom, although it's not the same old story from the 1950s and is responsive to her historically shifting value as a Hollywood commodity that interrupts her fans' relation to mainstream culture. As that young female poster herself exemplifies, moreover, there is indeed yet another story to Garland fandom. A second young female fan wrote in 1999 that she became "Judy crazy" following the telecasting of *The Wizard of Oz* in 1997, after which she spent the entire day watching a Garland birthday tribute on TCM. "And if it had not been for my mother stopping me I would have seen every one of them," she went on. "I love Judy, but my mother is against it. She knows all about the gay men that Judy was with and all the pills and drinks and she doesn't want me to have anything to do with Judy. But I can't just stop lovin' the only person I give a damn about" (9 March 1999).

Deemed irrelevant to explanations of Garland's historic gay following, young female fans such as these two have traditionally been absent in accounts of her star text, yet they seem equally attracted to its marginalizing stance toward mainstream culture; moreover, they are now making their presence evident on the Internet. In 1999, a strong, somewhat iconoclastic identification of female fans with Garland was evident in their profiles on the DataBase's defunct Internet fan club, in their comments in the DataBase's guest book, in their effusive testimonials on the memorial wall of another site, "The Judy Garland Photographic Page," and in the increasing number of webpages hosted by young women, such as "Fans 4 Judy," "Mitali's Judy Garland Page," and "Judy Garland: Forever Beautiful," with its all-female "Judy Guardians." Young, often adolescent female fans like the second one quoted above discover Garland through the annual TV showings of *Wizard of Oz* and encounter the legend only after a connection is forged with Dorothy's nonconformist longing to go over the rainbow. These fans identify with the character's resistance to heteronormality and its cultural regulation of femininity, and from there go on to read about Garland's up-and-down career and to appreciate her performance style and wit in this light. Even though these fans do not refer to her "camp," and perhaps are even uncomfortable or unfamiliar with the term, they highlight an alternative view of Garland as "crazy victim" that is as crucial to her camp appeal.

While omnipresent in the DataBase's Internet fan club in 1997, young female fans rarely wrote to the Judy List then, if indeed they subscribed to it in any sizable number. When they did post they were most often placed in an unacknowledged subordinate relation to the male fans who, writing with greater regularity and in more detail, and with more defensiveness about their relation to mainstream culture as Garland fans, dominated the terms of discussion. Once the list's gender gap began to close, the more active participation of female posters made clearer how the multiple formations comprising Garland fandom did not overlap but in fact competed with each other in the claims fans made for the authenticity of their own interested readings—readings that were themselves historically situated as articulations of cultural marginality.

The greater heterogeneity of list membership helps to explain why in March 1999 still another eruption of controversy shifted the ground of discussion about Garland's being a gay icon, reflecting more of an emergent awareness on the part of some fans of their *generational* differences from the dominant readings that still surround her star text. The discussion began when a woman wrote to complain about Michael Musto's campy foreword to Ethlie Ann Vare's *Rainbow: A Star Studded Tribute to Judy Garland*, a collection of excerpted publicity, fan magazine, and "serious" journalistic pieces. Noting that Musto's contribution "is not written as a fan so much as a critic," this poster complained about its "Judy-on-the-brink" view of the star as both "gay icon" and "tragic chanteuse," asking the list, "Do you use those terms? . . . I don't know about you, but I have NEVER been drawn to her by the drama of her personal life and its effect on her performances" (1 March 1999). A few days later she elaborated, angling her objection more directly toward Musto's camp rhetoric: "I have no problem with Judy's status in the gay community . . . That isn't what bothered me. My question was how many true fans, when discussing Judy, actually use the term 'gay icon' . . . or for that matter 'tragic chanteuse'? Don't you think that perpetuates an image which many in the crowd use as an excuse NOT to explore her talent?" (4 March 1999, second ellipses in original).

Aside from the expected explanations of why Garland's status as a gay icon is "pretty inarguable" (2 March 1999), the discussion that followed generated lengthy, often multiple responses from every segment of the list membership, and it centered on finding alternate terms for locating her appeal (her talent, her sexiness, her humor, her vulnerability, her delivery of raw, naked emotion). Some respondents made a point of disentangling the "gay icon" label from its cultural embeddedness in "tragic chanteuse." This thread, in turn, led some posters—straight and gay, male and female—to deny that their fascination with the star was related to their sexual orientation at all. But the debate also prompted a number of passionate recollections about how fans first became intensely fascinated with the star (most frequently, but not always, through *Oz*). For all the fans' discomfort with, as one writer put it, "the idea that something about themselves could conceivably have anything to do with something gay" (2 March 1999), what emerged quite noticeably from these various reflections, which drew on public myths and critical texts as much as personal narratives, was a greater acknowledgment of the historical dimension of the dominant reading that they contested as well as an articulation of the generational differences among fans themselves, many of them new converts to what the list calls "Judy-ism."

A more self-conscious generational awareness was in evidence among younger gay men, too, several of whom wrote to the list simultaneously. One writer agreed that "a Garland performance appealed to—in fact, filled a chasm for repressed gay men" but asked: "What about after Stonewall?" In particular, he was rejecting the argument advanced by D. A. Miller in *A Place for Us*, namely, "that musicals provided an outlet that subconsciously united all gay men (a thesis that can roughly be transposed to Judy Garland)." For the image that Miller presents "of a 13-year old boy just coming to terms with his sexuality, crying while mouthing the words to the Carnegie Hall concert in his basement . . . seems completely outdated . . . [it] doesn't seem applicable any more" (9 March 1999). Another fan agreed, remarking, "It seems to be more of an older generational thing, though there are many [fans] in my generation (early 30s) and younger" (9 March 1999). A third fan was even more specific:

> To the vast majority of gay men in their twenties—and to those now coming out in their teens—Judy Garland is little more than the actress who played Dorothy . . . This is not to deny the inexplicable force she played in the gay psyche during the 50s, 60s, and 70s—just that sometime during the 80s it began to diminish. Perhaps this is a natural balancing: Judy's heterosexual female following will become more present (it's always been there) and her gay male following will become less so (although it will never disappear), and Judy herself will be more and more recognized for her talent and not for her pathos. (9 March 1999)

These writers are trying to come to terms with gay Garland fandom as it has shifted historically and generationally, with the changes marked by the implicit presence or absence of camp as the factor shaping appreciations of the star's queer significance. In so doing, they bring out what, in his account of the transformation of camp during the past fifty years, Daniel Harris argues more explicitly: "the fact that [gay men's] love for performers like Judy Garland was actually a learned behavior, part of [their] socialization as homosexuals" (21). Regarding the cult forming around Garland concerts in the fifties and sixties, Harris sees it as a means of forging community and visibility for her gay fans. Gay fan formations around star divas like Garland, the critic explains, was "an emphatic political assertion of ethnic camaraderie, as was the gay sensibility itself, which did not emanate from some sort of deeply embedded homosexual 'soul,' but arose as a way of achieving a collective subcultural identity," and did so through camp (17). Thus Harris concludes about Garland fans that "they liked, not her, so much as her audience" (18).

Harris dismisses the value of Garland herself as the object of intense emotional and increasingly public investment by gay fans, but her significance for them was clearly more complex than he appreciates. Indeed, when placed in conjunction with Dyer's analysis of Garland's appeal to a "gay sensibility," what Harris has to say elsewhere in his book about pre-Stonewall gay fascination with film stars does suggest why the Garland cult was not separable from its object. In a homophobic society that required the invisibility of gay men and increasingly defined homosexuality as inverted or compromised masculinity, Garland's star text encouraged strong queer readings because of its potentiality for camp recognition, what Harris refers to as "the aestheticism of maladjustment" (10). That is, gay male fans inhabited a social identity which defined their own "in-between" relation to mainstream culture by transforming it into an identification with marginality as a performance of camp style, one embodied in the Garland image of difference within normality. As one list member recalled, after seeing *A Star is Born* in the 1950s, "for the next 3 days, I walked in a haze (which I now realize had a lot to do not only with the stunning display of talent, but with a force and a sense of style I was trying to cultivate in myself)" (9 March 1999).

The thrust of this return to "the gay thing" on the list was to historicize Garland's camp star text, but most fans nonetheless recuperated the discussion as evidence of her inherent and timeless appeal to "ALL KIND of people" (6 March 1999), "a cross-section of humanity" (9 March 1999). As in the earlier debates, these posters then tried to close the discussion by concluding that Garland fandom was simply a result of "good taste"—without appreciating the irony that "good taste" itself had once supplied the rhetoric of camp sensibility for pre-Stonewall gay men. These fans articulated their historical difference from an older generation as a purer appreciation of Garland's transcendent talent, as if there were now no textual mediation of Garland herself, the writers' own commentaries notwithstanding. Writers of both genders and of varying ages, for instance, testified with great passion that being a fan provides them with a principle of continuity for their identity: "Judy Garland has always been a part of my life" (10 March 1999); "I have thought about her everyday" (10 March 1999); "She seemed to fill the void" (11 March 1999); "She was a constant in my life" (13 March 1999); "My day is never complete without a dash of Judy" (13 March 1999). These claims personalize their dedication to Garland, while articulating how, in anchoring their sense of private continuity, their fandom reinscribes the marginalized cultural identity it seemingly assuages.

Although each debate about Garland's gay following on the Judy List pushed the controversy in different directions, taken together they highlight the instability of her star text to sustain a coherent, unified meaning in the present day. The Garland star text, as Dyer wrote of an older generation of gay fans, still speaks of a special relation to ordinariness—the camp appeal persists—but the inflection of this queer signification, what male and female fans take it to refer to in their own lives, has shifted considerably so that it now connotes more than a "gay sensibility." While the anxiety about Garland's gay associations, which galvanized the list's members into these debates, obviously raises a strong homophobic reaction to the inference that there may be something queer about their own fandom—whether with regard to sexual orientation, gender self-identification, or more simply "taste"—it has increasingly opened up a fault line in the list's discourse that registers as much discomfort with the culturally marginal status of their fan community.

Disagreements about Garland and the "gay thing" thus respond to the nonnormativity that her star text still signifies, but is now recontextualized in the commodity culture of contemporary fans. The need to normalize their dedication is then made most evident when fans read Garland in a way that authenticates both her legacy as a show-business legend and the relation of their fandom to mainstream consumer culture. Not only do they find their identities in that culture, they depend on it for Garland's ongoing commodification so as to insure that she remains a constancy in their lives as product, filling the void they otherwise feel. As one grateful poster exclaimed, when concluding his account of becoming a fan, "I can't believe that I can put Judy on ANYTIME I want to" (10 March 1999).

Collecting Garland product may secure the star's stability as a continuing source of pleasure, but it in no way guarantees the meanings or emotions attributed to the merchandise and memorabilia that appears to objectify her stardom. Consequently, with each eruption of controversy over her gay associations stressing the instability of Garland's star text, the Judy List records fans' efforts to normalize both that text and their fandom along the same lines as the DataBase. However, in contrast with fan pages such as the DataBase, which can fix a certain meaning for Garland through their archival concentration on one aspect of her career, the dialogic nature of the listserv— a site dedicated to arguing about her significance—foregrounds the lack of consensus, ideologically and generationally, which makes a star text like hers continually volatile, perhaps even more so now than during her lifetime, when fans did not have an opportunity for such interaction on a daily basis. At the same time that posters insist on viewing the list itself as a private space, a safe haven from the unsympathetic general public, debating Garland's star text in this forum places their fandom, which they understand in deeply personal terms, in a social setting. The public sphere of Garland fandom is continually implied by the intertextual frameworks of criticism, biographies, and media promotion that writers incorporate into their commentaries. For that matter, because of its electronic circulation and presence on the Web in a complete archival record available for anyone to read, the listserv itself makes the public sphere a requisite of membership in the fan community. In the face of their different readings of Garland, the most devoted fans are then compelled to defend the terms by which her star text is made legible for them: continually reinterpreting the relation of her life and her work, repudiating the dominant reading kept in circulation by the media, reconciling the clashing variants of fan formations, and disengaging their idol from her camp history.

With the marginality of their fandom disturbing their identification with mainstream consumer culture, list members' attempts to stabilize a new alternate reading and to authenticate it in "fact" often ends up appealing outside fandom to unsympathetic corporate interests as their means of accounting for and redressing the cultural displacement they experience because of their devotion to Garland. The more they concentrate her star text in the value of Garland product as their means of revising the significance of her stardom, the more uneasily these posters have to confront what John Fiske refers to as "the contradictory functions performed by cultural commodities which on the one hand serve the economic interests of the industry and on the other the cultural interests of the fans" (47). As the debates occurring before and after the A&E biography make especially clear, many Garland fans project an imagined entertainment industry that also has some presumed investment in normalizing her stardom while embracing all possible readings of it, even though in the manufacturing and marketing of Garland products—videos, CDs, biographies—that industry seems perfectly aware of her audience's marginality despite its increased diversity. Those same fans are just as quick to blame industrial exploitation for both Garland's personal troubles *and* the motives of those, profiting from her work and life today, who keep that dominant reading in place as the "preferred" one. The contradictory premise of this new alternate reading articulates fans' ambivalence toward the consumer culture that fails to appreciate Garland, and it accounts for the privileged status on the list of authors like Fricke and others; as fans and biographers, they are at once inside and outside the Garland industry, producers and consumers of it. This contradiction kept debates on the list ongoing, reiterating how the Garland star text was just that for fans—an unstable text that continually needed to be read on a daily basis, just like the Judy List itself: "Well so it goes . . ." mused one poster after supplying his fan-is-born narrative, "the dialogue continues . . . and we still love JG! To be continued . . ." (9 March 1999, ellipses in original).

Or so it seemed until 2001 when mounting tension between amateur and professional interpreters of Garland caused the Judy List to implode.

THE LISTSERV THAT GOT AWAY

The remarkable feature about Judy Garland's posthumous stardom is that she doesn't have to be alive to make another comeback: by now the triumphant return from adversity or obscurity seems permanently affixed to her star text. Such was the case in February 2001 with the broadcasting of ABC's miniseries, *Life with Judy Garland: Me and My Shadows*, based on daughter Lorna Luft's memoir, *Me and My*

Shadows: A Family Memoir. One effect of the program's promotion was a sudden preponderance of Garland imagery and sounds across the media. These ranged from a special collector's edition of *TV Guide* with multiple covers, magazine and TV interviews with Luft and star Judy Davis, renewed airplay of Garland vocals on the radio, a remastered CD of the Carnegie Hall concert from Capitol Records the same month as the miniseries, even a dedicated Garland CD page at Amazon.com. The cable channels also took advantage of ABC's publicity for the miniseries by running their own biographies. The E! Entertainment channel showed "The Last Days of Judy Garland: The E! True Hollywood Story" a month in advance of *Life with Judy Garland*. Lifetime jumped on the bandwagon, devoting an episode of its biographical series, *Intimate Portrait*, to the star. Not to be left out, A&E reran its two-hour biography the weekend before the miniseries.

Needless to say, the Judy List was abuzz with excitement by the time *Life with Judy Garland* aired. When that week's *TV Guide* appeared in stores with four different covers—three of Garland at various ages, one of Judy Davis decked out as the star—a female fan wrote:

> The thrill of walking into my neighborhood grocery store and being greeted with a myriad of images of Judy was almost too much for me to take in this morning!! Of course I bought all 4 [covers] and of course the cashier looked at me with a bit of questioning skepticism, but la di da. . . .
>
> I went straight-away to the article and any surrounding info and I have to admit I was soon in tears. Finally this wonderfully complex and dynamic woman will get her story told in its proper context. To squabble over the minutia is pointless, the depth and breadth of this wonderfully complex and dynamic woman will finally get the treatment she has always deserved. The production values appear to be "feature-film" quality and I really can hardly wait!!
>
> Mr. Fricke's article was superb and definitely "on-point"! It was icing on the cake to see his marvelous A&E biography again this weekend, too. After watching the recent dreck that other stations have stitched together, my appreciation of this documentary has doubly increased.
>
> Gosh, I'm almost giddy with excitement. It's funny, I went into

the store with my friend and her 9-year[-old] daughter. She saw the TV guides first, and grabbed my hand and said, "Auntie Kim, there's pictures of your family over there." We cracked up, but in a tiny, funny, true way, that's the way I always thought of Judy, a member of my family. (19 February 2001, ellipses in original)

This writer typifies how fans looked forward to the miniseries' impact as the occasion of the latest Garland comeback. The "giddy" excitement described here combines, on one hand, an expectation that Garland would finally be having "her story told in its proper context" with, on the other hand, the writer's own "tiny, funny, true" sense of "family" identification with the star. Familial affiliation implies intimacy as well as kinship, while also suggesting the insularity of Garland fandom, its isolation from mainstream consumer culture of the sort *TV Guide* ordinarily covers. In this sense and without regard for sexual orientation, the expectation that the miniseries would reach audiences unfamiliar with or unappreciative of the star would let the *real* fans come out of the closet about *their* life with Judy Garland.

The miniseries, well-reviewed and one of the most watched of the season, was actually the crescendo of a wave of new Garland product that had appeared throughout the short lifetime of the Judy List, all of it examined, appreciated, but also critiqued at length. Along with the A&E biography in 1997, these included Luft's memoir, the Ethlie Ann Vare anthology, and "Judy: The Box," a multimedia package from 32 Records (four CDs, a videotape, and a 102-page book), all in 1998. Pioneer released the Garland CBS TV series on DVD over a four-year period beginning in 1999, first issuing two stand-alone discs, then at year's end bringing out a set of fourteen episodes, stored, along with a paperback reprint of Coyne Steven Sander's *Rainbow's End: The Judy Garland Show*, in a cardboard box representing a theatrical trunk. In 1999 as well, Schiffer Books published, as part of its series on "collectibles," Edward R. Pardella's *Judy Garland Collector's Guide: An Unauthorized Reference and Price Guide* which encompassed and lavishly illustrated the many aspects of her career. 2000 saw Gerald Clarke's sensationalized and heavily publicized biography, *Get Happy: The Life of Judy Garland*, and, as an expensive gold CD from the high-end company DCC, the first remastered recording of the Carnegie Hall concert with the songs in their correct order and all of the star's patter included. (Capitol released its cheaper and differently mixed version the year afterward because of this one's success.)

As a result of the new biographies, too, Garland generated new interest for the media. *60 Minutes II* on CBS featured "Judy Garland's Legacy," a retrospective profile of the star in 1999 to tie in with the publication of the Luft memoir, and *20/20* on ABC reviewed Garland's "darkest days" the following year to do the same for the Clarke biography. Both newsmagazines had additional coverage of Garland on their networks' websites. ABC's was the more ambitious. It included a short article on "a star's demise" which focused on Clarke's "find," Garland's late-night, rambling, and angry tape recordings and a manuscript for a memoir she never completed; a transcript of the biographer's online chat with viewers following the broadcast; and a text of the *20/20* piece itself ("20/20: Judy Garland's Tragic Life," <abcnews.com>, downloaded 5 April 2000). In 2000 the *New York Times* website supplemented two reviews of *Get Happy* (one favorable and one not) with a story on Clarke and his research, a print interview with the author abbreviated from a longer audio one that was also made available for downloading, a letter of rebuttal from Lorna Luft, and material from the newspaper's archive—reviews of Garland's major films and news articles about her Carnegie Hall comeback, death, and funeral (<nytimes.com/books>, downloaded 26 April 2000).

Less mainstream attention to Garland more directly focused on the star's status as a gay icon. As part of its celebration of the twenty-fifth anniversary of Stonewall in 1999, the gay and lesbian magazine series on PBS, *In the Life*, returned to "The Judy Connection" with talking-head spots featuring "out" entertainers recalling the star's influence, Garland experts like John Fricke and the producers of the Judy Box CD-video set, and Lorna Luft, who came on to promote her memoir. The next year *Atlantic Monthly* and Salon.com reexamined the supposed death of gay camp diva worship as it had centered historically on Garland (Gross, Cave). Her cult status nonetheless persisted, evident in several items sold on eBay and directed to a gay audience during the years I am chronicling: a bootleg CD of those autobiographical tapes which she made at the end of her life; a digitally edited version of the theatrical poster for *Gladiator* (2000) with

Garland's face, taken from her "Get Happy" number (the same still used on the cover of both Clarke's and Fricke's books), incongruously inserted to peer over Russell Crowe's shoulder in camp commentary on his dour, oh-so-straight expression; and the video of "Christmas with Judy Garland," the Castro theater tribute.

Addressing consumers who inhabited the mainstream as well as those who did not, the renewed commercial attention to Garland motivated the pretext determining the import of *Life with Judy Garland* for fans. Specifically, this pretext kept in place a dualism which had dominated the listserv from the beginning, as it had the construction of Johnson's DataBase: a dialectical view of Garland forged from setting her "legacy," with reference to her body of work both for its artistic value and as evidence of her charismatic hold on audiences, against her "legend," with reference to the biography. "What a sad life," Barbara Walters commented at the end of the 20/20 piece, and as far as Garland fans are concerned this is the legend most instrumental in devaluing the legacy. The "sad life" marks the biographical trajectory of her story but also functions as the interpretive starting point, whether the aim is validating the legacy or demystifying the legend. There is, of course, another side to the legend, namely, Garland's portrayal of Dorothy Gale in *Wizard of Oz*: an iconic value of unblemished innocence existing in counterpoint to the record of studio abuse and addiction to prop up the full impact of "sadness" in the star's life story as a "crazy victim." This distillation of the legend still views Garland as an embodiment of suffering, the life lived tragically on the wrong side of the rainbow. What more intriguingly complicates the legend/legacy dualism is the way that Garland herself inflected it during the last decade of her life. She promoted her own "legend" as a camp raconteur exaggerating or fabricating stories of her years at MGM with great flair and ironic, self-deprecating wit on television talk shows, beginning with her famous appearances on Jack Paar's program.

Lorna Luft's memoir and her many television appearances promoting both the book and the miniseries are structured by this dualism. So too are John Fricke's chronicle of the star's "professional legacy" (9) as opposed to the legend of a life gone awry in *Judy Garland: World's Greatest Entertainer* and, on the other hand, Gerald Clarke's very different goal of documenting the unstable and unhappy woman behind the legend in *Get Happy*. Their projects, more-over, extend beyond the readership of their books since, like Luft, both authors have appeared in conjunction with the new Garland merchandise in one guise or other. In addition to their television appearances, Fricke wrote the *TV Guide* feature article on Garland for the miniseries and stressed the legacy of a great performer. Eight months earlier, and timed to the first airing of *Wizard of Oz* on TCM, Clarke wrote the spotlight piece for that magazine which concluded by summarizing his book's claims about the "real" Garland who later "found the image of Dorothy to be a kind of prison" ("Beyond the Yellow Brick Road," 24).

In his article, moreover, Clarke took direct aim at the fan community, writing: "Some of Garland's more fanatical fans, displaying symptoms that might have puzzled Freud himself, were outraged that I talked about her active sex life, her drug addiction and her emotional problems. 'We don't want to hear about these things,' they shouted in letters and through the internet. It was not Judy Garland they cared about—in other words, the real, vibrant woman I had tried to portray. It was Dorothy, a girl who never existed except on film" ("Beyond the Yellow Brick Road," 24). This accusation, which characterized Garland fans through their blind devotion to an unreal icon, implicitly set the agenda for reconsideration of the legacy as the real object of their fandom, igniting a fire which still burned when the miniseries aired. The reference to the Internet even suggested to some that Clarke might be a lurking member of the list. In contrast with Clarke, Fricke declared in *TV Guide* that Garland's diverse audiences today see "beyond the muckraking" ("She Made Us Love Her," 22). Similarly, Luft has made a point of graciously praising Garland fans. To be sure, in her book she makes some unkind comments about a few of the "Garland freaks," fans who had become friends and, at the end of the star's life, worshiped her but also "poisoned her with that worship, catering to her every whim in the sickest possible ways . . . These hangers-on were invariably male and usually gay" (203). But when she appeared on *In the Life*, Luft took pains to recognize the loyal gay fan base. "She did know she had a large gay following," Luft commented about her mother, "and she loved it." More to the point, Luft singled out the unwavering dedication throughout the past decades of these same fans who, she stated with gratitude, had "protected her [mother's] image and protected her memory."

Despite the importance of longtime fans, whether gay or not, in keeping the memory alive while the entertainment industry itself pretty much dismissed Garland as a cult taste, the commercial impact of *Life with Judy Garland* for the legacy had the residual cost of shutting out the most faithful. In between airings of the first and second parts of the miniseries, when posters were already starting to air their thoughts, Luft's husband, Colin Freeman, wrote to the list:

> For all of the people on the list who are enjoying the movie, she [Lorna] thanks you. For those who have decided to find every little fault that you can and nitpick, please let me know when your movie comes out about your mothers' life and what network it would be on!
>
> This movie was not made for you. It was made for the millions of people who did not know her mother's work and life after Dorothy. She did this for her mother's memory. JG deserves all the TV Guide covers, accolades and reviews. We have received many phone calls today from some famous and not so famous people saying thank you for bringing her back to the public eye. (26 February 2001)

Coming from official owners of the Garland legacy—Luft and her husband comprise part of the "Judy Garland heirs trust"—this post sought to regulate the reception of the miniseries by segmenting off the most dedicated fan base. For, as one list member angrily wrote afterward, if this movie was not made for the diehard fans, the ones buying the TV Guide covers and other merchandise, and eagerly following all the "accolades and reviews," then who *was* it made for? (28 February 2001). Like Clarke's TV Guide article, Freeman's post depicts fans not as the faithful but as the fanatical, and it then distinguishes them from the miniseries' target audience, the "millions" unfamiliar with Garland who are potential new consumers of her CDs and films. Throughout the Judy List's history, this is the split identity that fans have continually been negotiating, but before Freeman's post, they had not been called spoilsports for doing so.

Freeman's sharp words divorced Garland from her fan "family." His post pointed ahead toward a potential consequence of the miniseries' renewal of interest in Garland, namely, diminishment of the special role played by the faithful fans as protectors of her memory and defenders of her cultural significance as the twentieth century's greatest entertainer. The warning not to "nitpick" because the miniseries was made for the general public pointed up the much more vexing question of the faithful fans' own authority not only as knowledgeable interpreters of Garland's life, career, and art, but as the sentinels of her reputation. "I think," one fan wrote to a newcomer on the list to account for the hostile reaction to the Clarke biography, "there is a small % of Judy fans who see themselves as her avenging angels" (30 June 2000). Set off against these "avenging angels" on the Judy List, although actually just the more authoritative version of their watchful eye, were the professional historians of Garland's career, the most vocal of whom was always John Fricke. The media promotion of *Life with Judy Garland* intensified the determination with which Judy's "angels" of both camps sought to "protect" her reputation by interpreting her stardom "correctly." Indeed, what the Freeman post implied about the subordination of the dedicated fan's contribution to the legacy had already begun to play itself out on the Judy List the month before the miniseries was broadcast, with John Fricke's authority serving as a lightning rod. Challenges to his privileged position on the list as the definitive Garland expert led to charged exchanges among posters which the "giddy" fan was noting when she inserted her praise of his *TV Guide* article into her account of finding the magazine's display at her local market. The debate about Fricke occurred before and after the broadcasting of *Life with Judy Garland*, temporally framing the list's discussion of the merits of the miniseries, and it resulted in the "family feud" that abruptly ended the list three months after this latest Garland comeback.

As had always been his custom on the Judy List, Fricke wrote as the official chronicler of Garland's career. He painstakingly sought to correct fans' misinterpretations of her achievements with the purpose of disentangling the legacy from the legendary "sad life," usually by exposing the inaccuracies in or incompleteness of the so-called "record," whether as offered by a fan's interpretation of an event in Garland's life or career, or via a fan's reference to published material. Fricke, in other words, used the list as a forum to clarify the legacy for fans. Additionally, he offered fans a perspective from inside the Garland industry, explaining decisions about marketing or inclusion/exclusion of certain material on a CD or TV documentary, and so forth. Other Garland authors and industry professionals posted such information to the list, too, but Fricke wrote with more persistence and regularity, and because of his books, CD liner notes, TV participation, and contact with many list members either in New York City or during his personal appearances, he had the greatest public visibility as *the* Garland expert.

Fricke's privileged position on the list had been disputed previously but this time out he only succeeded in raising the stakes of what he called "The Legend Versus The Reality battle" (26 January 2001). Although his aim was pedagogical, his e-mail style was adversarial, brusque, often rude, not too different in tone from Colin Freeman's. The month before the premiere of the miniseries, challenges to Fricke's authority emerged in conjunction with "The Last Days of Judy Garland: The E! Hollywood True Story," one of the cable programs taking advantage of ABC's promotion for its dramatized biography. Criticizing the E! program's shoddiness, list members pointed to the contrasting "brand of knowledge and professionalism" of Fricke projects, such as the 1997 A&E biography (25 January 2001). The author himself weighed in to offer a back-story account of the E! producers' disregard for accuracy, going on to expose the opportunism and shoddy work of other Garland professionals, whether in their capacity as authors, TV or CD coproducers, or venders of bootleg material. Fricke was referring in particular to disagreements about the dubious expertise or motives of certain fans who had become producers or authors or both, and their status had been hashed over many times before on the list, resulting in the willing departure or forced expulsion of the people under attack and some of their defenders.

This time, Fricke's snippy posts moved one articulate fan—the same poster who would later explode in anger about Colin Freeman's condescension—to complain vigorously if also sarcastically about the "special treatment" Fricke received from the list's owner, Mark Harris. Fricke's often intemperate critiques were always published, it was charged, and he had license to attack people by name, whereas Harris returned or censored as personalized attacks comparable e-mails from the nonexperts with no commercial motive, fans like this angry

poster and his friends. In contrast with Fricke, this writer characterized himself as "a 'normal' fan of Garland's." He explained:

> I'm not trying to write a book, produce a documentary, or make
> a biographical film about Judy.
>
> I simply buy the CD's and other products and enjoy her artistry.
> I KNOW there are errors in practically everything done about
> Judy—just like with Marilyn and Elvis and other great icons. WE
> KNOW THAT!!! That's why I've made a point of reading ALL
> the books out there to form my own "informed opinion" on what
> Judy's life might have been like. And that's just what it is, "my own
> opinion." I'll never know all of it and neither will anyone else. The
> only one who could is Judy and she's not with us—hence all the
> people out there making a quick buck by writing the "be all-end
> all" biography—whether it's on paper or film or on the internet.
> (25 January 2001)

In the long thread resulting from this post, most list members defended Fricke's dedication, loyalty, and generosity to the fan community, and they of course applauded his own selfless "intention" as a
Garland author. "He just wants people to have an accurate representation of what Judy was and still is," wrote one member. "He, more
than any of these fly by nights, is still around, when just about ALL
the other authors have never mentioned Judy again after their book
hit the stands" (27 January 2001). Rushing to Fricke's side, fellow author Steve Sanders observed that he himself had never "read a post
(at least recently) so vitriolic, misinformed, and undeserving" as that
angry poster's unwarranted attack on Fricke's fairness:

> To my knowledge, I don't think John or I (or some of the others
> active on her behalf) have ever claimed to be all-knowing "Judy ex-
> perts," "foisting" information or opinion on an audience with the
> arrogance and self-importance some of Judy's so-called fans have
> manifested—both here and elsewhere. If we've been sometimes
> less than tactful, it's usually to correct the all-knowing factions
> who know nothing. I'm not talking about personal opinions, I'm
> referring to completely uninformed fans passing off their own sub-
> text, misinformation, or dementia as fact. More often than I can
> count, I've read posts about what Judy thought, who she would

be proud of, what she'd like, what she felt, at whom she'd spit . . . Yikes! John has never assumed anything but only offered information based on decades of hard research, interviews, and investigation. (26 January 2001, ellipses in original)

In his own defense, Fricke explained:

If I sometimes (SOMEtimes?! :) come across as pro-Judy—and want her professional and personal memory presented in a manner that does justice to those inestimable gifts—you'll just have to accept it as additional personal opinion and a manifestation of my enthusiasm for and gratitude to someone who has given me more pleasure and excitement and uplift and joy as an entertainer than any other . . . and whose personal AND professional reputation is often 'done wrong.'

But then he added, parenthetically: "It's especially disheartening to read some of the drivel posted here by those pseudo-solicitous, smug types who are determined to perpetuate the 'understanding' of Judy's problems—often based on inaccurate reports from everywhere—while vaunting their own self-assessed superiority" (26 January 2001, ellipses in original).

I certainly do not dispute the quality of Fricke's scholarship or that of the other authors writing in defense of his credentials or their documented charges of plagiarism made against certain people who had departed from the list; and I admit the post attacking Fricke, for all its insight about what normal fans do, *was* snide, particularly when the angry poster suggested that this author's criticisms might be defensively motivated by his own "waning" career. All the same, one gets the impression from reading the ensuing thread, though dominated by prolific defense of Fricke, that groups of like-minded fans on both sides of the battle were circling the wagons before the miniseries aired.

While Fricke was politely silent during the discussion immediately following the airing of *Life with Judy Garland*, the matter of his authority became an issue again some two weeks afterward and ran throughout March, so the miniseries by no means settled the matter. The second time around the challenge to Fricke's expertise arose when a new list member, inspired by the miniseries, wrote to inquire about the best books on Garland. After several people sent in their recommendations, Fricke replied with a tempered critique of Gerold Frank's biography, *Judy*, pointing out the restrictions placed on his research (i.e., certain things about people couldn't be disclosed when Frank wrote because they were still alive then). Fricke's comments resulted in a thread questioning his own biases in dismissing a rival author. At the same time, new list members wrote in with their answers to questions about Garland's life, engaging in the kind of amateur research or psychological speculation, often with supporting reference to comparable events in their own lives involving addicted or mentally ill relatives, which always caused Fricke to retort with impatience. As these two threads overlapped, he again stood out as the only bastion of accuracy in the face of the new "drivel" now being written to the list by the miniseries's most recent converts to Judy fandom. After defending his militancy about "Judy's reputation—WHEN the militancy [is] backed up by fact" (14 March 2001), Fricke finally declared, "I (JUST speaking for myself!) can't take it anymore." He objected specifically (and by name) to one poster's "ramblings" about Garland's addictions, another's "obsessive hysteria about Frank Gumm [and the charges of his having sex with a boy]," and a third's concern with a "knife throwing incident" that involved Garland with her two youngest children. Complaining about their " 'picking and choosing' random facts (often inaccurate and disproportionate)," Fricke exclaimed, "this List is getting to be a bitch to read" (24 March 2001).

Aside from rejoinders from those personally attacked, who then withdrew from the list, Fricke's defenders now did not excuse his tone as before, but defended only his authority as the leading Garland expert. One poster attributed the attacks on Fricke to "jealousy" (28 March 2001) and another saw Garland's "increased popularity among the general public" as a direct result of the author's "clear and thorough representation of Judy's career" (24 March 2001). Even Feltenstein weighed in indirectly with his recognition of Fricke's multiple contributions to the upcoming Rhino Handmade CD of *Summer Stock/In the Good Old Summer Time* (24 March 2001).

The first Fricke thread in January and its sequel in March functioned to legitimate his special position on the list by distinguishing his expertise and motives from those of the "bogus" experts: amateur interpreters who spun fantasies about Garland and entrepreneurial fans who had joined the Garland industry in some capacity but engaged in self-promotion and shoddy scholarship; implicitly, too, the defenders of Fricke positioned him standing firm in his objectivity to protect the legacy from the absent but still demonized Gerald Clarke, whose book perpetuated the sordid legend into the twenty-first century. The threads defined Fricke's singular authority by folding together his identity as amateur fan and professional author, in this way establishing the superior hybrid: the professional as opposed to unprofessional fan-historian. "Actually, I'd been the kind of passionate fan who researched Judy for my own pleasure since I was a preteen," Fricke explained when defending his credentials during the second thread. "As such, I was lucky enough to have become well aware of many of the different (oft-times conflicting) reports of various aspects of her professional and personal lives." Fricke's recollection of his once-incomplete understanding of Garland through media and biographical coverage, it is worth pointing out, is not all that different from that described by the angry poster who had initiated the first thread in January. Fricke then moved beyond this fan perspective, however, by noting that it ultimately helped him when researching his Garland book because it enabled him to "trace a sometimes more direct route among the surfacing material as well as the minefields of earlier reports, comments, and books" (13 March 2001).

In short, writing as another longtime and intensely devoted admirer of Garland, Fricke equated his unwavering dedication with that of the other fans on the list while, at the same time, he laid claim to that little something extra which exceeded *mere* fandom because of his expertise as a professional historian of Garland. As a consequence, the Fricke threads did not open up the list to public debate about the blank spots in the Garland text requiring dialogic interpretation of both the legacy and the legend; rather, the authoritative hybrid position granted to Fricke by consensual agreement among most list members more directly regulated their interpretative activity by virtue of their deference to his greater expertise, a credential wrapped up as his more intense yet objective expression of Garland fandom.

Was it just accident that a controversy about Fricke's authority in both January and March temporally framed the list's discussion of

Life with Judy Garland? I don't think so. The miniseries expanded the list's membership and generated the longest daily digest in its history. Almost all the posters praised the TV movie as a whole. Those who criticized it complained about minor details and condensations of the biography, some of the secondary performers, and the artificial recreation of Garland's most famous numbers. A minority also had difficulties with Judy Davis when she replaced the younger and more breathlessly innocent Tammy Blanchard. One early post complained that Davis would have benefited from adapting the illusionist techniques of female impersonators in order to look younger (25 February 2001). While some people objected to anyone bringing in drag as a standard, others concurred that Davis's appearance and her bearing were too harsh. The previously mentioned angry poster, the one who had openly challenged Fricke's authority in January, wrote at length in agreement with these criticisms. As well as berating Colin Freeman for waiting too long before telling fans the miniseries was not made for them, this writer commented, "A GOOD makeup artist (doesn't need to be a drag queen either) could have made Davis NOT look so much like A MAN IN A DRESS." Furthermore, he objected to the stiltedness of Davis's effort to recreate Garland move for move, and predicted "in time, this portrayal will be looked upon the same as Faye Dunaway's version of Joan Crawford. Campy and fun, but not REALLY her" (28 February 2001).

That kind of reaction hardly seems to be the preferred viewer response intended by the miniseries. *Life with Judy Garland* gives every impression of trying to prevent a camp reading of Garland by emphasizing the authenticity of Davis's performance as a faithful recreation. The miniseries's reproductions of "The Trolley Song" and "The Man That Got Away," for instance, work against the camp affect that I analyzed in this book's introduction when discussing these two signature Garland numbers. Yes, as some list members noted, Davis's impersonation stands out too noticeably as a simulation, undermining the authenticity which the painstaking attention to detail strives to achieve. Davis gets right the moves and gestures, as if she has studied the filmed numbers in order to mime them correctly, but an oddly wrong detail here and there, like her orange wig in "Trolley Song" (which just does not look or move like Garland's), makes the absence of the original all too palpable in the reconstruction.

These jarring details may momentarily disrupt the effect of the recreated numbers but they do not detract from their point. For all the fidelity to *filmic* detail, the intensity of Garland's performance style, which produces the dialectic of authenticity and theatricality that structures "Trolley Song" and "Man That Got Away," is given a *biographical* explanation. The miniseries recontextualizes the Garland style, accounting for its excess by supplying a fully legible content, the psychologized character of "Judy Garland," which restores the connotations of authenticity.

The handling of these two numbers in the miniseries mutes the camp dialect that Jack Babuscio sees in the star's intensity. "Trolley Song" now refers to the progress of Garland's love affair with Minnelli and also supplies the fictive occasion for her meeting Kay Thompson; its excessively upbeat delivery represents the high point of her career at MGM when she felt beautiful and her talent expressed it. On the other hand, before "Man That Got Away" reaches its finish, in the miniseries Garland interrupts the shoot. She breaks down and sobs uncontrollably, attributing her outburst to the stress of making *Star is Born*, her pent-up reaction to her mother's death, and by implication, because of the scenes surrounding this number, her drug use. When Garland says she cannot continue with "Man That Got Away" because its emotions touch home *too* intensely, her brief conversation with director George Cukor on the set afterward provides an explanation for her excessively torchy delivery; the fictionalized sequence removes any implications of either "crazy victim," the Garland who reportedly kept stalling production of *Star is Born* and drove it over budget because of neurotic, self-indulgent behavior, or camp ironist, the Garland whom Cukor recalled being "always funny" even when performing the film's most emotionally intense scenes (Haver, 164).

Many on the Judy List agreed that Garland was herself more "campy and fun" than the miniseries portrayed her. The most sustained thread critiquing *Life with Judy Garland*, in fact, dwelled on the absence of humor in the characterization of Garland as scripted and as performed by either Davis or Blanchard. A female fan wrote:

> Again and again, people on this list who have made a real study of Judy's life, who have contributed to major products disseminating her work and story, have stressed how important it is to

100

101

102

103

Judy Davis impersonates Judy Garland filming "The Man That Got Away" only to stop the shoot before finishing the number. *Life with Judy Garland: Me and My Shadows* (Miramax, 2001). Frame captures.

show people her wit, her love of life, her vivacity, but that seemed to be mostly missing from the pre-1950 portion of this show. I do wish the producers had taken this opportunity to give some of that context, and therefore more depth, to the usual "little girl lost" narrative. I think it's telling that the friends I watched it with, neither of whom knows any more about Judy's life than they've learned from me over the years, would fill the commercial breaks with exclamations of "oh, it's just so sad. What a horrible life." (27 February 2001)

No one called what was lacking evidence of Garland's "camp" wit, whether with reference to the performance style guided by Roger Edens or, after the MGM years, that ironic engagement with the legend which Garland herself orchestrated—but that is what posters described. Explained another female fan: "The extreme dichotomy of humor & tragedy—more or less always intermingled—is, along with Judy's warmth, something that folks just don't seem to be able to capture all that well" (5 March 2001).

There were, to be sure, a few posts that alluded to "the gay thing" and they did so with a camp's wit. Steve Sanders sent in the following "infonugget," overheard "while at dinner at a Mexican restaurant, the kind of place where the battery-acid margaritas act as strong enough vaccination to protect from their e-coli pink chicken burritos. Anyway, en route to the men's room were two rugged looking—I said, 'looking'—gentlemen in matching flannel shirts. Just I was walked [sic] past their table, one of the moustached men with great flourish said, "Judy Davis was just FABulous!" (5 March 2001). This anecdote immediately moved a poster to reply: "Oh, so THAT'S who Colin was referring to when he said that the movie was made for someone other than 'us'" (5 March 2001). On the other side of camp appreciation of the miniseries, Mark Harris proposed a queer reading that saw Garland's life story as a drama of passing beginning at MGM. Basing his interpretation on a scene that depicts Roger Edens telling Garland to be Francis Gumm when she sings, Harris observed: "Being one person inside and another to the rest of the world is something each of us have in common. Here on The JUDY List, from manager/webmaster to newly-joined high school student, from Judy's own family members to 'noted historians' . . . we're all 'Frances' struggling with our own 'Judy.' Sure goes a LONG way towards explaining the eternal allure for Judy's gay fans, doesn't it? . . . Her struggle is our struggle . . . That's why she means something so personal to each one of us in a similar, yet different way" (27 February 2001). None of these observations, which each offer camp insight about Garland's cultural significance beyond her biography or her talent, attracted any comment, so they passed without further notice.

In contrast with previous media events such as the A&E biography, then, the miniseries did not generate heated debates about what Garland's star text signifies about her fans as well as for them. Previously, those controversial disagreements on the list had dwelled on her legendary status as a gay icon, which epitomized the indeterminacy of her star text and the commercial insignificance of her work—the legacy—in the present day. As a result of the first Fricke thread, however, by the time the miniseries aired, the ground for that sort of debate had been relocated around the question of who were the more authoritative interpreters of Garland, the fans themselves or the professionals. Responsibility for safeguarding Garland's legacy, formerly the province of her longtime fans, was being handed over to the experts and to the Garland industry as a whole. The hierarchical positioning of professionals over fans then served to focus the latter's dialogue more exclusively on the text of the miniseries alone and not on Garland as a cultural icon inscribed with conflicting meanings for fandom and the general public alike. Yet as Gross had observed the year before in his *Atlantic Monthly* article, albeit without mentioning anyone by name, many "hard-core gay Garland fans" include "men who make a living as experts on her career" (66). According to Gross, they evade the historical phenomenon of this star's queer appeal as it may apply to their own fandom, instead publicly insisting on the universality of her audience. It is not just a coincidence, I think, that the transfer of authority on the Judy List from fan to expert, which occurred before and after the miniseries, similarly directed attention away from "the gay thing."

The poster who replied to Sanders's anecdote about those two "rugged looking" men discussing Judy Davis's "FABulous" performance may well have been right: marginalization of Garland's gay following could have been the unstated point of Colin Freeman's differentiation between "nitpicking" fans, that is the ones already most attentive to her value as an entertainment icon, and the "millions" addressed by the miniseries as potential new consumers. To attract a crossover audience, as had been remarked on the list in the past, Garland needed not "to be perceived as a gay thing by the general public." The legend of her long-standing history with gay fandom had to be revised, her camp affect effaced, in order to facilitate commercial renewal of the Garland legacy through the miniseries, and the elevation of the professional expert over the fan manifested this on the listserv, if only indirectly. Complicating the debate on the Judy List about who was more qualified to safeguard the Garland legacy, the professional or the fan, was therefore the same inescapable, if by this point unstated, anxiety about her fans' relation to mainstream tastes and pleasures. That anxiety had divided list members in the past, but it was now being deflected through the threads about Fricke's privileged status as the leading Garland historian, the author most committed to bringing her legacy to a larger audience.

On the list itself, anger at the apparent devaluation of Garland's most loyal fan base—the "us" that Freeman said the miniseries was not made for—ended up being aimed most virulently at Mark Harris, in no small part because of his close identification with the experts and the access to the Garland industry that they offered him. This happened three months after the miniseries aired, and it did not occur without a high degree of camp melodrama all its own.

A contentious gay fan waged battle with Harris at the Judy List's website. Early in May Harris reported an intricate but unsuccessful effort to sabotage the site. The offensive began with hacking of its BBS. According to Harris, the culprit wrote "whacked out, rude (and . . . surprise!) badgering and baiting posts . . . under a variety of names." As if parodying the list's regulation of fan dialogue, the offender used one name to ask a question, one to answer it, one to confirm the answer, one to agree and put down anyone who disagreed, and one to applaud the insight being offered. After Harris discovered the ploy, the offending fan invaded the software script so that it automatically posted blank messages every few seconds to jam the board. With some clever detective work, Harris found his perp: a list member who had already been expelled some years before for uncivilly voicing his opinions, and Harris then informed the Judy List of what this "sick, deviant mind" had tried to do—"in one post he starts a thread based on the fact that his 220 lb. Irish/American 'wife' looks like Judy" when "everyone knows" that "he's as Queer as Folk" (9 May 2001).

Two days later, Harris wrote a retraction. It turned out he had named the wrong person and the list's devious enemy was actually that angry poster already mentioned. *He* had set up the false suspect as a "fall guy," duped Harris with a series of fraudulent e-mails sending him on the wrong trail, replaced the suspicious posts on the BBS with obscene messages about Harris, joined and posted to the list under several e-mail aliases, all with the aim of "getting even" because Harris had prevented him and his friends from "trashing" both new unknowledgeable fans and the professional authors on the list. Reporting that this poster had complained in the past that people were afraid to post because of Fricke's rebukes, Harris countered: "You can see what lengths a screaming queen will go to when they feel they've been 'wronged'" (11 May 2001).

Vowing legal prosecution and worrying about further retribution, such as a mail bomb, Harris swore to keep the list going just to spite this nefarious scheme, yet by month's end he had given up. The 30 May daily digest contained a terse e-mail that offered control of the Judy List to whoever wanted to take it over. Although the expense and stress of keeping the list going had "all been for Judy," Harris wrote in a separate e-mail to a group he called "the good Judy fans," he had finally been worn down by the arrogance and nastiness of amateur fans claiming expertise they did not have. He criticized, as well, fans who used the list to insult Jim Johnson when the DataBase went off-line temporarily at this same time, reportedly because of harassment, too. However, Harris ultimately justified his decision by referring to the pathos of his own "sad life," citing his potentially fatal medical problems, clinical depression, unemployment, debt, and imminent homelessness. Despite his personal turmoil, he vowed, "SOMEHOW I will continue to have an Internet connection and Judy WILL continue to be part of my online life" (31 May 2001).

In his own tale of adversity, the Judy List's owner was almost sounding like the legend herself. The new Judy Group which he was organizing at Yahoo, with its membership restricted solely to the "good" fans, would be *his* comeback, he promised, as well as her next one. Of course by this time, the expelled offender and his cronies had already started their own alternate group on Yahoo so there were, in effect, dueling comebacks. As for the DataBase, it also returned, albeit with few updates from this point on as Johnson devoted more of his energies to other, less major stars and to maintaining a strictly encyclopedic site on classic musicals. The two competing Judy chat groups, in the meantime, existed alongside other relatively new discussion forums on Yahoo centered on specific aspects of the star's career or organized around particular fan formations. The dialogue about Garland therefore managed to go on despite the Judy List's somewhat unexpected attempt to regulate it in the name of professional expertise and, more indirectly, out of that ever-elusive fan hope of returning their idol to the mainstream. That kind of comeback will never happen because of "that little something extra" which still draws fans to Garland in the first place and helps to explain why she, more than any other star who worked at MGM during the studio era, continues to personify the camp appeal of the studio's musicals half a century later.

CONCLUSION

*I*ntroducing *Dangerous When Wet* (1953) on a recent night in August devoted to Esther Williams, TCM's host Robert Osborne acknowledged the silliness of its plot: the star enters an annual competition to swim the English Channel with the hope that winning the prize money will finance the purchase of a purebred stud bull for "the girls" on her father's dairy farm back home in the United States. Osborne nevertheless promised viewers they would still find many treats in this musical, mentioning in particular the numbers, notably an animated dream sequence putting Williams in the water with Tom and Jerry, and the cast of talented players supporting the star (Fernando Lamos as a French champagne salesman; Jack Carson as the promoter of a vitamin-and-alcohol spiked health syrup; Charlotte Greenwood and William Demarest as the star's parents, themselves health nuts; Barbara Whiting as her younger sister, in a part meant for Debbie Reynolds; and Denise Darcel as a "French bon-bon" who, Osborne's epithet notwithstanding, also tries to swim the channel). I know *Dangerous When Wet* delivered considerable pleasure to *me* when I found myself watching this musical again for the umpteenth time. Except for the dream sequence, which parodies the leading character's conflict over whether to dally with the seductive Lamos or keep to her training (his continental charms take second place to the swimming, which may be the reason she is dangerous when wet and safer when dried out), there is nothing extraordinary about this

Esther Williams musical except that it is pure MGM: silly perhaps, stylish yes, camp definitely.

Beginning with the same attractions that Osborne singled out for his viewers, my goal in *Incongruous Entertainment* has been to use camp as a focal point, a critical and historical lens, for reassessing the entertainment value of the MGM musical during the era of its production and afterward. As a result, I have organized this book around what many fans of the genre—such as those who watch these old films on TCM with nostalgic relish and tune in for every repeat of *That's Entertainment!* (1974), even though the musicals excerpted in that compilation are frequently shown in their entirety on the cable channel, too—still do not consider a legitimate pairing. After all, everyone knows that the MGM musical was designed primarily as frivolous, escapist entertainment for a mainstream audience. Camp, by contrast, was a queer social practice alien to the audience addressed by these films; it bespoke a viewing position located on the margins of dominant culture, one irrelevant to but just as much irreverent of the norms being reproduced by the films to guarantee their commercial success, even when it happened that Esther Williams was playing a champion athlete, swimming for the bull. But as I discussed in this book's early chapters, at the point of the MGM musical's greatest currency as "king of the box office," there was ample textual and extrafilmic motivation for camp as well as noncamp reception of these films: in the house style's lavish, over-the-top mise-en-scène and aggregation of numbers, in the witty, ironic affect of female star turns, and in the unstable masculinity staged by Gene Kelly's dancing.

From the vantage point of the musicals' production in Culver City, a camp idiom shaped the entertainment they offered to a mainstream audience during the studio era, and it was crucial to their popularity, even if this audience did not know it was watching camp. Probably the most relevant insight of camp for my study, in fact, lies in the recognition that both straight and queer affective responses to the same cultural object indirectly refer to each other. If the noncamp reading remains staunchly oblivious to signs of camp in the musicals, the camp reading engages ironically with evidence of their unimpeachable wholesome orientation in order to see that little something extra slyly lurking beyond it.

Camp, as I stated in my introduction, is the queer eye for the straight guise. Historically, it articulated a dialectical stance toward the dominant culture by inverting the latter's hierarchical binary thinking and turning it against the naturalization of normative values. Motivated by the imperative to pass as straight, queer men used camp as a strategy for seeming invisible to the straight eye while performing their own cultural identity as homosexuals, thereby inhabiting the mainstream covertly yet defiantly. Thus, in exposing the incongruity of cultural dualisms like "masculinity" and "femininity," "straight" and "queer," "normal" and "deviant," but also "good" and "bad" taste, practitioners of camp enacted a queer perception of how culture works to regulate value through the commodification of gendered identities and sexual desires. I have therefore sought to point out in this book how, in drawing on camp strategies, these great old MGM musicals similarly require viewers to negotiate the incongruous cultural dualisms that constitute the ideological ground of heteronormality, especially when the means of identifying with it is through the consumption of mass-produced entertainment. Furthermore, as this book's structure means to record, in examining the ways that camp and the MGM musical illuminate each other, I have followed the historical path of their interaction, examining how camp and the genre have each considerably shifted in their cultural value over the course of the past half century.

In terms of its reputation today, the MGM musical's affiliation with camp seems much less controversial, although this connection has also been muted by the added value of nostalgia on one hand, epitomized by the *That's Entertainment!* series, and by the phenomenon of mass camp on the other, predicted by *Singin' in the Rain* (1952). Camp nonetheless continues to be an assertion of dialectical resistance to the hegemony of straight thinking and, I myself cannot resist saying, it means to be dangerous when (the wit is) whet. It is thus important to realize that resistance *to* camp is as much of a crucial marker of its effectivity and visible a sign of its presence, as we saw in the discomfort registered on the Judy List by each recurrence of "the gay thing." Garland's status as a gay icon referred to more than her camp and her audience's, to be sure. All the same, camp crystallized and perpetuated her queer appeal and her fans' ability to bond with her, investing her performances with a greater sense of directness and intimacy for an audience of closeted men. This cultural meaning no longer has the same hold on the generations born after Stonewall and lacking the "Judy gene," as is often said with camp tongue in cheek. Still, every reminder of Garland's camp affect—from her MGM musicals to her concerts to her biography—raises the inference that there may be something queer about fans' own consumer tastes and, hence, their cultural identity, at least from the perspective of their being crazy about this particular star and crazy about her musicals, too.

That ambivalence regarding what camp signifies to an audience about its relation to commodity culture is not confined to Garland fandom but determines how the old-fashioned musical genre is perceived by the entertainment industries as a safe commercial property today: either as stolidly mainstream or as broadly camp. After I completed this book, Warner Home Video announced the long-awaited debut of the *That's Entertainment!* series on DVD in October 2004. Significantly, the cover art for the discs, which appeared on websites such as Amazon.com, retained the posters used for the first two entries but again altered the one for the third, replacing that drawing evocative of Judy Garland in her fedora and tuxedo jacket with one of Fred Astaire and Cyd Charisse dancing in *The Band Wagon* (1953). Restoring the image of heterosexual coupling initially used in that compilation's theatrical poster, the packaging gives the impression of disavowing the camp address of both *That's Entertainment! III* and the making-of documentary, still to be included as one of the DVD's supplements.

Two recent examples of musicals, one from Hollywood and one from Broadway, both explicitly incorporating references to MGM, further illustrate what I mean about the ambiguous value that camp, at once "out" in the open and closeted, now brings to the genre. *De-Lovely* (2004), produced by the newest corporate version of Metro-Goldwyn-Mayer, purports to recount Cole Porter's life story with authenticity because it acknowledges his homosexuality; additionally, it aims to introduce his songs to a new, younger audience, which is why, the filmmakers said in interviews, the Porter estate gave approval to the screenplay's candor. That made clear in the advance publicity, this musical biopic removes all traces of Porter's celebrated camp wit from his character, an absence emphasized all the more by Kevin Kline's performance and the dialogue written for him. True, the film cannot entirely erase the composer's camp because it remains in the songs, often inserted for no biographical reason and chosen without regard for their chronology; but the numbers are edited in a way that subordinates them to dramatic scenes visually and aurally, which blunts the songs' impact as numbers, obscures the camp wit of the lyrics, and directs attention away from the pop stars performing them. The sole exception, as I recall, is "Be a Clown." Lifted without acknowledgment from *The Pirate* (1948) and with awkward, claustrophobic choreography inspired by the Marx Brother's MGM comedies, it is recontextualized as a fantasy number to justify the Broadway artiste's selling out to a grotesque version of L. B. Mayer. While *De-Lovely* suggests that Porter's years at Metro apparently gave him access to numerous all-male pool parties which he took great advantage of, this musical is otherwise not very gay in either sense of the word. Frankly, I found *De-Lovely* so dispiriting, so mistrustful of pleasures specific to the genre regardless of their camp value, that when the time came for Porter's riding accident, I was rooting for the horse. I couldn't wait for it to be over.

Conversely, the 2001 Broadway blockbuster hit *The Producers*, in preproduction for a film version with much of its acting and creative talent intact, explicitly draws on audience knowledge that the musical is a camp genre with a lineage harking back to MGM. The two leading characters (originally played by Nathan Lane and Matthew Broderick, whom I did not see in the roles) intend to produce a big, fat flop so that they can take the money they have embezzled from investors and run off to Brazil. They choose a play most likely to fail outrageously because of its bad taste, "Springtime for Hitler," and put it in the hands of Roger DeBris, a cross-dressing gay director of musicals (played by Gary Beach, whom I did see on stage). The producers' crafty thinking that gay won't pay goes awry, however, when their show unexpectedly proves to be a critical hit because of its camp, from its jaw-dropping, eye-popping combination of Ziegfeld showgirl line and offensive Nazi symbolism to the number's leading man: the director himself takes on the starring role at the last minute and performs Hitler by channeling Judy Garland. Mein Camp it is! For all this number's hilarity—and it is a genuine showstopper—the central joke at the heart of *The Producers* is still made at the expense of camp, which is presumed to be gay in only one stereotypical sense of the word. The camp spectacle onstage is clearly set apart from the superior viewing position of the theater audience, who can comfortably laugh at both the producers' inability to predict a theatrical success given the preeminence of gay men working on Broadway *and* the gay director's own bad taste in taking his camp seriously and not recognizing it as "camp."

I end this book contrasting *De-Lovely* and *The Producers*, the former making camp a significant absence and the latter making its presence undeniable, simply to point out what I have been claiming about the MGM musical's greater subtlety all along. Despite the more widespread awareness of camp today in comparison with past decades, the dialectic tension between what counts as straight pleasures in the musicals' entertainment and what counts as queer ones still makes their camp attractions disarming and disturbing, especially to those viewers who would otherwise agree to the presence of camp in these films—that is, they would if they could only see the camp, because otherwise they just don't get it, so how could it be there? The answer, as I hope this book has shown, is to think more queerly about the MGM musical's cultural significance as camp; and to think more queerly, I have been arguing, is to think about its incongruous entertainment more historically and more critically as well.

NOTES

1   My understanding of these terms is indebted to Alex Doty's discussion of "queerness" in *Making Things Perfectly Clear* (xi–xix) and *Flaming Classics* (6–8); Eve Kosofsky Sedgwick's analysis of terminology in *Epistemology of the Closet* (16–18); and George Chauncey's account of the historical differences between "homosexual," "queer," and "gay" in *Gay New York* (14–23).

2   In the postscript to his essay, Ross cites Warhol's conscious celebration of mass culture's "leftovers" (74). See also Matthew Tinkcom's chapter on the artist's films as camp in the fullest, queerest sense of the word in *Working Like a Homosexual* (73–118) as well as in his essay, "Warhol's Camp."

3   This episode was cablecast on VH-1 on 18 January 1997. It is worth mentioning that another guest, Jess Cagle, then an editor for *Entertainment Weekly*, referred to Sontag's famous essay in order to define *camp* for the audience as a style privileging artifice.

4   The gender role-playing "dictated" same-sex pairings but was not always maintained or fixed to the person. Clubgoers contributing to the Garden of Allah's oral history mention butch lesbians who suddenly reappeared as femmes with the start of a new relationship. Similarly, many sources in the oral history reiterate that the female impersonators belied stereotypes because they partnered with butch men yet took only the "top" position in sexual intimacy. For that matter, even in makeup and high heels the performers could handle themselves unexpectedly well when hassled on the street, returning much more than they got.

5   See Bérubé (88–89) and Kaiser (38) for accounts of the army's all-male production of Clare Booth Luce's *The Women*, apparently done "straight" but nonetheless complete with a bathtub scene for the actor playing Crystal

Allen (the Joan Crawford role in the 1939 MGM film version), during which he stood up to expose his brawny body in a jock strap.

6   Let me make clear, though, that Dyer's point is not to deny a camp reading of the scene by any means, but to distinguish the number's representational strategies in constructing the star's authenticity from what he terms a "deconstruction" of its artifice.

7   In the next paragraph Babuscio goes on to explain that "in part, at least, Garland's popularity owes much to the fact that she is always, and most intensely, herself. Allied to this is the fact that many of us seem able to equate our own strongly-felt sense of oppression (past or present) with the suffering/loneliness/misfortunes of the star both on and off the screen" (46). Nonetheless, his commentary suggests that there is much more than an audience's recognition of transcendent emotionality at work in the performance's camp affect as it occurs on-screen.

8   Richard Lippe's reading of Norman's self-destructive behavior, however, does see the character enacting the turmoil of a closeted gay male in the 1950s. According to Lippe, Norman's self-destruction is unexplained by Moss Hart's screenplay but addressed indirectly by George Cukor's direction of the film's melodramatic narrative: "While [Norman and Esther] feel they have failed each other, it becomes obvious that the expectations and demands entailed by their respective gender-roles are overwhelming them" (53).

9   Haver further discusses the composition of the screenplay as well as the differences from the 1937 version (51–61), mentioning how hearing "The Man That Got Away" galvanized Hart's progress when he stalled between sketching the revised narrative structure and filling out its details. Lippe offers a more thorough comparison of the two films, as well as their lineage back to Cukor's earlier *What Price Hollywood* (1932).

10 One of Staiger's points is that the overwhelming "intensity," of the sort which Babuscio attributes to the camp style of Garland's performances, was already a key word in the fan discourse about her (166).

1 IMPROBABLE STUFF: CAMP AND THE MGM HOUSE STYLE

1   Unit production of films at MGM, a form of specialized labor which drew on studiowide resources to deliver specific types of product, was officially disbanded in 1947 because the system's large overhead became too great a liability in the face of postwar declines in revenue (Gomery, 70); nonetheless, production of musicals continued with Freed, Pasternak, and Cummings at the helm throughout the 1950s. Freed's was the most organized as a bona fide quasi-independent unit with a dedicated labor force, drawing on the same people most consistently, but that should not detract from the importance of the other two producers who specialized in the genre. According to Thomas

Schatz, from 1946 though 1955, 25 percent of Metro's output comprised musicals (industry-wide the genre's share was more like 4 percent), meaning that MGM made half of the musicals coming out of Hollywood during this decade. Of the eighty-one musicals produced at MGM during those ten years, Pasternak was responsible for twenty-seven, Freed for twenty-one, and Cummings for twelve (*Genius of the System*, 447). Not only were these films enormously successful, following a strategy of distinguishing the studio's "high-end output and its house style," but since "studio operations were geared to the output of musicals" (Schatz, *Boom and Bust*, 375), MGM needed to keep turning them out on a regular basis and doing so under the reliable stewardship of Freed, Pasternak, and Cummings, that is, until the studio started to collapse economically in the late 1950s.

2   Rubin goes on to argue: "Viewed in this way, the history of the musical becomes not so much a relentless, unidirectional drive toward effacing the last stubborn remnants of nonintegration, but a succession of different ways of articulating the tension and interplay between integrative (chiefly narrative) and nonintegrative (chiefly spectacle) elements" (12–13).

3   Kay Thompson's camp style can be seen in her one major film performance, Edens's own production of 1957's *Funny Face* (made for Paramount, not MGM, though with director Stanley Donen and other MGM personnel, because star Audrey Hepburn was under contract to Paramount). Thompson opens the musical with an Edens–Leonard Gershe number, "Think Pink!" which perfectly captures her camp collaboration with Edens, giving an on-screen indication of their off-screen labor at MGM in the 1940s. Playing the editor of a fashion magazine, Thompson decides to promote the color pink in the next issue; her song turns into a montage featuring model Suzy Parker, which imagines the world drenched in pink: fashion, decor, toothpaste, everything —"and that includes the kitchen sink" (as indeed it did in the 1950s, when pink was a big color in suburban housing). In the dance following the montage, even chorus boys painting the walls of the magazine's offices sing out, "Think pink!" The number well represents Thompson's distinctive performance style from her nightclub act after leaving MGM in 1947—she always sings much lower and deeper than everyone else, almost as if speaking yet perfectly on key, her gesturing offers as much inflection to her vocalizing as the voice does, and her figure dominates the surrounding ensemble. Yet for all her admonition to "think pink!" she herself never changes from her black and gray tailored suit. After the number's end, Thompson stands out as queerly nonconformist in contrast with her assistants, all wearing pink, the difference signifying an ironic stance toward all this pink glamour and, as the song also acknowledges, the rosy-red view of the world implied by the color as well as its association with femininity. When asked afterward why she isn't wearing pink like everyone else around her, Thompson replies in her throaty voice, "Me? I wouldn't be caught dead."

4   See Harvey, *Directed by Vincente Minnelli*, and Naremore, *The Films of Vincente*

Minnelli, for analyses of the director's style in terms of his mise-en-scène. In contrast with Minnelli, George Sidney—who happens to figure importantly in this chapter because of the attention given to his *Ziegfeld Follies* number and *Bathing Beauty*—lacks an esteemed reputation as a stylist and has certainly never been treated as an auteur. The one appreciative assessment of Sidney's career through directorial style (which, as an auteurist overview, does not take into account the contributions from others at MGM) is a recent one by Eric Monder. "His films," the critic concludes, "are virtually an index of popular culture in the 20th century, whose antinomies he unveils by contrasting and reframing what is considered vulgar and refined, commercial and artistic, old and new, masculine and feminine, harmonic and discordant, theatrical and cinematic, sensual and spiritual" (59). Although the aim here is to understand Sidney's career "beyond" the curiosity of camp (as Monder puts it), what is being pointed out about the director's films through their "antinomies" sure seems like camp to me.

5 For one account of the collaboration that went into production of a musical at MGM, see the oral history of the making of *An American in Paris* (1951) in Knox, *The Magic Factory*.

6 *Ziegfeld Follies* had a two-year gestation from its production, previews, and try-out run in Boston until its full theatrical release in 1946, but it turned out to be a huge hit. According to Fordin, "Here's to the Girls" was, in the near three-hour preview version, followed by Astaire in "If Swing Goes, I Go Too" and then a Jimmy Durante sketch. The latter drew no laughs and Astaire didn't like his "Swing" number, so both were cut (143–44). The addition of "Wonderful Men" afterward does not necessarily mean that the camp of "Girls" failed to work and needed the coda to clarify its satire; if that had been the case, the number could have been tinkered with or edited down, as others were following the preview. More likely, the coda was added to continue the opening number's camp tone and to insure more of a focused transition to the star-laden camp specialty numbers (directed by Minnelli) which follow.

7 MGM's other successful formula for musicals during the 1930s was the Jeanette MacDonald–Nelson Eddy cycle of operettas, starting with *Naughty Marietta* (1935), released the same year as *Broadway Melody of 1936*. However the operettas did not translate as well to the 1940s, either with regard to subject matter or musical style, as did the flashier, Tin Pan Alley–based series with Eleanor Powell. The operettas' influence, however, can be felt in the integrative aesthetic as it came to function as the standard for evaluating the film musical's development (Griffin, 23).

8 At around the same time as *Broadway Melody*, MGM also produced the lavish *Hollywood Revue of 1929*, featuring most of its star roster, in no small part to introduce their voices and try them out for musicals. Barrios gives an account of the first movie musicals which not only appraises *Broadway Melody*'s historical significance but also traces the rise and fall of the early talkie revue,

important for the genre's aggregate values. Related to the waning popularity of the revues, Jenkins offers a case study of the production of MGM's seemingly incoherent *Hollywood Party* (1934)—intended as a sequel to *Hollywood Revue*—showing how the extensive script revisions and disagreements about this musical's narrative make evident "the clash between classical Hollywood norms and the vaudeville aesthetic" (114).

9   Though following Williamson's argument here, I don't entirely agree with her that these anxieties in Williams's star image were ever fully "repressed" by the aqua-musicals. To be sure, MGM did not again cast Skelton as her romantic lead (even when the two costarred later on), instead pairing her opposite the likes of Van Johnson and Howard Keel (her two most frequent male costars); but even so, the male leads couldn't swim as well as she when they joined her in the water to do some side-by-side treading. Further, Williams's characters became more professional and ambitious, declaring little interest in romance to start with and, despite the plot closures that heterosexualized her, the water numbers became more daring in their stunt work. Williams was always much more than just another bathing beauty, particularly once Busby Berkeley was added to the mix when he staged the water numbers in *Million Dollar Mermaid* (1952) and *Easy to Love* (1953).

2 THE LADY IS A CAMP: GLAMOUR, STAR TURNS, AND THE BOYS IN THE CHORUS

1   In fact, there had been an original production number shot for the end of the film, but the glamour finale, combining "Ziegfeld Girls" with the montage, replaced it when the studio decided that *Ziegfeld Girl* needed to conclude with an explicit evocation of the Oscar-winning *Great Ziegfeld* in order to cash in on audience memories of the latter. Titled "We Must Have Music," the deleted number does not survive, but a portion was used in a short by that name publicizing the MGM sound department. From the surviving snippet, it appears that plans for the finale were very different from what ended up on the screen, since it involves Garland dressed as a drum majorette and dancing with the boys in the band. More on *that* in a moment.

2   To be fair, though, Garland's costume also seems designed to give her an illusion of having a longer upper torso—hence the bodice has inverted V's going down past her waist, the sash is layered over her hips—and to show off her long legs, considered her most glamorous feature.

3   On the history of blackface, see Gubar, Lhamon, and Lott, and on its significance for the film musical, see Clover, Gabbard, Knight, and Rogin.

4   The song's later use in *Singin' in the Rain* clarifies the address that is muddled here by making it a duet between Gene Kelly and Debbie Reynolds in the finale. Before that, in a fuller version ultimately deleted for the release print, Reynolds sings the song to an image of Kelly on a billboard.

3 DANCING WITH BALLS: SISSIES, SAILORS, AND THE CAMP MASCULINITY OF GENE KELLY

1   Untitled magazine clipping, circa 1946, no source; Gene Kelly clipping file, Margaret Herrick Library of the Academy of Motion Pictures Arts and Sciences. The anecdote appears as a lengthy caption to a signed photo of Kelly and is probably from a Sunday newspaper supplement such as *Parade*. It goes on to recount a second sort of self-effacing imposture, mentioning "how he even fooled his [future] wife once." When trying out for a job at Billy Rose's Diamond Horseshoe supper club, she mistook him for "that janitor— or stagehand," not the revue's dance director.

2   "Dancing: A Man's Game," *Omnibus*, NBC, originally broadcast on 21 December 1958, Museum of Television and Radio archive, Los Angeles. See Gerstner, "Dancer from the Dance," for a thoughtful examination of the program's aesthetic and cultural politics, which resulted in a highly problematic realization of Kelly's aim to depict "the creative process as *a process of masculinization* that stressed the male-as-artist was not an effeminate creature" (59).

3   See Genné, " 'Freedom Incarnate,' " for a discussion of how the sailor was used as a distinctive American type in 1940s dance, on film in Kelly's *Anchor's Aweigh* and onstage in Jerome Robbins's *Fancy Free*.

4   Along with a number of other derogatory labels that depicted effeminate men as women, such as "Miss Nancy," "old maid," and "Mary Jane," "the most popular of all female terms for men" was "sissy," first appearing in print in the 1890s (Rotundo, 272–73).

5   For example, Bruce Babington and Peter William Evans describe Kelly as "a breezy, brash, unashamedly American urban hero, not sophisticated enough to refrain from 'taking a bow every time he heard a clap of thunder' " (166). Michael Wood similarly refers to Kelly as "the indefatigable American," adding, "in or out of Paris, he is the practicing apostle of exertion and expertise as keys to fabulous success, and it is the American mood which found its metaphor in Kelly's brash confidence" (150).

6   There are similar moments of Kelly doing this type of broad impersonation of a fairy in *Cover Girl* and *On the Town* but not to the extent of this scene in *Anchors Aweigh*.

7   To be fair, Prock reads Kelly's career as dancer-choreographer through *Singin' in the Rain*, contending that its "historical reception and critical reception reiterate a [male/female] gender hierarchy posed by the film itself," which, in turn, conforms with Kelly's masculinist dance aesthetic as a whole (297). I agree in large part with this smart reading of the film, as I discuss later in this chapter. However, I do not share Prock's conclusion about Kelly's dancing overall, namely, that the star "is thus able to reverse the object of display from woman to man even while rigorously resisting his own objectification" (315). More to the point, although Prock rightfully stresses how Kelly's

anxiety about a male dancer's effeminacy informs his choreographic style with respect to subordinating his female partners, the critic does not go on to consider where that anxiety was located culturally and why it should have attached itself to Kelly's star image. In comparison, Gerstner's analysis of the Omnibus television program does critique Kelly's masculinist aesthetic as an unsuccessful effort to recuperate his dancing from postwar homophobic suspicions about a dancer's effeminacy. While referencing Kelly's musicals as part of the informing context of this aesthetic, however, Gerstner is primarily concerned with how the television media works against it.

8   Whenever I teach *The Pirate*, for instance, my students never agree on whose viewpoint the ballet is enacting. Gerstner also notices the number's slipperiness, calling attention to how director Vincente Minnelli's autobiography describes it as Manuela's whereas Hirschhorn's biography of Kelly, written in consultation with the star, refers to it as Serafin's (Gerstner, 57).

9   Comden and Green, 4–8; Harvey, "Stanley Donen," 5; Hirschhorn, 177.

10 The bit with the dummy's hand on O'Connor's knee in "Make 'Em Laugh" can be read as either a heterosexual or homosexual pass. According to O'Connor, he got the inspiration for this routine from an experience in his youth: while he was riding the subway in the 1940s, an "ex-fighter" type sat next to O'Connor, then moved closer, finally putting a hand on his knee, then his crotch. O'Connor recounts, "So I did a gay voice and said, 'Listen, my boyfriend will beat the shit out of you if you go any further!'" (Silverman, 160). This source of the dummy routine is also acknowledged in Hirschhorn's biography of Kelly, although there O'Connor's response to the groper is more engendered as "safely" masculine: "The guy won't take no for an answer and keeps on doing it until I have to lay him out flat" (183–84).

11 Adding to the questionable status of three men dancing as an "effective" masculine activity, Kelly staged such dances using his two female assistants, Carol Haney and Jeanne Coyne (his second wife and Donen's first one), to work out these numbers in place of the men. This practice is noted in biographies but was also known at the time. One newspaper article mentions that "Gene Kelly calls them his right and left hand, respectively, although they better might be described as his extra pair of feet," and goes on to note that the two women have stood in for Kelly's male and female costars, as well as a line of chorus boys or girls (Lowell E. Redelings, "Women Behind the Scenes," no source, Kelly clipping file, Herrick Library). The article is not dated in the file but it refers to Kelly's "new CinemaScope musical, 'Brigadoon,'" so it appeared at some point either in spring or summer 1954.

4 WHAT A GLORIOUS CLASSIC: *SINGIN' IN THE RAIN* AND MASS-CAMP RECYCLING

1   On the same day as the anniversary package's release, Warner Home Video also brought out on DVD a PBS television documentary about Gene Kelly,

Anatomy of a Dancer (2002), which makes the argument that he revitalized the movie musical.

2   Yet not without some bumps along the way. These first "all talking, all singing, all dancing" musicals attracted large audiences, but their box-office appeal did not hold up when moviegoers tired of hastily produced, poorly staged, and statically edited imitations of earlier successes, particularly the filmed revues. Thus, just three years after the introduction of sound, and "contrary to the general belief that hard times generated a desire for escapist fare" (Crafton, 359), the musical was already considered a recipe for box-office failure, so studios rethought the genre's viability. Studio as well as audience interest in the genre was then renewed in 1933 when Warners, responding to the competition from radio and the failure of its own revues, dusted off the backstage plot in *42nd Street*, and the rest, as they like to say in the movies, is history.

3   Prerecording and playback began, somewhat accidentally, with MGM's production of *Broadway Melody*: "The Wedding of the Painted Doll," another Freed-Brown song in the talkies montage, required a retake to make it more cinematic and, to save expenses, was redone without rerecording the orchestra and lead singer (who is mostly off-camera); in postproduction the new film footage was combined with the soundtrack already recorded live on-set from the number's first shoot (Barrios, 65).

4   To be sure, many present-day viewers may just know that these songs are recycled standards without being aware of their sources, and others may even assume that the songs were newly composed for *Singin' in the Rain*. Either way, comparisons with the vintage musicals can pass by without notice. On the other hand, the fiftieth-anniversary DVD now includes the initial rendition of the songs on a second disc, encouraging a viewer to watch as a cinephile with fuller knowledge of the MGM musical's history, which would have been more evident in 1952, as it looms behind *Singin' in the Rain*.

5   While Freed gets the brunt of the blame and shame whenever this story is retold, it is worth mentioning that he wrote the lyrics—his partner was responsible for the suspicious music. Since MGM owned rights to the Porter song, the similarity with "Make 'Em Laugh" may not have seemed like a big deal at the time to Freed, but it is nonetheless striking that he, not Brown, gets the dubious credit for the theft whenever the story is retold.

5 HOLLYWOOD'S MOST PRECIOUS JEWELS:
THE MGM MUSICAL'S RETURN AS A CAMP COMMODITY

1   Feltenstein is in fact echoing a quotation from Jack Haley Sr. in the pamphlet accompanying the 1996 boxed set, *That's Entertainment!: The Ultimate Treasury*.

2   These figures are based on Clive Hirschhorn's year-by-year catalogue of releases in *The Hollywood Musical*, 2nd edition (New York: Portland House,

1991). According to Hirshhorn's volume, *Variety*'s estimate of MGM's 1954 output was overly ambitious since the studio ended up producing ten musicals, the same as the year before.

3   I am quoting from the title page of the auction catalogue, prepared by the David Weisz Company, and then summarizing from its listing of the eighteen-day schedule.

4   My primary source of this latter-day history of MGM is Bart, *Fade Out*, as supplemented by Hay, *MGM: When the Lion Roars*; "MGM/UA Communications Co. Annual Report, 1986" (the first report of this newly formed version of the company); the 559-page report filed by Time Warner with the Securities and Exchange Commission for the merger with AOL and available on-line from the Commission's Public Information Server, Edgar (<www.sec.gov/ Archives/edgar>, downloaded 21 October 2000); Peter M. Bracke, "Special Report: The Liberation of MGM," which recounts the complicated intertwining and then unknotting of home-video rights to the MGM library (<www .dvdfile.com>, downloaded 6 July 2000); and press releases (from November 1994 through November 1995), documenting the formation of TCM on its website (<www.tcm.turner.com/pressroom>, all downloaded on 2 April 2000).

As postscript to what I am recounting, in 2003 Time Warner removed AOL from its corporate title, and in the spring of 2004 MGM was put on the block again, with both Sony and Time Warner aggressively bidding for it. Sony's offer ultimately prevailed. According to *Daily Variety*'s first report of the completed deal, once the larger company absorbs MGM, "After 2005, that label and the roaring Lion will be put to rest (Learmonth and Fritz, 17). The following day, however, the trade paper reported, "What is known is that MGM and its roaring lion logo will continue to operate as a separate label to produce and distribute roughly three films per year" (Graser, 1). Whether the logo disappears for good or not, the company being purchased had by this point little relation to the entity formed by Loew's in 1924. Ironically, though, the sale would be returning the MGM logo to the Culver City studio that had become the Hollywood plant of Sony Pictures. Coincidentally too, at the same time as the confirmed deal was being announced, Time Warner held a special screening in Beverly Hills of *That's Entertainment!* to show off the compilation's digital restoration prior to a DVD release, an event which occasioned additional news accounts of the studio's legendary fame and demise.

5   The Turner merchandising of the catalogue was not limited to the home venues I am discussing here—cable, CDs, and high-end video—but included the company's publication of several oversized books on MGM and its licensing of images from the famous films for products such as mugs, umbrellas, collectible plates, and dolls.

6   Other soundtracks in this series included the scores of *North by Northwest* (1959) and *Dr. Zhivago* (1964) and a double CD of numbers from the Busby

Berkeley Warner Bros. musicals, also in Turner's library because of the 1985 MGM deal.

7   For some reason, Feltenstein's actual role in the production of *That's Entertainment! III* is left unnoted by the film's long list of credits. The press kit, however, identifies him as "MGM's executive in charge of production for *That's Entertainment! III* and Senior Vice President/General Manager of MGM/UA Home Entertainment, Inc." and notes that he was "integral in compiling the list of films to be included."

8   See Feuer, *Hollywood Musical*, 42–47, and, on the Comden-Green scripted films for producer Arthur Freed, "Self-reflective Musical."

9   The segment's change to a camp tone is particularly, if artificially, evident in the laser-disc boxed set because it comes at the point where one has to take the first disc out of the player and put in the second.

10 "Ask John Fricke" (questions from August 1997), Judy Garland DataBase, downloaded 21 October 2000. Ellipses in original.

11 See Gluckman and Reed, "The Gay Marketing Moment"; Baker, "A History in Ads"; and Walters, *All the Rage.*

6 JUDY ON THE NET: GARLAND, CAMP, AND
CONTEMPORARY FANDOM

1   The Judy Garland DataBase was at <www.zianet.com/jjohnson> until 2000, when it changed to its own domain at <www.jgdb.com>. The Judy List website was at <www.judylist.com> until its demise in 2001.

2   As mentioned already, the Judy List's website contained an archive of its daily digests in zip-file format for easy downloading by the Internet public. List members were well aware of this availability, since at times they asked about the possibility of having its contents indexed. In quoting from the digests, I have respected the anonymity of fans and only refer by name to those people with a public identity as a Garland author, one acknowledged by their posts to the list. I include the list's owner and moderator in this group since he was interviewed by the press in that capacity. Finally, because posts were oftentimes written without use of a spellchecker, I have silently corrected typos and misspellings.

WORKS CITED

The American Film Institute Life Achievement Awards: Gene Kelly. 1981. World Vision Home Video, 1991.

Altman, Rick. *The American Film Musical.* Bloomington: Indiana University Press, 1989.

Archerd, Army. "Just for Variety." *Daily Variety,* 20 March 2003, 2.

Babington, Bruce, and Peter Williams Evans. *Blue Skies and Silver Linings: Aspects of the Hollywood Musical.* Manchester, England: Manchester University Press, 1985.

Babuscio, Jack. "Camp and the Gay Sensibility." In *Gays and Film,* edited by Richard Dyer, 40–57. Rev. ed. New York: Zoetrope, 1984.

Baker, Don. "A History in Ads: The Growth of the Gay and Lesbian Market." In *Homo Economics: Capitalism, Community, and Lesbian and Gay Life,* edited by Amy Gluckman and Betsy Reed, 11–20. New York: Routledge, 1997.

Barrios, Richard. *A Song in the Dark: The Birth of the Musical Film.* New York: Oxford University Press, 1995.

Bart, Peter. *Fade Out: The Calamitous Final Days of MGM.* New York: Morrow, 1990.

Barzel, Ann. "Dancing is a Man's Game." *Dance Magazine* (February 1959): 30–33.

Bergman, David, ed. *Camp Grounds: Style and Homosexuality.* Amherst: University of Massachusetts Press, 1993.

Bérubé, Allan. *Coming Out Under Fire: The History of Gay Men and Women in World War Two.* New York: Plume, 1990.

Bracke, Peter M. Review of *Singin' in the Rain.* Fiftieth Anniversary DVD. Downloaded from <www.dvdfile.com>, 10 September 2002.

Bronski, Michael. *Culture Clash: The Making of Gay Sensibility.* Boston: South End, 1984.

Burlingame, Jon. "Preservation Key in Growing Original Score Market." *Daily Variety*, 15 October 1997.

Burt, Ramsay. *The Male Dancer: Bodies, Spectacle, Sexualities*. London: Routledge, 1995.

Carpenter, C. Tyler, with Edward H. Yeatts. *Stars Without Garters! The Memoirs of Two Gay GIs in WWII*. San Francisco: Alamo, 1996.

Cave, Damien. "Descent of the Divas." Salon.com, 10 January 2000. Downloaded from <www.salon.com/people/feature>, 13 March 2000.

Charness, Casey. "Hollywood Cine-Dance: A Description of the Interrelationship of Camerawork and Choreography in Films by Stanley Donen and Gene Kelly." Ph.D. diss., New York University, 1977.

Chauncey, George. *Gay New York: Gender, Urban Culture, and the Making of the Gay Male World, 1890–1940*. New York: Basic, 1994.

Clarke, Gerald. "Beyond the Yellow Brick Road." *TV Guide*, 1–7 July 2000, 17–24.

———. *Get Happy: The Life of Judy Garland*. New York: Random, 2000.

Cleto, Fabio, ed. *Camp: Queer Aesthetics and the Performing Subject*. Ann Arbor: University of Michigan Press, 1999.

Clover, Carol J. "Dancin' in the Rain." *Critical Inquiry* 21 (1995): 722–47.

Clum, John M. *Something for the Boys: Musical Theater and Gay Culture*. New York: St. Martin's, 1999.

Comden, Betty, and Adolph Green. *Singin' in the Rain*. New York: Viking, 1972.

Costello, John. *Virtue Under Fire: How World War II Changed Our Social and Sexual Attitudes*. Boston: Little, Brown, 1985.

Crafton, Donald. *The Talkies: American Cinema's Transition to Sound 1926–1931*. Berkeley: University of California Press, 1977.

Chumo II, Peter N. "Dance, Flexibility, and the Renewal of Genre in *Singin' in the Rain*." *Cinema Journal* 36.1 (1996): 39–54.

Delamater, Jerome. *Dance in the Hollywood Musical*. Ann Arbor: UMI, 1981.

Dempsey, John. "Movie Channels Battle for the Top: AMC, TCM, FMC Try New Tactics to Win Auds and Advertisers." *Daily Variety*, 16 February 2003.

Dong, Arthur, dir. *Coming out Under Fire*. Zeitgeist Films, 1991.

Doty, Alexander. *Flaming Classics: Queering the Film Canon*. New York: Routledge, 2000.

———. *Making Things Perfectly Queer: Interpreting Mass Culture*. Minneapolis: University of Minnesota Press, 1993.

Dyer, Richard. "The Colour of Entertainment." In *Musicals: Hollywood and Beyond*, edited by Bill Marshall and Robynn Stilwell, 23–30. Exeter, England: Intellect, 2000.

———. "Four Films of Lana Turner." In *Only Entertainment*, 65–98. London: Routledge, 1992.

———. *Heavenly Bodies: Film Stars and Society*. New York: St. Martin's, 1986.

———. "It's Being So Camp as Keeps Us Going." In *Camp: Queer Aesthetics and the Performing Subject*, edited by Fabio Cleto, 110–16. Ann Arbor: University of Michigan Press, 1999.

————. "*A Star is Born* and the Construction of Authenticity." In *Stardom: Industry of Desire*, edited by Christine Gledhill, 132–40. London: Routledge, 1991.

Ebert, Roger. Review of *Singin' in the Rain*. *Chicago Sun-Times*. Downloaded from <www.suntimes.com/ebert/ebert_reviews/1998/06/061801.html>, 6 November 2003.

The Ed Sullivan Show (Toast of the Town). "The MGM Story." 1954. Classic Television Video, 1996.

Ehrenstein, David. *Open Secret: Gay Hollywood, 1928-1998*. New York: Morrow, 1998.

"An Evening with Gene Kelly." BBC, 1974. Rebroadcast, Turner Classic Movies, 23 July 1995.

Farmer, Brett. *Spectacular Passions: Cinema, Fantasy, Gay Male Spectatorship*. Durham, N.C.: Duke University Press, 2000.

Feuer, Jane. *The Hollywood Musical*. 2nd ed. Bloomington: Indiana University Press, 1993.

————. "The Self-reflective Musical and the Myth of Entertainment." In *Hollywood Musicals: The Film Reader*, edited by Steven Cohan, 31–40. London: Routledge, 2002.

Finch, Christopher. *Rainbow: The Stormy Life of Judy Garland*. New York: Ballantine, 1976.

Fiske, John. "The Cultural Economy of Fandom." In *The Adoring Audience: Fan Culture and Popular Media*, edited by Lisa A. Lewis, 30–49. London: Routledge, 1992.

Fordin, Hugh. *The Movies' Greatest Musicals: Produced in Hollywood USA by the Freed Unit*. New York: Ungar, 1984.

Frank, Gerold. *Judy*. New York: Harper, 1975.

Fricke, John. *Judy Garland: A Portrait in Art & Anecdote*. Boston: Bullfinch, 2003.

————. *Judy Garland: World's Greatest Entertainer*. New York: Holt. 1992.

————. "She Made Us Love Her." *TV Guide*, 24 February–2 March 2001, 20–24.

Gabbard, Krin. *Jammin' at the Margins: Jazz in the American Cinema*. Chicago: University of Chicago Press, 1996.

Genné, Beth. " 'Freedom Incarnate': Jerome Robbins, Gene Kelly and the Dancing Sailor as an Icon of American Values in World War II." *Dance Chronicle: Studies in Dance and the Related Arts* 24.1 (2001): 83–103.

Gerstner, David Anthony. "Dancer from the Dance: Gene Kelly, Television, and the Beauty of Movement." *Velvet Light Trap* 49 (spring 2002): 48–66.

Glenn, Joshua. "Camp: An Introduction." *Hermenaut* 11–12 (winter 1997): 2–21.

Gluckman, Amy, and Betsy Reed. "The Gay Marketing Moment." In *Homo Economics: Capitalism, Community, and Lesbian and Gay Life*, 3–10. New York: Routledge, 1997.

Gomery, Douglas. *The Hollywood Studio System*. New York: St. Martin's, 1986.

Graser, Marc. "Leo's Big Fadeout: Prod'n Pacts in Limbo; Tower Tenacy Ending." *Daily Variety*, 15 September 2004, 1, 25.

Griffin, Sean. "The Gang's All Here: Generic versus Racial Integration in the
    1940s Musical." *Cinema Journal* 42.1 (fall 2002): 21–45.

Griffith, Richard. *The Cinema of Gene Kelly*. New York: MOMA, 1962.

Gross, Michael Joseph. "The Queen is Dead." *Atlantic Monthly*, August 2000,
    62–70.

Gubar, Susan. *Racechanges: White Skins, Black Face in American Culture*. New
    York: Oxford University Press, 1997.

Harris, Daniel. *The Rise and Fall of Gay Culture*. New York: Ballantine, 1997.

Harris, Scott. "Gene Kelly Dies: Legendary Dancer was 83," *Los Angeles Times*,
    3 February 1996, home edition, A-1+.

Harvey, Stephen. *Directed by Vincente Minnelli*. New York: MOMA, 1989.

———. "Stanley Donen." *Film Comment* 9 (July–August 1973): 4–9.

Haver, Ronald. *A Star is Born: The Making of the 1954 Movie and its 1983 Restora-
    tion*. New York: Harper, 1988.

Hay, Peter. *MGM: When the Lion Roars*. Atlanta: Turner, 1991.

Hillier, Jim. "Interview with Stanley Donen." *Movie* 24 (spring 1977): 26–35.

Hirschhorn, Clive. *Gene Kelly: A Biography*. New York: St. Martin's, 1984.

Hofler, Robert. " 'Hairspray' Camps Out on B'way." *Daily Variety*, 19 August
    2002, 1, 33.

Howard, Edwin. "Gene Kelly: He-Man Dancer Perfected the Filmusical."
    Memphis Business Journal, 19 February 1996, 30.

In the Life. "June Pride Episode." June–July 1999. PBS videocassette.

Jacobs, Frank. "What's Entertainment?" *Mad*, June 1975, 4–10.

Jacobson, Matthew Frye. *Whiteness of a Different Color: European Immigrants and
    the Alchemy of Race*. Cambridge: Harvard University Press, 1998.

Jenkins, Henry. *What Made Pistachio Nuts? Early Sound Comedy and the Vaudeville
    Aesthetic*. New York: Columbia University Press, 1992.

Jennings, Wade. "The Star as Cult Icon: Judy Garland." In *The Cult Experience:
    Beyond All Reason*, edited by J. P. Telott, 90–101. Austin: University of Texas
    Press, 1991.

Johnson, Albert. "Conversation with Roger Edens." *Sight and Sound* 27.4 (spring
    1958): 179–82.

Judy Garland: Beyond the Rainbow. A&E. Cablecast on 27 March 1997.

Kael, Pauline. *I Lost it at the Movies*. New York: Bantam, 1965.

Kaiser, Charles. *The Gay Metropolis 1940-1996*. New York: Houghton, 1997.

Klinger, Barbara. *Melodrama and Meaning: History, Culture, and the Films of
    Douglas Sirk*. Bloomington: Indiana University Press, 1994.

Knight, Arthur. *Disintegrating the Musical: Black Performance and American
    Musical Film*. Durham, N.C.: Duke University Press, 2002.

Knox, Donald. *The Magic Factory: How MGM Made An American in Paris*. New
    York: Praeger, 1973.

Krauss, David. "A Classic Act: George Feltenstein and the Crown Jewels of
    Warner Home Video." Downloaded from <www.digitallyobsessed.com>,
    20 December 2003.

Lacher, Irene. "Fred is Her Co-Pilot." *Los Angeles Times,* 17 August 1997.

Larson, Allen Robert. "Alienated Affections: Stardom, Work, and Identity in United States 20th Century Culture." Ph.D. diss., University of Pittsburgh, 2003.

Learmonth, Michael and Ben Fritz. "Sony Ponies Up for Lion: Time Warner Bows Out, Paving Way for $5 Bil Purchase of MGM." *Daily Variety,* 14 September 2004, 1, 17.

Lhamon Jr., W. T. *Raising Cain: Blackface Performance from Jim Crow to Hip Hop.* Cambridge: Harvard University Press, 1998.

Lippe, Richard. "Gender and Destiny: George Cukor's *A Star is Born.*" *CineAction!* (winter 1986): 46–57.

Long, Scott. "The Loneliness of Camp." In *Camp Grounds: Style and Homosexuality,* edited by David Bergman, 78–91. Amherst: University of Massachusetts Press, 1993.

López, Ana M. "Are All Latins from Manhattan? Hollywood, Ethnography, and Cultural Colonialism." In *Unspeakable Images: Ethnicity and the American Cinema,* edited by Lester D. Friedman, 404–24. Urbana: University of Illinois Press, 1991.

Lott, Eric. *Love and Theft: Blackface Minstrelsy and the American Working Class.* New York: Oxford University Press, 1995.

Loughery, John. *The Other Side of Silence: Men's Lives and Gay Identities: A Twentieth-Century History.* New York: Holt, 1998.

Luft, Lorna. *Me and My Shadows: A Family Memoir.* New York: Pocket, 1998.

Madigan, Nick. "Coogan, Astaire Bills Signed by Gov. Davis." *Daily Variety,* 12 October 1999.

Mann, William J. *Behind the Screen: How Gays and Lesbians Shaped Hollywood 1910-1969.* New York: Viking, 2001.

Mast, Gerald. *Can't Help Singin': The American Musical On Stage and Screen.* Woodstock, New York: Overlook, 1987.

Matthews, Jack. "The Athlete Who Danced Our Dreams." *Newsweek,* 11 February 1996, 5.

McCullough, John. "Imagining Mr. Average." *CineAction!* (summer 1989): 43–55.

McLean, Adrienne L. "Feeling and the Filmed Body: Judy Garland and the Kinesics of Suffering." *Film Quarterly* 55.3 (spring 2002): 2–15.

Mellencamp, Patricia. "Spectacle and Spectator: Looking Through the American Musical Comedy." In *Explorations in Film Theory: Selected Essays from Ciné Tracts,* edited by Ron Burnett, 3–14. Bloomington: Indiana University Press, 1991.

"Metro Shooting Lotsa Musicals." *Variety,* 16 June 1954, 5.

Meyer, Moe, ed. *The Politics and Poetics of Camp.* London: Routledge, 1994.

Miller, D. A. *Place for Us: Essay on the Broadway Musical.* Cambridge: Harvard University Press, 1998.

Mizejewski, Linda. *Ziegfeld Girl: Image and Icon in Culture and Cinema.* Durham, N.C.: Duke University Press, 1999.

Monder, Eric. "George Sidney's Hi-Tech Vaudeville Show." *Film Comment* 30.4 (1994): 50–59.

Mueller, John. *Astaire Dancing: The Musical Films*. New York: Knopf, 1985.

Naremore, James. *The Films of Vincente Minnelli*. New York: Cambridge University Press, 1993.

Negra, Diane. *Off-White Hollywood: American Culture and Ethnic Female Stardom*. London: Routledge, 2001.

Newton, Esther. *Mother Camp: Female Impersonators in America*. Chicago: University of Chicago Press, 1979.

O'Neill, Brian. "The Demands of Authenticity: Addison Durland and Hollywood's Latin Images during World War II." In *Classic Hollywood, Classic Whiteness*, edited by Daniel Bernardi, 359–85. Minneapolis: University of Minnesota Press, 2001.

Parke, Andrew. Review of *That's Entertainment! Part III*. *Laserviews* 8.1 (January–February 1995): 34, 54.

Paulson, Don, with Roger Simpson. *An Evening at the Garden of Allah: A Gay Cabaret in Seattle*. New York: Columbia University Press, 1996.

Prock, Stephan. "Music, Gender and the Politics of Performance in *Singin' in the Rain*." *Colby Quarterly* 36 (2000): 295–318.

Proctor, Kay. "Hey Irish!" *Photoplay*, May 1943, 36–37, 94.

Reflections on the Silver Screen with Professor Richard Brown: Gene Kelly. AMC. Cablecast on 2 February 1994.

Roberts, Shari. "Seeing Stars: Feminine Spectacle, Female Spectators, and World War II Hollywood Musicals." Ph.D. diss., University of Chicago, 1993.

Robertson, Pamela. *Guilty Pleasures: Feminist Camp from Mae West to Madonna*. Durham, N.C.: Duke University Press, 1996.

Roen, Paul. *High Camp: A Gay Guide to Camp and Cult Films*. Vol. 1. San Francisco: Leyland, 1994.

Rogin, Michael. *Blackface, White Noise: Jewish Immigrants in the Hollywood Melting Pot*. Berkeley: University of California Press, 1996.

Ross, Andrew. "Uses of Camp." In *Camp Grounds: Style and Homosexuality*, edited by David Bergman, 54–77. Amherst: University of Massachusetts Press, 1993.

Rotundo, E. Anthony. *American Manhood: Transformations in Masculinity from the Revolution to the Modern Era*. New York: Basic, 1993.

Rubin, Martin. *Showstoppers: Busby Berkeley and the Tradition of Spectacle*. New York: Columbia University Press, 1993.

Sampey, Kathleen. "Judy Garland Remains a Big Star on the Web." Associated Press, 25 June 1998. Downloaded from <www.technoserver.com/newsroom>, 23 September 1999.

Schatz, Thomas. *Boom and Bust: American Cinema in the 1940s*. Berkeley: University of California Press, 1997.

———. *The Genius of the System: Hollywood Filmmaking in the Studio Era*. New York: Pantheon, 1988.

Sedgwick, Eve Kosofsky. *Epistemology of the Closet*. Berkeley: University of California Press, 1990.

Shipman, David. *Judy Garland: The Secret Life of an American Legend*. New York: Hyperion, 1992.

Silverman, Stephen M. *Dancing on the Ceiling: Stanley Donen and His Movies*. New York: Knopf, 1996.

Sinfield, Alan. *The Wilde Century: Effeminacy, Oscar Wilde and the Queer Moment*. New York: Columbia University Press, 1994.

Skolsky, Sidney. "Hollywood is My Beat." *Hollywood Citizen-News*, 19 August 1954, n.p. Kelly clipping file, Herrick Library.

Sontag, Susan. "Notes on Camp." In *Camp: Queer Aesthetics and the Performing Subject*, edited by Fabio Cleto, 53–65. Ann Arbor: University of Michigan Press, 1999.

Staiger, Janet. *Interpreting Films: Studies in the Historical Reception of American Cinema*. Princeton: Princeton University Press, 1992.

"Sten." Review of *Bathing Beauty*. *Variety*, 31 May 1944. Reprinted in *Variety Film Reviews, 1943–1948*. New York: Bowker, 1998.

Stewart, Susan. *On Longing: Narratives of the Miniature, the Gigantic, the Souvenir, the Collection*. Durham, N.C.: Duke University Press, 1993.

Stoop, Norma McClain. "Gene Kelly; An American Dance Innovator Tells It Like It Was—and Is." *Dance Magazine*, July 1976, 71–73.

Studlar, Gaylyn. *This Mad Masquerade: Stardom and Masculinity in the Jazz Age*. New York: Columbia University Press, 1996.

Taylor, Greg. *Artists in the Audience: Cults, Camp, and American Film Criticism*. Princeton: Princeton University Press, 1999.

Tharp, Twyla. "Gene Kelly: The Charming Maestro of Movement." *Los Angeles Times*, 7 February 1996, home ed., F-1.

Tinkcom, Matthew. "Warhol's Camp." In *Camp: Queer Aesthetics and the Performing Subject*, edited by Fabio Cleto, 344–54. Ann Arbor: University of Michigan Press, 1999.

————. *Working Like a Homosexual: Camp, Capital, Cinema*. Durham, N.C.: Duke University Press, 2002.

Torres, Sasha. "The Camped Crusader of Camp: Pop, Camp, and the *Batman* Television Series." In *Camp: Queer Aesthetics and the Performing Subject*, edited by Fabio Cleto, 330–43. Ann Arbor: University of Michigan Press, 1999.

Van Leer, David. *The Queening of America: Gay Culture in Straight Society*. New York: Routledge, 1995.

Vare, Ethlie Ann, ed. *Rainbow: A Star-Studded Tribute to Judy Garland*. New York: Boulevard, 1998.

Vartell, Paul. "Sour 'Notes on Camp.'" *Chicago Free Press*, 3 May 2000.

Walters, Suzanna Danuta. *All the Rage: The Story of Gay Visibility in America*. Chicago: University of Chicago Press, 2001.

Who's Who at Metro-Goldwyn-Mayer: M-G-M Anniversary, 1924–1944, 20 years of Leadership. MGM publication, 1944.

Williams, Alan. "The Musical Film and Recorded Popular Music." In *Genre: The Musical*, edited by Rick Altman, 146–58. London: Routledge, 1981.

Williams, Esther, with Digby Diehl. *The Million Dollar Mermaid*. New York: Simon, 1999.

Williamson, Catherine. "Swimming Pools, Movie Stars: The Celebrity Body in the Post-War Marketplace." *Camera Obscura* 38 (May 1996): 4–29.

Wills, Nadine. " '110 Per Cent Woman': The Crotch Shot in the Hollywood Musical." *Screen* 42.2 (summer 2001): 121–41.

Wolk, Martin. "Gene Kelly Dies: Imbued Dance with Blue Collar Style." Reuters, 2 February 1996).

Woll, Allen L. *The Hollywood Musical Goes to War*. Chicago: Nelson-Hall, 1983.

Wollen, Peter. *Singin' in the Rain*. London: BFI, 1992.

Wood, Michael. *America in the Movies, or 'Santa Maria, It Had Slipped My Mind'*. New York: Columbia University Press, 1989.

Zuiderveld, René. "Mother of Synchronised Swimming and Queen of Camp." *Gay News Magazine*, 28 November 2001.

INDEX

Durante, Jimmy, 62, 221, 246, 346 n.6

Durland, Addison, 79-80

Dyer, Richard, 24, 27, 101, 104, 114, 133, 145, 177, 179, 277, 279, 288, 294, 295, 300, 302, 307, 313, 344 n.6

Easter Parade, 59, 89, 120, 135, 148, 260, 277, 285

Easy to Love, 347 n.9

Ebert, Roger, 206, 210

Ebsen, Buddy, 63, 140-42

Eddy, Nelson, 139, 346 n.7

Edens, Roger, 31-32, 47-59, 52-53, 58-59, 62-65, 88, 93, 102-6, 111, 113, 120-21, 133, 138, 140, 144, 234, 240, 331, 345 n.3

Ed Sullivan Show, 121, 128, 135, 264, 265

Effeminacy, 12, 47, 66, 70, 114, 151, 153, 156, 158-61, 165, 171, 173, 179, 349 n.7

Ericson, John, 130-31

Ethnicity, 69-70, 78-87, 108, 112, 119, 146, 274. *See also* Whiteness

Farber, Manny, 207

Farmer, Brett, 1, 21-22, 50, 60, 180, 271

Feltenstein, George, 247-49, 267, 268, 279-80, 283, 284, 299, 300, 326

Female impersonation, 10, 94-96, 119, 328. *See also* Camp: and drag

Femininity, 12, 16, 35-36, 56-57, 69, 76, 81, 85, 86, 89-90, 92, 95-96, 98, 101, 104, 110-11, 136-39, 141-43, 148, 152, 179, 182, 186, 187, 194, 276, 309, 339, 345 n.3

Feuer, Jane, 32-33, 179, 210, 265-66, 269

Finch, Christopher, 106

Fiske, John, 315

Fitzgerald, Peter, 279-80

Fordin, Hugh, 51, 346 n.6

For Me and My Gal, 164

Forrest, Helen, 41, 72, 78, 79

Forrest, Steve, 130

Fosse, Bob, 156

Freed, Arthur, 31, 43, 47, 48, 53, 60, 62-63, 200, 206, 216, 222, 234, 255, 280, 344-45 n.1, 350 n.5

Freed-Brown song catalogue, 200, 201, 203, 204, 211, 213, 220-28, 234, 235

Freed unit, 3, 31, 45, 47-66, 67, 144, 200, 201, 203, 228, 295

Freeman, Colin, 321, 323, 328, 331-33

Fricke, John, 283, 285, 294-300, 304-7, 315-28, 332-34

Friedgen, Bud, 279-80

Garden of Allah, 12, 343 n.4

Gardner, Ava, 131, 268

Garland, Judy, 14, 19, 37, 43, 47-49, 51, 59, 62, 63, 92, 96-99, 101, 137, 141, 144-46, 176-77, 179, 194, 217, 218, 221-22, 225, 246, 254, 260, 262, 263, 266, 269, 277, 279, 283, 284, 287, 340, 341; Arts and Entertainment biography of, 48, 49, 51, 298, 304-8, 315, 316, 323, 332; as camp star, 52, 104, 121, 122, 133-34, 288, 291, 295-96, 299, 301-2, 309, 311-14, 319, 329, 331, 339-40; career at MGM, 31-33, 101-2, 104, 106, 120, 269, 292, 293, 295-98, 329; career of, after MGM, 120, 288-89; fandom and, 4, 247, 308-9, 317, 319, 322-27, 340; gay fan following of, 26, 133, 285, 289, 291, 295, 299, 302-14, 320-21, 332, 333; as gay icon, 288-90, 302, 309-10, 318, 332, 339; "Get Happy," 32, 120, 128, 142, 266, 277, 285, 319; and glamour, 101-11, 119-21, 124, 132, 133-34, 148, 277, 295-99, 347 n.2; in "The Great Lady Has 'an Interview,'" 51-52, 88, 91, 93, 120-32, 134, 144, 264-65, 299; Internet fan pages on, 291-99; legend of, 293, 298, 299, 301, 309, 313, 319, 322, 327, 331, 332; in "The Man That Got Away," 23-36, 38, 40, 328-29; in "Minnie from Trinidad," 106-21, 134, 144, 147, 277; in "The Trolley Song,"

Steven Cohan is a professor of English
at Syracuse University.

Library of Congress Cataloging-in-Publication Data
Cohan, Steven.
Incongruous entertainment : camp, cultural value, and the
MGM musical / Steven Cohan.
p. cm.   Includes bibliographical references and index.
ISBN 0-8223-3557-3 (cloth : alk. paper)
ISBN 0-8223-3595-6 (pbk. : alk. paper)
1. Musical films—United States—History and criticism.
2. Metro-Goldwyn-Mayer.
3. Homosexuality and motion pictures.
I. Title.
PN1995.9.M86C59 2005   791.43'3—dc22
2005006507